MARIE MASON POTTS

MARIE MASON POTTS

THE LETTERED LIFE OF A
CALIFORNIA INDIAN ACTIVIST

Terri A. Castaneda

UNIVERSITY OF OKLAHOMA PRESS : NORMAN

Publication of this book is made possible through the generosity of Edith Kinney Gaylord.

Library of Congress Cataloging-in-Publication Data

Names: Castaneda, Terri A., 1955– author.
Title: Marie Mason Potts : the lettered life of a California Indian activist / Terri A. Castaneda.
Other titles: Lettered life of a California Indian activist
Description: Norman : University of Oklahoma Press, [2020] | Includes bibliographical
    references and index. | Summary: "Biography of Marie Mason Potts, a Mountain Maidu
    woman, from her formative years in off-reservation boarding schools, through marriage and
    motherhood, and into the spheres of Native American politics and cultural revitalization."—
    Provided by publisher.
Identifiers: LCCN 2020015419 | ISBN 978-0-8061-6719-0 (hardcover)
Subjects: LCSH: Potts, Marie, 1895–1978. | Maidu Indians—California—Plumas County—
    History—20th century. | Land tenure—Political aspects—California—History—20th
    century. | Indian educators—California—Biography. | Indian women activists—California—
    Biography. | Sacramento (Calif.)—Biography.
Classification: LCC E99.M18 C37 2020 | DDC 979.4004/9741092 [B]—dc23
LC record available at https://lccn.loc.gov/2020015419

The paper in this book meets the guidelines for permanence and durability of the Committee
on Production Guidelines for Book Longevity of the Council on Library Resources, Inc. ∞

For
Dr. Charles Roberts, Choctaw

Grandson of Lesa Phillip Roberts (1890–1994), Mississippi Choctaw
and
Jesse Roberts (1888–1934), Oklahoma Choctaw

Son of Pearl Roberts (1920–1948), Choctaw

Professor Emeritus, Department of History
California State University, Sacramento

Contents

Abbreviations

AFSC	American Friends Service Committee
AICC	American Indian Chicago Conference
AIHS	American Indian Historical Society
AIPA	American Indian Press Association
AMNH	American Museum of Natural History
BIA	Bureau of Indian Affairs
CCI	Council of California Indians
CIA	Commissioner of Indian Affairs
CIB	California Indian Brotherhood
CIC	California Indians Congress
CIJA	California Indians Jurisdictional Act
CIIS	Carlisle Indian Industrial School
CLAI	California League for American Indians
CSUS	California State University–Sacramento
DAR	Daughters of the American Revolution
DNIWA	Del Norte Indian Welfare Association
ECMC	Engels Copper Mining Company
FIC	Federated Indians of California
GWP	Great Western Power
IBC	Indian Board of Co-operation
ICC	Indian Claims Commission
ICCA	Indian Claims Commission Act
ICI	Indians of California, Inc.
IDA	Indian Defense Association
IRA	Indian Rights Association
MIF	Mission Indian Federation

MIS	Mission Indian School
NCAI	National Congress of American Indians
NCIA	Northern California Indian Association
OIA	Office of Indian Affairs
PAHMA	Phoebe Apperson Hearst Museum of Anthropology
RRLC	Red River Lumber Company
SAI	Society of American Indians
SAS	Sacramento Anthropological Society
SCC	Sacramento City College
SCC	Student Coordinating Committee
SIM	State Indian Museum
SJC	Sacramento Junior College
SJIA	San José Indian Association
SSC	Sacramento State College
TGH	Treaty of Guadalupe Hidalgo
UCW	United Church Women
WNIA	Women's National Indian Association
WPC	Western Power Company

Acknowledgments

Marie Potts has set the better part of my travel itinerary for nearly two decades. This is perfectly fitting, as travel was one of the passions she pursued into her eighties. I did not have the pleasure of knowing Potts; she had journeyed on long before I arrived in California. But I met her in the archives, and like so many others, I was instantly taken by her intelligence, humor, and boundless energy. My initial research interests were very narrow. As a museum professional who had undertaken a doctoral degree while working as a curator at the Houston Museum of Natural Science, I was fascinated by her California State Fair exhibits. This was a segment of her life I could investigate independent of all the complicated and legalistic land claims history. Or so I told myself for several years. I was wrong. Land is everything, as I was about to find out in a very personal way.

In 2008 a colleague in Native American studies at California State University–Sacramento invited me to develop an exhibit in conjunction with a symposium she was organizing to honor one of our colleagues upon the occasion of his retirement. I put out a call to Native American students, faculty, and staff, hoping they would be willing to collaborate in representing the Native American community on campus. They came forward with gorgeous art, heirlooms, and stories, but I was especially anxious for the symposium honoree, Charles Roberts, to have a presence in the exhibit. I had known him for years. Many of my students had taken his courses in American and California Indian history. He was rigorous and demanding. I often ran into him in the university library, his chosen spot for reading his graduate students' theses. He took their work seriously, and they respected him for it. When I approached him about the exhibition, he thought for a moment and said, "Sure, why don't you come by the house and pick up a few things?" I stopped by a few days later. Emerging from a back room, he placed a battered shirt box, some photographs, and files of photocopied research material on the coffee table. Opening the box, he gently withdrew a purple 1940s-era scarf printed with a western rodeo scene and a black-and-white border of teepees, a small string of bracelet charms, a toy mechanical monkey bank, and a handwritten letter. "These were my mother's," he quietly announced. Pearl Roberts had died when Charles was a boy of seven. He remembered hoisting himself onto a ledge to see if he could spot her through the hospital window; this was his last memory of her alive. Leafing through some photographs of his grandmother Lesa Phillip, he explained that she had raised him after Pearl's death. His family had come west during the world war, following kin who had already settled in California. Handing me an article he had published about Lesa, he told me to use what I wanted. Entrusted with these precious mementos, I went back to the museum and began going through the material, including page after photocopied page of the Dawes Roll of the Mississippi Choctaw, and U.S. Census records he had used in his own research. Towns and cities in Mississippi and Louisiana where my ancestors settled only four and five generations ago leaped out, implicating me and my family in Choctaw removal. I sat that day in the stark silence and painful presence of this incontrovertible truth. It has never left me. This book is dedicated to Charles, a descendant of those who initially stayed—like Lesa's parents, Buckhorn and Lucie Phillip—and those removed to Indian Territory in the 1830s. He is a gentle and generous Choctaw scholar and teacher who has helped change the California world into which he was born, one classroom and colleague at a time.

I thank Marie Potts's many descendants for sharing time and memories of her with me, especially Pansy Marine's children Larry, Marvin Lee, Michael, Susie, Joe, and Judy, who have carried on their grandmother's dedication to Native culture. A diligent correspondent in the tradition of her grandmother, Susie Bear Yanes, Pansy's eldest daughter, has stayed in touch with me over many years, patiently waiting to see if I would ever manage to produce this book. This encouraged me to stay the course, and her warm response to an initial draft put much-needed wind in my sails. My thanks go out to all of Marie's descendants who have contacted me over the years. Some, like Mandy Marine and Peggy Fontenot, I have met in person. Others have reached out via email, including great-granddaughters Kelli DuFresne and sisters Kristi Marine Sii and Michele Marine LeFeau. To all the descendants of Marie's grandfather Hukespem: I hope this book does justice to your remarkable ancestor. May it inspire a massive family reunion, the likes of which have never been seen, in sight of Kom Yamani/Mount Lassen. (Melany

Johnson, I'm thinking of you!) To the Mountain Maidu people, your resilience and persistence shines ever brighter. My heart is with you as you work to reclaim and steward your ancestral homelands.

William and Carole Fairbanks generously offered their Los Osos home on the central coast as a base of operations during my first sabbatical, while they were on a cross-country trek. Words cannot express the depth of my gratitude to them. Watching fog lift from Morro Rock while writing at their kitchen desk, rock hunting at Spooner's Cove, exploring Montaña de Oro State Park's tide pools and bluffs to clear my weary brain, listening to waves crashing ashore as I drifted off to sleep, nurtured the very soul of this project. Lovers of learning, life, and family, of late-night conversations over a good bottle of wine, Bill and Carole are two of the brightest and kindest people I know. Both have dedicated their lives to education and to making the world more humane. Certainly, my sense of what counts as a rewarding academic life was recalibrated by their example. Along these lines, I want to thank my friends and colleagues for constancy of friendship, for warm and welcoming homes, and for always showing up with humor and good cheer, most especially Brian Baker, Aaron Cohen, Liam Murphy, Sheila O'Neill, Gail Pilas and family, Mary Reddick, and Alexanderia Russell.

Over the years, many individuals have shared their knowledge of California Indian history, land claims organizations, twentieth-century activists, and sources. Special thanks go to Rose Borunda, Richard Burrill, Steven Crum, Kimberly Johnston-Dodds, Dwight Dutschke, Susan Hanks, Farina King, Lucie Kýrová, Scott Lawson, Anne Luna, Brendan Lindsay, Stella Mancillas, Beth Rose Middleton Manning, Valerie Sherer Mathes, Eleanor Nevins, Annette Reed, James Sarmento, Joan Sayre, Khal Schneider, Rose Soza War Soldier, and Sheri Tatsch. This project has benefited from the support of colleagues affiliated with California State Parks, the State Indian Museum, and the California Indian Heritage Center Foundation, including Larry Myers, Connie and Al Striplen, Paulette Hennum, Jena Peterson, and Will Jorae. At the West Sacramento Historical Society, where the *Our Journey: The First Families* exhibit featured some of my work on Potts, the Federated Indians of California, and the All-Indian VFW Post at Bryte Memorial Hall, I thank April Farnham, Thom Lewis, and Ileana Maestas.

The Maidu Museum and Historic Site in Roseville, California, deserves mention here. After Pacific Western Traders closed its doors in 2014, the museum's monthly "Night Out at the Museum" helped fill a painful void, luring kindred spirits from near and far to a Saturday reception and lecture series showcasing the region's vibrant community of California Indian contemporary artists and culture bearers. Though some—Dugan Aguilar, Charley Burns, Frank LaPena, and April Moore—have recently passed on, the words and worlds they shared on these occasions inform the spirit of this book. April—who once said in reference to Marie, "That lady was one mover and a shaker!"—was just a young girl when her great-grandmother Lizzie Enos and Marie Potts became friends. Over a museum dinner in March 2015, she explained that while the political details naturally eluded little children, the excitement and sense of purpose these two great-grandmothers attached to their work was palpable to all. It was also here, at the Maidu Museum, that Shiwaya Peck shared with me her memories of Marie and other elders conversing with one another in Mountain Maidu well into the 1970s. I highlight these particular moments because they underscore the incredible vitality and intercultural exchange that infused the museum on these evenings, when it was a rich site of contemporary California Indian place-making, enlivened by the visionary work of California Indian artists like Tiffany Adams, Denise Davis, Jean LaMarr, Sage LaPena, Judith Lowry, and Alan Wallace. I have drawn inspiration from them all and extend my heartfelt thanks to Sigrid Benson and Mark Murphy for the opportunity to participate in this remarkable milieu by curating an exhibit about Potts.

CSUS has been my professional home for the last twenty years. When I was first hired, I was fortunate to have senior colleagues whose firsthand experiences with Potts confirmed the sense of her that I had developed purely through archival research. These individuals include Jerry Johnson, Frank LaPena, Kenneth Owens, and Dotty Theodoratus, who kept Potts's papers safe for many years and entirely altered my perception of Potts's work with anthropologists by telling me, "Oh, she was my teacher." Morgan Otis, for whom Potts taught basket weaving in the early Ethnic Studies Program, regaled me with stories of the cartwheels he turned to hire her under a credential of eminence. Gerald Heine, who produced the film *Chen-Kut-Pam*, screened it for me in the department lab, allowing me to hear, for the first time, the gentle voice of this woman whose archival and activist presence was so strong. My graduate students have constantly inspired me through their own work, much of which dovetails with Potts's life in this city. I especially want to pay tribute to the members of my graduate seminar Narrating Lives: Theoretical Perspectives on Life History as Ethnographic Method and Text for their intellectual contributions. In my department, I am indebted to Ana Guttierez, Judith Commons, and Karen Dively for assistance of every kind.

Craig Bates, Billie Blue Elliston, Richenda Hawkins, Paulette Hennum, Barb Landis, Tommy Merino, Herb Puffer, Jed Riffe, Dixie Rogers, David Risling Jr.,

Charles Trimble, and Kathy Wallace were central to the earliest phases of my research, and I want to acknowledge them once again. I owe special thanks to Dr. Robert Littlewood and Dr. Benjamin Swartz for sharing copies of their UCLA student term papers, discussed in chapter 8, and to the late Francis "Fritz" Riddell for his generosity of time and knowledge. Most of the analysis in this book was first tested in national and international conference sessions and symposia, where I benefited from interdisciplinary feedback. I thank all of these scholars—too numerous to credit individually—including those with whom I most recently presented: Vanessa Esquivido, Mark Minch, Brittani Orona, Nicolas Rosenthal, and Rose Soza War Soldier.

My research has been supported by a Faculty Scholarship Community Grant, Research and Creative Activity Program summer fellowships, President's Office Faculty Development Grants, sabbatical leave awards, and travel grants from the College of Social Sciences and Interdisciplinary Studies. I appreciate Dean Dianne Hyson's continued commitment to this critical faculty resource. A last round of research was made possible by a generous honorarium from the Shingle Springs Band of Miwok Indians. A substantial grant from the Historical Society of Southern California, in conjunction with the Ahmanson Foundation, covered expenses associated with image acquisition, rights and reproduction, and indexing. And here I also want to acknowledge the countless archivists, museum curators, and records managers whose assistance has helped to further my research.

This book came to fruition because Kathleen Kelly, my acquisitions editor at University of Oklahoma Press, convinced me that it was time to develop a book proposal and write the manuscript. She shepherded me with sage advice through every step, including the advance contract stage. Others at the press have been generous with their professional knowledge and expertise, including Adam Kane, Amy Hernandez, and Stephanie Attia Evans, in whose deft editorial hands this book was lucky to rest during its final passage. I am much beholden to copy editor Peg Goldstein for the firm but gentle hand with which she tamed the many unruly aspects of my manuscript; readers can rejoice.

The manuscript benefited from the vital contributions of two peer reviewers, William J. Bauer Jr. and Tanis C. Thorne. Their scholarly criticism, disciplinary perspectives, and organizational advice helped to forge and polish this book from beginning to end. It was immeasurably improved by their time and historical expertise; I extend my utmost thanks to both of them. As always, errors and omissions are my own. Two others reviewed the manuscript, and it is my pleasure to acknowledge them here. Mountain Maidu elder, historian, and ethnographer

Beverly Benner Ogle knew Marie. Like her, she holds a deep commitment to ancestral culture and lands, but more significantly, she shares Potts's passion for writing! And, to the benefit of us all, she also has Potts's tendency to sacrifice her own time and projects when others—myself included—come calling. A warm and welcoming person, Beverly is also a superb storyteller whose work I have read, cover to cover, several times over. I look forward to her next book and thank her from the bottom of my heart for reviewing mine. Donna Miranda Begay is a busy woman with endless commitments that keep her running between her Tübatulabal homelands and the city of Sacramento, where she has long been a vital and energetic leader in the Native community. I sought her out to review the manuscript for this reason and because she and her mother, Leona Miranda Begay, have such robust memories of Marie's time in Sacramento. My thanks go out to Donna for her thoughtful queries, for the sentiments and remembrances—some incredibly touching—embodied in her marginalia, and for her generosity of time.

Finally, I thank my family—Chris, Courtney, and Ramsey—for their patience and support. Since the summer of 2002, when I dragged them to the National Archives in Washington, D.C., and to the site of the former Carlisle Indian Industrial School—a sobering education if ever there was one—they have learned about Potts right alongside me. In the spirit of encouraging other scholars to pursue new insights into her life and activism, all royalties from this book are donated to the Marie Mason Potts Endowment at California State University–Sacramento.

Introduction

Try, for a moment, to visualize a California Indian activist. What comes to mind? Used in combination, the words *California* and *Indian activist* tend to conjure a very specific moment and image. If your mind's eye went immediately to Alcatraz and young men, you are not alone. As the women who were party to that occupation will attest, stereotypes tend to crowd out their own presence and contribution.[1] For California Native Americans, the problem of Alcatraz was much larger. This important milestone in American Indian activism was televised and riveting. The occupation (1969–71) captured the popular imagination and has never let it go. One unintended outcome was that national press coverage effectively conflated California, as a place, with images of American Indians whose homelands were largely out of state. Missed in this moment of rapt media attention was the island's status as the ancestral territory of the Ohlone people, indigenous to the San Francisco Bay Area, and—by extension—the very concept of California as "Indian Country" thousands of years before Native Americans from across the United States began arriving by way of military assignment, war industry employment, Bureau of Indian Affairs (BIA) relocation programs, university enrollment, and the like.[2] Alcatraz coverage was frustrating to many California Indian leaders because they were still waiting for the federal government to compensate them for theft of their ancestral homelands when California became the thirty-first state to join the Union. California Indian efforts to hold the federal government accountable for stealing their land consumed most of the twentieth century. These efforts also produced one of the state's most impressive activists. She lived through Alcatraz, lending material and moral support to its occupiers, and covering it with passion in the California Indian newspaper she began editing and publishing out of her home in the late 1940s. In physical appearance, she was the antithesis of the strapping young men the media tended to train their cameras upon at Alcatraz. This book tells her story.

Marie Mason Potts (1895–1978) was Mountain Maidu. Born in the northern reaches of the Sierra Nevada, she maintained a highly public and urban profile in the last three decades of her life as a political activist and editor of the *Smoke Signal* newspaper, headquartered in Sacramento, California. These years and accomplishments stand in stark relief to the prosaic life that federal Indian policy mapped out for Native women of her era. A graduate of two American Indian off-reservation boarding schools, Potts arrived at the first through no choice of her own. The same cannot be said of the second; she was a proud graduate of Carlisle Indian Industrial School, class of 1915. For more than sixty-three years, Potts wrote. She penned boarding school essays, *Smoke Signal* editorials, lectures about California Indian history and culture, and reams of correspondence related to state and national activism. These sources document her intercultural fluency, encounters with colonial power, and transformations in her response to it over the course of eight decades.

Life-Writing

Archival research is traditionally associated with historians and biographers, but the field of ethnography, or cultural description and analysis, also has a tradition of life-writing. In its early days, when anthropology was associated almost exclusively with oral societies, this genre entailed interviews, transcription, and translation—the latter involving both the linguistic and interpretive variety. These works and similar ones produced in allied disciplines have been roundly criticized within and outside the discipline and academy for publishing spiritual and esoteric knowledge, reproducing romantic and essentializing tropes, and simultaneously exploiting and eliding the colonial context that enabled and encouraged their production and consumption.[3] Colonialism holds the opposite position in the narrative that follows; it was the ever-present force within and against which Potts lived her life. Luckily, her inner strength and sense of self were equal to it. In this respect she was, and continues to be, a role model for many Native California people.

Subjects of early ethnographic life-writing were rarely literate, widely traveled for their time, or cosmopolitan in sensibility and experience. But Potts was all these things. The archival traces of her life are widely dispersed, seemingly everywhere, most assuredly yet to be identified and studied in full. The process of tracking them—or rather *her*—down, of plotting and following her cross-country treks, back and forth multiple times over, and situating her within her own time and place by populating these varied landscapes with the relevant cultural markers and political actors, is ethnographic fieldwork of an entirely different sort. Those who knew Potts in the Sacramento region, and there are many, both Native and non-Native, are often surprised to learn about her boarding school days and accomplishments, or the extent of her engagement with national organizations. Her grandchildren were well aware that she was always off to one or another meeting, but they did not always recognize the historical significance of her work. In the narrative that follows, Potts's voice is privileged wherever possible. It is one that emerges in abundant epistolary form and that she was careful to document and preserve in carbon copy, in oral interviews, and in a newspaper of her own.[4] Other voices, both contemporary and archival, contribute valuable context and perspective, but readers will discover that she had no trouble speaking for herself. In this regard, she is perhaps the only Native California woman born in the nineteenth century whose life and subjectivity are so thoroughly documented by her own hand. Assembling these sources into narrative form sheds light on both her life and the role of literacy in her generation of Mountain Maidu and California Indian people.

Ethnographic life-writing is a qualitative methodology and literary genre that highlights the variegated nature of human experience. History and culture are neither produced nor encountered as monolithic forms. Life-writing can answer questions about how individuals apprehend the material conditions and sociopolitical forces that define their life circumstances.[5] Potts was born into a Mountain Maidu world stripped of relative equilibrium by the gold rush and statehood. Her story brings that period of sweeping cultural change into sharper relief. It fleshes out empty corners and abstract contours of the region's intercultural history with concrete examples of how alien values and forms of power inscribed themselves upon the bodies and minds of Mountain Maidu people. Potts's story also illuminates the transformative power of human agency—the capacity to upend, circumvent, or exploit otherwise dangerous circumstances or negative effects, leveraging them for alternative ends. Life histories oriented to these potentialities can temper or challenge orthodox scholarly interpretations and recalibrate "common knowledge," dialing its accuracy up or down a notch. Even when a biographical subject's life course is more or less conventional, their story adds new texture to the larger portrait of how people lived out the conditions of their time. Potts's story does both of these things. It follows a predictable course in some respects. In others, it diverges radically from those well-worn and familiar paths; she exercised substantial personal agency within the stringent confines of settler colonialism.

Settler Colonialism

Potts's lifelong expression of nostalgia for her Carlisle years is one of many ways her life story complicates easy understandings of Native American encounters with colonial institutions. Just as life histories demonstrate that not all members of a given society respond uniformly to the same phenomenon, the field of comparative colonial studies reveals that not all colonial forms and trajectories are equivalent.[6] Distinguishing between one or another variant is not a purely theoretical exercise; it engages contemporary peoples, polities, and futures. This is particularly the case with settler colonialism, the form applicable to the United States and other countries founded by colonists whose primary motivation in leaving their countries of origin was to permanently resettle.[7] This scenario contrasts with a range of alternative varieties where resource production and/or extraction, human labor foremost among them, was paramount and where decolonization, at both the sociopolitical and intellectual level, is more straightforward.

Settler colonialism, in a very small nutshell, means the colonists never go home. At some point in the colony's existence—usually many generations deep—they pursue political autonomy from the mother country. Once it's in hand, they begin transforming the territory into a new "motherland," their own and that of their descendants. This means that while the colonial population achieves independence, the colonized do not. Their subjugation continues; what shifts is the seat of colonial power. To fully realize the colony's transformation into their homeland, settlers must wrest ownership and control of the territory—of land as the commodity resource and means of production—from the Indigenous population. Removal in the most literal sense, as in relocation to reservations or reserves—a tradition in Canada and the United States—is a common strategy. Other genocidal practices, ranging from mass murder to ethnocide, operate in tandem. Because its endgame is to rid the land of the Indigenous population, settler colonialism is constantly innovating new "population transfer" strategies, as the colonized come to recognize the latest—increasingly nuanced—measures by which they are targeted for "elimination."[8]

This process of swapping out the Native for the settler is always unfinished business, as tricky as it is bloody. The settler state's perspective on the colonized population is inherently contradictory. With one hand, it claims them as cultural patrimony—a romantic source of distinction from the originating mother country; with the other, it seeks to fully erase them. This desire to simultaneously inhabit and eliminate the Native body is the essence of colonial ambivalence. Settlers wrestle with the contradictions between their own historical struggle for freedom from colonial status and their oppression of others, *their* other. Colonial ambivalence expresses the irreconcilable conditions of settler colonialism, where the Native is simultaneously admired and reviled, humanized and dehumanized, denied autonomy and sovereignty, and forever the object of self-serving—some might argue genocidal—paternalism. Many of the institutions and actors that animate Potts's life story are the very embodiment of colonial ambivalence. This creates latitude and space for her to develop her own talents and ambitions.

Potts constantly breaches the fragile cultural and racial divide that settler society erects to discern her likeness to—and distinction from—them. She is fundamentally confusing. Indian and modern at the same time, she refuses to inhabit the settler identity and body that her literacy and schooling are meant to affect. She remains Native, wielding to her own advantage tools designed to reshape her sensibilities and identities, to eliminate her Native belonging. She crosses over into settler territory, lingers, takes from it what she wants, and crosses back. She does this with confidence and aplomb, and more rarely with anger and disgust. Potts was not the first to use settler colonial tools and practices to Native advantage, but she offers a brilliant example of how this was done by a California Native in the twentieth century.

The terms *settler* and *settler colonialism* are used throughout the text. While the form is centuries old, the terminology reflects recent social-scientific nomenclature. Potts did not live her life thinking, "I am going to subvert the settler colonial state," but she did so at regular intervals. Only rarely is there a hint of her wishing anyone real harm; her sense of human decency was bigger than that of the settlers who greedily gobbled up her homelands. The relationships she formed with most settlers were genuine and reciprocal; but they were also utilitarian and entirely necessary. They advanced her access to the material resources, legal knowledge, and symbolic capital that were critical to her desires and needs as a young woman, a mother, and an activist. As a heuristic device, settler colonialism situates these relationships and her firsthand encounters with colonial institutions designed to eliminate Native people —to "solve the Indian problem"—in a continuing historical process and power structure. And it situates settlers, and their descendants, squarely in that structure.[9] This book is intended to reach a wide audience, including Native and non-Native scholars, as well as a general readership. Those who approach the book from the latter position will not find themselves burdened at every possible turn with settler colonialism's full analytic and interpretive weight. Its quotidian influence in Potts's life will be easily recognized by students and scholars.[10] The cascading effects of land dispossession defined her life from beginning to end.

Organization of the Book

The natural division between Potts's early years and those of her activist career skews biographical depth toward the final three decades of her life. Four sections, the prologue through chapter 3, cover the period preceding her move to Sacramento. Chapters 4 through 10 address her activist years. The final chapters, 8, 9, and 10, take a more thematic approach. The prologue grounds Potts's life story in her northern California homelands, where her ancestors challenge their land dispossession by a homesteader. The traditional Mountain Maidu world of her grandfather's youth is counterposed with a landscape radically altered by the post–gold rush economy and value system. Marie is born into a cohort of cousins who are the offspring of Maidu women and newcomers from around the world. Chapter 1 follows her to a nearby boarding school, where she joins her older cousins. The school's mission origins and transformation into a federal boarding school are described in relation to Maidu people's response to it. Chapter 2 is set in Pennsylvania, at the Carlisle Indian Industrial School, where Marie stretches her social and intellectual wings to their full potential. Her gains are contrasted with her cousins' less fortunate fates. Life after Carlisle is described in chapter 3. Marie marries and starts a family, reunites with her mother and Maidu heritage, and suffers discrimination and domestic abuse. Throughout these challenging times, she is determined to ensure her children's educations and well-being, sending them off to boarding school as her personal situation declines. She survives, eventually relocating to Sacramento.

The challenges Potts faces in middle age foreshadow and fuel the activist spirit that emerges in chapter 4. California Indian land claims history and legislation are summarized, giving readers a sense of the turbulent political context that gave birth to the Federated Indians of California (FIC), the organization that launched her activist career. Marie's role as editor and publisher of *Smoke Signal* is analyzed in chapter 5. This work is clearly the realization of long-simmering ambitions and literary passions originating in her boarding school education and Carlisle's print and reading culture. Her creativity and astute political sensibilities shine in chapter 6. In California's centennial years, along with other FIC officers, she plays the generic, "real Indian" in patriotic venues and settler "pioneer" celebrations. This is a bit of a devil's bargain, but it generates fundraising opportunities and state support of FIC's land grievance against the federal government. However, behind the scenes Potts is just beginning to envision and organize a very different kind of gathering, one that brings California Indians together to celebrate their distinct cultural heritage. Chapter 7 documents Potts's remarkable work curating the inaugural All-California Indian Exhibit at the 1950 state fair. This exhibit, reprised for many years to come, brings her onto the radar of local and regional amateur and professional anthropologists. Chapter 8 explores her modernity and cross-cultural interests in relation to her Mountain Maidu heritage and the history of salvage ethnography. Potts's adventurous spirit and national activism are highlighted in chapter 9. She is constantly on the go, to the benefit of the FIC, National Congress of American Indians, American Indian Chicago Conference, and American Indian Press Association. Settling back into Sacramento, chapter 10 takes a more place-based approach, demonstrating Potts's dedication to being Native in the city: to carving out community, revitalizing dance, educating schoolchildren, and recognizing the cityscape's Indigenous antiquity. The conclusion brings the land claims case and her life to a close.

Terminology

A brief note about terminologies and names. Throughout the book some terms are used interchangeably. For instance, California Indians, California Native Americans, and Native Californians are all names for the collective group whose lands were confiscated upon statehood and who pressed suit against the federal government as "Indians of California." I use *American Indian, Native American, Native,* and *Indigenous* synonymously. This is not meant to elide their distinctions but rather to vary the prose and avoid a repetitive quality. The term *California Indian people* was commonly deployed by Potts and others of her generation, and its use continues among many contemporary California Natives. As the late Frank LaPena, professor emeritus of art and ethnic studies at my university, once explained to me, adding the word *people* to *California Indian* reclaims and humanizes a label that was otherwise generic, colonial, and legalistic. I use this terminology in that same spirit. Tribal nation names are used where known and typically as they appear in archival records. Mountain Maidu is the nomenclature presently preferred by the people indigenous to Potts's homelands, but they also recognize themselves as Northern Maidu (popular during Potts's own lifetime) and Northeastern Maidu. Occasionally these names are shortened to Maidu, a more encompassing term that also includes the Konkow and Nisenan speech communities, which are distinguished here by those designations. The terms *settlers* and *white people* are used synonymously; Potts used the latter most commonly, though on occasion she referred to homesteaders and other invaders of her homeland as settlers.

All spellings or transliterations of Mountain Maidu words or place-names are those of Potts, unless otherwise indicated. The decision to retain them as is preserves her voice and translation, and allows linguists, Maidu and otherwise, to appreciate popular mid-twentieth-century spellings and changes in vernacular renderings over time. The place Potts called Big Meadow was often referred to as Big Meadows (or the Meadows) by early settlers. Some Maidu have adopted this pluralization, which reflects early settler recognition that this mountain valley meadow had two lobes, a feature that became more pronounced after reservoir construction. The first superintendent of the Mission Indian School, the precursor to Greenville Indian Industrial School, distinguished Big Meadow families and pupils from the nearer Mountain Maidu camps and communities. His use of Big Meadows as a tribal affiliation became institutionalized in BIA records for a time. Singular or plural, this name refers to pupils whose families were Big Meadow residents. Greenville Indian School, as it was commonly known, is shortened to Greenville. The nearby town of Greenville, after which the federal government named the school, is always distinguished as such in the text to avoid confusion.

Finally, it is important to note that this is not intended to be an ethnography of the Mountain Maidu, although it contributes to a larger ethnohistorical portrait.[11] It is a life history that aims to illuminate how one individual apprehended, lived out, or refused the conditions and choices that unfolded in her family, time, and varied worlds—a "sample of one," with all the attendant meanings and possibilities.[12] It draws upon a rich, almost overwhelming, abundance of autobiographical forms and texts, and on infinite oral and written sources that can and must be read both against and "along the archival grain."[13] It is in this spirit of writing settler colonial history in a "minor key" that this profile of a California Indian activist is offered.

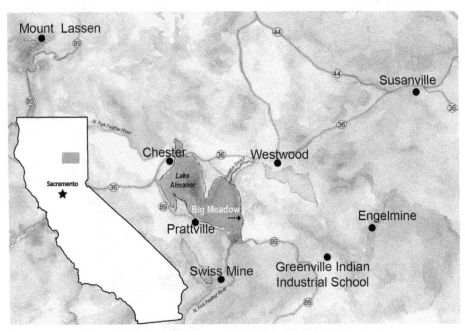

Map showing points of interest in Marie's early life (locations are approximate). An arrow marks the location of her grandfather's allotment, where she lived as a child. Most of her family's allotments were sited along the eastern shore of Lake Almanor, formerly Big Meadow.

Map by Nancy Wylie Design.

Prologue

Big Meadow Maidu

Many writers like to tell how Indians scalped the pioneers. They forget that we kept them alive in the wilderness during those rough winters.

—Marie Potts, 1960

In spring 1870, overland emigrant D. D. Blunt encountered a Mountain Maidu hamlet while visually surveying a stretch of acreage along the eastern rim of Nakám Koyó, which settlers called Big Meadows—or simply the Meadows. Having learned to suffer American presence with equanimity, residents found no cause for alarm and watched him continue on his way. A few months later, indifference turned to concern when he returned and began fencing off a section of their ancestral village. Soon he built a house, staking more visible claim to the 160 acres delineated in his preemption certificate. Long before Blunt arrived, an ancient footpath bisected the hamlet on a roughly north–south axis. When settlers graded it for wagon use, the Maidu erected a fence on the road's east side to protect a garden they had cultivated for fifteen years. Their residences remained on the west side, in closer proximity to the river that settlers called Hamilton Branch.

Blunt must have been perplexed when the Maidu did not simply pack up and leave once he settled in, but eventually he approached and tried to shoo them on their way. If puzzled before, he was surely astounded by their indignant refusal to budge, yielding no ground to the flimsy paper he produced. Material evidence of their long, prior occupancy was abundant. They did not fail to point it out. Here were their burial grounds; over there, eternal springs bubbled up to quench all creature thirsts. A dugout canoe reposed along the riverbank. Fallen trees formed strategic perches from which to spot the riparian life darting below. Basket traps were nestled in prime locations. He could see stretched and drying deerskins, fire pits, mortars, fishing nets, and basketry designed to serve every need, from cooking acorns to carrying infants. This was home, a settlement rich in memory and meaning, not some random spot to be vacated on demand.

Perhaps Blunt perused this domestic scene with some regret for his own role in Maidu dispossession. If so, he did not act on it, because Justice of the Peace John Seagraves eventually showed up to negotiate a compromise. Citing California's 1850 Act for the Government and Protection of Indians (Statute 133), Seagraves confirmed Maidu rights to traditional subsistence but insisted they reduce their land base. They agreed to confine themselves to a twenty-acre tract on the road's east side in exchange for a guarantee of their right to hold and inhabit these lands unmolested, in perpetuity. Terms were committed to writing, signed by Blunt and three nonliterate Maidu, who marked an X above their names: Doxam X, Dick X, and Bob X. Three homesteaders, John T. Hamilton, D. N. VanNorman, and John W. Starr, witnessed the negotiations and provided signatures. Perhaps they too harbored some sympathy for the Maidu's expulsion to the eastern boundaries of the village, but their vested interest was in retaining nearby a cooperative, and seasonally expendable, labor force.

In the Plumas County seat of Quincy, Seagraves documented the compromise in his September 26, 1870 docket:

State of California, County of Plumas, Seneca Township. At the request of parties interested, and under an act for the government of the Indians and protection of, passed April 22, 1850, page 82, Compiled Laws of California, Sec. 1–12, I proceeded to Mr. Blunt's ranch in Big Meadows, Township, County and State aforesaid, and set off for the use of the Indians residing thereon, all of that portion of said ranch lying east of the road and known as the Garden, belonging to said Indians, said land being in the SW1/4 of the NE1/4 of Sec. 10, 27 N, R8E, the same being bounded by a timber fence put there by Indians years ago, but still visible, said Indians agreeing and perfectly understanding the dividing of the same; also D. D. Blunt, the claimant to said land by government file, being present and agreeing to the same, all parties fully understanding the arrangement.[1]

Hereafter, the Maidu families restricted their lives to this small fraction of their original hamlet—dwelling, raising children, and burying loved ones in this ancestral place. Like their intrusive American neighbors, they "improved" the land. They rebuilt dilapidated fencing, erected a ceremonial roundhouse, diverted springs and streams, planted an orchard with twenty-two fruit trees, acquired and pastured livestock, grew hay, and built barns. They expertly adapted to limitations colonizers forced upon them, but this would not be enough.

Blunt vacated his preemption claim with the Marysville Land Office, in 1870, in favor of a homestead application. He filed this in spring 1873, in the Susanville Land Office, which inherited jurisdiction over Big Meadow upon its February 1871 creation. Five years later, on July 30, 1878, Blunt received his patent. A widower whose health was fading, he could no longer manage the ranch and was living in Quincy with his daughter and son-in-law, Mary and Aaron Drew.[2] Half the property was already sold to Abram Holmes, and on May 6, 1882, Alexander R. Thompson and Henry Kloppenberg bought the remaining eighty-acre portion, inclusive of the Maidu village. Thompson immediately moved his family into the ranch house and, by February 6, 1883, was sole title-holder.[3] Or so he imagined. Despite prior knowledge of the Seagraves agreement and the bustling hamlet on the property's southeastern arm, Thompson was bent on ejecting the Maidu. Having labored for a dozen years to accommodate themselves to the smaller but supposedly protected confines, they stood their ground. Thompson hired an attorney and sued.[4]

The case was heard August 28, 1883, in Plumas County Superior Court. Plaintiff attorney R. H. F. Variel asked in his filing for the defendants' "true names" to be known (they were previously enumerated as pseudonyms, "Joe Doe, Richard Rose and John Stiles, etc."), for the court to find their claim invalid, for his client to be issued a writ of possession quieting his title, and for Thompson to recover associated costs. The defendants' attorneys, D. W. Jenks and J. D. Goodwin, argued two lines of defense. First, the Big Meadow Maidu had never ceded to any nation, state, individual, or government the title to their aboriginal lands; nor had any government extended to them a promise or means of future sustenance and support. Second, in September 1870 they had agreed to vacate a portion of their village in exchange for permanent ownership and occupancy of the current site. Jenks and Goodwin argued that both Blunt's homestead patent and Thompson's title were illegitimate. To substantiate this claim, they turned optimistically to history and a sense of justice. They identified Doaksum Sr. as the "chief of a tribe or family of Indians known as the 'Big Meadows Indians' and called in their own language, 'Nahkomas.'" They asserted time immemorial ownership and occupancy of the land prior to October 1, 1492, previous to which their clients' ancestors had "discovered, entered upon and claimed and occupied said tract of land, and built dwellings thereon." They argued Maidu continuous occupancy and use, as well as development to the tune of three hundred dollars. As proof that title was never extinguished, they reviewed the federal government's failure to treat with Big Meadow Maidu or even to ratify the treaties negotiated with other California Indians, including those gathered at John Bidwell's Chico ranch on August 1, 1851.[5] Finally, attorneys for the defendants reminded the court that their clients' nonliterate status rendered them wholly dependent upon honorable and oral representations of the law, as when they conferred with Seagraves and Blunt.

Without benefit of jurors, Judge G. G. Clough rendered a short statement of findings on November 22, 1883, affirming Thompson's title and right to recover costs incurred to quiet it. Jenks and Goodwin were undeterred. On April 23, 1884, they appealed to the California Supreme Court on behalf of their clients, identified as "Doaksum Sr., Doaksum, Jr. and Perconnum, appellants, and John Doe et als., defendants." Humored by the notion that aboriginal title was not extinguished, Variel, in his pompous response to the court, summoned the language of conquest and racial superiority: "In fact, defendants asserted a title claimed to have descended from sovereigns occupying the premises away back in the misty past, before Columbus landed on the Western Continent. But they, at the same time, claimed that they had no written language or evidence of their title save traditionary lore."

Literacy was an uncommonly effective weapon of imperial conquest. Imposition of codified over customary law intentionally and disproportionately disadvantaged Indigenous peoples whose socioeconomic systems were rooted in orality. Even after Big Meadow Maidu affixed their mark to Seagraves's written words, they lost their rights. A cornerstone of the lower court's ruling was that Big Meadow Maidu had failed to assert title in a timely fashion—if indeed they held one. The U.S. Land Commission would have dismissed it, regardless. Yet the fact remains that the Maidu had no way of knowing the United States would preempt their lands as surplus public property. The Treaty of Guadalupe Hidalgo, which had ceded this formerly Mexican territory to the United States, theoretically protected private title granted under Spanish and Mexican rule. Even if Big Meadow Maidu possessed private title as recognized under English common law, chances are slim they would have managed to retain it. With rare exception, after American conquest, the combined effect of linguistic differences, nonliteracy, and state and

CELEBRATING 50 YEARS OF SERVING OUR COMMUNITY

Indian
HEALTH BOARD

American Indian Month Event

Save the Date!

May 27th, 2022
1:00-3:00pm

1315 East 24th Street
Minneapolis, MN 55404

Use your smartphones camera
to take a snapshot of the QR
code. This will redirect you to
the event page for the most
up to date event information.

federal failure to effectively communicate the process and deadline for presenting private title to the land commission, in concert with corrupt land speculators and ambiguous legal tradition, further alienated Indigenous people from their lands. Variel dismissed all linguistic contingencies and notions of customary law where Blunt's agreement was concerned. Instead, he compounded the insult by enumerating a litany of codified state and federal laws and precedents that supposedly rendered the defendants' claims to "Indian title" void.

Galled by this Maidu challenge to manifest destiny, Variel argued, "They assert an independent paramount claim, having its inception in the shadowy past, and which is alleged to be adverse, sovereign, and superior to that of either the United States Government or its grantors, whose existence and supremacy has been unquestioned, since a period long prior to the time when Columbus first unfurled his strange banners on the shores of the New World." He mocked, "Appellant's defense, although unique in its absurdity, has not the merit of entire originality," citing a similar, and unsuccessful, Louisiana Supreme Court case. Moving next to Seagraves's agreement, he quickly dispatched Maidu rights to occupancy and possession, arguing that the premise for the original agreement was flawed, since relevant sections of Statute 133 had been repealed. Moreover, Blunt did not hold patent at the moment of compromise and could not, therefore, define future disposition.

When the case initially moved forward on appeal, the local press declared that the California Supreme Court was famous for its "queer decisions."[6] This was not one. On February 25, 1886, it upheld the lower court's ruling. The editor of the *WASP* observed sardonically that when the Supreme Court justices solemnly contended that "the relation of the Indians to the lands they occupied, their title thereto, their power of alienation and the mode of its accomplishment were questions much discussed in the early days of our Government," they were obfuscating a central truth: "The value of these discussions to the Indian's interest was somewhat impaired by the fact that he was excluded from them. His part in them was a modest one—he was the thing discussed."[7]

Before California: The Ancestral Mountain Maidu World

Mountain Maidu settled into their alpine homelands at the convergence of the southern Cascades and northern Sierra long before settlers invaded.[8] "Time immemorial" expresses this depth of occupation in legal parlance and squares with Mountain Maidu histories.[9] Mountain Maidu make their homes throughout their ancestral territory and the wider world. For this reason, it is important to underscore that past tense is not used below to describe a people but rather to describe historical patterns predating and largely altered by American occupation. The Mountain Maidu language is closely related to the Konkow and Nisenan dialects spoken by neighboring groups, suggesting shared ancient ancestry. Immediately adjacent homelands and neighboring peoples include the Atsugewi and Achumawi to the north; Paiute and Washoe to the east; and Yana/Yahi, Konkow, and Nisenan to the northwest, west, and south, respectively. Maidu men traditionally found marriage partners among the Atsugewi.[10] After settler invasion produced refugee communities of displaced Native people, Mountain Maidu occasionally found it necessary to protect themselves from raiding groups, including those Marie's grandparents called Mill Creeks.[11]

Average annual temperatures ranging from the low twenties to the mid-eighties, heavy winter precipitation, and seasonal resource availability determined settlement patterns above all else. Marie's Big Meadow homelands are forty-five hundred feet above sea level. In fall and winter, preferred village sites were those strategically perched along the sloping ridge of vast bottomlands that became blanketed in snow, at times seven feet deep, during the coldest months. In spring and early summer, this location afforded easy access to lush meadowlands below and to higher conifer forests, where deer and other game retreated and where temporary summer camps were often established.[12] Before settlers came, Mountain Maidu sustained themselves through hunting, fishing, and gathering the profuse woodland and riparian flora and fauna available in temperate months. More importantly, they learned to preserve and store sufficient quantities of food to carry them through the severe winters, when resources were scarce and more difficult to harvest. From the earliest age, children learned through storytelling, ceremony, and observation to respect the interdependence of all beings. The fragility of life during long, harsh winters helped cultivate respect for medicine people and the wisdom of elders, whose deep knowledge of their environment was central to human survival. For all nature's predictability, its forces, including age-old human greed, brought aberrations in resource availability. Generosity was a guiding social value and necessary attribute for leadership, while principles of reciprocity governed everyday life.

The first American emigrants to homestead in Nakám Koyó were ill prepared to weather the severe winters and survived because Maidu people fed them from their own precious stores. Marie's grandfather, called Big Meadow Bill by Americans, was known for such life-sustaining generosity. "After I grew older, I heard many stories of the kind deeds and courtesies he extended to the white settlers as well as his own people. How he saved the lives of white settlers by taking them fish, jerky and dried roots, and showing them the edible tubers in the early spring."[13]

Ancestors

Big Meadow Bill earned the appellation Hukespem (Wise One) in adulthood, but as a twin, he was recognized as special from the moment of birth. He and his brother were born to a Hat Creek (Atsugewi) mother and a Mountain Maidu father sometime between 1835 and 1845.[14] In the mid-1860s, Bill participated in a cycle of violence between the Mountain Maidu and Mill Creek enemies, which

Figure 1. Marie's grandfather Hukespem, also known as
Big Meadow Bill, circa 1900.
Photograph by Eli Piazzoni.

was covered in the local press. The prelude to this sensational account occurred in July 1866. A settler traveling "over the mountain" from Taylorsville to Big Meadow, on July 31, reported that upon his arrival, an agitated and frightened Maidu man approached him. Exclaiming that Mill Creeks had killed two men and two women on the Meadow's west side that morning, he wondered if the traveler had seen any of his kinsmen coming from Indian Valley.[16] A customary pattern of reprisal and revenge explains why Big Meadow Maidu, in league with their Indian Valley counterparts, subsequently organized an avenging foray into Mill Creek country. A month or so later, adequately provisioned with armaments and food, they advanced on enemy territory. Their triumphal return home in mid-October occasioned an impressive reception described in a letter published by the *Plumas National*. Replete with stereotypic embellishment, one paragraph deserves note: "The lion of the evening was an Indian named Big Bill, the one who shot the Mill Creek; and as a token of regard his dark-skinned brethren and sisters kept brushing him with small twigs which each one carried. Another honor which they conferred on the successful warrior, was fasting him a certain number of days after the shooting of the enemy to appease the wrath the 'Great Spirit' might feel toward the tribe."[16]

According to Potts, Mill Creeks murdered Hukespem's first wife, Phoebe, with whom he had several children. The July 1866 attack likely marked the instance of Phoebe's death and may or may not have been the same point at which Phoebe's sister Mariah, Marie's grandmother, was kidnapped. According to Potts's account, several families were temporarily camped on the Meadow's west side while the men, employed by Americans, were working on a wagon road. At some point, the men left camp for several days to attend a Fourth of July "big time" at Bahapki, a Native village established by General John Bidwell on his Chico ranch. Cash prizes annually lured regional competitors to footraces and other athletic competitions. While the men were away, Mill Creeks reportedly crept into camp, committed murders, and stole two girls, Nellie Jenkins and Mariah. Potts guessed that Mariah was about fourteen.[17] If the kidnapping occurred the summer after Big Bill's mid-October return from Mill Creek, it fits neatly into the cycle of attack and revenge that Roland Dixon later chronicled.[18]

Carted off and enslaved, the two girls were bound nightly, hands and feet, to prevent escape while their captors slept. One night, as the story goes, Mariah wriggled close to Nellie and released her compatriot's hands. Nellie sat up, unlashed her ankles, and fled alone into the darkness. Mariah's captivity dragged on. Assigned to attend the wife and children of the Mill Creek leader, she absorbed enough of their language and setting to plan a getaway. This opportunity arose when Americans—probably vigilante militia, though she assumed soldiers—attacked. With her captors distracted, she slipped into a hiding place she had earlier discovered along a rocky gorge. Mariah remembered the onslaught raging for days. She waited patiently for stillness to settle over the canyon. Finding her way home was an exhausting ordeal. Some accounts have her gone midsummer to fall; others suggest she was captive more than a year and pregnant upon escape.[19] Intrepid young Mariah returned to mother Phoebe's surviving children and the five more she bore Big Meadow Bill. For the remainder of their lives, these two exhibited remarkable resilience in the face of adversity and socioeconomic upheaval.[20]

They witnessed the steady invasion of their forest and meadowlands by emigrant overlanders and argonauts from around the world. These newcomers commandeered rivers and polluted streams with mining tailings, fenced the open meadowlands for agricultural production, and carried counterproductive values into a social landscape steeped in centuries-old traditions designed to preserve the common good. Hukespem could deal swiftly with sporadic terror of Mill Creeks, but Americans posed a persistent form of violence to livelihoods and autonomy. Maidu watched these invaders with curiosity and occasional amusement. Initially, they coped with interlopers by getting out of the way, unable to foresee that within two generations their expansive homelands would be endlessly partitioned and depleted. Where once they exploited a wide swath of terrain flush with indigenous flora and fauna, husbandry of imported species now consumed disproportionate volumes of water and land, restricting their subsistence resources and movement.[21]

Transformations to the social landscape were profound. The 1860 census, California's first federal enumeration, offers a revealing portrait of Big Meadow and the wider Seneca Township. Notoriously ambiguous, even in their failings census records offer spectacular insight into socioeconomic conditions. The 1860 census records 480 individuals but entirely erases the Maidu people who populated this township. Absence from the formal record might be chalked up to several rationales, from language barriers to cultural and geographic distance. Still, the enumerator's failure to bridge such gaps with even a cursory estimate confirms that Maidu people did not figure into the new order of things, however much their land and labor—manual, sexual, and reproductive—were absolutely essential to it. Fifty-three Chinese gold miners, roughly 10 percent of the township's population, were last to be counted. While their numbers and enumeration foreshadow the

1882 Chinese Exclusion Act, their occupation and masculine gender align with the township's wider profile.

Non-Native women were scarce in 1850s northern California. This was certainly the case in Seneca Township, where 432 men and only forty-eight women were enumerated. Most were wives and minor daughters of American homesteaders or immigrants plying riparian channels for placer gold, although occasionally women worked in placer mining. Such was the case for thirty-nine-year-old Victoria Lara, a single Mexican immigrant house-holding with Erasmus Kercher of Saxony. The non-Native population was youthful, with most adults between twenty and forty years old; thirteen were age forty to fifty, and none were in their sixth decade of life.

Miners far outnumbered homesteaders in Seneca Township during the first decade of statehood. Some were Americans who journeyed overland, but most hailed from international ports of call. Making a protracted voyage around the Horn, or over the Isthmus of Nicaragua, they were unceremoniously disgorged into the rough-and-tumble streets of San Francisco. Anxious to transform their lives, here or back in their countries of origin, they scrambled and slogged their way into the Sierra foothills and up the North Fork of the Feather River. By 1860, Mountain Maidu country was populated with miners from Chile, Mexico, Turkey, England, Ireland, Baden, Prussia, Switzerland, France, and China. Between 1860 and 1870, Seneca Township lost one-fifth of its population, as placer mining's luster faded.[22] Meanwhile, ranching and dairy farming gained ground, both figuratively and literally, as Americans began claiming Big Meadow acreage by the thousands under the Swamp and Overflow Act. By the 1870s, first-generation homesteaders like Peter Olsen were protesting excesses allowed under this law.[23] During the 1860s, a residential base capable of sustaining schoolteachers, gardeners, craftsmen, blacksmiths, loggers, hoteliers, a few merchants, and at least two physicians developed. The Chinese mining community remained active, but some settled into cooking and gardening. Overall, more non-Native women, family households, and older adults populated the township. Some aged in place, but others were recent arrivals, such as fifty-three-year-old David Drew Blunt.

No Maidu are enumerated in Seneca Township's federal census until 1880, but those born in the 1860s and 1870s, like Hukespem's children, were integral to the wage-based economy, many by choice but never as equal beneficiaries. Older Maidu, such as Mariah and Big Meadow Bill, supplemented household resources through traditional means: gathering, hunting, and fishing. This mixed subsistence strategy was not simply a function of their marginalized position in the encroaching agricultural and cash economy. Like people everywhere, they preferred their own foodways and continued to pursue them, exercising a measure of autonomy over the pace and scale of acculturation.[24] Yet no matter how peacefully or purposefully Big Meadow Maidu labored in new or old ways, daily life was troubled by jarring worldviews and material outcomes that contradicted centuries-old values and expectations.

John Seagraves settled the Maidu's conflict with Blunt by defining sufficient land to meet their "necessary wants" as defined under Statute 133, Section 2. Contrary to humane pretense, this language encoded how dispossession was enacted statewide—on terms that satisfied the particularistic needs of local settler economies. Seagraves was not exercising moral suasion by negotiating an agreement between Blunt and the Maidu, but rather a California-specific mechanism for removal or transfer by degree. The four American signatories cast themselves as benevolent overlords to the Nahkomas while preserving their self-interest.[25] Despite forced dispersal of the Big Meadow Maidu from this ancestral hamlet, in ten years' time these same lands sheltered one of their descendants who would become a vocal advocate for her people and lands. Mountain Maidu was her natal tongue, but English-language literacy was her weapon.

Stolen Land and Lives: Genocide, Rejected Treaties, Social Reformers

After California gained statehood, the federal government initiated the process of expropriating Indigenous lands as "unoccupied" public surplus, a specious status to be sure. The Preemption Act of 1841 anticipated and fostered U.S. westward expansion.[26] American immigrants were already squatting on Native land when Mexico controlled Alta California, but after gold discovery and statehood, immigration accelerated, and Native resistance along with it. Miners and settlers wanted Native people out of the way and retaliated indiscriminately to "depredations" against their possessions and interloping presence by striking back at the collective California Indian body.[27] Vigilante militias, head bounties, and scorched earth tactics made manifest the unquenchable bloodthirstiness of California settler colonial ambitions. As one scholar notes, even seasoned military officers and Indian agents were stunned by the atrocities that presumably God-fearing people perpetrated on fellow human beings.[28] These were not shameful, secret, backroom dealings. The mid-nineteenth-century press observed this bloodshed with interest. The rare editorial condemned "civilized" society, but newsmen of the day were predominantly boosters of genocide.[29]

A month after California joined the Union, Congress passed legislation creating a treaty commission. George W. Barbour, Reddick McKee, and O. M. Wozencraft began their work in March 1851. In January 1852, they forwarded to the U.S. Senate eighteen treaties negotiated with captains and headmen of perhaps one-half to one-third of the autochthonous polities within state boundaries.[30] In California, settlers who had earlier insisted that Native people be moved out of their way were now beside themselves, certain that lands earmarked for reservations held vast mineral and agricultural wealth. In response, the state senate and assembly passed resolutions by a margin of twenty-five to six, renouncing the treaties and mandating that California's U.S. senators oppose them before Congress. On July 8, 1852, the treaties were rejected in executive session. Sealed and locked away in U.S. Senate archives, they were scrubbed from settler colonial memory as the citizenry, state government, and federal government continued to consume treaty-ceded and -reserved lands. Under pressure to resolve California's "Indian problem," the federal government created four military and several farm reservations, beginning with the 1853 establishment of Tejon Reservation.[31] Some reservations were populated through forced marches that remain impaled in the hearts of contemporary descendants.[32] Corruption, inadequate provisions, traditional enemies shoved into close quarters—a thousand problems large and small—rendered these measures largely ineffectual. Most Indian people remained homeless, without the meager protection of reservation lands. Continually pushed from ancestral homelands and temporary campsites, they struggled to survive. Many did not.

Social reformers and missionary organizations, including Philadelphia's Indian Rights Association (IRA) and the Northern California Indian Association (NCIA), took note of these cruel conditions and sought relief for people whose suffering lay squarely at the feet of the U.S. government. Their efforts led to "rediscovery" of the rejected treaties. Traveling to Colusa County in 1902, to identify land or patrons who could help the county's homeless Indian population, San José NCIA member the Reverend H. C. Meredith learned of an agreement signed around the time of statehood, promising land for Indian people. A local journalist had been the interpreter at these negotiations, and his uncle had been a signatory. Meredith's news incited NCIA research into this treaty and a memorial to the president for relief of homeless Indians. California's senator Thomas Bard and IRA's Samuel Brosius induced Senate clerks to search out the elusive document, and the sordid story of not one but eighteen treaties came to light.[33] The ensuing moral outrage fueled the long and contentious legislative process resulting in the 1928 California Indians Jurisdictional Act (CIJA), which allowed a suit for broken treaty promises to be brought against the federal government in the U.S. Court of Claims. Meanwhile, more immediate relief for homeless Indians was pursued through the Office of Indian Affairs (OIA), which appointed NCIA attorney and executive secretary C. E. Kelsey as "California special agent" in 1905. He was tasked with producing a census of non-reservation Indians documenting blood quanta and residential status; this list formed the basis for purchasing a series of small rancherias.[34] Culled from meager surplus public lands typically lacking arable soil and sufficient water, they were taken into trust by the federal government, becoming home to refugee communities of culturally and linguistically distinct peoples who intermarried, created new kin groups, and have since engaged in generations of place-making to recover and patch together traditions and aboriginal worlds ravaged by colonization.

Colliding Worlds: Intercultural Intimacy, Violence, and Love

When Alexander Thompson drove the Maidu from their village, John T. Hamilton was already deceased. An early comer to Big Meadow, Hamilton had settled on its east side, near the branch of the Feather River's North Fork now bearing his family name. Like other Big Meadow agricultural enterprises, his was dependent upon Maidu labor. Feudal relations were common between homesteaders and the Big Meadow Maidu families who were allowed—even encouraged—to camp on the margins of ranching operations that had subsumed their traditional territory and livelihoods. As an 1885 newspaper declared, "The Big Meadows tribe of Indians number about 200 and are divided among the different ranches, each having its separate campoody and set of retainers. The men find employment part of the year working for the ranchers, who are entirely dependent upon them."[35] Men became skilled cowboys and ranch hands. They defined new ways of being Maidu men. This included turning to employers for intervention when the likes of Blunt and Thompson threatened to erode the provisional accommodations they had made to settler presence. Maidu women's domestic, reproductive, and sexual labor was no less critical to this landscape, as Marie's ancestral family history demonstrates. The lives of Hukespem's children and grandchildren bore the diverse hallmarks of these fluid and turbulent times.

Land theft was only one frame through which Big Meadow Maidu apprehended distinctions between their own values and those of the Americans for whom they toiled. Treatment of Maidu women and children was another. Native women's vulnerability during the gold rush is legendary. Historian Albert L. Hurtado documents the rampant violence perpetrated against them without flattening a landscape of conjugal relations between non-Native men and Native women that included instances of love, mutual respect, convenience, strategic alliance, and the like.[36] Their more remote location delayed and diminished the wholesale nature of violence that women suffered in more southerly reaches of the Sierra, but this does not mean that Mountain Maidu women escaped rape, exploitation, and abuse. Like their southerly sisters, they brought their own cultural values and expectations to the realms of affection and intimacy into which they willingly entered during this period of intercultural encounter. As in other colonial and cross-cultural contexts, only occasionally were they met.[37] Yet it was children produced through these voluntary and involuntary unions who most keenly reflected the complexities of a settler colonial project that reduced identity and mixed ancestry to a blood-quantum calculus.[38] Post–gold rush news columnists regularly offered unflinching commentary on the county's reproductive demographics. Moral and racial anxieties were inseparably coupled in these discourses. In 1877 the *Plumas National* sniped, "It is said that the crop of half-breeds in the Meadows was never better."[39]

Seneca Township was astonishingly cosmopolitan for such a rural and remote setting. When the 1850s and '60s mining boom subsided, many non-Native miners joined the agrarian economy, finding wives among the second generation of overland emigrants. Others returned home long enough to court spouses or collect families left behind. As agriculture expanded, Big Meadow women worked as domestic laborers, often for the same families as male kin. Listed as "laundresses" and "washerwomen" in census records, these wives and daughters labored in settings where they were vulnerable to sexual exploitation, as evidenced by the growing population of unacknowledged children fathered by non-Maidu men, who freely abandoned their children's Maidu mothers. Native dependence upon settlers for wage employment and land occupancy "rights" buttressed Maidu women's vulnerability and limited their capacity to flee abusive circumstances.

These were the social conditions under which Hukespem's daughter Josie Bill gave birth to her first two children, Marie's half siblings, John and Lizzette Mason.[40] Their father, John E. Hamilton (b. 1862), was the only son of the elder Hamilton, party to the Seagraves negotiation. Following his death in 1878, Hamilton's widow, Sarah, maintained the ranch, raising her young children there. Josie worked as a ranch laundress well into the 1890s, and her first two children were conceived while John E. Hamilton was splitting his time between Big Meadow and Shasta County, where he owned property and, in 1890, met and married Samantha Thatcher. Josie gave birth to their first child, John, in November 1891.[41] Lizzette Pansy followed in 1893. In April 1894, Hamilton's brother-in-law John T. Becraft, another settler descendant, took over day-to-day management of Hamilton ranch, which his wife, Hamilton's sister Marietta, inherited after her mother's 1892 death. Josie's employment continued, while Hamilton attended to his Shasta County home and wife as her baby's due date approached. In March 1895, Samantha Hamilton gave birth. Their daughter lived, but Samantha died soon after.[42] In mid-fall 1895, Josie Bill gave birth to Marie, her third child and second daughter. Years later, after becoming a mother herself, Marie learned the truth of her conception. Unlike her brother and sister, she was conceived through rape. The indigenized name Bearcraft has been passed through several generations as her genitor's surname. Many years later, she offered some commentary on this subject to a newspaper reporter: "They called the child a half-breed. Some of the men weren't proud of it. I don't know why they were ashamed of fathering a child. But that's white society for you. My father was one of those sons-a-bitches."[43]

Josie's experiences of intercultural intimacy and Mountain Maidu motherhood are usefully counterposed with those of her sister, Jennie Bill Piazzoni. Brothers Christopher and Baptiste Piazzoni arrived in northern California in the mid-1860s, argonauts from Canton Ticino, on the Swiss–Italian borderlands. By 1870, almost three thousand of their countrymen had immigrated to California, typically with sponsorship from the Swiss government and previously migrated families. After trying their luck in the goldfields, most settled in rural areas and took up agricultural pursuits founded on generations of Old World expertise. California's dairy industry owes its start to Swiss emigrants, whose heritage is still visible in Monterey, San Luis Obispo, and Sonoma Counties.[44]

Big Meadow drew its share of Swiss farmers in the 1860s and 1870s. Its topography, high altitude, and snowy winters were no challenge; here was a diminutive version of the Alps. In fact, late-nineteenth-century tourists habitually likened the area to Switzerland in published letters and travelogues. Local residents swelled with pride at poetic renderings of sun-kissed meadows against a backdrop of snowcapped peaks and rivers rushing through sheer canyon walls. This was the landscape that drew miners and farmers to Seneca Township. The North Fork of the Feather River, which meandered lazily through marshy Big Meadow, dropped precipitously at its southern terminal, carving deep channels through ancient rock with stunning gravitational force. From the 1860s through 1930s, a small community of hardy folk, as eccentric as they were optimistic, inhabited the Seneca—or North Fork—district. Here along steep canyon ravines, a rugged stretch of narrow, unpaved road traces the contours of the North Fork at the summit of its mighty race down to the Sacramento Valley. Drownings like that of Caribou miner Henry Keep, in 1890, were dark reminders of its lethal and magnificent force: "It is said that the angry waters of the North Fork never give up their dead!"[45]

The brothers Piazzoni eventually found their way to Big Meadow and its promise of mineral wealth, but it was not their initial destination. When Chris Piazzoni left Intragna, Switzerland, he was headed for Petaluma, where he was recorded in 1870 at thirty years old. He and "Faldo," a relative aged forty, worked as "laborers," along with twenty-three-year-old "woodchopper" Baptiste. Christopher returned home for a time, which Guy Métraux notes was common among Swiss immigrants, before returning with another family member in 1876. He and eighteen-year-old Fidele Piazzoni, both listed as miners, arrived in New York from Le Havre, aboard the *Labrador*. By 1880, Baptiste, a lifelong bachelor, and Christopher had settled in Plumas County, staking multiple claims in the Seneca mining district.[46] The Piazzoni "Swiss Mine" cabin still stands in Plumas National Forest, three miles west of the once wild and woolly mining town of Seneca. Christopher settled down to a prosaic Big Meadow life. The U.S. census shows that in 1880, the household of this single "farmer and dairyman" included twenty-year-old Italian-born Francisco Berini (or Perini), a "servant."[47] Immediately adjacent were Hamilton Ranch, the contiguous portion of Blunt's ranch—now owned by Abram Holmes—and the "moveable" households of some fifty Maidu, including, Old Doaksum and Mary, John and Roxy [Roxie] Peconum, John and Mary Meadows, and Old Bill and his wife, Mary. Old Bill is listed as a "hunter"; Mary (Mariah) is said to be "keeping campoody." Sixteen-year-old Jennie is single, hinting at the courtship that soon turned these neighbors into affines. Two years later, Thompson banished them.

Jennie's marriage to Piazzoni bestowed a level of belonging on the Bill family denied them by American settlers, such as Thompson and the fathers of Josie's three eldest children. Perhaps Piazzoni's immigrant experience, his "exogenous otherness," made him more enlightened and humane.[48] Certainly, his household was one of the most linguistically diverse in Big Meadow, with children, parents, and extended kin regularly interacting in Maidu, Italian, and English. The intimate encounters among this second generation of Mountain Maidu, American, and Swiss peoples produced a third generation of cousins who shared a remarkable intercultural heritage. Sadly, some did not survive the negative repercussions of being Indigenous in late-nineteenth-century California.

1

Big Meadow Maidu Schoolgirl

Please Mish Tubody, I want needle . . . to sew doll.
—*Marie Mason, fall 1900*

M arie was born in the crisp fall months of 1895, when apple orchards were
being harvested.[1] Welcomed into the fold of her large extended family, she
joined the multitude of mixed-ancestry siblings and cousins comprising the second
generation of her family to be born since Americans began arriving in Big Meadow.
By now, Mountain Maidu tradition was irrevocably altered. Homesteaders and
miners brought change; but so too did federal policy shaped thousands of miles
away in Washington, D.C., and in the drawing rooms of wealthy eastern elites.
From these distant and lofty perches, "Indian reformers" launched an assault on
tribal estates, religions, languages, and cultures.[2] Although the architects and
advocates of this campaign articulated their vision in the language of "Americanizing" and "civilizing," its goal was forced assimilation or ethnocide. Bearing in
mind that land is the critical commodity in settler colonialism, it is easy to see
how removing tribal peoples to western reservations once served settler colonial
logic.[3] However, as westward expansion exhausted available lands, reservations
fell under new scrutiny. In the same way the ideology of manifest destiny furthered
settler colonialism, so did late-nineteenth-century Americanizing and civilizing
ideologies.

The concept of a communally held tribal estate was always contrary to American capitalist ideology, but now its last refuge—the reservation—was assailed as
a vector of poverty and disease. Reformers set about "rescuing" Native people
through the 1887 General Allotment Act, or Dawes Act. This legislation aimed to

produce citizen-farmers by dividing reservation acreage and distributing it among
adult heads of households; "surplus" lands were then opened to settlers. Far from
benign or paternalistic, the Dawes Act devastated Native societies. Reservations,
for all their shortcomings, endowed American Indians with a land base, tribal
sovereignty, and a measure of protection against genocidal instincts that, in
California, Christian "civilized" settlers acted upon with unapologetic savagery.[4]

Allotment operated in tandem with a powerful apparatus and symbol of settler colonialism: the boarding school. The earliest and most celebrated of these
schools, powerful sites of forced assimilation in Australia, Canada, and the United
States, was Pennsylvania's Carlisle Indian Industrial School, founded in 1879
by retired army captain Richard Henry Pratt. After the Dawes Act was passed,
off-reservation boarding schools proliferated across the American West. Removing
children from their families and communities, the traditional agents and sites
of enculturation, they promised to detribalize and Americanize the younger
generation. White Christian women were the most enthusiast proponents of these
schools, finding no contradiction in their claims to superior moral and maternal
values while simultaneously supporting the separation of Native children from
their own mothers.[5]

Marie and her extended family experienced these reforms in a highly local-
ized fashion. Mountain Maidu rights of occupancy were ever diminishing, and
their condition was grim indeed when the Indian Office began allotting them
surplus public lands in 1894, under authority of the Dawes Act. Though short-
lived and inadequate to their needs, this process brought Marie's kin a moment
and measure of security in the wake of rejected treaties, no reservation, and the
ever-encroaching capitalist economy.[6] Like allotment, the Bill family experience
with boarding school was equally idiosyncratic. It began with the development of a
mission school, south of Big Meadow, that her large, intercultural family exploited
strategically. While Christian reformers, organizations, and institutions foreclosed
on some Mountain Maidu traditions, Native people demonstrated intelligence and
resilience in their interaction with the school and its early administrators, who
were drawn from the local community. Taking a wide-angle view, this chapter
demonstrates how Marie's kin exercised Native agency to greatly varying effect.
Marie's experience was even more distinctive, as she arrived just as the school
was experiencing a changing of the guard. The federal government's authoritarian hand became increasingly visible and inflexible in their small community.
Marie's childhood and adolescence were shaped by forces beyond her youthful
control, but she proved to be a quick study—bright, ambitious, and lively. For

better or worse, the school eventually became her anchor in a sea of constant change.

Chenkutpem: Big Meadow Granddaughter

In 1894, Hukespem and Mariah, along with their children and a handful of grandchildren, were each granted 160 acres of federal trust land through the Dawes Act of 1887. Most Bill family allotments encompassed portions of their ancestral hamlet along the eastern rim of Big Meadow, from which Thompson had expelled them a decade prior, though Hukespem's was the only one with water, so most of the family camped there.[7] Although Marie, born the following year, was never allotted, she was blessed with knowledge and memories tied to this place and her beloved grandparents. The enchantment of falling asleep as a panorama of stars glistened down on murmuring glades and the vast forest floor never left her. The pine canopy sheltering their cedar bark house came to nocturnal life with the baritone strains of owls holding forth in wizened dialogue. Her grandfather's hunting prowess and ability to care for his family was a lasting point of pride. How amazed she was in later years to realize what a profound education Hukespem imparted as she ambled along playfully at his side, absorbing instruction about the expansive realm of beings that shared their small corner of the universe. These were lessons about mutual respect and generosity toward all beings that she carried later into urban contexts and that informed her steadfast commitment to giving freely of her own time and money, even when she had little of either to spare. Tender remembrances of these fleeting years were embodied in the name Mariah gave her: Chenkutpem (One with Sharp Eyes). The appellation was endearingly tied to the special relationship Marie and Hukespem shared. A little sprite, she awaited his daily return from hunting and fishing expeditions with anticipation for the treats he invariably brought her. Training her gaze on the slim apertures between towering sugar pines, Marie would announce his imminent arrival while he was still off in the distant woods. The superior vision of her granddaughter and namesake reminded Mariah that she and Hukespem were growing old. This energetic little child who brought such joy to their household would soon join her siblings and cousins at school.[8]

Mission Indian School

Between 1890 and 1897, a humble precursor to the federal, off-reservation boarding schools that multiplied across the western landscape emerged in fits and starts about fifteen miles southeast of Big Meadow. The government did not

originate the school, but its affiliation with Christian reform organizations like
the Women's National Indian Association (WNIA) fostered its development. In
1897 the government purchased the land and buildings comprising the Mission
Indian School (MIS), changing its name to Greenville Indian Industrial School
(hereafter called Greenville).[9]

The school's small size, rural environs, and historical origins endowed it with
a different character than other off-reservation boarding schools. It grew from
the modest efforts of two ranching cousins, Amelia Martin and Charles Hall.
Around 1888, Martin began missionary work in Indian Valley. She ministered to
the ill; offered women lessons in cooking, sewing, and housekeeping; and taught
Sunday school for children and adults. Her school was originally hosted in Abro
Johnson's home, but opposition from other camp members forced its relocation to
the Martin ranch. Around this time, several Maidu fathers living near Hall were
angered when their children were denied public school admission, so he began
instructing them in basic subjects. Soon he began looking for funds to purchase
school supplies and to construct a suitable building on his ranch, several miles
east of the village of Greenville.[10] In 1889 Hall turned to civil rights activist Albion
W. Tourgée for suggestions. Soon to distinguish himself as plaintiff's attorney in
Plessy v. Ferguson (1896), Tourgée, in turn, contacted Amelia Quinton, WNIA
president. Thus began the MIS.[11]

Quinton nurtured Martin's Sunday school efforts, but her real interest was the
fledgling day school. Through a combination of appeals to the federal government
and national publicity in the *Indian's Friend*, she harnessed the tremendous
evangelical passion and philanthropic potential embodied in white women's
late-nineteenth-century commitments to maternalism. The rise and fall of this
movement within the ranks of WNIA and the federal Indian Service is well documented, as is its particularistic expression in 1890s California. Despite occasionally
unflattering portraits of WNIA's longtime leader, there is no denying Quinton's
force. She expertly leveraged the organization's collective energy and her own
prominence within the movement to draw government funding and donations
by the barrelful to the modest doorsteps of this rural California outpost.[12] The
latter came most consistently from the Philadelphia, Jamaica Plain (Boston), and
New Orleans chapters. After 1894 support also flowed from a new chapter, the San
José Indian Association (SJIA), but the entire WNIA network followed Greenville
through decade-long incremental growth and setback, construction and fire,
and mission day to government boarding school transition. Long after Quinton
negotiated its government sale and transfer, WNIA affiliates were encouraged

to remember "our old love Greenville" at Christmas, when teachers needed help with presents for children and parents.[13]

The school drew federal support from the start, as Quinton was able to convince the Office of Indian Affairs (OIA) to pay Hall's salary as MIS's first teacher. He resigned a year later to move out of state, and in October 1891 Edward N. Ament replaced him. Seven students met in the one-room building the WNIA had paid Hall and several Native fathers to build in 1890. Holding his post for a decade, Ament indelibly shaped the school, local perceptions of it by Native and non-Native communities, and its reputation among reformers from San Jose to Washington, D.C.[14] Edward and his wife, Florence "Floy" Ament, were earnest Christians, believing righteously in their own benevolence. A graduate of Oakland's Heald Business College, Ament regularly solicited donations of clothing and funds for school supplies in Plumas County and San Jose, where SJIA provided vigorous support.[15]

In 1892, when Floy was hired as assistant teacher and school matron, MIS boasted twenty pupils. Addressing the Plumas County Teachers Institute, Ament claimed that his students took quickly to writing and drawing but found arithmetic challenging. He bemoaned his lack of patience, as teaching Native students required this virtue in abundance: "Many of them live in smoke-begrimed campoodies, and subsist on acorns and fish, with now and then a week or so of more civilized food. And yet we expect them to come into school looking clean and fresh; we expect well-learned lessons from pupils who have breakfasted on acorn flakes, pick up raw acorns at noon, and will go home to acorn soup at night. This food, we must admit, is not a great brain stimulant at best."[16] On some points, Ament was flatly incorrect. Acorn is a valuable source of nutrition.[17] On others, he was strikingly clear-minded—at least in part: "Indians are naturally superstitious and loth to step outside of old customs and traditions, and thus *many of the older ones are convinced that education is only another means of wiping them off the face of the earth.*"[18] Indeed, many were unwilling to send their children to Greenville. Others were anxious to do so regardless of ideological and material hurdles.

Ament hewed a rigid Christian line. One of the many townspeople he invited to tour the day school in its early years was Methodist Episcopal preacher S. W. Albone. Although he was duly impressed, what really captured his attention was learning how Ament handled the sudden and nearby appearance of a k'um, or "sweat house, a work of the past, [where] the Indians go on Sunday evening to dance and drink." Heading over on first notice, Ament and his brother William lectured them about the ills of dancing and drinking and "sang to them."[19] This anecdote is enlightening. First, it demonstrates that some parents were willing to forgo ceremonial expression—or suppress public knowledge of its continued vitality—to keep their children in school; this was common practice for many Indigenous peoples under colonial regimes. Maidu were no different. Second, what parents clearly sought for their offspring was educational advantage, and literacy above all, not Christian conversion.[20] Third, they were willing to move residence and ceremonial sites to get it.

Big Meadow Maidu Parents: MIS Transitions from Day to Boarding School

In 1892 the fathers of ten Big Meadow Maidu children traveled to Indian Valley, hoping to find nearby employment so they could enroll their children at MIS, still just a day school.[21] This impulse was not without precedent or design. On a summer 1891 California tour, Quinton had preached at Big Meadow, agitated for a Big Meadow Sunday school, and purportedly "induced some of the Indians to move over to Greenville in order to attend school."[22] Unlike fathers who moved to Greenville in 1891, those who went in spring 1892 did not find jobs and returned home frustrated. Even during milder months, when wagon roads were passable, daily round-trips of thirty miles from Big Meadow to Greenville and back again were prohibitive. Certain that lack of schooling would disadvantage their children, the fathers met with public school superintendent Benjamin R. Foss in May to lobby for a school. He reported a planned follow-up meeting and the Maidu desire that white people attend and "assist them in securing the school."[23] A tally of forty school-age Big Meadow Maidu seemed to bode well, but support never materialized, despite WNIA's own optimistic projections in July 1892: "This [Quinton's 1891 trip] has led to the great increase in the desire for help at Big Meadows. Some bright young ladies, the Misses Abbott and others will no doubt help in the new enterprise in their own town." While the *Indian's Friend* was making this announcement to its national readership, local residents were learning official state requirements for public school access: "Indians who have given up their tribal relations" were entitled to public education for their children; those maintaining tribal relations could expect their children to be lawfully excluded.[24]

This news galvanized Quinton, who pressed Commissioner of Indian Affairs Thomas Morgan for help in developing boarding facilities. She and Ament had already cited hunger, poverty, and three-mile treks through snow by Indian Valley pupils as incentives for boarding school status. The effort of Big Meadow fathers to get their children schooling punctuated these points. WNIA offered to build the structure if OIA would contract for student room and board. Slowly, the federal system's massive cogs began to grind. By fall 1894, thirty-six of Greenville's eighty students were boarding. Quinton then decided the government should cover day pupil lunches. Why should they eat a "cold potato" from home while their boarding peers dined on more substantial fare?[25] Morgan conceded.

Quinton's sale of MIS to the government two years later came with high Native costs. In Greenville's early day and boarding iterations, pupils were there because parents made the difficult choice to send them. Education was not only or always a motivating factor. Some parents sought for their children greater food security, warmth during winter months, and daily supervision when they were called away to work or lost the family members who typically cared for them. They gambled on Greenville providing such things. Regardless of limited options or knowledge of the school's ideological endgame, parents still held the balance of power. This small degree of autonomy was lost under federal administration; the school superintendent was now compelled to follow federal policy, including an 1891 compulsory attendance law. As with all else in these perilous times, Native parents could not predict the future. But for Big Meadow Maidu who had lived through *Thompson v. Doaksum*, knowing their children could compete in a world dominated by the written word must have been paramount.

Arrival, Escape, and "Rescue"

Marie's carefree life with Hukespem and Mariah wound to an abrupt close in June 1900. In February, OIA budgeted $150 for student recruitment and transportation; the government wanted beds filled. The Aments often found the commissioner's expectations tedious and absurd, but they were dedicated to the school's Christian mission, and on occasion these aligned with his demands. For a decade, Floy had ministered to the sick, checked on elderly Maidu, and distributed medicine, clothing, and toys sent by the barrelful from WNIA affiliates. She was a familiar presence in Big Meadow, where between late spring and early summer, she made three trips to visit camps and collect students. Recent acquisition of a covered wagon made these excursions decidedly more comfortable and efficient.[26]

Perhaps Marie was more curious than scared on the road to Greenville, but this quickly changed. Boarding pupils were bathed upon entry—and in some schools subjected to haircuts and destruction of tribal clothing. She was not going to escape this ritual. Marie surveyed her strange surroundings while Floy stripped her down. Spotting a tub of steamy water, she was terrified to find herself suddenly inhabiting it. Unable to speak or understand English, she drew on experience. Knowing that Mariah used big tubs to cook acorn mush, Marie ascertained that she had been plucked of her clothes for this same purpose! Bolting out of the tub and door, she sprinted naked and frightened into the countryside, as far as her little legs would carry her—two miles or more, she recalled. Woefully, her escape was thwarted when an older pupil caught up to her on a bicycle. For the next twelve years, minus a few summer weeks here and there and two years in public school, Greenville was home, not because she boarded there for so long that she forgot her grandparents' camp or her mother's existence but rather because it became an important site of family practice and belonging. The pupil who came after her was her fourteen-year-old cousin Eli Piazzoni, the eldest Greenville pupil in the Bill lineage. Marie was the youngest. In fact, at age four, she was the youngest student in the entire school. In between fell multiple siblings and cousins. Half siblings John and Lizzette Mason were eight and six. John Piazzoni was twelve, Amy (also known as Emma) was ten, Rose was six, and Alice was five. The youngest Piazzoni, Pauline, was home, an infant of not quite one. Older cousins had come and gone. Hukespem's grandchildren were among Greenville's earliest boarders. For instance, grandson Tommy Tucker, Flora Bill Dick's son, was boarding by 1896, as were granddaughters Tina and Anna, as well as step-grandson Rueben (or Rube), Charley Gould's children. Eli and John Piazzoni arrived not long after, excelling academically.[27]

Eli's "rescue" of Marie was simultaneously an act of betrayal and an expression of love, a poignant testament to the condition of being colonized as a people and determined to exercise the protective ties of family and kinship that boarding schools sought to undermine. Bundling up his naked little cousin in his shirt, he pedaled back to Floy and the waiting bath, assuring Marie in their shared Maidu language that she was not going to be cooked alive. Ament believed in saving the souls, washing the bodies, and transforming the domiciles of his students. "The first and most essential lessons are those of economy and cleanliness," he argued, "and it is really surprising to see how soon they learn to have a care for their clothing. We hear such remarks as 'I can't "bear" now; I've got on new pants.' 'Tommy Tucker, hand up your hat.' 'Johnnie Jim's got a hole in his shoe.' 'Cornea Washoe, how did you broke your dress?'"[28] Ament was expert at soliciting donations of shoes and clothing.[29] Speaking here to a generous San Jose audience, he continued, "Expressions like these would not be noticed from white children, but from Indian children it notes a decided advancement."

Ament's discourse on girls' physical appearance tells us how he and Floy perceived children like Marie upon arrival: "When the girls first come they are queer looking objects indeed; their hair which is stiff and uncompromising, is allowed to fall forward from the crown and is cut off, just covering the eye-brow, while the side and back locks hang unconfined over and in front of the ears. Sometimes it is quite long, but generally it is 'bobbed' straight around the neck. One's first impression is their heads must be square; but how soon all this is changed!"[30] Just as he had drawn upon his pupils' own words to demonstrate their acquisition of appropriate regard for their clothing, he turned to student conversation about new hair grooming practices: "Where's that curling irons? Roxy wants to curl Otie's hair." "I don't know. I don't see that curl irons today. I think Nellie got it."[31] New clothing and hairstyles were only part of Greenville girls' transformation, as this image of young Marie shows.[32]

Ament deployed his pupils' names and words to great effect in his public recitations. It is not by happenstance that he retains their grammatical imperfections. It is strategy. This was, to bend one scholar's turn of the phrase, "how a [boarding school] Indian should sound."[33] Their partial fluency or "broken

Figure 2. Greenville School girls, circa 1905. Marie leans forward on the far lower left, a wide grin across her face. Alice Piazzoni is fifth from the left. Behind her, with a pin on her lapel, is Marie's friend Ellen Reeves.
Trubody Collection, Plumas County Museum, Quincy, California.

English" reinforced his audience's stereotypic expectations and bolstered the importance of boarding as an assimilative mechanism. Boarding facilities, Ament argued, forced immersion in English language and American traditions. By contrast, a day school format provided only four hours of exposure, after which pupils returned home to Native tongues and ways.[34] His efforts paid off, setting the stage for expansion.

School facilities were small and primitive between 1894 and 1896, when Marie's cousins and siblings began boarding, but she arrived to a government-funded building celebrated as the county's most modern structure. The first floor housed the superintendent's office, girls' and boys' dormitories, a dedicated and plumbed kitchen, plumbed washrooms, and a spacious dining and social commons. The second story included housing quarters for the superintendent's family and other employees. Several outbuildings served storage and industrial needs. The wide porch was a favorite gathering place for socializing and formal photographs.[35]

Marie was assigned the surname Mason and spent her initial year learning English.[36] Though a kindergarten had been added the year before, her formal

Figure 3. Greenville School girls, circa 1911. Marie is on the far left, back row. Assistant Matron Selina Twoguns is at the far left, front row.
Trubody Collection, Plumas County Museum, Quincy, California.

schooling did not begin until fall 1901.[37] Siblings and cousins eased the trauma of dislocation. Tribal tongues were discouraged by staff, and occasionally fellow students joined the refrain to speak only English. Having kin with whom to speak Maidu, however clandestinely, helped make comprehensible an unstable and otherwise inexplicable social landscape. The Aments' sudden departure, an interim superintendent's arrival in November, quarantining of pupils with chicken pox, vaccination of children and staff, and the arrival of Superintendent Charles Shell all occurred within six months of her arrival.[38] A quick study in English, Marie quickly charmed Greenville's seamstress, Emma Trubody. In a letter thanking WNIA for Christmas donations, Trubody explained that she and the kindergarten teacher, Miss Pope, had spent their evenings leading up to the holiday sewing clothes for fourteen dolls purchased with funds from the Jamaica Plain Indian Association. They had also made thirty-six sewing bags filled with scraps of lace, silk, velvet, and assorted notions—needles, thimbles, ribbons, buttons, spools of thread, and the like—sent by the New Orleans Indian Association, "so every girl from Alice to Marie—who has barely learned to say and is always saying 'Please Mish Tubody I want needle,' and when asked what for 'to sew doll,' received a sewing bag, and all but four of the older girls received dolls."[39] Floy's evening fancywork classes started the summer Marie arrived. Little girls met on Tuesday and older ones on Saturday. Trubody took over after Floy departed. Marie was clearly anxious to join her cousin Alice in these classes.[40]

Realms of Play: Mountain Maidu Cultural Persistence

Marie and her peers fascinated the daughter of Augustus (Gus) R. and Clara Bidwell, who split their time between Oakland and their Plumas County property. From the late 1890s through the early 1900s, Elsie and her younger brother Bruce frequented the school because their father had been appointed to supervise its expansion and modernization.[41] Five years older than Marie, Elsie was an avid reader of the *San Francisco Chronicle* children's page, to which she submitted missives detailing life in Big Meadow and surrounds. In May 1902, a *Chronicle* editor remarked, "Here is another interesting little contribution to our native races, who are, alas, fast becoming civilized almost beyond recognition": "GREENVILLE—It seems so good to see spring again. The fruit blossoms are out and the hills are covered with flowers. Pretty soon the picnic time will come. We will have lots of fun then. The Indian girls here have such 'high-styled' names. Here are a few: Agnes, Jessie, Rosie, Bessie, Amy, Mildred, Belle, Kate, Hazel, Christine, Edna,

Alice, Stella, Sadie, Ada, Pearl, Ines, Lillie, Ethel, Ivy, Martha, Marie, Augusta, Mable. Your constant reader, ELSIE BIDWELL." A summer resident of Big Meadow, Elsie had greater familiarity with pupils there, which is apparent in the high percentage she names: Marie, three Piazzoni sisters, several Peconum and Rogers girls. She was not alone in anticipating picnic season. Each May the school hosted a community-wide Decoration Day picnic, bringing local residents, parents, pupils, and teachers together in a convivial environment. But what really captivated Elsie were Maidu girls' private realms of play:

> When we first came to the mountains we lived in the woods near a large Indian boarding school. The little girls played around the trees in groups of five or six. They sat on the ground in a circle with a great deal of laughing and jabbering in Indian. We wondered what they were playing. One day, as my brother and I were gathering flowers, we came upon a doll's playhouse made of irregular scraps of boards and brick, gathered from a house that was being built near there. There were bits of bark, broken pieces of china and old tin cans for furniture and it looked so cunning that we thought we would like to surprise the little Indian girls by putting in something from our own dollhouse. So when the girls were away we put in some little Japanese dolls. For a few days they stayed there, and I suppose the Indians play with them. But one day we peeked in and saw their clothes were taken off and put on the stick dolls. I don't know what became of the dolls themselves. The stick dolls were little sticks with bits of calico wound around them. They were all rather small. Some of the girls had bisque dolls given them by friends, but they never played with them out of doors and they made stick dolls for every playhouse.[42]

Decades later, she expanded on this portrait, recalling material evidence of inventive play found "among the rocks and trees, on the hillsides adjacent to the school grounds." Maidu girls were willing participants in school games like croquet, but these did not replace their own imaginative pursuits, such as fabricating miniature Maidu camps. "Some were regular 'campoodies,' and in them were odds and ends of broken glass and china . . . pictures cut from catalogues, and most interesting of all, evidences of their own ingenuity, such as tiny baskets and dolls papoose cases, chains and furniture made from bark and stones."[43]

Marie later recalled Bidwell's school visits: "We played together and tried to teach the daughter how to speak our Indian language."[44] Indigenous pupils and parents retained, integrated, and taught instructors about their own traditions.

Figure 4. Greenville School students and teachers at a Decoration Day
picnic, circa 1903. *Circled, from left to right*: Marie's sister Lizzette, cousin
Alice Piazzoni, and friend Edith Peconum. Teacher Emma Trubody
stands behind the children, wearing a wide-brimmed hat.
Dorothy M. Hill Collection, Meriam Library Special Collections, California State University–Chico.

For instance, under syncretic cover of the school's 1895 Decoration Day picnic,
and surely others as well, Maidu practiced components of their Spring Ceremony,
or Bear Dance, when "they made a flying rush to the river, throwing into the
swift current grass and flowers, signifying a casting away of 'hatred, malice,
hatred and all charitableness' for the year."[45] The chains Elsie observed in their
playhouses, adaptations of traditional weaving to acculturative forms and price
points, attest to the school's grounding in Indigenous place. "There are probably
yards and yards of them still in Greenville homes," Bidwell wrote.[46] Pupils made
them in summertime, collecting and peeling new fir shoots. They were shaped
into interlocking links while green and malleable, and the going price was five
to twenty-five cents per yard, depending upon the size of links, which typically
ranged from a quarter inch to an inch.[47] Baskets, by comparison, were a highly
regarded and expensive art form, traded and sold locally by Native women, collected by tourists and museums, and featured for sale by WNIA's Industrial
Department in the association's monthly periodical, the *Indian's Friend*. California "work baskets, card trays, and decorative pieces," which sold for between

seventy-five cents and one hundred dollars, were advertised with the tagline "The finest baskets in the world come from our Pacific Coast."[48] In her 1901 "Course of Study for Indians Schools," superintendent of Indian education Estelle Reel asked reservation agents to send the finest basket specimens and their weavers' names, so they could arrange to hire them as teachers, since the art must be "revived by children of the present generation." She urged its teaching as a component of historical instruction, encouraging teachers to exhibit student work in classrooms to stimulate competition and to remind them that the more "Indian a basket is, the higher price it will bring."[49]

Greenville was ahead of this curve. In 1895 SJIA donated money to hire an "Indian woman living near the Greenville school to give the girls in the school a lesson once a week in basket making. This woman is industrious and capable and makes especially fine baskets."[50] Identified as a pupil's mother, she had an ally in Floy, who recommended her and insisted she be paid for her work, confiding to WNIA that she was clean and her baskets "very pretty."[51] The girls' handiwork was sold through the association's Industrial Department to support missionary work, including the cost of shipping donations of clothing and supplies to Greenville. WNIA cleverly tapped into a thriving market for Native crafts of every type, from moccasins to beadwork and basketry. Industrialism's social ills fostered antimodernist sentiment. Rebellion, among the middle and upper classes, found robust expression in the arts and crafts movement, where white women wove "Indian" hobby baskets as an antidote to the psychosocial pathos of the very same modernity to which they were righteously forcing Native peoples to assimilate. Catalogs supplied patterns, materials, and instructions, but Native-made basketry was prized as the embodiment of authentic life. World fairs displayed Indigenous art and artists, including basket weavers. When a "model" Indian boarding school was proposed for the 1904 Louisiana Purchase Exposition, social reformers were jubilant. Vehemently opposed to Wild West shows and midway displays that hyped stereotypical imagery of Native people as savage and violent, they wanted to show off the human products of their reformer labor. However, as one scholar observed, when "Show-Indian students replaced Show Indians," the public failed to demonstrate enthusiasm.[52] Book learning, blacksmithing, crocheted collars, and other fancywork bored romantic sensibilities and accosted an eastern imaginary animated by "authentic" objects and pursuits linked to "frontier" states.[53]

Despite WNIA's early promotion of basket weaving, in 1910 Greenville's Superintendent Frank Mann bemoaned its decline and the passing of expert practitioners. Young women were not interested in keeping it afloat, he lamented, seemingly oblivious to the role boarding schools played in destroying the fabric of family and socioeconomic tradition that ensured its respect and reproduction. Yet the very next year, Marie was enrolled in a basketry course, building upon skills and knowledge Mariah and Josie had already begun imparting.[54] The traditional stick dolls and miniature "campoodies" Bidwell stumbled upon are vivid reminders that Maidu women had been successfully cultivating "domestic arts" and "maternal" values in their daughters for centuries, reproducing their culture without Christian or American intervention. Yet the driving premise of WNIA and the federal boarding school system was that Native people, women in particular, must be taught to cook, keep house, clothe, and mother children. Intent on reorienting Native people toward the nuclear family, reformers encouraged husbands to exercise patriarchal authority over wives and children, and wives to maintain "proper" Christian domiciles. The "womanly arts" were enshrined as the foundation for producing Americanized families and households, where fathers and sons tilled their allotment's soil while mothers and daughters labored happily—and only—in the domestic sphere. As one scholar affirms in her study of federal "fathers and mothers," Indian Service employees were expected to model these gendered dimensions of domestic married life.[55] Indeed, the Aments and their successors promulgated this ideology in the classroom, the countryside, and the church. For nine years Ament preached on Sunday mornings and taught afternoon Sunday school. Upward of sixty parents and students regularly congregated to hear him extoll Christian monogamous marriage over customary or polygynous counterparts. Committed to Christian lives and domiciles, Floy diligently penetrated the outlying countryside, visiting Native camps. In no time, her correspondence reproduced the discursive imagery of Native families and homes that peppered the *Indian's Friend*, where her WNIA peers regularly vented their horror over "dirty" and "primitive" conditions from which they self-righteously removed children.[56]

A Settler Colonial Curriculum: Learning to Read, Write, and Labor

Sunday sermons and field visits to Native homes were important, but children's schooling was the gravitational center of assimilation. Academic instruction included reading, writing, geography, and arithmetic. This comprised about five hours of classroom work, split between morning and afternoon sessions. Industrial training and recreation filled the remainder of the day. While boys learned to shoe horses, repair wagons, and farm, girls trained in domestic arts. Simple sewing, which Marie was so anxious to begin, progressed to embroidery,

crochet, and fancywork. Upper-grade girls learned pattern making and dressmaking, and machine sewing, helping to produce school uniforms.[57] They trained in
cooking, setting a proper dining table, washing and ironing, singing, and playing
musical instruments. The year Marie was born, Ament solicited help in buying
an organ. Generosity from WNIA affiliates enabled the purchase of two, one
for the dormitory and the other for instruction and chapel services in the main
building.[58] Physical grace was cultivated through dance and synchronized hoop
drills that young girls often performed for visitors.[59]

    Biographical studies of boarding school alumnae over the last quarter century
show how rarely Native women could afford the luxury of laboring solely in their
own homes. Instead, these lessons in domesticity prepared female students to
labor in white homes.[60] Marie can be counted among them, but neither Greenville
nor her experience is so easily encapsulated. Some scholars argue that boarding
schools were designed to produce an underclass in permanent servitude to settler
colonial society; others highlight gaps between reformer intent, federal policy
mandates, and onsite administration, noting that variegation in the latter produced
distinctive patterns of assimilationist practice *and* resistance to it. This uneven
grain existed not only between institutions but over the lifetime of individual
schools. Scholarly calls to transcend generalizations about boarding schools
and alumni are not denials of profound suffering, death, and intergenerational
trauma. They are challenges to discern distinctions; to acknowledge variations
in personnel, in community reception, and in student response. They are calls to
identify individual and collective modes of survival, resistance, and persistence.[61]
Close mining of oral and archival records shows that despite Greenville's active
and inherent denigration of Native peoples and domiciles, parents and children
occasionally deflected its corrosive potential, navigating its presence *as* families
and its possibilities *for* family.

The Subversive Bonds of Mountain Maidu Kinship

Unlike most off-reservation boarding schools that drew rural students into distant
and alien urban settings, Greenville drew students from the nearby countryside
in its early years.[62] This allowed parents to vest it with alternative potential. John
Kinney, recently widowed and without means to care for his young daughters,
Maude and Katie, saw the school as a safe haven while he was living and working
on a nearby Indian Valley ranch, but he spent every Sunday at school visiting his
girls. The Aments made much of this and the deep affection they demonstrated for
one another. As Christians, and beneficiaries of WNIA's missionary patronage,

they reported how touching it was to witness six-year-old Katie kiss her daddy good-bye and offer an evening prayer that Jesus make her papa "a good man" and her a "good little girl." Indeed, this is a stirring anecdote, but not because it evinces Christian conversion. Rather it reminds us that parents made tremendous sacrifices in these rapidly changing times. Two years after the *Indian's Friend* recounted Katie's prayerful wish in the May 1895 edition, John Kinney withdrew both daughters; little Maude died eight months later.

Schoolchildren missed and longed for their siblings and cousins back home no less than they longed for their parents, and vice versa. Some Greenville pupils found ways to bridge that distance. This happened in spring 1895 when a father arrived from Big Meadow with a basket of fresh mountain trout. At the close of the visit, his three daughters deposited in the basket treasures for their little brother and sisters. Wanting to be sure this was permissible, the father showed Ament these contents: "There were a few little toy dishes, three or four marbles, a doll, and a handful of little dried figs I had given them the day before."[63] This display of love and generosity was not unusual. Five-year-old Rosie Piazzoni, "at the lead of her class of six or seven," was similarly inclined and clever when deciding that her little sister Alice, back in Big Meadow, should have a string of blue beads just like the one she had just earned for finishing her first reader. Tucking this prized possession away, she approached her teacher with a different book, explaining that she planned to read it and earn a second strand of beads, as the others were for her sister.[64] These gestures toward absent siblings speak volumes. Separating siblings was no less cruel than separating parents and children.

Marie's siblings and Piazzoni cousins were anxious to welcome her. Once the Aments learned she was below OIA's five-year-old admission threshold, she was allowed to stay only because they intervened with pleas and assurances that she was "smart" and capable of schoolwork.[65] Six months after Marie's arrival, the couple resigned.[66] They had grown the school's capacity beyond their own limits, working seven days a week. In early years, a two-month break helped them recharge, but this ended under federal administration. Students were expected to remain on-site for years at a time. Ament challenged this policy, explaining somewhat insubordinately that he would be hard pressed to keep parents and children apart given the school's proximity to their homes. He was correct; parents continued to ask for their children to be sent home for vacation, and some older pupils went on their own dimes.[67] Break or no break, students missed their youthful kin cohorts. When younger family members joined them at school, they gained some comforts of home. They could celebrate birthdays, Decoration Day picnics, and Christmases together. More importantly, they could make daily mischief and memories, tease and look out for one another, safely "talk Indian," and bask in the sense of security that family fostered.[68] As is demonstrated in a recent study of Scottish adoptee birth family reunions, it is this latter repository of everyday "unmarked" exchange that generates the profound and enduring bonds of kinship.[69] These social acts, marked and unmarked, also produced "fictive kin" at off-reservation boarding schools, generating vast cross-tribal networks of alumni, who reflect on these years and experiences with nostalgia that descendants find difficult to comprehend. During the first half of Greenville's existence, despite efforts to detribalize and Christianize, families used the school strategically. When new superintendents arrived, instituting curricula not in their children's best interest, parents intervened when they judged it necessary. For instance, in 1906, when John Peconum learned that coeducational dancing was part of the exercise curriculum, he threatened to withdraw his daughters, demanding that Mountain Maidu tradition be observed. Unmarried men and women did not dance together.[70] The Peconum boys, watching out for their sisters, had relayed this development to their father.[71]

For almost a decade, the Bill cousins enjoyed a semblance of family life at Greenville, venturing home to Big Meadow for longer and shorter stays. Marie also boarded for long stints, but in May 1905 she left for a year, continuing her education in public school at Prattville. In June 1906 teacher Mabel Locey promoted her to fourth grade. She was back at Greenville in September but called home weeks later when her stepfather, Abe Lowery, became ill.[72] He died in January or February of 1907. Finishing out the school year in Prattville, Marie returned to Greenville that fall, but not before another family crisis ensued.

In August, Marie's brother was involved in a fatal altercation with a Maidu man and family friend.[73] Although the act was later ruled self-defense, John Mason fired the bullet that eventually killed thirty-year-old Billy Lowery. Half Lowery's age, John was jailed for a week, until the circuit judge arrived in Prattville to hear testimony. Witnesses confirmed that alcohol was to blame for the August 24 shooting at a Humbug Valley big time. Lowery apparently cracked his pistol butt on Mason's head several times and verbally threatened the adolescent's life. The local paper subjected Lowery to extensive character assassination and cavalierly pronounced both to be "bad Indians."[74] Multiple news stories offered an unfiltered glimpse at the racist underbelly of a local community unable to apprehend its own role in this sad drama through the introduction of alcohol.[75] "It seems a rather difficult task to kill this notorious and dangerous half-breed,

Billy Lowery," the writer opined, when it seemed he might live. Two years earlier he survived a brutal stabbing in Quincy. When he finally succumbed, a near-celebratory headline proclaimed, "End of Billy Lowery," and the article reported, "Billy Lowery, the half-breed Indian noted for the many troubles he has caused himself and others is dead."[76]

A cascade of loss ensued. John "Bull" Mason was Marie's eldest sibling. She must have been devastated by community condemnation of him as a "bad Indian," but she was doubly stung when two months later, John and Lizzette left for Chemawa Indian School in Oregon.[77] "John Piazzoni arrived from California on Wednesday with his cousins John and Lizette Mason," proclaimed the November 29, 1907, *Chemawa American*. Piazonni had been transferred there in 1903, along with several other aged-out Greenville students.[78] His cousin's presence and his own athletic prowess helped ease Mason's transition to Chemawa. He played a season of football, ran track, and won the April 1909 Salem–Portland relay race. Academic hurdles were another matter. Despite years of Greenville schooling, he tested into second grade.[79] This does not mean his classmates were small children; young adults populated elementary grade levels across the boarding school system.[80] Striving to close this gap, Mason passed his third-grade exams in June 1908 and joined the Reliance Literary Society the next fall. With other Greenville alumni, Joaquin Meadows, Frank Mose, and John Peazzoni (as he spelled his name in adulthood), Mason excelled in his woodcraft and industrial training classes.[81] Two years younger, Lizzette took her sixth-grade examination at the end of her first year and, with her future sister-in-law Rhoda Silverthorne, was active in YWCA leadership.

Meanwhile, twelve-year-old Marie, bereft of her siblings' companionship, completed fourth grade. Her fifth-grade year (1908–1909) progressed as usual, but when school resumed in September 1909, Marie was not there.[82] Hukespem had died. Although the mission school now belonged to the federal government, Quinton and WNIA kept a missionary in the field. In 1906 and 1907, he documented crushing need among elderly Maidu, including Mariah and Big Meadow Bill. In late November 1908, the county board of supervisors approved $7.50 per month to be drawn, on Marie's grandparent's behalf, from the county's hospital fund. The Reverend John Johnson of WNIA was assigned to purchase supplies from a designated Greenville merchant and personally deliver them.[83] Hukespem died just weeks after this round of aid expired. Perhaps it eased his final days.

Marie returned to begin sixth-grade studies on October 29, 1909. That summer, 1910 census takers enumerated Mariah in Indian Valley Township, domiciled

with her daughter and son-in-law Susie (Bill) and Thomas Buckley and their
fifteen-year-old granddaughter Elsie, Marie's cousin.[84] Just down the road were
newlyweds Josie Bill and Johnny Roy and their eighteen-month-old daughter.[85]
Like Josie, Johnny Roy was a Big Meadow Maidu employed at a nearby sawmill.[86]
Josie had achieved a measure of stability in her personal life, but this intimate
domestic sphere was not one into which fifteen-year-old Marie comfortably
figured, tethering her more tightly to school as the principal site of home and
belonging. This was doubly problematic. Seventh grade was Greenville's highest
grade level. She was poised to age out the next year. She had seen this happen to
her cousins and others. Some, like Roxie (Jake) Dexter, now school laundress,
had nowhere to go. Marie had to be worried.

An Uncertain Future

Marie finished sixth grade with resolve, despite her late start and the radically
altered world around her. Her siblings and cousins were scattered far away, Josie
had a new husband and baby daughter, her beloved Hukespem was dead, and Big
Meadow was about to be inundated by a hydroelectric project, all heralding deep
uncertainty. She was not the only person pondering her future.

In 1911 Superintendent Mann told the commissioner of Indian affairs that he
worried about his pupils' limited futures and the white community's ambivalence
toward the school. This problem had not existed under Ament's administration,
but the near-constant rotation of superintendents under federal administration
affected community relations. Racism was accelerating. Public schools were not
taking their share of Native students, and many Native parents were not pursuing
their children's enrollment to shield them from overt discrimination.[87] Mann tried
resolving this tension by hosting events that brought the two groups together in
settings that demonstrated his pupils' intelligence and achievement, but he was
skeptical that this would alter their socioeconomic fortunes. A 1907 recommenda-
tion that students be trained to enter the dairy industry had fallen on deaf ears.
Mann knew this rural setting posed limited opportunity. Old weavers produced
"beautiful specimens," but the "laborious" nature of the art could not maintain
the interest of young Maidu women trained in domestic arts, who earned fifteen
to twenty dollars per month. Maidu young men made between $1.50 and $2.50
per day working as ranch hands, in summer resorts, for mine companies, and at
sawmills. Requests for Maidu laborers came faster than Mann could fill them.
Greenville now had agency status, and he was disappointed in the quality of the
land allotments he oversaw. They were hit and miss in terms of enabling long-term

agricultural versus short-lived timber production for those Maidu lucky enough to even receive one. Few men owned herds and ranching operations. Boys were lured permanently away from school by age fourteen with the promise of steady wages. Girls eventually followed as domestic laborers in white homes.[88] Marie knew intimately the routine life awaiting her after adolescence. She had to be pondering her life after Greenville.

Interviews with boarding school alumni show how ingenious students were when it came to outwitting matrons and disciplinarians whose overactive imaginations led to preemptive strikes on innocent forms of socializing.[89] At Greenville, the outlying woods where Marie and her friends had once played house with stick dolls were places to escape for adolescent flirtations and midnight snacks from nearby fields and orchards.[90] Marie and Hensley Potts, a Konkow student, were already romantically linked. Her good friend Ellen Reeves had recently married Walter Potts, Hensley's brother. Marie was not inspired to follow suit. Her attention was turned eastward, where Eli and his sisters had been drawn. At the end of her seventh-grade year, 1910–11, a new superintendent arrived. Willard Campbell, formerly of Pipestone School in Browning, Montana, had special sympathy for Marie's situation. An orphaned White Earth Chippewa student, Ada Curtis, had been living with his family the previous year and had accompanied them to Greenville. During the 1911–12 year, Campbell tutored Ada and Marie in eighth-grade work, and Marie informally earned her "keep" as a lower-grade teacher's assistant. By summer 1912, when Marie showed Ada around Big Meadow and Chester, these two were good friends.[91] When Greenville's laundress resigned in June, Curtis applied for this federal Indian Service position. They were friends with another young woman, Selina Twoguns (Seneca), who helped Marie imagine new possibilities.

Finding Female Role Models

Twoguns perhaps recognized a bit of herself in Marie, because she began recruiting her to her alma mater almost immediately.[92] Twoguns had not intended to go into the Indian School Service. Graduating in spring 1910, she immediately enrolled in Carlisle's postgraduate business program, but initial course work inspired her to head out into the world. Taking the civil service exam, she quickly landed a position as Greenville's "small boy's matron," arriving in May 1911, just weeks before the school year's end.[93] Sitting down to complete the "Records of Graduates and Returned Students" that August, she was overcome with gratitude and nostalgia. Like many Carlisle alums, she believed her years there would forever be the crowning experience of her life. Her youthful devotion is preserved in her graceful longhand and fading sepia-toned ink. Designed to verify ongoing commitment to assimilationist ideals, gather evidence of "civilized" lives and housing, and generate testimonials worthy of school propaganda, the questionnaire closed with a final appeal: "Tell me anything else of interest connected with your life." Twoguns confided,

> One thing, I am trying my very best to paddle my own canoe assisted by the things taught me during the years I spent at Carlisle. I was not sent there to school, but I wanted to go myself and I am not, for a minute, sorry that I went. It has fitted me to earn my own living, not only that, but to earn it honestly. Now, may I take this opportunity to thank you and all your assistants for all they have done for me during my long stay at Carlisle, I'll admit those days were my happiest although I am very much pleased with the West.[94]

"The West" still held romance in those early months. Before long, she felt trapped in this rural mountain setting, where reaching the closest train station was an ordeal.

Marie, Curtis, and Twoguns shared common experience as long-term boarding school students.[95] Any differences among them receded in the long shadow cast by their upbringing in educational milieus designed to promulgate assimilation.[96] As it turned out, Marie already knew about Carlisle, and not just because her cousin Eli and his sisters were there. Boarding school periodicals, especially the *Carlisle Arrow* and *Red Man*, circulated widely among feeder institutions, and the *Plumas National* had been extolling the virtues of the famous Indian school and its athletes for longer than Marie had been alive.[97] But Twoguns kept up the pressure, writing Carlisle superintendent Moses Friedman in February 1912 for a photo of her graduating class. She posed proudly in the front row, beside friend and fellow business student Sarah Hoxie, a Nomlaki from California's Round Valley Reservation. Perhaps Marie's cousins had already mentioned this Covelo student, but here was photographic proof that a California Indian woman had gone east to Carlisle, graduated, and returned to work in the Indian Service.[98]

Nearing seventeen years old, Marie was more or less on her own. She longed to see the wider world, not simply through books or newspapers or graduation portraits but for herself. Intellectual curiosity fueled her ambition and imagination at least as much as Carlisle propaganda and family ties. Greenville was remote and in these years drew most students from the regional population, but Indian

Service employees from far and wide cycled in and out, exposing pupils to life beyond the northern Sierra. By her very presence, Twoguns embodied possibilities that Marie could now imagine for herself. Curtis's predecessor, Lottie George, a twenty-five-year-old Shoshone from Idaho and a Haskell Indian School graduate, had done this as well. Marie was already leaning toward adventure when Twoguns again wrote Friedman:

> Marie Mason is one I am very anxious to have the chance of getting all that Carlisle gives its students. She is an all around good girl and exceptionally bright in every thing she undertakes. Very ambitious and on her own accord she has been working since our school closed, had a place engaged long before she went for her vacation. She has learned all that this school can give its pupils in all lines. I would like to take her with me to Carlisle when I go, also Ada Curtis, another nice girl. . . . I think Mr. Campbell will write you concerning the girls.[99]

The "place" Marie had secured entailed working at a Chinese restaurant in Susanville. She waited tables by day and tutored a Chinese student, likely the restaurant owner's child, in the evening. Marie's cousin Tommy Tucker walked her home from work at night to guarantee her safe arrival; she was probably boarding at his Susanville home. Tucker's mother, Flora, and his stepfather, Billy Dick, were deceased, so he was living with his grandfather Hukespem's younger sister's daughter, Emma, and her husband, Cap DeHaven.[100]

Less than sanguine in his response, Friedman worried that his travel budget might not accommodate California fares.[101] Greenville superintendent Campbell, carrying on his own correspondence, had yet to learn this. In mid-August he told Friedman that he had two or three prospective Carlisle students in mind; applications would be forthcoming. Ada Curtis was "a splendid girl in every respect and wants especially to take up and perfect herself in sewing, dressmaking, etc." In reference to Marie, he declared, "We have another girl, a Digger half-blood, who has finished the seventh grade at this school and I want her to go to Carlisle also. She is very bright and an excellent girl in every respect. . . . [I]n regard to transportation, you had better place immediately to my order at Keddie, California, on the Western Pacific, as many tickets as may be needed. How about the incidental expenses, etc.? Should they take sub-vouchers for incidentals?" Campbell forwarded Marie's and Ada's applications on August 22. Having yet to receive a response from his earlier letter, he underscored, "These are both splendid girls, and if accepted, I am sure will be a credit to your school."[102]

Carlisle required a parental signature for applicants eighteen years and under. Campbell explained, "Marie Mason does not live with her mother, who has no jurisdiction over her and, consequently, she signed the application herself, which is alright. Ada Curtis' parents are both dead and she has been living with us during the past year, but is anxious to get some more education and thinks Carlisle is the place to go."[103] Turning back to the young woman he had only come to know in the last year, he wrote, "You will find Marie a bright girl and I trust you will let her take up the things she is best fitted for."[104] After Friedman telegrammed in late August to say the girls would have to pay their own expenses, Curtis decided to stay on at Greenville until December to earn her train fare and other expenses.[105] Marie and Twoguns, on the other hand, bought their Western Pacific tickets within the week. They would board at Keddie, on Monday, September 9, and arrive in Harrisburg, Pennsylvania, by week's end.

Forging Her Own Path

Big Meadow and Greenville could not have been further removed from Washington, D.C., yet federal policy and reformers worked their way into the most intimate corners of Mountain Maidu life. Native people adapted to Christian missions, ideologies, and institutions in the same way they had to settler invasion four decades earlier: making the most of new possibilities while retaining practices and beliefs that defined them as Maidu. While some families refused to send their children to day or boarding school, others decided the advantages outweighed the losses and risks. In the years preceding and for many years after her arrival, Marie had close family at Greenville. She sewed and played dolls, learned letters and geography, spoke Maidu, and built a fund of memories with them through both marked and unmarked kinship exchange. She remained tethered to Big Meadow and her grandparents, going to family allotments and camps on a regular basis. After her cousins' and siblings' California departures, her stepfather Abe Lowry's death, Josie's remarriage to Johnny Roy, the birth of a younger half sister, and Hukespem's death, Marie's daily connection to family was attenuated. Greenville superintendents and teachers, her "surrogate family," were just as mobile and impermanent, with new ones rotating in and out every few years. Luckily, Superintendents Mann and Campbell recognized her exceptional personality and academic potential. Native and non-Native personnel saw it too. The fictive kin who animated Marie's daily life in this home away from Big Meadow cultivated her sense of self-worth and encouraged her to continue her education. Coming of age in a world where post–boarding school life entailed some combination of marriage, motherhood, and domestic servitude in white households, Marie looked around for new role models. She found them in her cousin Eli, who had graduated from Carlisle, and in young Native women like herself, who found employment in the Indian School Service. Determined to forge her own path, she took a daring leap.

2

Carlisle

In Pursuit of a Lettered Life

From far off Pacific, the famed Golden Gate, Comes Marie, A Medum, the pride of her State.

—The Arrow, June 4, 1915

Marie matriculated at Carlisle in September 1912. Ferried out to Pennsylvania by her highly adventurous spirit and academic ambition, she found herself confronting new standards for both. Prepared to encounter a vastly different place, she was stunned by the sheer scale and diversity of the campus after years at a tiny rural school that drew its students from local and regional surrounds. A different set of academic standards prevailed; she had catching up to do. Spreading her social wings, Marie hosted parties and made new friends. Her senses were under constant and wonderful assault as she absorbed new curriculum, places, and people. Carlisle cultivated new academic talents and passions, leadership skills, and cosmopolitan desires, and it also brought her back into proximity with her Piazzoni kin. Rose was her schoolmate once again, while Eli, looming larger than life in Marie's childhood memories and in his alma mater's estimation, was just around the corner. Now a husband and father, he personified the boarding school success story. Yet these accomplishments paled in relation to what he most desired during these years and failed to achieve. This chapter documents the vicissitudes of Native life for the cohort of Hukespem grandchildren who grasped the lifeline and promises held out to them by Americanization and made their way into a wider world. As a young woman, and the last cousin to head out to Carlisle, Marie had much to gain from this experience.

To Philadelphia and Beyond

Stagecoach was the only way to get from Greenville to Keddie, where Marie and Selina Twoguns were slated to board the Western Pacific, heading northeast along the "Scenic Feather River Route." The stagecoach trip alone was a new adventure for Marie—one she remembered with enough awe to find it worthy of telling her grandchildren about five decades later.[1] Riding the rails for four days must have been nothing short of wondrous. They chugged across the Sierra Nevada, the Rocky Mountains, and the Great Plains. The North Fork was spectacular in its untamed beauty and roaring descent to the Sacramento Valley, but it was a far cry from the bustling riparian corridors of the Ohio and Mississippi Rivers. Gazing down from their trestled perch, seventeen-year-old Marie had a bird's-eye view of paddle wheelers and barges below. The journey was an education all its own, bringing a new materiality to places and things she knew only from newspapers and books. Four days later she saw Philadelphia, a city she came to love. They had escaped the treacherous weather conditions, harrowing rail accidents, and other calamities that had imperiled her cousin Eli's life on his December 1901 journey. Brimming with anticipation, they boarded another train for the final leg into Harrisburg, 120 miles away. She could not have anticipated how different Carlisle's fifteen-acre, parklike campus would be.[2]

A Less-Storied Arrival

Marie's arrival at Greenville had been punctuated by confusion and terror. Afraid she was about to be cooked alive, she ran for her life—a story repeated throughout her life. A dozen years later she arrived at the premier American Indian boarding school of her own initiative and on her own dime. The only surviving trace of her arrival is a hardbound, government-issued ledger stamped "5–932, Department of the Interior, U.S. Indian Service." A hand-lettered title identifies this otherwise prosaic artifact, the female student register: "Consecutive Record of Pupils Enrolled." Ruled pages are divided into four columns for data entry. Twenty-seven lines down, on page 238, she appears:

2767 | Marie Mason | Digger | September 15, 1912

Among the new term's first arrivals, entries both preceding and following her own document diverse tribal nations, "Onondaga, Chippewa, Seneca, Sioux, Seneca,

Tuscarora, Chippewa, Menominee, Digger, Seneca," bearing out Friedman's low prioritization of applicants from far western states.[3] Not everyone could pay their own way, skewing tribal representation in favor of nearer nations.

A double-sided index card, "Descriptive and Historical Record of Student," documented vital statistics taken upon each pupil's entry. "Number: 2767, English Name: Marie Mason, Agency: Greenville, Cal., Nation: Digger." Fields for "Band" and "Indian Name" were left empty. "W. S. Campbell, Super., Greenville, Cal." was given as her home address, and "Sister, Lizzette Mason, Prattville" was squeezed in at some later date. The card is thoroughly devoid of Josie's name or address, a fact underscored by the presence of an "L" entered in the field for mother under "Parents Living (L) or Dead (D)." Her father's status is marked "D."[4] Perhaps this was Marie's way of dispensing with questions about her paternal origins. Alternatively, perhaps Josie told her he was dead. Her other data included "Blood: ½"; "Age: 17"; "Height: 5' 5¼"; "Weight: 140½"; "Sex: F."[5] Her religious affiliation is recorded as Methodist. Her decade of prior schooling is recorded in the proper spot, as is "distance from home to the nearest public school": one and a half miles.

Founded in 1879, Carlisle was now in its final years; it would close in 1918. Public schools were increasingly under pressure to accept Native students, and Native parents were encouraged to send their children to them, especially if they were in close proximity. Superintendent Friedman did not support this new trend, feeling it threatened and discounted Carlisle's reputation and legacy. Even before O. H. Lipps arrived to replace him, these two were sparring about the "coeducation" of Indians and whites. Lipps was an early advocate for rapid integration of Native students into state-funded public schools, while Friedman defensively noted that Carlisle had done more to get Native students employed alongside whites than any other place or strategy.[6]

Academic Setbacks and Solutions

Marie's grammar school instruction had ended at seventh grade, although both she and Ada Curtis had received independent lessons at the eighth-grade level from Campbell. When she matriculated, Carlisle's curricular structure entailed grades one through ten. Marie's placement examinations consigned her to seventh grade, an unexpected and disappointing outcome. She had no choice but to enter the freshman "departmental grade."[7]

From September 1912 through April 1913, she boarded at Carlisle, spending half days in academic course work and half in household arts. Making good progress in the latter, she had advanced from shirt-making to dressmaking class by January

1913. A welcome and familiar face soon joined her there. Curtis had finally arrived from Greenville. They had fun moving through the ranks together.[8] Such camaraderie was important for more than obvious reasons. Carlisle students, like those everywhere, formed social networks that functioned on multiple personal and professional planes. Important sources of moral support and emotional sustenance for pupils far from home, they later functioned as networks of professional capital. More importantly, they were critical conduits of informal knowledge that pupils used to navigate Carlisle's social and academic corridors. Marie tapped into this vein of back-channel expertise when she learned from "the girls" how she could bypass the internal system of course work and annual grade-level promotion that would extend her time to graduation longer than originally anticipated.[9]

The Outing System: Traces of Richard Henry Pratt

Carlisle's founder, Richard Henry Pratt, was a vociferous proponent of forced assimilation. As an army veteran, he was all too familiar with the bloody outcomes of military campaigns entailing the systematic slaughter and imprisonment of Native people.[10] His oft-quoted and infamous dictum "Kill the Indian in him and save the man" voiced his recognition of the role that culture versus "blood" played in defining and reproducing collective identities and traditions. His preference was to kill Indigenous culture rather than people.[11] On superficial glance, this seems an almost startling gesture toward humanitarianism, one scholars still seek to situate and understand in all its historical complexity.[12] Before being pushed out of Carlisle in 1904, Pratt butted heads with many parties, but he had especially long-standing issues with missionary-based reform groups whose work was more communitarian in orientation. The "Indian problem," he argued, could only be solved at the granular level; the individual must be removed from the reservation and severed from family and tribal relations. Despite Pratt's disdain for religious reformers, he was a well-read self-promoter who could be very persuasive from the secular pulpit provided by his own disciples. At the 1891 annual meeting of the Board of Indian Commissioners, Pratt harangued endlessly about the distinctions between blood and culture—or "habit." His long address closed with three parallel points: "Savagery is a Habit," "Civilization is a Habit," and "Language is a Habit." Referring to the last, he cited a range of instances where language acquisition was demonstrated to be a feature of cultural learning, including one that involved French scientists placing an infant in the care of a mute: "The child was not permitted to hear a word of any language for 8 years. It was then found that it could imitate with great perfection the songs and calls of birds, of animals, of insects it had heard, but could speak no word of any human language. I add this to the case of Quanah's mother, of Steven and his mother, Dr. Montezuma, the young Cheyenne, and to hundreds of other like cases within my experience and knowledge, and am forced to conclude that LANGUAGE IS A HABIT."[13]

Pratt's screed contains two mutually supporting points. First, culture—or "habit"—is plastic. Molded in one environment, it can be entirely remolded in another. Second, the molding environment comprises a force of its own in sustaining and reproducing acquired habits. Carlisle and other off-reservation boarding schools were designed to disenfranchise Native people from their Indigenous languages just as much as they were meant to teach them English. Monolingualism, not bilingualism, was the goal. Places intended to destroy Native values and behaviors, boarding schools were equally sites for instilling new ones.[14] The "problem," as Pratt knew, was that the most effective environment for this process of re-enculturation to take hold was the home, not the school—not even the one of his own invention.

The 1912 *Carlisle Indian School Catalogue* warned rather sternly that it was a place for students "with a definite purpose in view and who really 'mean business.'" During these years, it accepted students between fourteen and twenty-one years of age "of good character," who could prove at least one-quarter blood quanta.

> It is the aim of Carlisle to train the Indian youth of both sexes to take upon themselves the duties of citizenship. Indian young men and young women are given thorough academic and industrial training, which prepares them to earn a living, either among their own people or away from the reservation in competition with whites. It is primarily a vocational school for both sexes. Its graduates and ex-students are engaged as efficient workers and leaders among their own people on the reservation, and as teachers and officials in the government service, and are successfully competing with whites, away from the reservation, in the trades and professions.[15]

Students spent equal time daily on academic course work and the industrial training programs of their choice. The "trades," from baking and blacksmithing to printing and wheelwrighting, were restricted to boys. Girls were steered into household arts. For decades, Carlisle promoted this program as a pathway by which young women could secure employment as domestic servants in white homes. Pratt was long gone when Marie matriculated, but his influence lived on.

Ethnocidal crusades are won by striking a fatal blow at the collective cultural body. Women are the critical targets in this process, since biological and social reproduction are equally necessary to cultural survival. Pratt's campaign hinged on reordering the most intimate corners of the domestic sphere.[16] Forced assimilation to settler conceptions of proper marital relations, gender roles, family forms, household composition, physical shelter, sexual behavior, reproductive standards, and economic productivity were the off-reservation boarding school's raison d'être. These values were embedded in academic curricula, but they were most patently present in the program of industrial training that required Carlisle students to go on "outing" to "country homes." More than sites of apprenticeships where students applied skills learned in cooking, sewing, and laundering classrooms, white homes were equally, if not more so, venues in which to observe and absorb the more abstract dimensions of settler society, including the subordinate and domestic disposition women were expected to assume in the context of patriarchal marriage and motherhood.[17] Although Marie pursued household arts as her course of industrial training, not all women gravitated to this program. Some, like Sarah Hoxie and Selina Twoguns, trained for work in clerical and business settings. Others went into nursing, and still others went on to normal school and teaching careers, an option Marie briefly considered toward the end of her Carlisle tenure. This is not surprising, as she prioritized academics even on outing.

Outing was Pratt's brainchild, and eventually it was exported to boarding schools across the West.[18] He claimed that it originated with his search for a mechanism to help Native students become full participants in "the American family"—writ large and small.[19] The Quaker-based Indian Rights Association and wide network of Friends in Philadelphia were a boon for this project, as Pratt revealed in a brief memoir published in *Red Man* during Marie's first summer in Pennsylvania:

There was a distinct disadvantage in having the Indians close to Carlisle, because it was too easy to make frequent visits, to run away and return to the school. The third summer, homes further away from the school were secured, particularly among the Friends in Bucks County and in the country about Philadelphia. This feature of the school proved throughout the years one of the very best and most important helps to its great success, because it enforced the theory of school by practice and quickly accustomed the pupils to civilized life. Indian boys and girls isolated from their fellows, surrounded by English-speaking people, advance in English and civilization far more rapidly than is possible in any Indian school.[20]

Conceding that many homesick pupils ran away from their initial outing place-ments back to the surrogate home Carlisle had become, Pratt solved the problem by finding patron homes too distant for such retreat.

Pratt was unceremoniously forced into retirement in 1904. Between then and Friedman's April 1908 arrival, Pratt's replacement—Major William Mercer—came and went, choosing a military over an educational career. Throughout these transi-tions, the outing program remained, and its stable of "country" patrons expanded well beyond Philadelphia city limits. Unbeknownst to Marie, the ouster of yet another Carlisle superintendent was about to take place, as accusations—most related to fiscal malfeasance—were quietly fomenting in the background of her freshman year. The outing system was implicated, since Friedman stood accused of a raft of irregularities related to athletic funds, enrollment numbers, and outing program earnings. His guilt or innocence in these matters was never satisfactorily answered, but the parties lodging the complaint—including current and former students, along with OIA personnel—pegged accusations of disciplinary laxity to those of malfeasance, amplifying the atmosphere of near hysteria surrounding Friedman's downfall.[21] One of the natural challenges in running a school filled with adolescent and young adult pupils was managing their attraction to the classic diversions of adulthood—from smoking and drinking to sexual activity. Friedman was apparently ill equipped or lacking in motivation when it came to handling these matters, even when offending students were on campus and breaching school code right beneath his nose. Students who went on outing were naturally adept at finding ways to entertain themselves and exercise their independence. In fact, they tested the expectations and constraints of "home" under every single superintendent, whether on or off campus, as have adolescents everywhere.

To Friedman's credit, he resented and sought to protect students from country patrons who simply wanted servant girls or farm laborers without reciprocal obligation to fully integrate them into the family fold, where they stood a chance of enjoying the privileges that should accrue to them as responsible "fictive kin," however staged and temporary.[22] Regular field visits and outing agent reports detailed the nature of the home environment, student well-being, and each party's assessment of the outing placement—discerned through separate interviews with pupils and patrons. While patrons often had years of experience with Carlisle students, pupils arrived to their first outing experience equipped with only what they gleaned from peers in advance.

Students were expected to spend a minimum of one year on outing and to attend the neighborhood public school.[23] The highly gendered dimensions of the outing system were still in evidence three decades after its creation. Assimilation was the goal for male students. They "work side by side with white mechanics, and not only acquire a knowledge of their trade as it is conducted in the 'dollars-and-cents' world, but they also gain a thorough familiarity with the conditions surrounding the American workman."[24] For female students, practical experience in household arts was the manifest purpose, but tacit expectations were clear. This intimate setting allowed them to observe the proper role and place of women in the domestic sphere, to acculturate to the nuclear household and the patriarchal settler family form. Pratt explained:

> No other branch of the educational work is of so much benefit as the "Outing." No school can give home training on a small scale as the Indian should learn it in order to become Americanized. In the majority of country homes to which pupils go, they are considered as members of the family and are as carefully trained as are the sons and daughters of the family. Many a "country mother" has kept a hold on an Indian girl for years after her return to the reservation, and through correspondence has fastened the influence of civilized life on the rude home-making in those isolated spots.[25]

"Rude home-making in those isolated spots" and country mothers who maintain years of influence on Indian servant-daughters echoed the maternalist discourse of Quinton, Floy, and WNIA. Despite Carlisle's commitment to the "country home" as the core site of instruction, the household arts—in either the literal or euphemistic sense—were hardly the corpus of knowledge female students sought out or acquired in these experiences.

Venturing Forth

Marie spent a total of seventeen months on outing. Her first was four months long and took her to the Fred Rapp household in Llanerch, a suburb on Philadelphia's west side, about 130 miles east of Carlisle.[26] After a month in their primary residence, the Rapp family packed up and headed for their summer place in Ocean City, New Jersey. Marie still held fond memories of that summer six decades later.[27] Home was a two-story flat above a drugstore at East Eighth and Westley, with a private apartment entrance. Outing students had a third-floor bedroom. The beach was an eight-minute walk away. It was a glorious experience. Seventeen-year-old Marie had come all the way from the other side of the country to catch her first glimpse of an ocean. She spent three long months inspired by an entirely different vista than the beautiful mountain peaks and meadow valleys of the northern

Sierra. She marveled at the endless Atlantic horizon out there, on the far side of the world. Excursions up and down the Eastern Seaboard brought new delights. Earlier outing records for the Rapp family are more complete and lend additional texture to Marie's experience. In July 1910, three years before Marie joined them, outing agent Mollie Gaither visited the Rapps at their summer abode. All six children were still at home, ages fifteen, twelve, seven, five, three, and one. The two oldest were young adults when Marie joined them three years later, but even Rose La Rose (Shoshone Nation, Ross Fork, Idaho), who helped care for all those children, thought Mrs. Rapp was very likeable and the work tolerable: "A kind motherly woman, plenty of work but she can stand it." The pay was $2.50 per week.[28]

Marie's natural sense of adventure was sharpened by these experiences. They cultivated her lifelong love of travel, a near restlessness that pushed her out into the world whenever opportunity knocked. Modest means conditioned her mode of transport but never influenced the decision about whether or not to travel. She was always on the go—up to the North Slope of Alaska, down to New Orleans, into the deepest recesses of Carlsbad Caverns. Hither and yon she went, as she had learned to do at Carlisle. Travel was like a metronome, ticking out a lively rhythm that kept her engaged in Indian affairs, full of energy, and ever curious about the next horizon to be conquered. During her first summer on outing, she mastered train travel and returned to Carlisle that fall eager to venture further afield. The perfect opportunity awaited.

Carlisle students were savvy and strategic when they applied for outing, exercising a significant degree of autonomy and self-interest in fulfilling the requirement to spend a year "out." The student pipeline about living conditions, "country parent" attitudes and expectations, nearby social and recreational opportunities, neighborhood schools, and cityscapes was robust. Marie learned about a public school in New Jersey allowing students to advance through grade levels by examination versus annual promotion. She was determined to go; otherwise she would be looking at three more years of school. Knowing her peers had managed grade-level promotion by this means gave her added confidence. Thus it was academic ambition—not household arts—that drove her choice of outing city. This particular country patron, Rebecca Edwards Love, was well-known to the school. Love was a wealthy Philadelphia-born Quaker (b. 1843) and widow. Two girls had recently served the family. Lena Blackchief, a Seneca from Akron, was with them from April 1912 through April 1913, returning to Carlisle a month prior to Marie's departure for summer outing with the Rapps, leaving plenty of time for Marie to meet and hear about Lena's outing experience.

Marie managed her schoolwork, along with the cooking, serving, and other household duties, with diligence and success. The *Arrow* chronicled her academic progress. The October 3 issue revealed that she was among five girls out for winter. She and Jane Gayton sent "word that they are very much pleased with their Outing homes." The November 28 weekly announced, "Marie Mason, who is attending school in Moorestown, New Jersey, is now in the 8th grade." In January, "Marie Mason who is attending school in Moorestown, N.J., is doing good work in her study," having advanced to ninth grade. Finally, "Marie Mason, who is attending public school in Morristown [*sic*], N.J. expects to finish this spring."[29]

She returned August 27, 1914, ready for grade ten, Carlisle's senior year. Intelligence and determination were two qualities she had in abundance, so it is not altogether surprising that she advanced through two grades that year. Decades later, she recalled the accomplishment with pride. "The first year I went to Carlisle, the second year I went to a school in New Jersey. . . . That's where they train the dogs for the blind," she offered as an aside, making it clear that she had kept up with Moorestown over the years. The Seeing Eye program began long after she was resident there. As to progress, "I did real good, because they promoted you not because . . . they gave you exams and they promoted you according to your knowledge rather than just promoting you from year to year. And that was why I went out there." Asked how this system worked, she replied, "Well, we had what we called country homes. We would sign up to go to the country. That's what we called the country and they took care of us. They were our country parents."

"Was this a religious thing?"

"No, no" she replied. "We worked for room and board."

"And you went to this school because it was a good school, but you got into the home because it's in the neighborhood of the school, or how? Were the parents working in conjunction with the school?"

"No," Marie explained, "they just accepted the students from Carlisle. That was a big deal out there. Everybody wanted students from Carlisle. Carlisle was worth something, you know? You just mention Carlisle and you were in."

In a different interview, her assessment of the program's assimilationist foundation was crystal clear: "They called it our country home. As in going to the American country."[30] She had known from the start that *country* did not signify a rural-versus-urban landscape but rather the totality of the culture to which she was being assimilated. Friedman was gone when Marie returned to Carlisle in August, removed at the end of April and replaced by Lipps. These two got along famously and would later cross paths in California, when Lipps was assigned to the Sacramento Indian Office. But this transition in superintendents was not the only change in her Carlisle world.

Cousins

In 1914 Rose went home to care her father, now in his seventies. The April commencement ceremony where Rose was awarded her dressmaking certificate featured Maidu soloist Otie Henry. Ada Curtis was present too, taking home certificates in dressmaking and domestic arts. Henry Roe Cloud, newly graduated with a master's in anthropology from Yale, was their commencement speaker.[31] Four decades later, Marie would meet and work with his wife, Elizabeth Bender.

Rose's departure must have been bittersweet for Eli; at least their father would have the comfort of one daughter in old age. Father and son once imagined that life in the East would be less perilous for the Piazzoni girls. Eli could watch over them at Carlisle. He had certainly tried, but settler colonial worlds played themselves out then, as now, in unpredictable fashions and tempos. Like its offspring scattered across the West, Carlisle was marked by deep strains of colonial ambivalence that influenced the choices of outing patrons, superintendents, teachers, and alumni. Motivations cannot be read like so many tea leaves. Boarding schools were unequivocally sites of death, but sometimes they were imagined as places of refuge. Greenville had once served the material needs of Hukespem's descendants: food and shelter from harsh winters, protection while their parents were off working in settler homes and fields, and an education in the language and alien ways of interloping Americans—all things parents sought for their cherished children in giving them over to its care.

In December 1901, when Eli's parents sent him off to Carlisle, a boy of sixteen, they hoped it would equip him with a trade and steady employment. He, likewise, anticipated a brighter future for his sisters when he brought them east in the summer of 1905. Their mother had died the month before. Amy, Jennie's eldest daughter, passed away soon after, leaving Christopher to parent their five surviving children. Pauline was four years old, and her mother was an invalid under the care of the school physician, when her father enrolled her at Greenville in October 1904. Eli was at Carlisle and John at Chemawa, but her sisters and three Mason cousins were there. She would have regular meals, a roof over her head, and care while he worked at the dairying business. In May 1905, Eli completed Carlisle applications for his three surviving sisters and mailed them to Prattville for their father's signature. It never occurred to him that five years later he would be arranging for Alice's body to be shipped to him in Wyebrook, Pennsylvania, where he lived and worked, choosing a casket and a lambskin lining for it, signing her death certificate, and laying her to rest so far from their Big Meadow Maidu homelands. Yet there he was, stumbling blindly through this nightmare at twenty-five years old. Somehow he managed this heavy loss. But death was greedy and hovered patiently at his door.

Marie was on outing in Ocean City when it claimed Pauline, despite the watchful eye and care of her outing mother, Mrs. Walter Scott. In early spring she reported that her charge had suffered a couple of colds and was down a few pounds, but "Pauline was a tubercular child . . . is now pretty well and we think growing stronger all the time." On May 1, 1912, she remained optimistic about her prognosis: "Pauline is now enjoying far better health than when we took her in July 1905. She then had tubercular glands and ulcerated eyes." Tuberculosis had stalked her relentlessly for nearly a decade. Marie was waiting tables in Susanville, California, when Pauline first began to falter. On June 26, 1912, she was admitted to Carlisle's hospital—"Diagnosis: Pulmonary TB." Page after page in her medical chart shows diligent efforts to forestall the inevitable. Box after box ticked hourly with endless descriptive data: time, temperature, pulse, respiration, and nourishment—"milk and eggs," "did not go to supper," "refused nourishment," "extra milk and eggs." When she was discharged a month after Marie's arrival, Pauline's chart declared her "greatly improved." In Ivyland, Pennsylvania, she enjoyed a month or two of school and play on the Scott family farm, where Marie visited her, along with Rose and Eli.[32] But on November 15, 1912, she was admitted to Pennsylvania State South Mountain Sanatorium for Tuberculosis, in Mont Alto. Friedman received a March 7 update: "Present condition: Moderately progressive for advanced pulmonary tuberculosis with signs of beginning intestinal tuberculosis." Pauline's school file preserves a touching letter written on March 13, 1913, to an outing sister, "Miss Youngs," inquiring about their good friends Daisy Chase and Alta Printup. It enumerated her nuclear family members, living and deceased: three dead—mother and two sisters from consumption—one sister living, father living, two brothers living. She looked forward to returning to Carlisle but died in Mont Alto on June 16, 1913, at twelve years old. Another Mountain Maidu girl forever far from home, she is buried on the sanatorium grounds.[33]

Friedman sent Christopher Piazzoni word of this tragic news by both telegram and letter: another daughter—his youngest child—now gone. Posted to Prattville that very afternoon, the letter took a month to reach its recipient. Prattville was already remote, but Piazzoni was still further removed, off in Seneca,

California, where Baptiste was working their mining claims. Even so, mail was being forwarded to their Swiss Mine cabin, and he was unable to fathom how its delivery had gone so awry. Pain was etched in every stroke of his reply: "I hasten to thank you and all those in attendance for your courtesy and kindness during my hours of bereavement. Believe me, I appreciate every act." Pauline's outing parents also felt her loss. Earlier that fall, despite her own frailty, she had impressed her "country father," Walter Scott, with her compassion when lightning struck several farm outbuildings, burning them to the ground, despite the valiant efforts of two male pupils who saved the animals and tried to douse the flames. Praising the boys in his letter to Friedman, Scott added, "A tribute is also paid to Pauline Peozzoni's [sic] courage and presence of mind in saving the chickens."[34]

The plight of Marie's Piazzoni cousins is as instructive as it is heartbreaking. For all their efforts to make boarding schools work to their own advantage, Native people encountered colonial dispositions and forces beyond their control.[35] Eli's sisters entered Carlisle and began schoolwork as usual, but as soon as possible, Eli had them placed with trusted outing families. Graduating in 1907 to much fanfare, his commencement was attended by VIPs from Washington, D.C., and Pennsylvania, who watched him demonstrate the mechanics and fitting of the steam engine.[36] Quickly landing employment as a driver and mechanic for wealthy Philadelphia capitalist William Potts, he earned twenty dollars per week. An automobile owner himself, Eli chauffeured Carlisle boys in complimentary "tours" like those he gave to other nearby residents to supplement his income. On May 26, 1909, Eli married Clara Scott, the daughter of his first "country parents," the Scotts, with whom he had gone on outing in 1902. He was seventeen at the time, and his outing "sister" was twelve. Lore has it that their romance began soon after.[37] Thus his own little sister's outing parents were his in-laws. Pauline lived with the Scotts during her early days in Pennsylvania and again in her final year, as did Alice prior to her 1910 passing. Though Presbyterians, the Scotts had deep Quaker roots in Pennsylvania. Longtime outing patrons, they benefited from student labor while feeling magnanimous about helping Carlisle students assimilate to American settler society. Clara's younger sister, Beatrice, even taught at Carlisle for a year. Slated for transfer to Hoopa Valley School in October 1910, she took a local job instead.[38]

Eli worked to keep his family together by all means possible, but he could not stave off the ravages of TB. Gratitude to Carlisle and his outing parents is evident in frequent alumni updates.[39]

Figure 5. Carlisle Indian Industrial School class of 1907,
including Eli Piazzoni (*second row, fifth from left*).
Cumberland County Historical Society, Carlisle, Pennsylvania.

I spent most of my time in the country. I can never repay my country
father and mother for their kindness to me. I was fortunate enough to be
with a family who had two girls. At night we all sat around a big table and
studied our lessons. It was not only school lessons I received, but I learned
good manners and a great many nice little ways that my country father
and mother taught me. When school closed, my country father taught me
the proper use of all farming implements, the proper care of horses and
cattle, and the proper way to behave when we went away from home either
to church, town, picnics, or any public places. The things I have learned at
Carlisle and under the outing are paving my life's path now. I do appreciate
it. I am getting along so nicely with my fine home, many friends, and a
loving wife and two children, a boy and a girl.[40]

Perhaps Carlisle's imminent closure accounted for these depths of sen-
timentality. On the other hand, it is hard to discount Eli's sincerity. The
Scotts had been loving surrogate parents to him and his siblings in the
absence of their father, loss of their mother, and the death of one sister after
another. "Digger" children and "half-breeds" in boarding school and BIA

records, they were family to the Scotts, who later followed Eli and Clara to California.

Marie's Senior Year

Back at Carlisle by August 28, 1914, Marie settled into the girls' quarters with anticipation. Much of the cosmopolitan disposition she exhibited later in life traces back to these youthful days, where classrooms, literary societies, and dormitories were brimming with students who brought distinct languages, traditions, and histories to their interactions, despite a curriculum designed to orchestrate their internalization of a national narrative in harmony with settler colonialism. Marie's senior year course work comprised geography, elementary science, arithmetic, business forms, orthography, and penmanship, as well as literature and history. The latter combination of subjects entailed three consecutive series: "Reading for Ideals"; "The United States and Its Relationship to the History of the World in General"; and "Sociology Applied to the Indian Race." Some members of "the Indian race" studiously digested these lessons by generating counternarratives and impassioned dialogue back in their residential quarters—and throughout their lives. Marie turned out to be one of them.

Carlisle's student newspaper, the *Arrow*, reveals that Marie blossomed into a confident leader and intellectually engaged young adult during her senior year. She was highly sociable from the start, as the September 1914 *Arrow* reported: "Marie Mason hosted a melon party for some of her friends: Estelle Bradley, Mary Welch, Amy Smith, Minnie Charles, Lena Watson, Lucy West and Mary Lonechief."[41] Her guests were drawn from Chippewa, Cherokee, Little Lake Pomo, Cayuga, "Digger" (Konkow), and Pawnee nations, respectively. By early October, she was helping lead Sunday-evening Protestant services, one of many students to serve in this capacity over the coming year.[42] In October she and Kenneth King led the service, and Marie read the poem "What's the Use?"[43] She participated in group Bible verse recitations and led services again in January.[44] In mid-April, as graduation drew near, Marie and a male peer represented the senior class in chapel exercises, where she read "Polonius' Advice to his Son."[45]

The YWCA was the principal benefactor of Marie's boundless energy and the forum in which she honed her considerable leadership skills. She played minor roles at early fall meetings and was elected president in late October, when the prior president, Estelle Bradley, left her postgraduate program to go home.[46] The faculty sponsor offered advice, but Marie approached the position democratically, canvasing members about topics of concern. In January she spoke on "Christian

Work among the Indians." Student reporter Florence Edwards proclaimed it was "an excellent talk on this subject."[47] Reading between the ideological lines, one can surmise that Marie gained valuable research, writing, and public speaking experience through these endeavors.

When not engaged in more substantive matters, Marie continued to host parties. A reporter writing under the byline "One of the guests" captured the spirit of these occasions:

> Thursday evening Marie Mason gave a party in honor of Blanche Jollie's birthday. The guests were Blanche Jollie, Amy Smith, Otie Henry, Mary Welch, Emily Moran, Theresa Lay, Rose Snow, Elizabeth Janis, Ella Fox and Mary Lonechief. The first thing required of the guest was for each to give a hearty laugh. Otie Henry won the prize in the contest. Then a yell was given for the guest of honor, Blanche Jollie, Rah! Rah! Rah!—1–19, Blanche Jollie. The refreshments were cake, pie, hot biscuits, crackers, ice cream and coffee. The girls then repaired to the Mercer society room where a short musical program followed: Piano solo, Theresa Lay; Indian dance, Elizabeth Janis; Vocal solo, Otie Henry; quartette, Mary Welch, Amy Smith, Otie Henry and Marie Mason.[48]

Quartettes, solos, Indian dances, and refreshments galore—this party was far more entertaining and sumptuous than the "melon party" Marie hosted her first year. Piano access was an entirely new privilege that Otie brought to the mix.

While Marie was on outing, her Mountain Maidu peers Otie and Rose, along with Konkow Lena Watson, were initiated into the Mercers, one of two women's literary societies. Marie belonged to the Susan Longstreth Literary Society, or Susans, named for a Quaker patron who had befriended Pratt and dedicated herself to advancing the literary arts at Carlisle.[49] Male counterparts were the Standards and the Invincibles. These societies cultivated familiarity with the Western literary canon; engaged students in discussion of current events, ranging from women's suffrage to U.S. imperial intervention in the Philippines; and developed their competitive spirits through regular debate. Students alternated judging and declaiming, thus honing skills in research, reasoning, argumentation, and public oratory. Even before the Friedman debacle, legislators, social reformers, and the OIA knew the time had come to shutter Carlisle, and the Susans chose this topic for debate that winter. According to Alta Printup's February 1915 article, the meeting commenced with roll taking. Those present responded to their name by quoting a line from poet Eugene Field.[50] Following the usual songs, recitations, and readings came debate: "*Resolved:* That Carlisle should be abolished and a military academy established in its place."[51] Marie and partner Maude Cook argued in the affirmative, but students adjudged Josephine Holmes and Nettie Kingsley to have made a superior case in the negative. Fidelity to Carlisle reigned supreme.

Given Carlisle's requirement to write home once monthly, Rose probably heard from Marie via private correspondence, just as Marie heard from her Carlisle cousins in years prior, but Rose was also a faithful *Arrow* subscriber and thus able to stay abreast of her Carlisle friends' news. Otie belonged to YWCA and Mercers, participated in Sunday-evening services, and continued her dressmaker's training. Lena stayed busy with YWCA and Mercers while meeting milestones in her nursing program.[52] *Arrow* coverage of Rose's life back home commenced with the October 23 issue: "The lessons I learned while in Carlisle have been of great use to me. I have now a flock of fine chickens." Several pages in, Rose "writes from Seneca, California, that she is keeping house for her father." In March, "Rose Pezzoni [*sic*] wrote from Seneca, Cal., that they are having plenty of sleigh rides as snow is two feet deep in that section of the country." By May, Rose had moved to Greenville, and Chippewa Ada Curtis was "enjoying herself at home in Minnesota." Handiwork she entered in the Cumberland County Fair proved newsworthy. In early November, Blanche Jollie reported that Curtis's "centerpiece" was among the sewing room's prize-winning fair entries.[53]

Marie's industrial arts training turned to laundering her senior year. Course work was intensive. Carlisle's dressmaking courses equipped the school with uniforms, dresses, kitchen linens, and residential bedding; its extensive laundry needs were also handled by female students.[54] By March they were learning "how to wash and iron table linen, doilies, dish cloths, and tea towels; how to heat irons and how to take care of them."[55] Later came lessons in woolen washing, starch making, and the proper heating and care of irons. In mid-April, Marie and another graduating senior, Mary Kewaygeshik, went "from the laundry to the sewing room so that they may work on their graduating dresses." These had to be completed in two short weeks.[56] On May 1, after a senior picnic at Mount Holly Park, they gathered at the campus bandstand for their class portrait. Marie stands shoulder to shoulder with Bessie Gilland (Sioux) on her left and Margaret Brown (Tlingit) on her right.[57]

Names of the graduating class members were published in March. They were in constant motion during these months, completing an elaborate series of graduation rituals, but the class of 1915 had a rather unique experience. Lipps invited

Figure 6. Carlisle Indian Industrial School class of 1915,
including Marie Mason (*third row, fourth from left*).
Cumberland County Historical Society, Carlisle, Pennsylvania.

Pratt to Carlisle's thirty-fifth anniversary, October 6, 1914. The following day, Pratt held a private audience with the seniors. Weeklong celebrations began on May 16, Baccalaureate Sunday. The former president of Dickinson College presented the address amid elaborate decorations installed by underclassmen. Seats reserved for the seniors were draped in their red and white class colors. The banner with their class motto, "Fidelity," decorated the auditorium stage. Seniors filed in to student orchestral accompaniment. Commencement exercises were on May 20 and attended by Commissioner of Indian Affairs Cato Sells. At Lipps's invitation, Pratt returned to present diplomas. This must have been a heady experience for the seventeen women and thirteen men who strode across the stage that day, women in "gowns of embroidered voile, with corsage bouquets of pink roses"; men in tailored uniforms. Speeches by salutatorian Minnie O'Neal (Shoshone) and valedictorian Hiram Chase Jr. (Omaha) inspired underclassmen and impressed members of the visiting public, who annually came in droves to witness these impressive ceremonies.[58] Eli, Clara, and her parents watched as the little cousin Eli had "rescued" from the Greenville woods, and who followed him out to Carlisle, accepted her diploma from Pratt. Now there were two Carlisle graduates in Hukespem's line.

A Lettered Life

A diploma and set of certificates in household arts were not all Marie took home from Carlisle. In these years, she developed a voracious appetite for reading and gained confidence in public speaking. She benefited from peer-to-peer education in a cross-cultural milieu that proved to be subversive ballast for assimilationist curricula that sought to tamp down expressions of Indigenous identity and language. Carlisle was a site of rich contradiction. Speeches and gatherings of former students who had founded the Society of American Indians (SAI) frequently made the *Arrow*'s pages, including a 1912 story about the print shop fulfilling SAI's stationary order. *Red Man* and the *Arrow* boasted about the breadth of tribal nations at Carlisle. Like Marie, many were politically minded, intellectually talented, and proud of their tribal heritage and identity. The *Digger* label—unquestionably a term of opprobrium—that followed her every movement, school record, and achievement did not express the individual or collective identity to which she related. The senior class teacher, Emma H. Foster, respected this in her "Tribal Lay of 1915," a poetic tribute to the rich intercultural world they comprised. She singled out every senior with descriptive praise: "From far off Pacific, the famed Golden Gate, Comes Marie, A Medum, the pride of her State."[59]

Talents and dispositions cultivated at Carlisle served her into old age, especially the ability to express herself in writing. This was evident by spring 1915, when the *Arrow* published the following testimonial.

What Have I to Give?
by Marie Mason

What have I to give the world? I can give to the world the best that I have and know; I can be kind and generous, where generosity is needed; I can help others, where I am capable of helping.

What have I to give to my people? I can give many things to my people. When I go back to my people I can teach them what I have learned, tell them of the world I have seen, heard, and known.

What have I to give to myself? If I am good and kind to others, they will be the same to me; if I help them, they will, in turn, want to help me; if I have given to them the best I had, they will want to give to me of the best they have; if I have taught them anything, they will want to teach me of what they know.

"Silver and gold have I none, but such as I have I give unto thee."

What have I to give to the world? "Give to the world the best that you have, and the best will come back to you."[60]

The content and placement of these verses immediately beneath a message from Pratt underscores the ideological indoctrination that suffused the *Arrow* and Marie's education. Yet she did go back to her people and in due time, she gave them everything she had to give—her time, her cultural knowledge, her intellectual and literary talents.

Another sample of prose documents a more extroverted side of its author. The *Arrow*'s June 1915 "Annual Senior Number" showcased the accomplishments of the class, including at least one literary composition from each student. One pupil penned his autobiography; another recounted her trip out to Carlisle; yet another forecast the future of every classmate—predicting that Marie and her friend Julia Frechette would be living in New York City, continuing the work of the YWCA foreign missions. Marie's contribution to this assemblage was an essay of more than one thousand words entitled "A Trip to Philadelphia." It leaves no doubt that she had developed a taste for urbanity and the energy of the city during her Pennsylvania sojourn. The excursion she chronicles occurred in late February, when she traveled to Philadelphia with her YWCA group, ostensibly to see the popular baseball player turned evangelist, Billy Sunday, preach.[61] The sense of exhilaration conveyed in her opening paragraph animates the entire essay:

I had just given up all hope of ever seeing Philadelphia again, when one day, after our YWCA meeting, the advisory member came up to me and asked if I would not like to hear Billy Sunday. Of course, I would not let such a chance go by; and, although the time set for going was three weeks off, I immediately began preparing for the trip. After three weeks of delightful anticipation, the day arrived, and twelve eager girls were up and ready to go long before it was time. After we were actually on the way it seemed to us excited girls that we could get on faster if we should get out and push the train, although it would have been easier to walk than to push.[62]

She gives due space to the revivalist encampment, or "tabernacle," and to Billy Sunday's sermon, but what really comes through is how enraptured she was with being in the city, shopping at Wanamaker's department store, and standing on a rooftop from which they could survey the magnificent cityscape and see all the way to Camden, New Jersey. They toured Betsy Ross's home on their final day, but first they visited the University of Pennsylvania. The buildings were "very beautiful, with ivy climbing over the walls." One left a lasting impression: "In the museum we found the Indian relics of most interest to us, but some of us were disappointed to find that we were not represented there."[63]

Her Sensibilities Are Transformed

Marie's disappointment in not finding her own people represented in the University of Pennsylvania museum foreshadows her engagement with museums and exhibits some three decades later. It also shows that she was searching in these years for her place, and the place of her people, in relation to the world that lay beyond Big Meadow and Greenville. All aspects of her Carlisle experience had profound implications for her future; they molded the exuberant personality and lively intellect of an adolescent girl into those of a confident young woman, able to interact with people from all backgrounds and walks of life. The fearlessness she demonstrated in finding outing situations that allowed her to advance her academic standing is an attribute she displayed throughout her long life, tackling whatever problems stood in her way with pragmatism and determination. Her affinity for travel and adventure, her literary talents, and her fondness of parties and laughter all resurface in her activist years as reminders of a young Maidu woman who went east.

Eli's influence on her as a model and mentor cannot be discounted. Eleven years older, he looked out for her, as he did for his sisters. Through her own perseverance and good health, she managed to mirror his success, graduating with an academic degree and two industrial arts certificates. Hukespem's grandchildren clearly met their changing times and circumstances head-on, yet their fortunes were varied and unpredictable. While Marie thrived, TB wreaked devastation upon her Piazzoni cousins. No amount of Americanization or clinical care could save them from their Big Meadow Maidu mother's fate. Their story leavens and rounds out an otherwise rosy portrait of Bill family experiences at Greenville and Carlisle. It is a reminder that boarding schools served purposes that the federal government never anticipated and that contradicted those for which the schools were designed and funded. As blunt instruments of forced assimilation, they sometimes failed to meet their mark, not because American Indian children failed to live up to settler society's vision of their potential but rather because Native families lived up to theirs, looking out for one another in whatever new and old ways they could. Eli did this by bringing his sisters east and watching out for his cousin Marie; Rose, in turn, by going home to care for her Swiss-Italian father. These three Carlisle alumni, grandchildren of Hukespem, continued to take pride in their educational experiences after returning home, using them to make their way in a society not yet willing to acknowledge the humanity, talents, and intelligence of California Indian people.

3

Life on the Margins

Marriage and Motherhood

Finally, one of the ladies came and said, "They object to your children going to Sunday school." And I said, "Well if that's the kind of Christianity you have, I object to them going too."

—*Marie Potts, 1955*

Intellectual ambition and sheer determination propelled Marie to Carlisle and through countless exhilarating experiences, including her May 1915 commencement. She now faced an uncertain crossroads. She could stay out east, continue her education, and become a teacher or Indian Service employee; or she could go home to Plumas County. She chose the latter.

Big Meadow No More

Discharged from Carlisle on June 15, Marie headed out to Wyebrook, Pennsylvania, where she spent the next three months with Eli and his family. She may have been employed by his benefactor, William Potts, during these weeks, but without doubt, she was spending her days and nights trying to decide what to do with herself now that she had achieved her long-standing goal of a Carlisle education. Years later, when asked why she decided not to remain out east like many of the school's alumni, she confessed, "Well, I could have gone to normal school there and become a teacher, you know, and I kind of liked that, but I don't know. Somehow, I got to thinking about my mother and cried myself to sleep several nights and decided, well, I want to go home."[1]

Marie's train rolled into Keddie the first week in September.[2] Mount Lassen, or Kom Yamani, welcomed her home with billowing gasps and smoky hiccups, remnants from the four-mile-high display that had accompanied its late May eruption, making national news—even in Carlisle.[3] Change was everywhere as Mountain Maidu pursued livelihoods on the periphery of the capitalist economy. Yet life "on the margins" was literal as well as figurative for Big Meadow Maidu, who had been pushed to the geographic edge of their rich meadowlands by a massive dam project. Marie's ancestral camp was gone—"drowned" with the rest of Big Meadow under a hydroelectric reservoir. Magnitudes of impact can be measured in infinite registers and from multiple points of reference, but affect is a powerful barometer of loss. This is what makes the language of "drowning" so apt.[4] It evokes imagery of a watery death, the smothering of cherished life forms and places too diverse to count or fully comprehend. Human and nonhuman relatives, realms of prosaic and spiritual life, places steeped in cultural expression and continuity—all were snuffed out like the flicker of a faithful candle.

Unlike residents who watched the reservoir fill to capacity over several years, Marie stood on its bank in September 1915 and was struck by its abrupt presence and massive scale. The full weight of this loss grew in magnitude as she matured. She recalled that Augustus R. "Gus" Bidwell, once a trusted local figure, had conspired with Great Western Power Company (GWP) agents to deceive both Maidu and white homesteaders about the future of the ranchlands being so rapidly consolidated by San Francisco real estate broker A. H. Breed. Bidwell "approached Indians and offered to buy their allotments for $50.00. . . . I heard one Indian say, 'What's the matter, white man crazy.'"[5]

By the time Marie left for Carlisle in fall 1912, GWP had claimed, through purchase or condemnation, most of the 25,480 acres comprising Nakám Koyó— whole villages, streams, fishing sites, burial grounds, and mythological places like Big Springs, or Wisótpinim, that figured into ancient Mountain Maidu histories.[6] New employment opportunities and excitement about a reservoir billed as the country's largest may have delayed it for a few years, but the magnitude and finality of their loss was profound. It was yet another forced removal in a rapid series that her own grandparents had lived out, from the gold rush to homesteader invasion to *Thompson v. Doaksum*. Land condemnations began in 1902, under Western Power Company, GWP's precursor.[7] Perhaps Big Meadow Maidu wondered if local homesteaders and hoteliers destined to be similarly displaced were finally getting a taste of their own medicine, or at least a fraction of the pain they had inflicted on their Indigenous neighbors. Local historians have described the sense of betrayal Big Meadow residents felt when forced to part with property their families had worked for three generations, but this was hardly comparable to the Big Meadow Maidu depth of place and time.[8]

Although its obliteration was under way when Marie left for Carlisle, in 1915 she arrived home to an irrevocably flooded Big Meadow, a landscape full of tender sites of memories she could never visit again. Decades later, as she fully understood that this brazen act of theft was enabled by the federal government, for a capitalist enterprise serving remote cities and shareholders with no stake in the history or quality of local life, she became increasingly angered at the double dispossession of her ancestral homelands—first by colonization and second by inundation to create the reservoir known as Lake Almanor. Crisscrossing the countryside in her activist years, meeting with tribal representatives whose treaty lands had been condemned for similar hydroelectric works, she recognized the assault GWP had waged upon her own people's cultural vitality and memory. Years of public speaking—and tales of her birthplace and childhood—inevitably evoked commentary about Lake Almanor's spectacular beauty. "You should have seen Big Meadow," she would quietly reply.

A Series of Betrayals

GWP rose to power during Marie's Greenville years, procuring—by hook and crook—all public forestlands, Maidu camps, and private property that fell within the reservoir's projected contours. Gus Bidwell initiated the process in 1901 by selling GWP his family's Meadow View Hotel and surrounding property comprising 720 acres. It ended in 1909 with the town of Prattville going up in smoke. Residents had ridden a roller coaster for the entire decade, initially assured they were not only outside the flood zone but also about to own lakeshore property. When the contours expanded in 1906 to incorporate Prattville, most residents refused to sell, so GWP bought and shut down two hotels that sustained local merchants and service providers. Aiming to force the town's hand, GWP was outwitted by saloon proprietor Frank Sorsoli, who built a twenty-eight-room hotel. With livelihoods dependent upon accommodations for seasonal recreation secured, the town held its own until a suspicious fire broke out on the afternoon of July 3, 1909. Residents watched in horror from their Independence Day baseball game and picnic a mile distant. A headline said it all: "$75,000 Blaze Wipes Out the Town of Prattville: the Sorsoli and Prattville Hotels, the Abbott and Costar Stores, Sorsoli Saloon, Redhead Blacksmith Shop and Dwellings were Destroyed."[9] Years later, Fred Davis Sr. made a remarkable donation to the Chester-Lake Almanor

Museum: Prattville School's hand bell. Davis was the company physician hired to serve the construction crew headquartered near the dam site at Bidwell's old Meadow View Hotel, renamed Nevis in 1909.[10] A tag affixed to the bell, which bears no signs of fire damage, indicates that it was removed from the school on July 2, 1909, the day before the fire—a curious coincidence, or not. Had GWP conspired with someone to commit arson—someone compelled to salvage that bell beforehand as an artifact of childhood nostalgia? Generations of children passed through the school's doors, including Marie, from 1905 through 1907. Townspeople never believed rumors of "Indians playing with fireworks" behind Abbott's store. In the fire's wake, most residents conceded defeat, but Sorsoli rebuilt. The hotel business was bust, but nearby dam construction promised sufficient saloon patronage, much to the chagrin of GWP, which continued its assault on Prattville.

Soon demolition began. Immense groves of towering sugar pines that had witnessed the unfolding of time—some sporting trunks seven feet across—were toppled and floated to the sawmill; barns and farmhouses raised by emigrant great-grandparents in the 1850s were reduced to rubble and dust. Marie's ancestral hamlet, taken first by David Blunt and then by Alexander Thompson, could not survive GWP's watery grave. Like the Americans who blithely pushed Hukespem's generation to the brink of existence, the community now found itself staring down the barrel of a corporation that could not have been more cavalier in its take-no-prisoners approach.[11] When the lake was expanded a decade later and GWP was forced to relocate cemeteries, a company representative lamented that it would have been easier to "read the service for burial at sea," if only those sentimental townsfolk would just look the other way.[12] Distrustful and bitter, they could not. Yet Big Meadow Maidu suffered more.

Lumber baron T. B. Walker, whose fame is overshadowed by that of Paul Bunyon, his company's advertising icon, first turned his gaze to the northern Sierra in 1894. Having depleted the Minnesota timber stands that built his Red River Lumber Company (RRLC), he was anxious to expand his empire. Thousands of trees in the reservoir's basin posed a practical problem for GWP. To Walker, they represented a gold mine; hence they were a source of welcome capital for both companies. The job of cutting and milling was no less massive than the targeted trees. A self-contained company town, "Walker's Camp," arose just east of Big Meadow in 1912.[13] Christened Westwood in 1913, it is a quaint reminder of the once-bustling RRLC. Though Native men and women worked in the timber industry, collectively they lost far more than the beauty of Big Meadow. Maidu allotments on the lake's perimeter and down in the North Fork district were seduced away from Marie's family members and many other Maidu before and after the reservoir's development. Quick cash for rocky, timbered land they had no fiscal wherewithal to develop or subsist upon was foolish to refuse in the face of daily need. Dam construction commenced in 1910, but the livelihoods and community resources the valley once offered began to dwindle even before 1908, when GWP stopped issuing permits to seasonal visitors for recreational use of its properties. The decline in fishing and camping clientele drove out residents who subsisted on related wage labor, including Big Meadow Maidu like Marie's kin, who dispersed to other camps and towns.[14]

Finding Her Way Home

In some respects, Marie was no more certain about who and what counted as "home" in September 1915 than she had been four years earlier, when she began pondering the implications of aging out of Greenville. Although John Mason had settled in Washington State, most of her immediate family still lived in Indian Valley, where they had moved near the time of Hukespem's 1909 death. This included sister Lizzette, mother Josie, stepfather Johnny Roy, and Marie's younger set of half siblings; six-year-old Alta Roy, born at Big Springs in December 1908, now had a baby brother, Charley. Despite this fact and Marie's later profession of homesickness for Josie, when pressed for a home mailing address upon her Carlisle departure, Marie gave the contact information for a Washoe girlfriend and Carlisle alumna: "Greenville, c/o Mrs. Edgar [Lillian] Parrett," marking the first of many times she would invoke her now expansive boarding school network.[15]

Marie evidently harbored uncertainties about where—and to whom—she would return. This was more than a practical problem. Josie had been picking up her mail at the school post office since at least 1910; why not "Greenville, c/o Josie Roy"? As with Campbell's earlier insistence that Marie was "not under her mother's jurisdiction" and the glaring absence of Josie's name in Carlisle's vital records, we are left to wonder if these two suffered a major falling-out over Marie's decision to matriculate at Carlisle. Had Josie counted on some relief at home—perhaps help with Marie's new half sister, Alta—once Marie finished at Greenville? Or was something more significant amiss, something beyond adolescent petulance at her mother's new marriage to Johnny Roy? Superintendent Mann, who had first commended her to Carlisle and Friedman in 1911, had publicly condemned Roy in a court trial earlier that year, accusing him of providing liquor to two young men, one of whom was a boarding school pupil.[16] Carlisle students were mailed the remainder of their outing earnings following discharge; was Marie worried that these funds might go missing or awry if sent to the Roy home? Perhaps the use of Lillian Porterfield Parrett's address reflected nothing more than Marie's determination to retain her independence. In any case, her choice speaks volumes about Greenville's status as a permanent anchor in her life. In fact, she lived there several months upon return, meeting new pupils and catching up with older ones, such as Konkow student Frank Day, whom she taught during her final year, when Twoguns was the young boy's matron. She also reconnected with her old flame.

Mission Chapel Marriage

Hensley Henry Potts was a Greenville alumnus. His paternal grandfather, Levi Newton Potts (1835–1917), had emigrated from Ohio during the 1850s, initially settling in Rough and Ready, a Nevada County mining camp.[17] By 1870 he had relocated to Yuba County's Foster Bar. Around 1868 he married a young Nisenan speaker named Ellen (daughter of Lucy and Charley Toley), who bore their first child, Henry—Hensley's father—in 1869.[18] Mendel, Levi Jr., Mary Ellen, Titus, Irene, and Esra followed. Henry's marriage to Alice Nye, the daughter of Pennsylvania miner James Nye and an Indigenous Yuba County woman, yielded four sons and one daughter: Walter, Hensley, Earl, Ernest, and Maude. Two half brothers later joined their ranks.[19] Hensley, born July 4, 1893, in Dobbins, began attending Greenville in 1904. "He never knew his mother," Marie later remarked. She died around November 1900.[20]

English was the language of Marie and Hensley's courtship and marriage. "He was a Konkow Indian—a branch of the Maidu, but we didn't speak the same Indian language. He finally learned a little Maidu," she teased.[21] They were married at Mission Chapel three months after her return. Civil and religious marriage was an exciting marker of assimilation for institutions like WNIA, Greenville, and Carlisle. In March 1908, the *Indian's Friend* rejoiced when widower Abro Johnson married Mary Washoe, and again in 1911 when Ellen Reeves married Walter Potts. The local paper carried a brief announcement of Marie's marriage: "At the Greenville Indian Mission, Plumas County, Cal., December 29, 1915, Mr. Hensley H. Potts and Miss Marie Mason, Rev. G. E. Reader officiating."[22] The *Arrow* elaborated considerably, demonstrating the importance that Carlisle attached to gender and family norms: "Mr. Edgar K. Miller, superintendent at Greenville, Cal., sent in the following item to Mr. Lipps. "I wish to report to you the marriage of Miss Marie Mason, which took place at this agency, December 30 [1915], by Reverend Reader, missionary here. She married Mr. Hensley Potts,

Figure 7. Mechoopda Indian Band, including Hensley Potts (*lower right*).
Dorothy M. Hill Collection, Meriam Library Special Collections, California State University–Chico.

one of the progressive young Indians of this jurisdiction. He has steady work at Engel's mine and seems to be industrious. He earns three dollar a day. Marie is one of our 1915 graduates and her many friends at Carlisle wish her and her husband a long and happy life.[23]"

Greenville superintendent Edgar Miller dispatched this news in record time, knowing its material and symbolic value. The art and trade of printing was his bailiwick. Prior to his 1915 Greenville appointment, he ran two boarding school presses, Chilocco's, in Oklahoma, and previous to that Carlisle's, where he led the "printer boys" in production of the *Indian Craftsman* magazine. This publication mirrored the sensibility and quality of Gustav Stickley's *Craftsman* magazine to such an extent that the latter's publisher forced Carlisle to abandon its title; whence came *Red Man* in 1910.[24] Just sixteen months before his Greenville transfer, Miller articulated his continuing commitment to boarding school print culture in the *American Printer*.[25] And like Lipps, who also published the story in record time, he recognized the value of reporting exemplary behavior to boarding school pupils and alumni peers, though Marie was surely pleased to share this news.

Wedding details beyond those published remain elusive but may be partly deduced through reference to the 1911 wedding of Walter Potts and Ellen Reeves.[26]

"Large pupils," meaning older students, were in attendance for this object lesson in Christian matrimony. Girls baked wedding cakes, and the school was festooned with flowers and streamers of pink and white. Employees and students performed songs and instrumental music during and after the ceremony. Hensley was his brother's best man, while Greenville alumna Lula Oshem stood for Ellen. Perhaps Walter now returned the favor for Hensley, and Ellen or her cousin Rose stood with Marie. Dissimilarities are certain. Ellen's parents attended her wedding, while both Josie and Lizzette are curiously absent in Miller's account of the marriage. Ellen wore a bridal gown and veil, but costs and planning probably placed these outside Marie's reach. It is far more probable that she wore her white Carlisle graduation dress. Wedding finery was certainly the antithesis of Engelmine, where Marie settled into married life.

New Motherhood in a Copper Mining Camp

In the late 1870s, German immigrant Henry Engels Sr. managed a San Francisco foundry that freighted its raw material by train from the Great Lakes, an expense that motivated the family to prospect Plumas County's Lights Canyon. Identifying copper deposits, sons William and Henry Jr. moved out to develop the mine. Wealth eluded them until the turn of the twentieth century, when copper values skyrocketed in tandem with the electrical industry. Attracting new capital investment, Engels Copper Mining Company (ECMC) formed in 1906. Demonstrating their flotation extraction method at the 1915 Panama-Pacific Exposition in San Francisco, ECMC garnered fame and investors, fueling dramatic expansion. Both Walter and Hensley worked there in 1916 when four hundred employees walked out. News coverage ignored labor issues, focusing instead on employee behavior during the brief strike, "when some of the uncontrollable element proceeded to imbibe fire-water."[27] By now ECMC was processing four hundred tons of ore daily and hoping to reach five hundred in coming months.[28] Substantial dependence upon Native laborers as miners, millers, and muckers is evident in the "fire-water" reference above. Soon, two more Potts brothers, Levi Jr. and Ernest, joined them. Two mining camps housed employees, and a lively community called Engelmine emerged, complete with a movie theater, orchestra, and rival baseball teams—the Lower Camp Angels and Upper Camp All Stars.

Here the couple welcomed their firstborn, Josephine Berg, on October 22, 1916.[29] Walter and Hensley registered for the selective service in the summer of 1917. The world war brought forth a groundswell of patriotism in rural Plumas County, and the Native community shared fully in the competitive spirit that drove each town to best the other in Liberty Bond investment.[30] It was a banner year for ECMC, with almost $300,000 going to shareholders, but this year also marked the end of Hensley's ECMC employment and the collapse of Walter and Ellen's marriage. Liquor was Walter's downfall—as it had been for his father. Three days before Christmas, Ellen, now mother to four children, filed for divorce on grounds of extreme cruelty.[31] Mining camp life surely exacerbated drinking problems that already plagued the Native community. Plumas County's Anti-Saloon League ran a full-page ad in July 1909, detailing four years of accidents, brawls, and deaths attributable to liquor, a significant portion involving Native people.[32] As always, white commentators danced nimbly around the obvious connection between their own intrusion and alcohol availability and abuse.

Marie and Hensley welcomed Jeanne Emerald on May 14, 1918. With a second babe in arms and Ellen gone, Engelmine proved lonelier and less hospitable. Marie's sister was facing similar challenges. On January 8, 1918, Lizzette married a Wintu man, Sandy Silverthorne, in Redding. Silverthorne worked for Bully Hill Mines in Copper City, Shasta County.[33] Their only child, Rhoda Pearl, was born on December 18, 1918. Eight days later, Sandy died. Out of tragedy a ray of sunshine emerged. Gathering up her infant daughter, Lizzette moved home to Josie. It was just a matter of time before Marie and her growing family followed.

Reunion with Her Maidu Mother and Culture

The two sisters and their mother came together for several fleeting years, which Marie forever cherished. Josie and Johnny were raising Alta and Charley on Roy property, behind the Greenville school and chapel, that stretched north toward the hills, off Mission Indian Road. This forested landscape was a welcome respite from the scarred landscape of the copper camps where the two sisters had begun married life. Here, the bonds of kinship and tradition were sutured back together. Josie's daily presence in her daughters' lives was a new experience. Marie's boundless curiosity and thirst for learning found new outlets, as she worked alongside her mother, harvesting and processing acorns, roots, bulbs, and basketry materials. She began weaving again and daily spoke the language of her ancestors and Big Meadow childhood. "We have a pretty language, I think!" she once remarked with genuine pride.[34] These were days when she renewed her love for it, binding up precious new memories in its lyrical tones.

Pain soon wedged its way into this rosy interlude. In 1920 along came an infant son who was not long for this earth. William died on March 22, 1921, barely a year old. Marie went into labor as he was drawing his last breath. The couple's third daughter, Nora Beryl, was born on March 23, 1921. The joy of a new baby was alloyed to the bottomless grief of losing a child, but Marie soldiered on. She began weaving again. A fire had consumed Josie's house in the winter of 1920, destroying baskets she used and treasured. Marie began working on a sifter to replace the one her mother had lost, but life with young children was all consuming. She set her weaving aside—for decades—but she was immersed in her own Native community, making memories she would conjure with nostalgia in later life. During these years the Roy property was the site of big times: "feeds and 'pow-wows,'" as the local press called them. Her world was enlivened by the old dances, food, games, language, and socializing of her grandparents' generation.[35]

Diminishing Fortunes and Bill Family Descendants

The size and membership of Marie's household and extended family underwent dramatic transformation throughout these years. Daughter Pansy Lizzette was born on December 18, 1922, and Kitty Marie followed on August 9, 1924. In between their arrivals, Lizzette, now remarried and living in the town of Greenville, succumbed to tuberculosis. Orphaned on November 1, 1923, six weeks shy of her fourth birthday, Lizzette's daughter, Rhoda, was taken in by her grandmother. Then death visited again: Charley Roy was riding alone in the woods behind his house when he was bucked from his horse, suffering a badly broken leg. He dragged himself home, but the injuries soon snuffed out his young life. The next year Josie Bill Roy followed him to the grave on December 16, 1926.

Bill descendants, once strong in numbers, were slipping away. Hukespem and Mariah's son, Charley (Bill) Gould, died three months before Lizzette. Their daughter Flora (Bill) Dick passed away around 1905 at Potadi, the Maidu camp near Bidwell's Meadow View resort, where she was working.[36] Her firstborn, Tommy Tucker, was gone too. Among Greenville's first boarding pupils, Tucker was the cousin who looked after Marie in Susanville in the summer of 1912. A member of the 363rd Infantry, he was killed in France on September 28, 1918, and laid to rest in the Meuse-Argonne American War Cemetery. His remains are among 486 graves marked "unknown."[37] Sad irony abounds in this inscription; it mirrors the "unknown" inscribed on the line for "father" on countless government records, from census to enlistment documents.

The cliché that there are no secrets in small towns is a fitting reminder that only rarely were fathers of unacknowledged children truly "unknown." Like the second-generation American ranchers who fathered but never acknowledged

Josie Bill's first three children, Tommy Tucker's father, William Warren "Warnie" Holmes—son of Aaron Holmes, grandson of Isaac and Elizabeth Holmes—was a descendant of American emigrant homesteaders. After Tommy's birth in the late 1880s, Flora married William "Billy" Dick and had three more children before passing away.[38] Like many male pupils, in early adolescence Tommy was lured away from boarding school by the prospect of earning a good wage. He did so in Tehama County, living with his stepfather and half siblings, later joining the household of his mother's cousin, his "aunt" Emma and her husband, Captain "Cap" DeHaven, in Lassen County. It was here the DeHavens' received word from General John Pershing: "He bravely laid down his life for the cause of his country. His name will ever remain fresh in the hearts of his friends and comrades. The record of his honorable service will be preserved in the archives of the American Expeditionary Forces [AEF]."[39] His death, like that of so many other California Indian veterans lost in World War I, is even more poignant because so many were not even citizens and served voluntarily.[40]

John Peazzoni also served in the AEF, overlapping with his cousin Tommy.[41] Assigned to an army transport job, he mustered out on July 15, 1918, after six months of training at Camp Meade. Discharged a year later, he rejoined Eli and his family in Wyebrook, where he had lived for most of the decade. Rose Piazzoni was still living at the Swiss Mine cabin, three miles west of Seneca, with her father and Uncle Baptiste. After Christopher died in February 1922, she moved to Oakland and worked as a seamstress. Baptiste died on December 20, 1925. At least that is the day his mining partner, Will Perry of Greenville, discovered him, pick in hand, some eighteen hundred feet deep in one of the adits he had been tunneling for years. He is buried on the slope above the cabin on Owl Creek where he chased his fortune for five and half decades.[42] It was almost in reach when family from Pennsylvania, Oakland, Greenville, and surrounds gathered to lay him to rest. Eli, John, and Rose inherited the mine and cabin, and Eli began looking for employment in California. In spring 1926, he landed a teaching position at Pomona's Lincoln High School and moved his family out; his in-laws soon followed. Marie later explained that to find employment, he was forced to elide his Maidu heritage in favor of his Swiss-Italian roots. John Peazzoni stayed in Wyebrook, working for the William Potts family.[43] Susie Buckley, the daughter with whom Mariah lived after Hukespem's passing, died after 1910.[44] Alta Roy was seventeen years old when her mother, Josie, died. Marrying Harry Rivas Thomas shortly afterward, she became stepmother to two young children. Her father, Johnny Roy, lived with them.[45]

Figure 8. Rose Piazzoni with her brother Eli (hat in hand) and his son
Walter Scott at the family's Swiss Mine cabin along Owl Creek in Seneca,
California, circa 1930. Carved into the lintel is "FROM 1874 TO 1926."
Plumas County Museum, Quincy, California.

Indian Schools: The More Things Change . . .

After Josie's death, eight-year-old Rhoda Silverthorne joined Marie's household,
now comprising six girls, ages four to nine. Marie was dedicated to helping them
thrive socially and educationally. Greenville Indian School, so close in proximity
to the Roy property, was not an option when Marie's eldest daughter, Josephine,
came of school age. Neither, as it turns out, was the closest public school.

In 1921 Greenville Indian School burned to the ground. Its demise was
foreshadowed a decade prior, when OIA assigned it agency status, expanding
Superintendent Campbell's responsibilities exponentially. In addition to the
school and children, he was now charged with the care and practical affairs of
Native people in six counties: Butte, Plumas, Shasta, Sierra, Tehama, and Yuba.
Pleas for more staffing so he could venture into the field, survey the needs of ill
and aged Indians, and tackle the problem of ranchers illegally grazing livestock
on Indian allotments fell on deaf ears. He resigned in mid-1914 to go to law school,
and his replacements were short-lived. When Edgar Miller arrived in Spring
1915, he managed to have two counties jettisoned from his jurisdiction—Shasta

and Tehama—both situated beyond mountain ranges that were impassable during winter, but the agency remained understaffed even as school enrollment increased.

Miller argued endlessly that Indian children were better off with a public school education but also regularly informed OIA that if it insisted on keeping Greenville open, it needed to modernize the twenty-year-old dormitory, upgrade sanitation facilities, offer vocational training for older boys, and provide regular medical care, including dentistry. Politically savvy, Miller also bent the ear of Congressman John E. Raker, who pressed for congressional appropriations. Although largely unsuccessful, these efforts demonstrate Miller's commitment to the local community, albeit largely in terms of white, economic interests.[46] With Washington's refusal to allocate sufficient funding or close the school, Miller sought work-arounds.

In the late 1920s, Miller oversaw Josie's sale of both Lizzette's and Mariah's allotments to RRLC. At the same time, he helped her pour the proceeds into the purchase of valuable acreage adjacent to the school.[47] First patented in 1880 to homesteader Andrew Jackson Hickerson, the property was inherited by his descendants upon his 1899 death. While Josie may have independently thought to acquire this property, Miller's excitement over its acquisition suggests clever designs upon it: "The sale of this property was recently brought about through Agent E. K. Miller of the Indian School, at a reported price of $5,000, the purchaser being the wife of Johnny Roy, representing the best class of Indian families who have had the advantages of the training of the school. It is understood that the school will derive an additional water supply from a portion of that belonging to the Hickerson property."[48] Miller's vision of enhanced water capacity for the school property was legitimate; among the challenges he reported as evidence that OIA should abolish the school was "inadequacy of the water system—(in the summertime there is not enough water for domestic use; none for fire protection or irrigation)."[49] Further, his effusive language describing Josie as "representing the best class of Indian families" to have benefited from a Greenville school education seems suspect, as it praises not only the graduates but also the local value of an institution he constantly professed should be closed.

Fire had plagued the school and its wooden structures throughout its existence, and this continued under Miller's watch. In June 1919 a blaze broke out in the attic of the two-story laundry, costing the government $2,500. Six months later, the second-floor agency office went up, prompting Miller to write the commissioner on January 19 about the school's fate. His preference for closing the school so he could focus on agency work is evident in his insistence that if the government wished to maintain the school, it must budget improvements of $60,500. In December 1921, while Washington fiddled, the dormitory and school building burned to the ground, the additional water supply from the Roy property notwithstanding. Miller told his old friend Lipps, now at Nez Perce Indian Agency, how much he missed the children: "Became so attached to them it seems now like working in a cemetery without their presence . . . was sure glad that I was here when I was for I know that every effort was made to save the building and that there is no question but that the old flue caused the fire."[50] No lives were lost, but 104 pupils were dispatched to government schools across three states: Sherman and Fort Bidwell in California, Chemawa in Oregon, and Stewart in Nevada. Forty-seven went home to parents or guardians, some of those forty-seven perhaps entering public school.[51]

Hoping to Rebuild: A Congressional Delegation, a Big Time, and a Bear Dance

After thirty-one years, the school held memories for both the Native and non-Native community, some of whom on both sides immediately sought its restoration.[52] Three years later they were still at it. In April 1925, the Greenville Chamber of Commerce held a meeting to prepare for a June congressional visit bringing OIA representatives to town: "A delegation of some forty Indians . . . made speeches advocating rebuilding of the school. Some splendid talks were made by the Indians, chief among them being the speech of Hensley Potts, a young Indian who had been educated at the Greenville Indian School."[53] In June hundreds of Native people arrived at the old school grounds to set up camp. "The stone foundation of the school building that burned several years ago had been transformed into a furnace and open-air kitchen. Six sides of beef had been roasting all night and morning for the barbeque. There was a huge cauldron of beans cooked with two sides of bacon and coffee with plenty of rich cream."[54] Native people took control: "Everything was prepared and supervised by a chef and a steward from Westwood, and served cafeteria style, Indians first. About 900 people were fed. While waiting for the barbeque the Indians entertained the crowd, which was a large one, with games, the most amusing one being the grass game. After the barbeque some of the Indians danced the bear dance. One wit among them made things lively by facetious remark about the onlooking 'pale faces' extending urgent invitation to different persons to join in the dance, all of which was received in the gayest of good humor."[55]

Financial contributions for the gathering came from the Greenville, Lassen, and Westwood chambers and from Taylorsville, Crescent Mills, and Genesee, affirming the vital role the school had once played in the regional economy. The congressional party was duly impressed, but the government stood its ground.

Marie and Hensley were among many alumni who harbored nostalgia for their alma mater. Their experience of the school dated to its earliest years, when local teachers and superintendents still populated its ranks. The school engendered lasting social networks and was the site where their own romance blossomed. Their cooperation with the local white community to forestall its final closure sheds important light on the nature of the school and agency as not merely Native resources but as indigenized places. Their own children were making memories and indigenizing a different "Indian school."

Lincoln School

When Josephine reached school age in 1922, she joined Marie's younger siblings at Lincoln School. Rhoda, Jeanne, and Beryl followed in due time.[56] Lincoln was the de facto public "Indian school" until it burned down on June 9, 1941.[57] Despite decades of effort by both the federal government and the Greenville Agency to have Indian students integrated into local public schools, the idea gained little traction in the white community. Damaging stereotypes persisted, unchanged since 1892, when the local paper had published the state's formal clarification of the terms by which they were permitted access to public schools: "If the parents of Indian children still maintain their tribal relation, the children are not entitled to attend the public schools, unless they are living under guardianship of a white person. If parents have given up their tribal relations, they are entitled to send their children to the public schools; but they must keep their children in proper condition; otherwise it is proper and right for the Trustees to exclude them from the schools."[58] The phrase "proper condition" encoded a suite of assimilationist expectations that Native people continued to recognize as blatant shorthand for racial prejudice.

Segregated and physically decrepit by comparison to the county's other schools, Lincoln was located in Lights Canyon, six or seven miles from the Potts home. "They had a little school way down in the valley and all the Indian children had to go to that little school," Marie later explained. "The town people didn't want them in town and they furnished them transportation. I think the government paid the transportation. And paid part of the expense for the teacher to teach the youngsters." Affirming the obvious discrimination, she recalled, "Well, I was living right on the edge of town and MY children had to go down to this little school. . . . [W]e were Indians and they didn't want Indian children mingling with their children in town." Asked if parents rebelled, she chuckled, "No we just sorta accepted it, until years later when the school burnt down; they had to accept the children then!"

Built in 1873, Lincoln served many white pioneer children in the late 1800s, but it had not been modernized since and was substandard by all accounts. In 1920 Lincoln's teacher approached the county for improvements, noting that with only nine pupils, and four of those in elementary grades, they were unable to participate in team-based athletic programs. But low enrollments were only part of the problem. The county would not even provide the school with basic sports equipment. Moreover, "the desks are ancient and mutilated and show that many little fingers have been more industrious with their knives than with their books."[59] This appeal got Lincoln a coat of paint and not much else.

Mulling the differences between the public school climate in Big Meadow when she was a child and the climate her daughters encountered in 1920s Indian Valley, Marie observed:

> As far as public schools were concerned, that was the only time that we had trouble. I mean the people didn't want our children going there, yet I lived in another town [Prattville] and I went to a public school; there was no objection. In fact, my whole family went during the summer months. And nobody objected to it; they just accepted us and took it for granted that we were entitled to the school just like anybody else. But that depended on the community and the people. More or less. For one thing, this [Prattville] was a small community and they had to have the pupils in order to get a teacher. So, they welcomed the Indian children.[60]

Discrimination hewed along strategic lines. Indian people had no trouble getting work, when jobs existed: "[A]ll the ranchers hired the Indians. In fact, they preferred hiring the Indians than they did hiring some drifters." Purchasing power was much like labor power: "Well in Greenville, they didn't bother the people. There was no racial prejudice as far as the restaurants or barbershops. . . . [I]t was just the school and the Sunday school. They even asked me to take my children out of Sunday school. They didn't want them there 'cause they were Indians."

After her Carlisle experiences, Marie had simply assumed her children would be welcome in any church setting. She was slow and shocked to learn otherwise. It was a white woman who let the cat out of the bag: "My youngsters went to

Sunday school every Sunday and finally one of the ladies came and said, 'They object to your children going to Sunday school.' And I said, well if that's the kind of Christianity you have, I object to them going too." Noting the logical conclusion to this revelation, she added indignantly, "Well, if they didn't want them in Sunday school, they surely didn't want them in church." Maidu people had acculturated, become fluent in English, taken up the colonizers' religious faith, adapted to the capitalist economy, and gone about their business as modern people. And settler society was still as gob-smacked and unnerved by their similitude as it had been forty years prior, when the local press had mocked, "Civilizing—We are told that Diggers in Indian Valley have put up a couple of dancing halls, and on stated occasions heir [sic] the services of a string band, and give a grand ball with all the extras thrown in. At the rate which they are going we shall soon looks [sic] for them to adopt white kids, and expect to have an order for a couple hundred ball programmes, to be headed 'Grand Grasshopper Ball.'"[61]

The Potts girls left Lincoln after the 1926–27 school year. The Christmas celebration that year was covered in the press and bore a striking resemblance to those chronicled by Marie's Greenville teachers in the 1890s and early 1900 editions of the *Indian's Friend*. Her girls took center stage in the program of performances. Boys and girls gave their parents decorative pillows, for which they had helped sew "cross-stitched tops and ruffling."[62] Fortunately, the one-room school, with tiny enrollments, was blessed with one very hardworking teacher. Despite the segregated environment, Marie fostered her girls' intellectual development and ensured their exposure to other forms of learning. Following in her mother's academic footsteps, Josephine earned reading club diplomas from the Plumas County Free Library in third and fourth grade.[63] The next year, the three oldest girls headed off to Stewart.

Retreat to Lake Almanor

Work drew the couple up to Prattville and Chester in the late 1920s, a friendlier social landscape for Marie. Lake Almanor was fast becoming a destination for boating enthusiasts, resort development was on the rise, and GWP was in the early phases of dam and reservoir expansion. The couple cobbled together a living in the seasonally based economy and wage labor market. In the winter months, Hensley took odd jobs doing road repair and snow clearing, but from late spring through early fall, recreational tourism was in full swing. Marie worked as a chambermaid at Almanor Inn and other resorts, and Hensley carved out a reputation in the growing sport–recreation industry, where his passion for hunting and fishing was put to productive use.

Even before the couple moved up to the lake, Hensley was sought after for his expertise in tracking, a skill honed in adolescence. Regional press coverage extolling his expertise began in 1918, when he was hired to lead the search team for a surveyor who had gone missing on an ill-advised trek from Engelmine to Susanville. The mountainous countryside required deep knowledge to navigate. Caught in a snowstorm, the surveyor died from exposure.[64] The next fall Hensley made news again when deer season opened: "The largest buck ever shot in this valley was brought in recently by two of our best Indian hunters, the Messrs. Potts and Orr. His antlers tip-to-tip measured 24 inches."[65] Hensley's reputation continued to grow in the regional press, and in 1924, when Smithsonian naturalist and ethnographer C. Hart Merriam—recently retired from the U.S. Biological Survey—headed into Mountain Maidu country on privately funded field expedition to document Indigenous place-names, flora, and fauna, he carried with him the names of two Greenville-area consultants, "Jim Lassen, 90," and "Hensley Potts, young."[66]

While also working as a domestic laborer in Chester homes and resorts, Marie worked alongside her husband in running a boat concession. Unsurprisingly, local promoters and news correspondents elided this fact, preferring to highlight fishing and hunting as masculine pursuits and realms of knowledge. Before long, Hensley Potts was a household name among Bay Area sportsmen bound for the High Sierra thanks to sports page coverage like the following: "Driving a Chandler car, four local nimrods last week started on their annual hunting trip, first picking up a guide in Big Springs in Plumas County. The guide, Hensley Potts 'knows his stuff,' with the result that the party came back with two of the largest and finest mule tails ever seen here."[67] Native identity, romanticized as a source of natural expertise, worked to Hensley's advantage.[68] One *San Francisco Chronicle* fish and game editor wrote, "Hensley Potts, the Indian Guide at Lake Almanor, who has built up quite a reputation for himself in getting fish when others fail, reports that he has never seen deer in more abundance in that section. Already the sportsmen from the southern part of the State are arriving at Hamilton Park."[69] Some stories published directions to the business, suggesting that the family had well-placed patrons in the larger community: "The run of rainbow trout at Lake Almanor is in great shape and large numbers of these big fish are being taken in channels just off the boat house of Hensley Potts, the Indian guide. . . . The fishing headquarters operated by Potts is located just across the causeway from

Chester. For bay region anglers the best highway to reach this fishing ground is across into Plumas County from Red Bluff. Potts has a free camp ground and rents boats and tackle."[70]

Separate Households, Separate Registrations for the California Indian Roll

By the late 1920s, the same problem that had destroyed his brother's and father's marriages caught up with Hensley.[71] Marie was not safe when he drank and could not rely upon him to meet his responsibilities to the family. By April 1930, she was separated from him. Census taker Randall Gay, whose family knew and employed Marie, recorded her marital status as "widowed." This must have been her choice, as it was a status she occasionally invoked in other contexts, right up to his death in 1952.[72] Hensley lived several blocks away. Though they were separately domiciled, the couple's livelihoods were still entwined. Hamilton Park did not renew Hensley's boat concession, so he moved the business just a couple miles north to Gould Swamp. A sign posted nearby, along Highway 36, advertised "Hensley and Marie Potts Hunting Guides." This marshy terrain on the lake's north shore was named for the same rancher from whom Marie's uncle Charles had acquired his surname. Charley's stepson, Rube Gould, was allotted here, and the property remained a base of operation for Potts and Bill family fishing, hunting, and even ice production, demonstrating that Native kin continued to share land and cooperate economically, as they always had.[73]

On July 22, 1930, Marie, Hensley, Eli Piazzoni, and Henry, Ellen, and Ike Jenkins filed consecutively into Quincy's Plumas County Courthouse to make application and attest to one another's Native identity claims so they could be added to a government "Roll of California Indians." Hensley listed his occupation as "guide" and claimed material assets totaling $150. The couple's five girls were enrolled with him. Marie's application, which included her niece Rhoda, listed her occupation as a "housewife," with no material assets. "Housewife" hardly covered the full scope of her work, which included caring for their girls, especially Kitty, who was not yet in school. Her certificate in "domestic arts" put food on the table and a roof over their heads. Like her mother, Marie worked for white families as a seamstress, laundress, and housekeeper, and later as a soda jerk in Spaulding's Drug Store in Susanville. When Hensley needed help, she went along as an extra guide. "Often I'd kill the deer because they didn't know how. Then I'd hear them bragging like hell about their great shot."[74] She also hunted deer for subsistence, having a like-minded hunting partner in Ethel Thieler, whose first husband, John, was a child when his family's Big Meadow homestead was condemned for reservoir construction. Before moving home from the Bay Area to their "country place," Ethel filed for divorce. The two women developed a close friendship that extended to their children. Expert at brain-tanning buckskin, Marie earned extra income in these years making "Indian" moccasins and vests for local children, including Ethel's son Don.[75]

Ensuring Her Daughters' Futures

The Potts girls were educated in both public and government boarding schools. After Lincoln, the three oldest went to Stewart Indian School in Carson City, Nevada, while Pansy completed eighth grade in Chester, with Kitty.[76] Like their father, Beryl, Pansy, and Kitty were musically inclined, and Marie cultivated their talents at literally every step, enrolling her two youngest in dance school in Chester. In 1935 they tapped their way through Greenville's Townsend Club picnic. In 1936 Beryl, Pansy, and Kitty entered Sherman Institute, where all three sang and played in the marching band: Beryl on snare, Pansy on trumpet, and Kitty on French horn.[77] Decades later, their mother still swelled with pride remembering a photograph taken at Sherman featuring Carlisle alumnus Jim Thorpe holding the microphone for Pansy while she played guitar and sang.[78]

Boarding school was more than a family tradition. The struggle to make a living during the Depression affected Hensley and Marie's livelihoods. As tourism waned, the guide and boat rental business slumped. Marie took in laundry and sewing. Hensley found work in WPA road and dam construction.[79] Boarding school reduced the financial strain and shielded the girls from their parents' deteriorating relationship. Hensley continued to lose his battle with the bottle, and Marie paid the price, despite their separation. Friends watched helplessly as this played out in her life and in the press. Arrested for drunkenness in December 1937, Hensley served thirty days in jail. Released in mid-January 1938, he was arrested again in late October and tried on charges of wife battery.[80]

Marie was hurt more severely than even she realized. Two months after the assault, when swelling in an injured foot subsided but debilitating pain lingered on, she consulted a physician. Only then did she learn it was broken and she would have to be hospitalized to fix it. Turning to the Sacramento Indian Agency for help, she explained, "I am not able to make the money for a reset of the bone and until the bone is reset and well, I'll not be able to work; I mean the kind of work one gets in a place like here, where you have to be on one's feet all the time. If it's possible I would like to have this taken care of right away as I am dependent on myself for a living."[81] While she is forthright about her struggle to support herself, she does not indicate the source of her injury or her status as a battered wife—not an unusual choice for her time. What she does express loud and clear is frustration over her languishing Carlisle education: "at least the kind of work one gets in a place like here." The agency approved her admission to Fort Bidwell Indian Hospital in Modoc County, and Plumas County funded her transportation there and back. She took her little grandson with her; there was no one else to care for him because his mother, Jeanne, was living and working out of town. Always protecting her daughters' best interests, Marie was raising her unmarried daughter's son as her own. After serving jail time, Hensley got out of town, moving down to Placer County to work on the North Fork Dam.

Sanctuary in Sacramento

Marie returned to her little Riverside Avenue rental after being released from the hospital, but her Chester days were numbered. Her daughters were forming families of their own. Beryl graduated from Sherman in May 1940. She was home long enough to marry John Gorbet, before returning to Sherman to earn a vocational diploma and "watch over Pansy and Kitty."[82] At the close of the school year, Beryl returned to Greenville, where Hensley now lived and worked for GWP's successor, Pacific Gas and Electric. The rest of Marie's daughters had begun gravitating to the Capital City.

Josephine relocated to Sacramento in 1937, where she worked for an architect. Jeanne followed in short order, moving in with her sister. Before long, Josephine met and married a man named John DuFresne.[83] Marie's first granddaughter, Aglaee Marie DuFresne, arrived in January 1939, Claire Ann followed in November 1939, and Robert Louis in December 1941. Another granddaughter, Nancy Zoe DuFresne, came along in August 1942. Younger sisters Pansy and Kitty were finishing up high school during these same years. At Sherman, Pansy met and fell in love with Lawrence Joseph Domingo "Dummy" Marine, an alumnus who returned in 1938 for the school's community work program. Enlisting in the Marine Corps in October 1940, he was stationed at San Diego's Camp Elliott, where the couple married in February 1941.[84] Returning to Sherman, Pansy graduated in May. Afterward, she and Kitty joined their sister in Sacramento, where Kitty entered Grant Union, a school her nephews remember her choosing for its superior music program. She graduated in January 1943, after a year and a half of class work and marching band. By now Marie—or Nana as she was called by her grandchildren—was there too.

Marie was drawn down to Sacramento, in December 1942, when nineteen-year-old Pansy was stricken with polio. For eleven months the two were sequestered in the back room of the small house Pansy shared with her sisters, while Marie administered an exhausting regimen of home therapy. She labored day and night to keep her daughter, now mother to a baby son, free from the paralysis that confined so many to iron lungs and wheelchairs. Pansy pulled through; she nursed a slight limp for the rest of her days, but it never slowed her down. As for Marie, she returned to Lake Almanor now and again, hunting rifle in hand, but henceforth Sacramento was home.[85] She was separated, though never divorced, from Hensley, and the move afforded her protection from domestic violence, reunited daughter Jeanne with her son Marvin, and brought Marie into close proximity with her other grandchildren. Perhaps she also sensed that Josephine's days were numbered. She died on June 30, 1944.[86] DuFresne left his job in the Vallejo shipyards and returned to Sacramento with the couple's four small children, moving in with the rest of the Potts clan.

Their home at 2727 Santa Clara Way literally brimmed with Hukespem descendants. Some relief came in October 1944. Kitty, a plane mechanic at McClellan Air Force Base, was transferred to Hawaii's Hickam Airfield. Marie, Pansy, and Beryl sent her off with a surprise farewell party attended by coworkers and neighbors. Among the latter was Benjamin Hathaway, who lived across the street.[87] Curator of the State Indian Museum (SIM), Hathaway had a gargantuan private collection of Native American material culture. Some of it was stored at home, but most of it was newly installed in a purpose-built adobe structure on the historic grounds of Sutter's Fort. Hathaway was to play an interesting role in Marie's future, but not before Kitty returned in 1945 and John DuFresne moved with his children to Virginia City, Nevada.

Life settled into a gratefully predictable rhythm.[88] It did not last long. Their house was about to become grand central station for Native California people coming to and through Sacramento. Today, the lot where it once stood hosts a twenty-first-century bungalow, but the original house was built in 1919 by Lorenzo D. Wilgus, a Civil War army veteran, and his wife, Mary Parker VanNorman. Mary, from Hat Creek, Shasta County, was the widow of D. N. VanNorman, signatory to Blunt's agreement with Marie's Big Meadow Maidu ancestors.[89] It seems highly improbable that the Bill descendants knew this history when they purchased the home in 1942, but it adds deep irony to its eventual status as a vibrant California Indian urban place.[90]

A Portrait of Strength and Resilience

Marie's decision to go home after Carlisle brought her back into the sphere of extended family and maternal love, Mountain Maidu language and culture, marriage, and motherhood. Yet these fortunes were also tarnished. All around her, the effects of colonization and land loss continued to play themselves out in the lives of Maidu people. The persistent loss of kin to tuberculosis, the utter transformation of her beloved Big Meadow, and the demise of the school she once called home loomed especially large. The grief and loss she and Hensley felt over their former boarding school's demise may seem surprising, but there is some logic in this. First, Marie was the rare pupil who by sheer accident of timing escaped the most violent moments and authoritarian superintendents in the history of two different boarding schools.[91] Families whose children died fleeing abuse and homesickness surely wondered why anyone would rally to rebuild Greenville. For them, it was a place of sickness, psychological abuse, corporal punishment, and death.[92] The local press regularly invoked the discourse of incarceration to describe the "escape" and "capture" of runaway pupils.[93] Horrific tales of violence and death, together with the cultural and linguistic loss these institutions perpetuated, mark them as repugnant sites of genocide for contemporary descendants.[94] But not all Greenville alumni apprehended their own experience as one of a thousand cuts to the Indigenous body. Neither did they have the wherewithal to fully benefit or divorce themselves from the capitalist economy or local white community controlling it. Like Marie, many Maidu were never allotted. Left to integrate as best they could into an economy built on stolen ancestral lands, Maidu people like Marie and Hensley could ill afford to express open hostility toward employers and colonialist institutions that systematically subjugated them for seven decades and then capitalized on their dependence.[95] Expressions of boarding school nostalgia among Marie's generation were not about erasing or denying their own or others' negative experiences. The psychological complexities of trauma survival, coupled with the material exigencies of life as a second-generation refugee in one's own homeland, challenge reductionist conclusions.[96] For some Native people, the school was a locus of stability in an unpredictable world. It was also a site of substantial memory-making—of shared experiences at school picnics, church services, Christmas celebrations, weddings, and funerals, two and three generations deep. It was not only a place that shaped them but also one they actively transformed in large and small ways. From their perspective, the school comprised an Indigenous space and place, a site where their collective belonging was privileged rather than questioned or resented.[97]

These years back home were real proving grounds for Marie. Racism and discrimination, domestic violence, and loss of kin were rude awakenings for this gregarious Carlisle graduate, who had once enjoyed a lively social life and a sense of control over her own destiny. Her vivacious youthful spirit was quelled by the limited economic opportunities available to women—and a Maidu one at that. Toiling as a domestic laborer in Greenville and Chester, she had no time or outlet for the academic talents that blossomed so profusely at Carlisle. Her children and grandchildren were the constant center of her world, and Marie dedicated herself to giving them the opportunity to pursue the bright future she had once imagined for herself. They were well along that path when she moved to Sacramento in 1942, ending twenty-seven bittersweet years of life on the margins of Big Meadow.

4

Federated Indians of California

A Mountain Maidu Activist Is Born

I think it's about time we Indians of California woke up and
realized what is going on around us regarding our claims and
make some effort to do something about it.

—Bertha Stewart, a California Indian

On January 11, 1947, Marie Mason Potts and several hundred California Indians squeezed into a meeting room at the Sacramento County Courthouse to discuss their land claims grievances. Little did she know how profoundly this gathering would shape her life course. Like other California Indians, she had been following newspaper coverage of K-344, the U.S. Court of Claims trial authorized by the 1928 California Indians Jurisdictional Act (CIJA). Predictably, they were not the only people interested in the trial's outcome or monetary significance. A raft of white attorneys, legislators, and Indian reform organizations waited with bated breath to claim credit, money, and power. Some had spent decades fostering distrust and fanning the flames of land claims factionalism. The Federated Indians of California (FIC) emerged in this moment of political promise and discord. It was the vehicle that launched Potts's activist career. Potts takes a backseat in the early part of this chapter, which describes how FIC came into being and introduces the cast of characters, friend and foe, who animated her life henceforth. In the former category, a Tolowa woman named Bertha Stewart is foremost. She and Potts got along famously. Together they channeled California Indian frustration into a coherent and productive organization with high visibility at the state capitol and a thumb on the state legislature's pulse, much to the chagrin of rival organizations and activists.

Prelude to the Federated Indians of California

In the mid-1920s, as the legislation that eventually culminated in CIJA was wending its way through congressional committee, attorney and California Commonwealth Club member Chauncey S. Goodrich explained how American legal tradition consigned California Indian people to subordinate status relative to their ancestral land: "The fee simple to lands obtained by conquest, cession or purchase rests in the sovereign, the United States. But the right of the Indian to a continued occupancy of the land he has tilled or roamed has been universally recognized throughout our history."[1] This passage invites consideration of two points. First, California's earliest formal statement relative to Native land was the 1850 Act for the Government and Protection of Indians, which, to quote Goodrich again, "is fair to say was for government rather than protection." This is evident in the case of *Thompson v. Doaksum et al.*; the plaintiffs' attorneys invoked it, albeit unsuccessfully, in their Supreme Court appeal, citing occupancy and subsistence rights set forth in both the Treaty of Guadalupe Hidalgo and the 1850 act.[2] Second, with his statement that the United States has "universally recognized" rights to occupancy "throughout our history," Goodrich wags a guilty finger at "the sovereign" for its failure to protect California Indian people from genocide.[3]

California Indians Jurisdictional Act—Addressing Unfulfilled Treaty Promises

CIJA authorized a suit against the federal government, in the U.S. Court of Claims, for failure to deliver to California Indians the lands and accouterments of agricultural civilization—clothing, schoolhouses and teachers, livestock, and so forth—promised in the treaties. In 1927, anticipating that Congress would finally approve legislation granting a trial, the California legislature passed a bill appropriating state funds for the California attorney general (AG) to press the suit. Until May 1928, when CIJA—or the Lea Act—finally passed, legislation had failed to either be recommended out of committee or to pass Congress. Only through significant compromise did it clear these congressional hurdles.

Stipulating that there could be no recovery of land, CIJA invoked the oblique language of "equitable" compensation. Yet even this was handicapped. The monetary value of the promised treaty lands, encompassing 8,518,900 of California's 75,000,000 acres, was capped at $1.25 per acre. Likewise, promised goods and services would be tallied at this same, 1852 value. Interest was barred by judicial code, so there was no chance of realizing a final award remotely equivalent to contemporary land values. Further, the United States insisted on a stipulation permitting the sum of all federal expenditures dedicated to California Indians during the intervening years to be deducted from a Court of Claims judgment against them. This included 611,227 acres of executive order reservations, rancheria land purchases, day and boarding school costs, and the like.[4] Finally, CIJA called for any award monies to be held in trust against future costs of California Indian support rather than distributed on a per capita basis. Despite this, the act called for a roll enumerating all "Indians who were residing in the State of California on June 1, 1852, and their descendants now living in said State." This was the roll to which Hensley, Marie, and Eli made application in Plumas County in July 1930. Descendants living outside California, like John Mason and John Peazzoni, were ineligible to apply, though many did and were stricken from the final roll approved in 1933. This suite of problems—vesting responsibility for the case in California's AG, limiting recovery to the value of lands promised in the eighteen unratified treaties, allowing offsets totaling *any and all* California Indian expenses (versus those relevant to the treaty parties whose acreage established the monetary cap on "equitable relief"), no per capita payment, and a roll contingent upon California residence—was tinder for the firestorm that erupted in Sacramento on the cusp of enactment of the Indian Claims Commission Act.

Indian Claims Commission Act—A Second Chance for California Indians

The 1946 Indian Claims Commission Act (ICCA) ambitiously aimed to settle all tribal grievances against the federal government.[5] The notion that a commission might provide a superior forum for such work did not spring to life overnight but was significantly boosted in 1944, when the National Congress of American Indians (NCAI) formed. The beleaguered process by which Native nations had to petition Congress for special legislation (such as CIJA) to sue the federal government was recognized as an undue burden on all parties.[6] Given the highly specialized nature of American Indian jurisprudence, a dedicated commission made sense. Only later would Native people realize that Congress acted on ICCA as a stepping stone toward termination.[7]

California Indians were still reeling from word that the $17,500,000 finding in their favor was to be reduced by federal offsets totaling $12,029,099 when word came that ICCA, rejected in 1945, was again up for congressional consideration and likely to pass given World War II's end. Through this channel, California

Native people could sue for the rest of their stolen ancestral lands—the whole of California minus lands covered under CIJA. Many Indian leaders had emerged during CIJA's Court of Claims trial, known by its filing number, K-344. They were ready to do battle again via ICCA, but there was little consensus on how to proceed.

K-344's dismal failure to "equitably" compensate California Indians was undeniable. Many blamed the three California AGs who were in office during the course of the trial, particularly Ulysses S. Webb, who filed the original petition in 1929. After a 1930 amendment clarified the roll's subjects and procedures, he was allowed to revise it. With discovery under way, Webb wanted to strengthen the state's claim, as the United States was posturing toward an extremely adversarial position, suggesting that California Indians were never legally entitled to occupancy and use rights. As his successor, Earl Warren, later articulated to the court, CIJA was grounded in moral versus legal obligation, but Webb knew the trial would be won or lost on legal standing. Deploying language that established aboriginal ownership from time immemorial, Webb also added a section that plagued the case to the end, naming three private Washington attorneys to assist in prosecution.[8] The court rejected this because the act stipulated California's AG as the plaintiffs' attorney. From this moment forward, bills attempting to overturn the decision were introduced into Congress nearly every session.[9] As they ground through committee, those California Indian leaders not consulted about these amendments were infuriated at the prospect of private attorneys claiming any portion of the award when California had appropriated funds for the AG to try the case. The individual who put his shoulder to this effort was a controversial figure in California Indians rights named Frederick G. Collett.

The Specter of Frederick G. Collett

A defrocked white missionary once affiliated with Amelia Quinton and the Northern California Indian Association, Collett and his wife, Beryl, subsequently lost the association's endorsement over fiscal irregularities. Forming the Indian Board of Co-operation (IBC) in 1910, they continued their activism to gain Indian children public school admission, relieve homelessness, and fight racism.[10] Collett helped convince John Raker to sponsor early federal legislation, introduced in 1920, addressing the homelessness and poverty caused by treaty rejection.[11] Anticipating that the bill would encounter difficulties in Congress, Collett began fund-raising among Indian people in 1919. Establishing IBC "Indian auxiliaries" throughout central and northern California, he pressed local Indian leaders into collecting member dues that would fund his lobbying efforts in Washington. He also urged them to accompany him—at their own expense—to testify before Congress. Even after CIJA named California's AG as the attorney of record, Collett continued to collect money from Indian people under troubling pretenses.[12] For instance, in 1932 he sent out the following frenzied plea for money and misrepresentation of the trial process in an IBC circular:

> Now is the time for auxiliary leaders to make definite plans to raise quickly their share of the money needed for their organization work and Court of Claims suit. Every Indian and his neighbor should help raise money to rush this case to an early settlement. It cannot be done without money to meet the expenses. It is the duty of persons who receive this message to hold group and auxiliary meetings to give this information to others.—Indian Board of Cooperation, F. G. Collett, Executive Representative.[13]

This raised eyebrows and ire in and outside the Office of Indian Affairs, and among many Native leaders, adding to incontrovertible proof of fiscal corruption already accumulated by Commissioner of Indian Affairs John Collier, the San Francisco–based Northern California Indian Defense Association, and the Sacramento Indian Agency.[14] Collett's robust criticism of the commissioner and BIA steadied their focus on him, but other organizations held him in similar disdain.

One of Collett's most formidable foes was the Los Angeles–based California Indian Rights Association (CIRA), which launched an aggressive print campaign against him in the mid-1930s. Labeling him a racketeer, CIRA aggressively disputed that he held power of attorney for all California Indians; indeed, his claim to this was not even an artful stretch of the truth.[15] Collett's auxiliary membership rosters, the basis for this assertion, were outdated and accumulated partly through fear and extortion. What he wanted was a slice of the CIJA award. Supported by his auxiliaries, he spent nearly a decade in Washington getting bills sponsored to amend the act so that private attorneys could be employed on a contingency basis.[16] These efforts failed repeatedly.

1945 Berkeley Convention

In September 1945, two California Indian organizations held a joint meeting at the Friends Church in Berkeley: the Indians of California, Inc. (ICI, formerly IBC) and the Mission Indian Federation (MIF), an activist coalition of southern California tribes founded in 1919 to seek freedom from the BIA.[17] The timing is noteworthy. Robert W. Kenny, Warren's successor after the latter was elected governor, had by now decided that there was no further recourse under CIJA and filed a stipulation agreeing to a K-344 award of $5,024,842.34, which was accepted by the Court of Claims on December 4, 1944. The funds were to be deposited in the U.S. Treasury, earn 4 percent interest, and be spent "to the benefit of the Indians of California." Anticipating ICCA's imminent passage, Kenny planned to file a second grievance on behalf of California Indians.

California Indians were clamoring in all quarters for per capita distribution of the K-344 award. Many showed up to Collett's convention, where "delegates" were selected solely from among his ICI membership. Proving that neither his motives nor his modus operandi had changed, he brought three bills pending before Congress (H.R. 3604, 3605, and 3606) to a straw vote. Unsurprisingly, his delegates approved them, promising later amendment as Indians saw fit. This was classic Collett—obtaining approval from a handful of people supposedly representing the entirety of all California Indians before the final terms of a bill were known. That neither ICI nor MIF had authority to speak for all became crystal clear in the coming year, but the meeting was significant for other reasons. First, Collett's H.R. 3606 proposed that "California Indians" elect delegates with the authority to name private attorneys for any grievance filed before the Indian Claims Commission (ICC), their fees to be deducted from the K-344 judgment funds. Convention delegates voted to approve this, with no discussion of fee caps, allowable expenses, or the like. Second, it was here that a new organization emerged. Calling themselves the Bay Area Indian Federation, they were shopping around attorney Reginald Foster, who wanted to represent California Indians before the ICC.

The 1945 Berkeley convention lit a fire under anti-Collett Indians observing the proceedings. They decided to call a meeting of their own. On March 25, 1946, thirty-two California Indian leaders met at the Sacramento Civic Building with Kenny; his recently retired special counsel, Frederic A. Baker; and Winnifred R. Codman, former state—now national—chair of the Indian Citizenship Committee of the Daughters of the American Revolution (DAR). Kenny contended that ICCA, still pending before Congress, offered an avenue to ameliorate K-344's failures. Gearing up for a gubernatorial primary run against Warren, he arrived with relevant statistics, most drafted by Baker while AG special counsel. Afterward, a *Sacramento Bee* article, "Indian Group Draft Bill for $93,000,000," proclaimed "delegates to the convention of the Federated Indians of California, which represents Indian councils and communities from all parts of California, met in Sacramento to draft a bill which is to be presented to congress" and introduced by Ellis Patterson, House Indian Affairs Committee. "Speakers included William

Fuller of Tuolumne, who called the convention, Ethan Anderson and Arthur Treppa of Upper Lake, Stephen Knight of Ukiah and Andrew Moro of Los Angeles."[18] The embryonic coalition passed a resolution condemning the bills that delegates had approved at Collett's Berkeley convention.[19]

Subcommittee Hearings: Public Skewering of Collett

After ICCA was approved on August 13, 1946, Assemblyman Don Allen of Los Angeles sponsored a resolution calling for statewide meetings with California Indians.[20] The Subcommittee of the Assembly Committee on Governmental Efficiency and Economy of Investigating Conditions of Indian Affairs in the State of California was formed, with Allen as chair, charged with reporting back to the legislature. The press regularly beat him to the punch.

California Indians attended their first hearing at the capitol on August 29, 1946, with Allen and John Evans, one of two additional subcommittee members. Headlines from the *Oakland Tribune*, "California Indians Accuse Agent," and *San Francisco Chronicle*, "Indian Fraud Plot Charged," captured the mood. Mildred (Hoover) Leonard, a Shasta descendant from Sacramento, remarked, "[W]e Indians are tired of being milked for funds to support certain individuals ... [who] promised us $100,000,000.00 would be forthcoming from the Federal Government." Leonard's sentiments were echoed by Grover Sanderson (Karuk) from Humboldt County, followed by Bertha Stewart (Tolowa) of Smith River Rancheria and Del Norte Indian Welfare Association (DNIWA), who explained that her community had stopped giving Collett money a decade before, but "he still claimed to represent 300 Smith River Indians."[21] William Fuller (Mi-Wuk) reported that he had known Collett since 1921. "He has had few living expenses, because in many cases he has lived with the Indians, used their automobiles, and been fed and clothed by them. He must have taken $200,000 or $300,000 from us since I've known him."[22] Arthur Treppa and Ethan Anderson (Pomo) from Lake County, John Porter (Miwok) from Ione, and Martha LeMay from Auburn Rancheria reiterated these claims. To quote Stewart, at least one Collett "diehard" was there. Lala Curl (Wintun) of Redding was vice president of IBC's Redding auxiliary. Calling Collett a friend, she confessed that his frequent pleas for money were often ignored, though she had sent him three hundred dollars in the last eighteen months.[23] At least two non-Natives spoke. A Sloughhouse rancher, Mr. Granlee, accompanied Martha LeMay to advocate for El Dorado County Indians, and Codman reported that during her 1937–38 stint of BIA fieldwork, helping aged Indians register with the county for California's Old Age and Blind Pension program, she learned that many were conned into paying to be on Collett's "roll."[24] Moving on to Ukiah, they heard from IBC founding member Stephen Knight (Pomo), who was even more vociferous in charging corruption. His rapid disillusionment led him to form the California Indian Brotherhood, in 1926, to suppress Collett's influence.[25] In Eureka, they heard similar testimony from Alvin Hostler (Hupa) and Stewart, making a second appearance on home turf. In all, approximately two hundred Indian individuals and group delegates spoke. Allen presented his report to the legislature with excerpts from oral testimony and thematically grouped findings: "The Problem of Roll Call," "The Problem of Per Capita Payment," "The Problem of Offsets," "The Problem of Selecting a Legal Representative," "The Problem of the Indian Bureau," and "The Problem of Liquor Serving." Each of these, save the last, played a defining role in factionalizing the California ICC landscape.[26]

Bertha Stewart Emerges from the Shadows

The March 25 *Bee* article that reported the Kenny meeting and FIC's formation failed to acknowledge the presence of Bertha Stewart, but subcommittee hearings brought her to the fore. Coverage of the August 29 capitol hearings included a staged photograph of the budding land claims coalition. Seated at a desk strewn with documents, Stewart and Assemblyman Allen are engrossed in conversation. Peering over their shoulders from behind are Assemblyman Evans; Fuller, "President of the California Federation of Indians" [sic]; Anderson; and Sanderson—who would soon split from FIC.[27]

Educated at Chemawa, Bertha Aldona Grimes Stewart (1900–99) was an astute politician whose many years of DNIWA leadership honed her communication skills and insight into the workings of state and federal government. Unequivocally the driving force behind FIC's formation, she enjoyed strong support from Fuller and Knight, both of whom provided damning anti-Collett testimony in a July 2, 1934, Senate subcommittee hearing.[28] Stewart's affiliation with Baker and Codman also buttressed her cause. Baker lived in Berkeley, had offices in San Francisco, and was special counsel for the California AG's office from 1940 to 1944, a job requiring frequent trips to Washington, D.C. It was here that Stewart met him, at a 1940 Senate hearing for K-344. She began corresponding with him in September 1941 while working for CIRA. She first met Codman in March 1946, at the Kenny meeting. Codman's involvement in Indian affairs began in the late 1920s, after she joined the Sacramento chapter of DAR. Initial work at Auburn Rancheria evolved into state and national DAR positions that brought her into sustained contact with California Indians, BIA personnel, and Commissioner Collier. In fact, she was so well connected that when NCAI treasurer George LaMotte resigned his position in early 1946 and moved to San Diego, he reached out to Codman for contacts to initiate his "West Coast Directorship." She passed along Stewart's Smith River address, and LaMotte wrote her on July 1, enclosing two newsletters and an outline of NCAI goals. Explaining how he had come by her name, he launched into a warm but urgent call for FIC to join NCAI: "We need your group membership."[29] Stewart praised NCAI's ambitions and assured him that FIC, which had met only once, would join in the near future.

FIC Begins to Flex Some Muscle

Forty California Indian people showed up to FIC's second meeting, on December 7, 1946. Governor Warren, accompanied by Lieutenant Governor Goodwin Knight, promised state support for an ICC claim.[30] Stewart and twelve men formed an executive committee.[31] Collett and Purl Willis (MIF) had already executed an attorney contract, now awaiting Interior Department approval. Hoping to derail it, the committee passed an eleven-article resolution denouncing the contract, Collett, and his claim to represent them. They entered the resolution into FIC's minutes and forwarded copies to the president, interior secretary, commissioner of Indian affairs, governor, and California senators and representatives. Accompanying it were three repudiations. The first, signed "William Fuller of Tuolumne; Henry Miller of Ione; Sam Lopez of Crescent City; and Albert Wilder of Orleans," read:

> We, the undersigned duly enrolled members of Indian tribes of California, hereby formally declare that the use of our names on papers sent during the year 1946 to Indians of California by Frederick G. Collett indicating that we are now officers or committeemen of any organization with which he is connected was wholly unauthorized by us and without our knowledge or consent. On the other hand, such action meets with our express disapproval. We are not now nor have we been for many years connected with Frederick G. Collett in any work among California Indians, a fact with which he was familiar.[32]

Arthur Treppa of Upper Lake signed a similar statement, and Ethan Anderson and Elmer K. Moore, also of Upper Lake, signed another. A December 9 letter inviting *all* California Indian people and groups to seat a representative on FIC's committee included copies of these Collett repudiations.

Potts Steps Forward at the January 1947 Sacramento Convention

In late December 1946, another letter from Stewart, Frank Gorbet, Chief Joseph Red-Horse, and Sanderson encouraged "All California Indians" to attend a January 11–12 meeting in Sacramento. FIC arranged accommodations at Traveller's Hotel and promised "a special effort . . . to clear up any misunderstanding among groups of organized, unorganized, or interested Indians."[33] Their sincerity is validated by a telegram Stewart sent to MIF's Adam Castillo on January 1: "You are urgently requested to attend important Indian meeting County Court House Sacramento January eleventh and twelfth. Other organizations sending delegates. Your group should be represented. Federated Indian of California [sic], Bertha Stewart, secretary." Although invited, Collett delegates withdrew from the December meeting at the last minute, circulating false reports of its cancelation. Stewart's personal telegram was intended to subvert a repeat performance. The meeting agenda clarified FIC's plan to unify everyone under a single claim to be pressed by the AG, perhaps in collaboration with private attorneys.

Potts was among the 250 to 300 California Native Americans who crowded into the Supervisor's Room at the Sacramento County Courthouse for the January 11–12 convention. Fuller gave a brief address and then called for election of a chairman and secretary for the day to avoid accusations of FIC control. Recent news items, including "withdrawal"—or termination—arose. Now serving as FIC's pro bono "legal advisor," Baker addressed these based on his long tenure in the Office of Indian Affairs: "[W]ith the removal of the Indian Bureau there would also go hunting and fishing rights, free government hospital and medical care, tax-free lands, etc.; on the other hand, Indians would gain freedom from Federal control over their lands and attain the same rights and privileges as any other citizen of the state."[34] In preparation for an afternoon speech, he also outlined differences between contingent and stipulated fee contracts. Assemblyman Allen discussed legislative support for an ICC claim, believing that California had an obligation to "represent the Indian free of charge, thereby eliminating temptation to selfish outsiders, giving all of any award that might be won to the Indians instead of paying a large percentage to attorneys." In the afternoon Baker blamed Collett and Willis for K-344's lengthiness, enumerating bills introduced without California Indian consultation, and the bribery to which they had allegedly resorted when those bills failed to pass. Collett was given the floor and "tremblingly made a feeble attempt to deny the charges," Stewart wrote in her account of the meeting. "Anyone with a spark of intelligence knows that Mr. Baker would not publicly make statements charging misrepresentation, fraud, racketeering methods . . .

unless those charges have been proven to be facts."[35] This comment perfectly captures FIC's preoccupation, Stewart's most especially, with eradicating Collett's influence. A final agenda item that day pertained to the attorney contract Collett submitted for Interior Department approval. Clyde Thompson, a 1945 Berkeley convention delegate, had earlier agreed to read it aloud. When the time came, he declined. This must have been highly encouraging to Reginald Foster, the Bay Area group's attorney of choice, because he immediately joined Sanderson in distributing petitions to be named ICC attorney. This group now called itself the Bay Area California Indian Federation. Three factions were in evidence that day: FIC, ICI, and the Bay Area group, though CIRA was there too, quietly weighing its options.

On January 12 a temporary "joint committee," comprising representatives from the three groups, convened. Potts was one of fifty-two individuals who had signed up the previous day to populate its ranks, marking her earliest appearance in FIC records.[36] Their agenda featured open discussion of "1) Disposition of Trust Funds, 2) Attorneys, 3) Treasurer's Report, 4) 10-Minute Talk by Mrs. La Motte [NCAI], 5) Power of Attorney—Do the Indians Want to Retain It or Revoke It?" The first agenda item listed four options that had circulated for months:

    a. Do we want all the fund per capita before any additional award is won, or

    b. Do we want to leave a million dollars in the treasury for attorney fees, etc. or

    c. Do we want to have the fund in the treasury accumulate interest until our entire claim is settled, or

    d. Do we want the fund paid to California Indians on a new roll or do we want it paid only to Indians of California on the 1928 roll?[37]

A penciled addendum adjacent to item 5 on Stewart's archived copy reads, "Collett group disrupted meeting here to avoid discussion." A handwritten note reminded Chairman Sam Lopez to solicit Sacramento-area volunteers to help with FIC work. Potts was listening; her activist future was sealed.

Assemblyman Allen met with those who lagged behind after the meeting adjourned. This resulted in three pieces of legislation: one called for a formal investigation of Collett and Willis, AB 372 permitted the AG to try the ICC case if Indians so desired, and AB 374 appropriated $45,000 to fund that action.[38] Those who felt the state owed them amends for its 1852 role in sabotaging treaty ratification supported this position. Those who conflated CIJA flaws and outcomes with the AG's office, were unconvinced that it could bring a compelling case, or were generally distrustful of state and federal government wanted to ensure that private attorneys handled the claim.

A Frail Alliance: Sacramento Junior College Convention, March 1947

Several days later the joint committee announced a general convention for all California Indians, March 29–31, at Sacramento Junior College. The committee met on its own the day prior, at the William Land Park community building. Penciled on the back of a flyer sent "To Committee Members Only" is another of Stewarts's historical footnotes: "It was at this meeting that Sanderson tried to force Foster on the California Indians by attempting to make them sign petitions endorsing him–Bert."[39] It was also on this occasion that the competition figured out how to rally the local press to its own ends. The *Bee* announced that the next FIC meeting would be May 3, in San Francisco, claiming that an "executive committee" was vested with "broad authority to enter into contracts pertaining to the claims, to hire counsel if it so decides, and to draw up bylaws for the government of the federation."[40] Already populated by Andrew Moro, William Fuller, Bertha Stewart, Arthur Treppa, Grover Sanderson, Edna Calac, Stanley Miller, Joseph Red-Horse, David Risling, Harrison Williams, Fred Wicks, Sam Lopez, Lela Dunlap, Alvin Hostler, Frank Singley, Theron Worth, Albert Miller, Evelyn Patapoff, Robert Spott, John Porter, and Frank Gorbet, the committee would accept one member from every tribe, band, or group in the state.

This was a short-lived invitation to a short-lived committee. Sensing trouble afoot, Chairman Lopez called a 10:30 P.M. meeting after the Bay Area group left for home. Gathered in the college auditorium, they discussed Collett's latest machinations and their own lack of resources to press a claim. Pansy Marine and several other volunteers agreed to assemble the next morning to formulate a plan whereby Allen could seek a larger state appropriation. Minutes from this eleventh-hour meeting were taken by "Acting Secretary Kitty M. [Potts] Moesch" and record the active participation of her mother, Marie Potts. A few days later, the three Potts women underscored their commitment in the local press. "Indians Are Invited to Meeting to Organize," read the *Bee* headline. "Kitty Moesch and Mrs. Pansy Marine today announced plans for a meeting of California Indians living in Sacramento or vicinity to organize a branch of the Federated Indians of California." Their objectives were clear: "California Indians are seeking payment for lands taken from them by white settlers in the Nineteenth Century."[41]

FIC was determined to prevail, and Fuller issued a press release calling for California Indians to attend a May 4 Sacramento meeting. Disseminated to the statewide press, the story was picked up on May 1 by the *San Bernardino County Sun*. The tone and stereotypical language were par for the mid-century course: "Sacramento, April 30 (UP) A Tuolumne Indian chief, William Fuller, will lead the Federated Indians of California in a two-day business pow-wow here Saturday. The descendants of the red men will come to talk about wampum—$5,000,000 worth of wampum judged due them from the federal government as payment on their lost lands. The money, however, is being held in trust in the white man's capital, pending arrangement of a means of payment to the individual treaties.... The teepee for the weekend will be the Sacramento Courthouse." The frail alliance embodied in the executive committee that the *Bee* had touted the previous month was fully withered by the time this meeting rolled around.

"One Hot Meeting" and Other Signs of Disunity

In San Francisco, the Bay Area group worked the May 3 executive committee meeting to its own advantage, and the embattled factions arrived in Sacramento desperate and determined. Baker later claimed that it was here that the Bay Area group's program was "ignominiously defeated and Red Horse, Sanderson and Risling took their few followers and held a separate meeting in the Land Hotel."[42] Baker's decade-old respect for CIRA evaporated when Moro sided with this group after Foster promised to support CIRA's push for a per capita bill and no reopening of the roll to add California Indian descendants who were out of state residents at the time the 1928 roll was produced. Stella Von Bulow, taking it all in from home, was exhausted and resigned as CIRA secretary. Things might have gone differently, she told Baker in an August letter, had FIC been "friendly." CIRA tried to compromise, she argued. After searching for an attorney who would take their case and work alongside the AG, they found none willing to do so on contingency or without retainer. In March Foster informed Moro that a new organization that included FIC board members was emerging. "Then everything blew up in the May 3 meeting; the reporters who took in the meeting were anything but complimentary—it was reported and quoted that Mrs. Stewart said that if Indians could not agree they could go their separate ways, a poor statement to make at such a time." Furthermore, Von Bulow insisted, there were FIC members whose character could not stand the scrutiny he had given Red-Horse.[43] She was not wrong about lack of civility. A typescript note among these archival records offered a hurried update, reading in part, "Oh yes, we held a meeting at Bakers till one o'clock, Evert Wilder, Chief Eagle Feather or Mr. Sanderson, Fuller, Baker, and myself, and I want to say it was one hot meeting. I thought once I would have to pull G. S. and F. B. apart at a time or two and I don't mean maybe, but I guess a meeting ain't good unless you get mad."[44]

This image of a near physical altercation perfectly characterizes California Indian land claims politics and passions. Under the leadership of Foster, Ernest Risling, and David Risling Sr., the group Baker prematurely pronounced "defeated" later incorporated as the Council of California Indians (CCI).[45] Castillo and MIF, temporarily affiliated with ICI, soon discovered they could file independently. Meanwhile, the three rival intertribal organizations vied for dominance. Each bore an appellation intended to represent the entirety of California's Indigenous population, comprising a mix of tribal nations and landless Indians. The cascading effect of treaty rejection a century prior continued to haunt California Indian people's efforts to achieve justice through ICCA, as these groups soon faced the startling possibility that none would be allowed to file.

FIC Sends Fuller and Stewart to Washington

The explosive May meeting galvanized FIC. Months of wearying diplomatic labor failed to achieve unity, but they forged ahead. Substantial benefits accrued from these early months: publicity, a record of meeting attendees showing tribal and/or group affiliations, and a sensitive finger on the pulse of California Indian people. Bills were being introduced hand over fist in both Congress and the state legislature by multiple parties, and the ICCA's five-year filing deadline was now only four and a half years away. At the May meeting, Codman suggested taking their case straight to Washington. Fuller and Stewart were elected as FIC's first delegates. Funding for the trip was in short supply. Rumors were not. Word spread that FIC had magically accessed the $45,000 Allen aimed to appropriate if California Indians signed a contract with the AG office. Instead, Baker drove his own car and all three paid their own expenses.

They left for Washington on May 20 and stayed through July 5. A "Record of Washington Delegates, 1947," kept on a wide-ruled newsprint tablet, bears the signature of "Mrs. Bertha Stewart."[46] Eighteen stained and crumbling pages document their busy and productive trip. Stopping at the Chicago BIA offices en route, "We checked the Calif. Ind. Roll and listed the application numbers of those who were rejected from the 1928 roll to determine how many were rejected for non-residence." In Washington they attended Senate and congressional hearings and met with committee chairs and bill sponsors. They researched documents

in the Public Lands Commission offices, met at the Smithsonian with linguist
John Harrington, who spent the next Sunday consulting with Fuller on California
Indian languages; had dinner and a "good conference on the activities of the
National Congress" with Ruth Bronson; examined Collett and Willis attorney
petitions and contracts at OIA; and prepared for their own hearings.

Stewart, whose FIC office was "permanent secretary," wrote the membership
on June 9, 1947, reviewing bills pending in the House and Senate, conferences
with the acting and assistant commissioners of Indian affairs, and meetings with
Ernest Wilkinson, whose firm was named in Collett's controversial contract.
They talked about fee structures and Collett petitions containing signatures of
underage children. They also learned that Castillo was trying to extract MIF from
the contract, claiming that Collett had duped him into signing it. The eighth and
last item Stewart addressed was their meeting with the ICC commissioners, who
were establishing rules of practice and preparing to disseminate filing instructions.
Stewart welcomed other FIC delegates to join them if chapters could afford to send
them and asked that donations supporting delegate work be sent to Treasurer Henry
Miller, of Ione. On July 2, she wrote again. They were about to introduce bills in the
House and Senate calling for K-344 per capita distribution, and then leave for home.

FIC Files California's First ICC Claim: Docket 12

The Washington trip spurred the group to action. FIC voted to file a claim. Chapter
delegates immediately began documenting their membership to prove FIC's
authority to represent them and to ensure that neither Collett nor Foster could
claim to speak or file on behalf of "all California Indians," as had happened
under K-344. This later proved unnecessary, but in September 1947, eroding rival
group misrepresentation was paramount. The typescript statement "We, the
undersigned hereby approve the plan of the Federated Indians of California to
file their claims against the United States before the Indian Claims Commission,
through their own chosen representatives as permitted by the law and the General
Rules of Procedures of said Commission, reserving the question of the selection of
Attorneys, if such is deemed necessary for future consideration" appeared at the
top of mimeographed pages, along with designated columns beneath for name,
age, degree of blood, and address. [47] Most bear legal signatures, but occasionally
a thumbprint appears alongside a printed name or, alternatively, two witnesses
are listed.[48] For instance, when Marie collected signatures in Lassen and Plumas
Counties, she and Grace Sabini served as witnesses in Susanville for seventy-five-
year-old George Peconum and eighty-three-year-old Ida Peconum. If delegates

ran out of forms in the field, they simply typed the statement onto a blank page and continued working.

The next month Stewart communicated important news to the membership using a brand-new forum, the *News Letter*. She sent the first of only three issues, which was typed and duplicated on manila paper, on October 1, 1947: "This is to inform all Indians of California that the Federated Indians of California are the first and only group of California Indians who have filed their claims with the Indian Claims Commission." Their brief, naming Fuller, Stewart, Archie McWhinney, Calac, and Treppa as FIC's representatives, became Docket 12 on ICC's calendar.[49] Using the names she and Fuller had collected in Chicago, she then wrote nonresident California Indian descendants whose applications to CIJA's 1928 California Indian roll had been rejected in 1933, urging them to contact their political representatives with support for two FIC bills (H.R. 4008 and S. 1565) that would reopen the roll to them. Hoping to gauge support for the bills prior to Public Lands Commission hearings slated for San Francisco, she asked them to let Assistant Secretary Pansy Marine know their mind.[50] Letters to FIC began pouring into 2727 Santa Clara Way and continued to do so for the next thirty years.

FIC Headquarters: An Office and an Urban Chapter

The January and March 1947 meetings had failed to unify California Indian people, but they established Sacramento as FIC's base of operation. In mid-July, Stewart first raised the need for an office at an afternoon executive committee meeting. Conferring afterward with Pansy, Potts returned for the evening session, offering a "small house in her back yard that needed fixing up, with six months free rent to be used as an office."[51] A motion to accept the offer carried unanimously. When the six-month period expired, FIC would pay six dollars per month and a share of utilities. They gained far more than headquarters and a street address in this agreement.[52] Proximity to the capitol and courthouse, and geographic centrality for central and northern California Indian people, was hard to beat, although Stewart chose to emphasize other attributes: "We are in temporary quarters at present but we hope to be in our permanent quarters at this same address. Our office will be small and humble compared to the office of Mr. Foster on Market Street in San Francisco but it will be ours and open to all Indians for all information and help on Indian problems. This office will be owned and controlled by Indians, so feel free to drop in at any time."[53]

Meanwhile, a new pattern for FIC gatherings was evolving, largely due to the generous hospitality of FIC's Sacramento chapter. Gone were the contentious days of squaring off with rival groups. Group delegates or individual members could travel to Sacramento on Saturday afternoon, socialize and swing to the rhythm of a big band that evening, attend Sunday's FIC meeting—where they would be served lunch—and still make it home before the workweek started. Stewart expressed her appreciation for this demonstration of generosity in her November *News Letter*: "There will be a benefit dance Saturday night December 6, 1947, at the Eagles Hall located at Southside Park, on 6th Street between W and X Streets, Sacramento. This dance is being sponsored by the Sacramento Chapter of the Federated Indians of California. This group is responsible for meeting arrangements, entertainment, and have served free meal to Delegates. The splendid cooperation of this group is to be highly commended and everyone who can should attend this dance in appreciation of their efforts. (Rumor has it that something special will be awarded as a door prize at this coming dance.)"

The Sacramento chapter was FIC's only urban chapter, one of nineteen scheduled to report at the December 7, 1947, FIC meeting. With the exception of Sacramento, all represented tribes, counties, or nearby towns: Del Norte Indian Welfare Association, Ione, Lake County, Mission Indian chapter of NCAI, and so on. Proximity to the capitol endowed the chapter with sociopolitical clout and administrative responsibility; it also made significant fiscal contributions. For example, from September 1947 through November 1948, it contributed $283 to the treasury, well above other groups and second only to individual member and meeting donations of $354 for the same period.[55] The group's hospitality and financial success were products of Marie's strong leadership.

The Sacramento contingent initially got off to a rocky and informal start following the January convention, with Frank Gorbet as ad hoc chair. By mid-April, when Kitty and Pansy placed a notice in the *Bee* to attract new members, those already involved were demanding Gorbet's resignation, citing procedural and bylaw infractions. Of greater concern were his ties to Ed Ainsworth, a half brother affiliated with Auburn Rancheria. This group was still loyal to Collett, though this would change.[56] Gorbet apparently shared membership rosters and other strategic data with Ainsworth, and FIC threatened to go to court if he did not hand over all records and property to the Sacramento chapter. He resigned immediately, perhaps even happily, as chapter responsibilities were intensifying.[57]

At the April 25 meeting convened by Kitty and Pansy, fifty-three-year-old Marie was elected chairperson. She immediately began professionalizing operations. After seeking formal approval from Fuller to create an affiliate group, she had members sign notarized affidavits, much after the fashion FIC used to verify its authority to represent individuals in its ICC filing. The Sacramento chapter affidavit read: "We the undersigned members of the Sacramento Chapter of the Federated Indians of California, cooperating with other similar associations with common object to serve the interests of the Indians of California; that associations extend over the State of California; that this association acts for said Indians in the community adjacent to its place of meeting, Sacramento, Sacramento County, California and represents the said Indians who have hereby affixed their signatures."

Initial lists were notarized in July 1947, with more coming mid-August. When Lloyd Joseph was elected delegate to FIC's August 17 executive council meeting, Potts signed the authorizing document. Misrepresentation and commitment to the chapter were serious concerns, and Potts established an impressive governance structure to manage this. Months before the mother organization approved governing documents, the Sacramento chapter adopted a constitution and bylaws, with seven articles addressing everything from member eligibility (direct descendants of California Indians) to twice-monthly meetings, parliamentary procedure, delegate duties, and fiscal liability limitations. Resolutions were to be presented in writing and read at two business meetings before being brought to a vote. Offices were declared vacant after three consecutive absences.

In February 1948, the chapter elected new officers: Tommy McWhinney, chairman; Archie McWhinney, vice chairman; Kitty Flores, secretary; Marie Potts, chapter delegate to FIC. Work never ended for the three Potts women, as they juggled duties at both the local and statewide levels: Marie was FIC recording secretary as well as chapter delegate, Pansy was FIC assistant secretary, and Kitty was FIC publicity agent as well as chapter recording secretary. Santa Clara Way was literally overflowing with land claims work. Soon an even more expansive vision of common purpose emerged.[58]

From Newsletter to Newspaper

The *Smoke Signal of the Federated Indians of California* debuted in January 1948. Kitty Potts Flores, FIC's first publicity agent, served as inaugural editor. Tucked away on the third and final page was a brief statement: "Note of interest to our followers is that the News Letter has been re-named. The *Smoke Signal* was adopted because this means of communication was formerly used by our ancestors. Also, we ask you to pass on the *Signal* after you have thoroughly digested its contents. In this manner more of our people can be benefitted by our services."[59] The language "our followers," "our ancestors," and "our people" spoke volumes about the editorial staff's ambition to reach beyond FIC to the wider population of California Indians. The paper features a two-column format, and the front page, though lacking a formal masthead, gestures toward the one that will eventually grace the paper. Centered in all caps is the paper's name. Hand stenciled on the left is a buckskin-clad Indian, his back to the reader. Two puffs of smoke ascend as he draws his blanket back from the flame. On the far right sits a reader's teepee, door flap open, beckoning the signal inside. These small images, no larger than a square inch, underscored the *Smoke Signal's* Native origin, content, and readership. They lent graphic force to the newspaper's appeal for solidarity among California Indian people by capitalizing on romantic mid-twentieth-century imagery associated with American Indians.

The inaugural edition proudly declared, "The *Smoke Signal* is edited and controlled completely by California Indians."[60] Demonstrating the FIC's credo of transparency, it led with a summary of the January 11 meeting, including delegate reports on local activity from "Mrs. L. Dunlap—Middletown Group; Mrs. B. Stewart—Del Norte Indian Welfare Association; Mr. A. Treppa—Upper Lake Group; Mr. W. Fuller—Tuolumne Group; Mr. A. Lorenzo—Yolo Co. Group; Mrs. M. Potts—Sacto Chapter FIC; Mr. M. Watson—Oroville Group; Mr. J. Porter—Mother Lode Council." The Mission Indian chapter of NCAI and groups from Hopland and Glenn County reported by mail, while no updates came from Wilton, Lookout, Yurok Tribal Council, and the Northern California Indian Federation of Hoopa. This enumeration was informative and generative. By the next meeting, new chapters were forming in El Dorado, Oroville, and Ukiah. For decades, Collett had solicited money in community settings but never disclosed amounts; they were determined to be different. Publishing the treasurer's report in full, they listed sums generated from each source, right down to the penny. The grassroots nature of their activism is evident:

$50.00 Mission Ind. Ch. NCAI

$53.00 Proceeds of Benefit Dance of Saturday, Jan. 10th

$20.00 Sac'to Chapt. FIC

$5.00 Yolo Co. Group

$5.00 Tuolumne Group

$10.00 Personal Donation-Rosetta Backman

$47.45 Donations at meeting

$190.45 TOTAL[61]

Closing out this front-page column, readers were reminded that FIC's February 8 gathering was on the horizon: "This meeting will be preceded by another Benefit Dance sponsored by the Sacramento Chapter, on Sat. February 7th at the Muir Clubhouse, at 21st and C, in Sacramento." The *Smoke Signal* charted an early course by reminding readers at every turn that FIC was trustworthy and unique: "Did you know that the Federated Indians of California is the only Indian organization in California that is completely led and controlled by California Indians?" Pithy one-liners were a hallmark of the paper for three decades, but they began as unsubtle reminders of the differences between land claims organizations: "This is not a masterpiece of journalism, but a good publication of truth."[62] Barbed innuendo directed at Foster and Collett, and allusions to FIC's superiority, served as handy filler between articles and stories. No feelings were spared. FIC believed that mercenary white attorneys and meddlers drove rival organizations. During their Washington trip, Fuller and Stewart acquired a copy of the attorney contract Clyde Thompson had declined to read at the January 1947 convention. The *Smoke Signal* ran it word for word so readers could scrutinize its terms and conditions in the comfort of their homes. Committed to California Indian people, they refused to sit quietly by and watch elders be abused for personal gain. Stewart was incensed by rival group tactics: "Statements have been made at several meetings throughout the State that those persons who are going among the California Indians with Foster's petition are being paid $1.00 a name for all the names they get signed to the petition. One man in Yreka said he was only getting $.75 a name while another man in Klamath said he was getting $50.00 a week. It's a sad situation when members of our race are misled into selling their people for a dollar a head."[63] Petitions and circulars distributed by ICI and the Foster group were riddled with misinformation. The *Smoke Signal* systematically called these out, countering false assertions with truths.[64] Confused readers were encouraged to seek clarification.

The inaugural edition featured a "Question and Answer" column that barely scratched the surface of queries that poured into the office after Stewart's December newsletter invited member questions. The Sacramento Indian Office could have addressed many of these, but FIC aimed to forge common bonds among all California Indian peoples and communities. Some inquiries compelled the Potts women to make phone calls or trips to the Sacramento agency, but this paid its own dividends, helping them build a reservoir of knowledge and resource materials. Four months after the paper's debut, Kitty wrote the BIA in Washington, D.C., citing the good working relationship FIC enjoyed with the Sacramento agency, and asked that any materials "affecting the Indians" be sent directly to FIC's office.[65]

Smoke Signal Correspondent Fred Baker

The *Smoke Signal* aspired to educate and empower California Indian people to make informed choices. Rampant confusion about the two distinct claims cases clouded the scene. Four issues into production, the paper announced it would publish a serialized version of "History and Proposed Settlement Claims of California Indians." Released in pamphlet form when Kenny decided to settle K-344, this narrative traced the history of California Indian land use and rights from preconquest to the present. The series and first *Smoke Signal* excerpt were prefaced with an important attribution: "Our legal advisor, Mr. Frederic A. Baker, contributed to this history through his extensive research work on this subject." Kenny's "Foreword," printed immediately beneath, echoed this. As these excerpts rolled out, Baker sometimes wrote addendums adding clarity to this complicated history and legislation. For instance, he explained how CIJA "straight-jacketed" the AG's ability to achieve equitable compensation. He penned a column on the 1943 Outland-Downey Bill, H.R. 3622, "To Appoint a Commission to Settle the Claims of the Indians of California"; this was his own solution to winning fair compensation. It called for suspending the CIJA case at the eleventh hour, when it was evident that federal offsets would cancel out any meaningful recovery. Instead, a commission would hear and decide the claim with a broader scope of recovery than CIJA allowed. The bill failed, but his explanation of this effort lent moral and legal capital to FIC.

Baker first became known in California Indian circles through his meticulous work on the 1928 CIJA enrolling commission. Traveling throughout California to oversee the application process, he gained an in-depth understanding of the circumstances California Indian people faced. He brought this insight to his subsequent work for the AG, and FIC was now the exclusive and pro bono beneficiary of his cumulative knowledge. Nearly every *Smoke Signal* hammered home this point, first argued by Stewart in her November 1947 newsletter. Telling members that FIC had entered into contract negotiations with Judge John Preston of Los Angeles, she remarked, "Mr. Baker, our legal advisor, who in our opinion has helped our Indian people more than any other single individual and who has always refused to act as a private attorney in the California Indian case . . . refused to act as Chief Counsel but consented to assist Mr. Preston." For his part, "Mr. Preston, who served nine years as an Associate Justice of the Supreme Court of

California . . . told our committee he would not consider being our council without Mr. Baker's assistance. Mr. Preston also stated that in his opinion the petition filing our claims [Docket 12] was the best that could be written on the subject. This petition was prepared for us by Mr. Baker without charge for his service, and just another instance of his unselfish interest in the welfare of our people."[66]

Baker wrote reams of correspondence for *Smoke Signal* publication, certain to the bitter end that only through a united front would California Indians achieve equitable compensation for their stolen ancestral lands.

More Than an Office: A Publishing House and Newspaper Staff

The permanent quarters Stewart envisioned in 1947 began to materialize in fall 1948. Pansy applied for a building permit and FIC treasurer John Porter came down from Ione in late November to assist with interior renovations.[67] The following January, FIC reimbursed Pansy for building materials and office supplies totaling $175.63. The office now housed a rented typewriter, a mimeograph machine, and reams of *Smoke Signal* paper. A file cabinet held ever-growing mailing lists, longhand minutes taken at the Sacramento chapter and general FIC meetings, mimeographed typescript copies distributed for corrections, and a bounty of general correspondence—arriving by May 1948 at a pace of about four letters per day.

A library began to grow: American Indian law books, BIA publications, legislative reports, and the NCAI *Bulletin*. Little wonder that the *Smoke Signal* called for office volunteers in the second issue. When the call for nomination of officers came up at the general meeting, "the [meeting] chairman," who happened to be Potts, "reminded the members that the officers elected should live in the vicinity of the Federated offices, as all work was voluntary and without pay, and very inconvenient if those who did the work lived too far away."[68] In December all three Potts women were reelected.

The newspaper was free to members and others on FIC's mailing list during January, February, and March 1948, but treasury funds were meager and expenses many. At the February meeting, FIC voted to send delegates to Washington for hearings on S. 1565 and H.R. 4088, bills it had introduced calling for $250 per capita payment of K-344's award. Calac and Stewart were elected as delegates, with Potts as alternate, highlighting an attribute distinguishing FIC from rival organizations: women played prominent roles. They also voted to prioritize delegate travel and lodging expenses over those of the *Smoke Signal* in the event the treasury could not sustain both. The newspaper was produced entirely through volunteer labor, but paper, ink and stamps were costly. The humble publication had already won the hearts of meeting attendees, who proposed a small subscription fee. A "Late Notice" on February's last page explained the fiscal situation and gave members a voice in the final decision by way of a mail-in survey. The response was overwhelmingly positive. Two issues appeared in March, each noting the new one dollar annual subscription fee beginning in April.[69] As always, readers were encouraged to share the paper far and wide.

Transitions: A Masthead and New Editor

FIC celebrated its two-year anniversary at its March 1948 meeting. The Sacramento chapter provided lunch as usual, but this time it was a veritable feast served in the courthouse's Veteran's Memorial Hall. Pansy and Baker took turns at the piano providing musical entertainment. Fuller offered a prayer to the Great Spirit and gave Baker the honor of cutting a birthday cake "decorated with an Indian head in the center, 'FIC' and '2 Years' in each corner." The March 7 *Smoke Signal* paid tribute to the occasion, with Fuller's prayer placed below the front-page fold. Above it, an elaborate though naively rendered drawing evokes symbolic imagery. A round cake reading "Happy Birthday to the FIC" features two flickering candles. From each, a tall plume of airy smoke rises to frame a set of portraits. Enshrouded in one plume are three figures—a man in a feathered headdress, a woman in braids, and a younger man behind in a single-feathered headband. The other plume features four individuals dressed in modern attire. Two are readily identifiable: Chief Fuller wears a business suit and his signature spectacles; beside him, Stewart sports her classic coif and trademark pillbox hat. They are clearly meant to represent contemporary renditions of their ancestral feather- and braid-wearing, counterparts framed by the other plume. Behind them stand two men in business suits, likely Baker and Preston. Allusion to California Indian ancestors is also evident in the phrase "United in Body, Spirit, and Mind to Right a Wrong of Many, Many Years," centered beneath a formal masthead.

Gone was the teepee of the first two editions. The smoke-signaling Native journalist continues his work, in much grander illustrative form, before a backdrop of rolling hills and panoramic skies. Buoyant puffs of smoke cluster into letterform: "The Smoke Signal of the FIC." FIC's motto—"In Unity is Strength"—is handwritten between grassy patches on the gentle slope below. Spanning the page width and set off between solid black lines are the volume number, publisher's address, and publication date. The work of using a stylus and a Mimeoscope, or light table, to reproduce these details in stencil form required the precision of a draftsman and a good measure of artistry, but the reward was incalculable. The masthead endowed the *Smoke Signal* with new journalistic authority and foregrounded the publisher's Native identity. It also heralded a change in editors.

Marie took over as *Smoke Signal* editor fourteen months into the newspaper's thirty-year run, when Kitty resigned as publicity agent in March 1949. Her husband, Lieut. Kesner Flores, had been transferred to Camp Roberts several months earlier, and FIC business proved too abundant and pressing to manage long distance. Stewart lauded Kitty for her invaluable contributions to the organization, the *Smoke Signal* especially. Unanimously elected to replace her, Marie was already a vital member of the newspaper staff and a central cog in FIC's political machinery. FIC members had come to know her tireless work ethic by virtue of her Sacramento chapter fund-raising efforts and political fieldwork, both of which were in abundant evidence in the pages of the newspaper during its inaugural year.

For instance, while dances were the Sacramento chapter's primary fund-raising vehicle, in winter 1948 Potts instituted door prizes to help raise delegate funding. The first was a quilt of her own making, with the winning ticket to be drawn at the January 1949 dance. Accordingly, the *Smoke Signal* initiated a new feature that month, highlighting dances and door prizes in the right-hand column, just beneath the masthead:

****

DANCE

DANTE CLUB 1511 P. ST.

SACRAMENTO CALIF. JAN. 22, 1949

BEAUTIFUL DOOR PRIZE

LOTS OF FUN AND OLD ACQUAINTANCES

WATCH THIS SPACE FOR NOTICE

****

Potts was nothing if not resourceful. Once competing for treasury funds, the *Smoke Signal* now pulled its weight through both subscription fees and free advertisements for chapter fund-raisers, with proceeds from the latter filling the delegate expense coffers that officers had earlier worried would be drained by newspaper production.[70] The next edition advertised "Card Bingo and other Card Games at Federated Indians Office, 2727 Santa Clara Way . . . March 19, 7:30 P.M.," the night before FIC's March 20 meeting.[71]

Many members came to know Potts through her 1948 fieldwork, when she traveled with Stewart or Fuller to communities like Bald Rock, Chester, Covelo,

Susanville, and Ukiah. Often documented by the mainstream press, these trips served the dual purpose of member recruitment and forewarning California Indian people about rival organizations that aimed to separate them from their hard-earned money under false pretenses.[72] The February 1948 *Smoke Signal* reported on a trip to Challenge, California, where Stewart and Potts spoke in Maggie Wagner's home: "Dinner was served prior to the meeting to all attendants, who numbered near fifty." On occasion, Potts undertook fieldwork more accurately characterized as intelligence gathering, traveling to Collett strongholds to witness his ICC pitch. On August 22, 1948, she was taking notes in the audience at a Redding meeting when ICI delegate Alfred Gillis opened the floor to questions. Unaware of her affiliation, he called on Potts. Standing to be seen and heard, she informed the audience that contrary to information Gillis had just reported, the Sacramento agency expected ICC attorney contracts for all three intertribal groups to be approved, warning them, in so many words, to be vigilant, pay attention to proposed legislation, and communicate directly with the Sacramento Indian Office when necessary. According to a *Smoke Signal* account of these proceedings, a "Guest Editorial by The Nite Owl," Collett was instantly apoplectic. "At this point, it seems that Mr. Collett changed colors approximately three times and the pencil he twisted in his hand was virtually demolished."[73] Potts both "made the news" and wrote news copy under Kitty's editorship, and she simply could not resist smacking Collett another time or two in the very same issue. The forum she chose was her popular "Via the Grapevine" column. She began by congratulating the new Mr. and Mrs. Homer Joseph, recently married in Stockton; "Mrs. Genevieve Williams, mother of the groom and Miss Rosina Barnes journeyed from Chester, Plumas Co., California to witness the ceremony." After reporting that the new couple would make their home in Genesee, she inserted her usual rows of asterisks marking transition to a new subject: "Whoever said 'You can fool some of the people some of the time but can't fool all of the people all of the time,' must have had Mr. Collett in mind. Those who know the facts are with the FIC. Of course, there are those who Barnum spoke in reference to when he said, 'There's one born every minute.'" Then another row of asterisks and hearty well wishes for ailing Arthur Treppa, who was "back on his feet at Sunday's meeting." Cue the asterisks for a third-person appearance: "When Mrs. Potts spoke at the Redding meeting she was strenuously rebuked for 'interrupting the meeting.' It couldn't be that Collett would prefer to withhold some information, would it?" Back to easy pleasantries she turned: The FIC office had recently enjoyed a visit from Mr. and Mrs. Jack Willburn, parents of Stewart's recent grandchild, the first baby announced in the *Smoke Signal*.[74]

Potts did not lack for talent in her layouts. Her knack for switching topics and tones at just the right intervals allowed her to fold political commentary into lighter material, ensuring it would be read. This is not to deny that purely social news had inherent political value. The "Grapevine" tethered grandparents to grandchildren, relocated Indians to home communities, and servicemen and -women to kith and kin. It built circulation and strengthened California Indian sociopolitical webs. Mercifully, it also leavened the weightiness of the land claims news that brought the *Smoke Signal* into being but never limited its content or reach. As the remaining chapters show, Potts's election as publicity agent and editor opened new vistas and activist avenues that transcended FIC's land claims politics.

Back in the Thick of Things

By an entirely random stroke of luck, FIC and Potts found one another. It is impossible to imagine how the organization would have fared had this intelligent and energetic Mountain Maidu woman not been living in Sacramento when the K-344 case was ending. Likewise, had Stewart, an equally smart and politically savvy California Indian woman, not been at the helm, it is unlikely that Potts would have been motivated to turn her life upside down on FIC's behalf. Was she in it for the land claims payment? Undoubtedly—her own and those due her children and extended kin. Their ancestral lands had been stolen, after all. But this alone would never have been enough. In FIC she found a social and intellectual forum not unlike Carlisle. FIC pushed her back out into the wider world with new purpose and commitment. After decades of marriage, motherhood, and life on the margins of white society, she was back in the thick of things, energized by the social networks, new horizons, and creative possibilities FIC engendered. Factionalism was rife and sometimes vicious, to be sure. It bears stating that the highly adversarial relations described in this chapter were historically situated. The same leaders who struggled fervently for their organization's dominance in the 1940s and 1950s came together in the 1960s and 1970s to forge new alliances at the anvil of solidarity and self-determination. By then, Potts and the *Smoke Signal* were practically household names.

5

Smoke Signal

A Native Journalist Comes to Life

Reginald George of Weimar, California, now stationed in
Germany, states he was very happy to see the *Smoke Signal* of
the FIC. Makes Injun Louie very happy to know that his *Smoke
Signals* can be read way over in Germany.

—*Smoke Signal, August 1951*

Potts's three-decades-long tenure as the *Smoke Signal* editor commenced in
March 1949. Two issues into its second year, her imprint was already indelible. She had realized from the start that the newspaper had a much grander
purpose than simply disseminating land claims news to FIC members and other
California Indian people; what she envisioned was a true newspaper, by and for
California Indians. Her intellectual curiosity, literary inclinations, exposure to
boarding school newspapers, and wit-sharpened tongue found full form in the
Smoke Signal's pages.

The 1950s coincided with her own middle age. Her girls were grown, she was
separated from Hensley both physically and emotionally, she had lived the legacy
of a landless California Indian descendant, and she was committed to land claims
justice. She was primed to once again express herself in writing. As the *Smoke
Signal* editor and publisher, she has a vehicle and reason to do so. After thirty
years, the possibility of intellectual fulfillment was at her fingertips once again.
She reached for it and never let go.

Reawakening Her Boarding School Sensibilities: Student Print and Reading Culture

The *Smoke Signal* awakened long-slumbering literary sensibilities from Potts's Carlisle years. There, she occupied a different position relative to the print culture world. She fed her voracious appetite for reading in the Carlisle library. She saw some of her writing published in the *Arrow*, but outing destinations, club activities, and social experiences made their way onto these pages with far greater frequency. Like all students, she had a print presence and occasional voice, but as a female student, her ability to shape Carlisle's print culture was marginal, her access to editorial instruction and the mechanics of print production nonexistent. Did she linger in the *Arrow* "newsroom?"[1] Was the print shop an inner sanctum she longed to inhabit? The enthusiasm with which she took on the *Smoke Signal* suggests so. Maybe she slipped across the threshold of these spaces every now and then. Or perhaps, like Native literary critic Robert Warrior, she could only wonder at the materialities, large and small, of print production: "I imagine the industrial smell of wet ink on newsprint and the whirring repetition of drums spinning, churning out copy after copy of souvenirs, newspapers, class materials, and whatever else the school's print shop manager found to keep the shop and the boys busy."[2] Photographs of Carlisle's print shop and famous "printer boys" were frequently counterposed with those of female students at sewing machines and laundry presses. The former held unrivaled currency, circulating widely during the school's heyday as evidence of Carlisle's commitment to Western gender norms. Not as propagandistically valuable were images of cerebral labor and work spaces. Ranking among the small percentage of Carlisle pupils to complete an academic course of study, Marie had abundant experience with both.

One scholarly analysis of Carlisle's reading culture includes four historical photographs. Two show students working in the library, and another features two girls studying in their dormitory room. The most impressive, however, features the girls' reading room.[3] Here, an imposing library table dominates, but a newspaper reading rail running the full length of two walls competes for viewer attention, as do spindled chairs that face it at regular intervals. Lining the rack, literally edge to edge, are more than a dozen broadsheet newspapers. Magazines and journals occupy five girls seated around the table, but two more are visible at the far end of the room. Backs to the camera, they are giving the press its due. This is surely where Marie read about Mount Lassen's long rumble to volcanic life and followed the planning and grand opening of San Francisco's Panama-Pacific International

Exposition. It was library research and intellectual labor that stood her well in Susan Longstreth Literary Society debates. Challenging Collett and his supporters on their own turf was nothing new. Research, debate, and religious oratory at Carlisle turned out to be good preparation for the land claims activism occupying her days and nights. She was not trained in journalism or print production, but the *Smoke Signal* bore witness to her intelligence, ambition, mastery of course work, and love of reading more generally. It is evident in her use of literary devices, eye-catching headlines, and clever layouts. Carlisle gave her an appreciation for the power of the well-placed quotation, perhaps from a Greek philosopher or P. T. Barnum, who knew an awful lot about fools.

Plastered wall to wall with dailies and weeklies, Carlisle's girls reading room wonderfully symbolized the print-saturated world of the early twentieth century and women's traditional place within it. In a society not yet transfigured by radio or television, newspapers and the industrial printing press were the height of technology for rapid and broad dissemination of information. Carlisle's "printer boys" gained partial entrée into the news business through vocational training, but women figured into it principally as consumers or readers versus editors, publishers, or newsmakers. Notable exceptions exist, but the likelihood that Carlisle students learned of them on campus or outing was slim.[4] However, newsmakers like Pauline Johnson, Laura "Minnie" Cornelius Kellogg, Sarah Winnemucca, Lucy Thompson, and Zitkála-Šá, Native women who made themselves and their political causes legible to the dominant society by conforming their physical appearances and rhetorical styles to arcane and romantic stereotypes, attracted mainstream press and drew plentiful attention from Carlisle's female students.[5]

Men controlled politics, economics, and world affairs in settler society. Women were not just excluded from meaningful participation; they were assumed to be intellectually inferior and uninterested in these "masculine" domains. The newspaper industry, whose daily bread was reporting developments in such arenas, reflected these patriarchal attitudes. By the turn of the twentieth century, women had carved narrow inroads into the public sphere of print production as authors and editors of periodicals focused on traditionally feminine realms: domesticity, social reform, and Christian charity. Amelia Quinton's editorship of WNIA's the *Indian's Friend* embodied this trend. From within these restrictive confines, Victorian-era women editors slowly gained literary traction elsewhere.

Sarah J. Hale, editor of the nineteenth-century periodicals *Ladies' Magazine* and *Godey's Lady's Book*, used her position and periodicals to increase the visibility of women's writing. Hale's multipronged strategy entailed publishing women's fiction and poetry, reviewing women's books and other literary contributions, and recognizing the diversity of genres in which women wrote. Hale waged a campaign encouraging sister editors to follow suit. By arguing for professional recognition of female writers, she advanced the radical notion that writing and print culture were realms where women could pursue independent livelihoods.[6] Role models like Hale and Quinton were rare, but rarer still were women editors without the wealth and social standing these two enjoyed. Even Marianna Burgess, editor of Carlisle's the *Indian Helper*, came to her position via her schoolteacher appointment in 1880. Though highly competent and independent by standards of the day, she inhabited a masculine editorial persona. Boasting a circulation of twelve thousand paid subscribers in 1897, the paper generated public support for Carlisle by highlighting its Americanizing work. It regularly featured alumni success stories, but current students also figured into its pages, where they were disciplined through criticism and faint praise. Adopting a panoptic "Man-on-the-Bandstand" identity, Burgess harnessed the masculine authority pupils associated with Richard Henry Pratt while also indulging the gendered expectations of mainstream readers who vested editorial power and gravitas in men.[7] Burgess left in 1904, well before Marie arrived.

Some of these historical trends are embodied in the *Smoke Signal* and its editor, but others are entirely upended. While the paper bears multiple hallmarks of the boarding school press, the assimilationist script is flipped. Where the former existed to pacify and silence tribal resistance, the *Smoke Signal*'s entire raison d'être was anticolonial in its land claims origins and agenda. Where settler colonial censorship governed the content and layout of the *Indian Helper*, *Redman*, and the *Arrow*, the *Smoke Signal* was California Indian authored, owned, and edited—by a woman at that. As she sat down at her typewriter to do her editorial work, did she think about the *Cherokee Phoenix*? Surely, Carlisle students learned about the oldest Native American newspaper. Did she remember *Arrow* stories of the founding of the Society of American Indians and its *Quarterly Journal*, which ran during her time there? Warrior's observation that the "immense history of Native American education" is "daunting" because "it seems so simple to judge and also so difficult" is apropos.[8] It would be easy to assume that Marie's decision to go to Carlisle was driven by settler colonial compliance versus curiosity, intelligence, and ambition, and that her boarding school education successfully replaced her Mountain Maidu identity with an anti-Native one. Three and a half decades after her 1915 commencement, such assumptions were obviously outlandish. Volunteering her intellectual labor to FIC while supporting herself as a domestic wage laborer, Potts used the academic knowledge and confidence wrested from her boarding school education to educate and empower California Indian people.

Print Production

Lacking vocational training in printing, Potts mastered the stencil-duplicating technology of the mimeograph. Widely marketed in the first half of the twentieth century as an inexpensive and alternative printing press, this was revolutionary grassroots technology in the late 1940s FIC office—yet to be popularized by the underground press or groups like Students for a Democratic Society (SDS). A journalist's description of the mid-1960s SDS headquarters on Chicago's West Side detailed an array of countercultural ephemera and protest posters. Here, amid wholly expected salutes to class consciousness, union labor, and sardonic political cartoons, an image of a mimeograph machine was stuck to the wall, and "[j]ust beneath it someone had written the words 'Our Founder.'"[9] Potts would have chuckled knowingly at this. Fifteen years earlier, the mimeograph at 2727 Santa Clara Way became her "founder," muse, and print shop floor.

No longer marginal to the print production world, she was printer, publisher, editor, copywriter, circulation manager, illustrator, humorist, and cartoonist. Her enthusiasm mirrored the youthful exuberance that Carlisle's intertribal milieu brought out in her, a social vibrancy well documented in the *Arrow*'s portrait of her as an energetic and adventurous young woman. On the eve of Christmas 1948 and her transition to editor, Potts was developing the signature touches for which she and the paper would become known. A border of holly leaves and berries framed a handwritten message in December's issue, placed just beneath the masthead: "Greetings to You at Christmas Time and Best Wishes for the New Year." Although Kitty's superior talent with the stencil and stylus was highlighted by the too-faint tracings of Potts's lettering and botanical illustration, the back page bore the confident imprint of Potts's season's greetings. Though the piece is anonymous, the humor and self-deprecating style identify "the poor substitute": "EDITOR'S NOTE—Due to the absence of the *Smoke Signal* staff, the office has had to take over."

FROM A POOR SUBSTITUTE

As I sit in the FIC office,
Trying to think of a greeting to send,
To the folks who receive our small paper

And a wish with a holiday trend.

My mind is so blank it feels empty,

So if this sounds unbalanced to you,

Forgive me for not being fancy

Boring you till you turn blue.

The purpose for writing this greeting,

Was to decorate the front of the page,

Any yells being heard from the office

Will be the Publicity Agent in a rage.

So just to make everyone happy,

I'll stop this writing for fear,

I'll forget the most important message,

"MERRY CHRISTMAS AND HAPPY NEW YEAR"[10]

This is the same personality who required all the girls to "give a hearty laugh" as the first order of business at Blanche Jollie's birthday party.[11] That the *Smoke Signal* "staff" was enjoying herself is patently obvious. Right at home with pen and paper, typewriter and stencil, writing and editing, Potts found unending inspiration in her Carlisle experience. Several years later, when she was being interviewed about termination legislation, interviewer Frank Quinn posed a leading question about her Carlisle education, assuming it to have been both forced and purely vocational, as was then the trend at Stewart and Sherman. Claiming and narrating her own history, she firmly set him straight, praising teachers, experiences, and course work that took both subtle and manifest form in the *Smoke Signal*. The same youthful spirit and conviviality that dances off the *Arrow*'s page is paralleled in her social briefs: "Joaquin Meadows, former student of Greenville Mission, Calif. and Chemawa, Oregon, after 40 years of absence, came home to visit his relatives in Plumas Co."; "ALMOST a stranger. Very glad to see Ethan Anderson again. Former Carlisle student"; "1st Lt. Kesner C. Flores of Sacramento is stationed in Japan"; "Mr. and Mrs. Victor William, Chairmen, reported a successful benefit dance held for the Federated Indians, March 12, at Rocklin, Placer County (THREE CHEERS!)."[12]

The *Smoke Signal* is laced with literary references undoubtedly dating to Carlisle. In November 1949, she used the prime real estate of the opening column to share the poem "Don't Quit," which is widely attributed to nineteenth-century Quaker poet John Greenleaf Whittier. She offered the preface "Dedicated to the 'Faithful Few,' first verse to the Treasurer."[13] The back page featured "A Thanksgiving

Soliloquy (with Apologies to Shakespeare)" of still called village. "Is this a leg
of turkey I see before me, The 'ball-bat' upward standing?" it asks in tribute to
the holiday fowl. On it goes for some twenty-two more lines before concluding,
"For it is done and I go; the bell invites me. Hear it ye students, all; for it is a
knell—'That tocxin of the soul, the dinner bell.'" The attribution accompanying
this play on the words of the famous British playwright and his countryman Lord
Byron proves that Potts drew upon an archive from her Carlisle years; it is signed
"—OH Lipps, Superintendent, Carlisle Indian School, from the THANKSGIVING
MENU, Thursday, November 26, 1914."[14]

Potts's literary education shows up in unexpected places. A 1950 story, "Apache
Vote Interest High," reports that the Phoenix League of Women Voters traveled
"200 miles to show the Apache Indians how to vote," with sample ballots, ballot
boxes, and a voting booth. To this story clearly taken from the mainstream press,
she added, "Editor's Note: The Phoenix Chapter of the League of Women Voters
is to be commended for the services rendered the Apache Indians." Although a
solid line demarcates the end of her commentary, she obviously had more to say,
adding immediately below, "There is only one cure to public stress, and that is
public education, to make men thoughtful, merciful and just. —John Ruskin."[15]

Quotations from the Western canon reveal literary knowledge and love but may
also express the material conditions of her editorship. Though she archived some
issues of the *Arrow*, there is no evidence that she owned any Native literature, even
old copies of *Red Man*, which carried Native song and "folklore." Bernadette Lear
correlates a dramatic decline in library acquisitions in Carlisle's post-Pratt years
with increased focus on vocational education. Furthermore, *Red Man* was not
produced for students. Thus it was the rich reservoir of Western literary quotations
acquired in the Susans, where memorization of prose was integrated even into
roll call, that Potts must have drawn upon as editor, although she clearly also
scanned the mainstream press for Native-focused news and role models. When
Osage chief Fred Lookout died, she carried the news, highlighting his Carlisle
education. "Gone to the Great Beyond" headlined an obituary and biography
of Henry Roe Cloud, Carlisle's 1914 commencement speaker. "Indian Mother
Honored for 1950" introduced a front-page column about Elizabeth Bender Roe
Cloud being named American Mother of the Year, its placement a testament to
Potts's obvious admiration.[16]

Decades later, Potts began using her editorial voice and authority to share
Maidu knowledge and experience in brief cultural vignettes, recognizing that a
younger generation was seeking its place within contemporary Native society.

Yet even in the paper's early years, she aroused nostalgia and cultural pride with stories of traditional foodways and ceremony:

SUSANVILLE HOLDS ANNUAL BEAR DANCE

The Indians in Susanville held the traditional Bear Dance at Indian Heights, Sunday June 6, 1948. Although threatening rain kept the crowd at a minimum, the ceremony continued as scheduled. A real "feed" with acorn soup and all was given by Katie Juaquin [sic] of Janesville prior to the Ceremonial dance. Mr. Jack Cunningham of Greenville played the role of the "bear."[17]

Engaging readers in recovery and intergenerational transmission of Native words and practices, she asked in June 1950,

"What's the name of that thing?" has been the question heard from every direction and all walks of life. The object is the baby basket that Indian mothers carry their babies in strapped on their backs. Every tribe has their own name for this basket. The Maidu tribe call it "tutu," translation meaning "nest." The Mewuk name is "hiki" (I like in it). With every tribe is a different name. The common name has been "baby basket" or "baby cradle." I have heard it called "papoose caboose." What's your name for it?? [18]

This sparked conversations among grandparents and grandchildren, mothers and daughters, basketry buyers and weavers. She solicited stories from readers about their cultural histories and traditions. Social news was easy to come by, but lack of response to calls for this kind of material greatly frustrated her. She knew it would be as educational and interesting to others as it was to her. It was slow going at first. Perhaps others were busy, uncertain about their writing skills, or not sure exactly what she wanted. Potts suspected otherwise. In 1952 she told a correspondent,

Quite some time ago you mentioned running stories in the Smoke Signal; I haven't forgotten. I was so busy at the time I just didn't write. I think it is a splendid idea. Could you supply some of these stories? After a start, someone else may be willing to contribute a story or two. I find some Indians very reluctant about giving out any information for the public. Their pet peeve seems to be that we [FIC] are making money on it and they don't like to see their own people make money but will gladly tell things to the white people.[19]

Even after she broadened the paper's coverage of cultural issues, its selling point remained policy and political concerns. Florence McClintock, a BIA field nurse, expounded enthusiastically, from Alturas, "Thanks, too, for the paper. I enjoy reading it. I get more information from that than from the Office. I am enclosing a dollar for the paper."[20] McClintock was atypical. Most subscriptions served extended families or households rather than individuals. In July 1960, Potts wrote Baker to confirm a meeting date so she could notify the membership, some seven thousand to eight thousand individuals. Notices went to households, not individuals, but even so, "It takes two or more days to cut stencils, run them off on the mimeograph machine, address and staple them," she explained. "Our subscriptions are picking up. We have had quite a few new ones; that of course makes us very happy. And the most of them are Indians. They hear so many false reports and write in for information and of course we send them a copy of the *Smoke Signal* and that does it."[21]

Injun Louie: Protagonist and Editorial Alter Ego

A lively character named Injun Louie animated the *Smoke Signal* from 1948 until the paper's demise in 1978.[22] He played many roles over the years; his most durable was as Potts's editorial alter ego. Setting the gendered dimensions momentarily aside, it must be noted that Injun Louie seems at first blush radically out of step with the image FIC wished to project as a professional organization of California Indian people. Making his debut in single-frame cartoons in the paper's second issue, he stumbles into *Smoke Signal* readers' lives as an affable, be-feathered, teepee-dwelling character. The central protagonist in FIC's battle against the federal government and competing land claims groups, Injun Louie gave visual expression to the persistent stereotypes and caricatures that infected every political, social, and economic encounter California Indians had with settler practices, values, and institutions. In this respect, Louie and other FIC and *Smoke Signal* imagery, including letterhead featuring a dye-cut stencil of a silhouetted man in a feathered headdress, fails to meet our twenty-first-century expectations.

Why would a newspaper written, edited, and published entirely by and for California Indians reproduce stereotypical, "generic" American Indian imagery rather than draw upon California-based tribal, regional, or diasporic themes? Recent scholarship on the visual economy of indigeneity provides a clue. One scholar's work, although principally concerned with the role that film, photography, and archives have played in the context of Andean ethnographic realms and pursuits, illuminates the power of the visual in narrative production.[23] In the United States,

American Indians are appropriated as core elements of a settler colonial narrative and creation story, where they buttress claims to distinction from the mother country, even as distinctions between Native nations are systematically erased in a settler imaginary that carelessly fuses disparate cultural elements to institutionalize an iconography of the easily (un)recognizable "Indian." Produced, circulated, and consumed in the most intimate and banal corners of the domestic sphere, from the kitchen to the garage, this imagery conveys affection and admiration for "vanished" American Indians without taxing consumers of household products or the U.S. national narrative with the difficult work of acknowledging settler violence or the diversity of Native nations displaced by colonization.

Native Americans had a very different relationship to such imagery when the FIC was founded. In the late 1930s, when Marie's younger daughters were attending Stewart and Sherman, forced assimilation was no longer federal policy. Yet wholly by design, its impact was still there. This generation of students, deprived of the ancestral tongues and cultural heritage that had been systematically stripped from their parents' and grandparents' everyday lives, often celebrated their shared identity as Native peoples through pan-tribal imagery symbolizing pride and persistence in the face of federal efforts to eradicate them—and their differences. The world wars also cultivated appreciation of Plains warrior imagery among Native people; this was the tradition and narrative Kitty had drawn upon when choosing the *Smoke Signal* name and early masthead graphics. Even Stewart and Potts, first-generation graduates of Chemawa and Carlisle, appreciated the symbolic currency of this imagery without it usurping their respective Tolowa and Mountain Maidu identities or sense of belonging.

Injun Louie operated in this symbolic realm. Everyman's "Indian" and no tribe's "Indian," he masterfully navigated the *Smoke Signal* pages. In the years of political mobilization immediately following ICCA's passage, Injun Louie showed what a "smart" Indian did: he enrolled with FIC and read its all-Indian-controlled newspaper so as not to be duped by those taking advantage of uninformed Indians. He poked and prodded ambivalent and politically apathetic California Indians, whose response to yet another federal promise was "Yeah, right." Cartoons of Injun Louie dreaming about achieving middle-class status—abandoning his teepee and camp for the tract home and car made possible by per capita payments—certainly enticed some individuals to join the FIC.

Injun Louie's haplessness and generic "Indian" identity were graphically rendered in seemingly innocuous cartoons, but the captioning in Hollywood "Injun speak"—or Hollywood Indian English (HIE)—deftly deployed the stereotype of functional illiteracy to prod California Indians out of their complacency while simultaneously criticizing the yawning gap between federal promises and actual practice.[24] On rare occasions, "Injun Louie" held forth in lengthy editorials, discursively constructing the illiterate savage in monosyllabic pidgin English, cleverly turning the image of cruelty and incivility back on settler society through scathing denouncements of the "Great White Father" and "Big Boss."[25]

There was genius to this discourse, which gestured toward critique of a *Plumas Independent* column carried in the early 1930s; without doubt, Potts would have read it. It was written by settler descendant Lee Laufman under the pen name Beggar Bill, a nickname for Maidu Bill Baker, husband of Daisy. Laufman had known Baker his entire life, and the column may have begun as a means to record Baker's remembrances, but it continued long after his death as the weekly "Injun Wolley Letter," reporting news for Indian Valley ("Wolley"), one the many Plumas County valleys and towns that the weekly covered via locally authored columns. Laufman slips back and forth between "Injun talk" and standard English: "Last week, Beggar Bill much sick, no can write for paper. Just sit around house all day per two hours. Just now feelum heap good, so will write for paper. This not much good weather for make things grow. Two cold and plenty storm. Storms tell me not too many nice days for June." Voice changes were often abrupt and characterized by perfect spelling and grammar regardless of topic, as when the above weather commentary was followed by news that a man recently had had his arm amputated at Westwood Hospital after breaking it while working on his car. Native news might follow in the very same voice: "The Indians of this valley staged a Bear Dance near Greenville Sunday. Quite a few of the red-men of other camps were present. 'Beggar Bill' was then dressed in the war paint of the tribe. Several of the braves indulged in too much fire water, which put them out of commission for the dance."[26] Since Laufman writes as Beggar Bill, readers can never be sure to whom these stories and discursive imagery refer—settlers or Indian people.

Ho-Chunk media activist and Carlisle alumnus (1893–99) Charles Round Low Cloud's "Indian News" is instructive, here. One scholar's analysis of this Native journalist draws our attention to the editor's decision not to copyedit Low Cloud's column, published from 1930 to 1949 in the Black River Falls (Wisconsin) *Banner-Journal*, despite the author's regular request for assurance that his spelling and writing were adequate. This decision reinforced demeaning stereotypes and muted his activist voice, which in the column's last years spoke directly to Ho-Chunk ICC grievances.[27] Speaking humorously back to the stereotypes, as did

Injun Louie, is a wholly different project than publishing a column theoretically designed to endow a subaltern population with a mainstream media voice while refusing its author the professional copyediting offered other columnists. Among the first generation of Mountain Maidu to command English-language literacy, Potts surely recognized the underlying derision in Laufman's use of HIE to record Baker's stories and "Injun Wolley" news for non-Native, mainstream-press readers.

The *Smoke Signal* enjoyed a small base of mainstream subscribers in the 1940s and 1950s, but they were regularly treated to a hefty dose of anticolonial anger and sarcasm. As California land claims inched laboriously forward, Injun Louie increasingly turned his voice against the United States, rendering caustic critiques of the federal government's consistent prioritization of other countries' post-wartime needs over those of Native Americans. Cartoons condemning the snap-of-the-finger speed with which Congress enacted the Marshall Plan for war-torn Europe highlighted its policy failures and foot-dragging at home. Never mind the long-suffering, war-torn California Indians patiently awaiting per capita payments from their CIJA award. Uncle Sam could dole out $13 billion to Europe in a nanosecond but continually failed to ameliorate the colonial legacy of racism and poverty at home.

For decades, Potts sent Injun Louie across the country as the affable and occasionally inept figure who greeted subscribers in postcard form when subscription

Figure 9. Injun Louie *Smoke Signal* renewal postcard.
Courtesy Marine family.

renewals were overdue. And more than occasionally, she appropriated his identity and attributes to apologize for incorrect mailing labels or failing to get the paper out earlier, or simply to remind subscribers that it was produced entirely through volunteer labor. The *Smoke Signal*'s June 1950 back page captures this side of her humor and editorial sensibility. Three images occupy the top two-thirds of the page. At ten o'clock a fisherman in waders, a collared button-down shirt, and a wide-brimmed hat reels in a fish at least half his size; the rod arcs dramatically under its weight. At two o'clock, two men are enjoying a summer swim. Glancing up from his lap, one sees the other diving right into his path. His terrified expression cannot help but draw a chuckle. At six o'clock sits the editor's long-suffering alter ego, laboring over the typewriter. The message is clear: while the rest of the Federated Indians are out enjoying themselves, she is slaving away. Injun Louie wipes his forehead with a soaking handkerchief, as bulging beads of perspiration drip from his braids and be-feathered brow. One drop strikes the floor with such weighty force that it shatters into droplets that leap up and outward. Though Potts's illustration is naive and unschooled, her humor is sophisticated.[28] The fly fisherman and swimmers Louie so obviously envies are missing his own premodern trappings of feathers and braids. They are modern people going about their everyday business and recreational pursuits while she inhabits the prodding, provoking, masculine role of Injun Louie, their volunteer *Smoke Signal* editor. The bottom third of the page is reserved for one of her rhyming editorial commentaries:

THE SPLOTCHES YOU FIND ON YOUR SMOKE SIGNAL
IS THE HONEST SWEAT OF MY BROW
WHILE YOU'RE FISHING AND SWIMMING AND SITTING IN THE SHADE
IT TOOK WEEKS OF HARD LABOR TO GET THIS THING MADE.
IF YOU HAVE ANY IDEAS OF A CARTOON, PLEASE JOT IT DOWN
AND WE WILL GLADLY PRINT IT, WHEN THE MONTHS OF JULY-AUGUST
COME AROUND. (AND THAT'S NO JOKE)   Ed.

Centered beneath was a "Reminder: Don't forget the next dance on AUGUST 5, 1950. It will be held at the Muir Athletic Club, 21st and C Street, Sacramento, California, and the next DANCE on September 2nd at the same place. When you come down for the Fair, kill two birds with one stone. Throw in some glad rags and be sure you don't miss this dance." These opportunities to dress up and dance the night away were relished by FIC members. Although shirtless Louie figures most prominently in the *Smoke Signal*'s pages, other images of California Indian men as business suit and tie–wearing people were important foils to Louie's eighteenth-century trappings and pidgin English.

Visual imagery never stood alone in the *Smoke Signal*. Potts peppered the news with jokes and riddles. Some simply made fun of white people: "Tourist question to aged Injun Louie: 'To what do you attribute your old age?' After much deliberation aged Injun Louie replied 'Me Injun Louie born many, many moons ago.'"[29] Others highlighted the corruption and ineptitude of those purporting to have Indian interests at heart despite all evidence to the contrary. White people's dishonesty was ever-present fodder, underscoring the hypocrisy embodied in the racist paternalism California Indians navigated in their everyday lives. In the March 1949 issue, Uncle Sam holds a cash bag marked "Billions for Europe." Injun Louie proclaims that he has patience and can wait a "heap long" time. In 1963 Louie is old; his son Aloysius has grown up and moved on. Uncle Sam hands Louie a tiny bag marked "47 cents an acre," the paltry per capita amount at which California Indian ancestral lands were finally valued. Louie has changed with age, but Uncle Sam, the unjust federal government, remains true to form.[30]

Racist stereotypes work by isolating a set of traits; defining them as fixed or immutable; encoding them with biological, intellectual, or cultural inferiority; and then deploying them as symbolic of the whole. This was never lost on Potts. Even as Injun Louie's persona and role evolved over the newspaper's long life, mainstream society continued its damaging caricatures. She mobilized that caricature of a premodern, generic "Indian" to bolster and subvert, to anger and to motivate California Native Americans. Injun Louie reminded them exactly how they were perceived by mainstream society and challenged them to counter that stereotype through political action. The question of whether or not Potts or other editorial commentators internalized racist stereotypes is an important one, but the uses to which Injun Louie was mobilized lay this question to rest. In the same way the *Smoke Signal* deployed Injun Louie to "draw and speak back," so do countless contemporary Native American artists and cartoonists, from Zuni cartoonist Phil Hughte, who caricatured anthropologist Frank Hamilton Cushing's naive and nosy fieldwork at Zuni Pueblo, to Ricardo Caté, cartoonist for the *Santa Fe New Mexican*, who entertains with his own version of an Injun Louie.[31] This is a universal feature of contemporary indigenism, as anthropologist Richard Lee observes: "Perhaps the least heralded weapon in the arsenal of the indigenous and a key to their survival is the use of humor. The indigenous groups I am most familiar with, aboriginal peoples in Canada and Ju/'hoansi in Botswana and Namibia, use deadpan humor as a tension releaser and, when necessary, as a devastating weapon.

Ever since I was taken in by the elaborate scam of the Christmas ox written up in 'Eating Christmas in the Kalahari' I have had a healthy respect for the wit and irony of Ju and their compatriots in the indigenous world."[32]

Potts nurtured and sustained the bumbling and lovable Injun Louie because she understood humor's productive value well before Deloria tutored anthropologists and others about Native wit by making them the butt of his literary levity. "Humor, all Indians agree, is the cement by which the coming Indian movement is held together," he expounded. "When a people can laugh at themselves and laugh at others and hold all aspects of life together without letting anybody drive them to extremes, then it seems to me that people can survive."[33]

The *Smoke Signal* shows that Marie held much of her own life together by recourse to wit and laughter, perhaps especially during her years working alongside Hensley as a hunting guide. Her wit spilled with abandon into every issue of the paper. It spanned the long miles between readers, evoking a chorus of laughter across the state, reminding California Indian people who and what they were eternally up against, despite cultural and political differences among them:

> An Indian was being packed out of a hunting trip in Shasta Co., by an Indian guide. It seems that after a day's journey, the tourist who had two rifles with him complained about his pack being too heavy and asked the Indian guide what he could do about it. The Indian guide told him to leave one of his rifles in the hollow of a tree and they would pick it up upon their return. The tourist rather hesitant asked if it would be safe in the tree, as the rifle was quite valuable. "Why sure it will be safe," replied the Indian. "There hasn't been a white man in these mountains for years."[34]

Injun Louie was a brilliant foil.[35] He was Potts's front man when readers, many of them men, had to be coaxed into standing up for the cause, donating time, renewing their subscriptions, or showing up to FIC meetings. Censure of Uncle Sam was more palatable coming from Injun Louie. His word carried more authority and force in Native worlds acclimated to settler colonial gender norms. Yet, possessed of so much naivete and ineptitude, Injun Louie cast serious doubt on the logic of patriarchy, even as his affable persona dulled Potts's razor-sharp edge when dealing with racism, laziness, or political complacency.

Louie endowed the *Smoke Signal* with a memorable editorial presence and voice during years when Potts was reticent to affix her name and authority to work she so clearly treasured. Humble gestures of voice and authorship dominated in these years: "ed.," "Editor," or more rarely "MP."[36] Potts had none of the resources her "sister editors" of an earlier era enjoyed, women like Hale or Quinton, whose work was underwritten by social privilege and family money. Yet aside from the attorneys working their claims case, she was doing the lion's share of FIC's work by 1950. She confided to Baker, in 1953, that she heard complaints "from people about not having meetings, but of course it would be from people living close in. Also complaints about not having *Smoke Signals* oftener; I realize what they mean but sometime I just don't seem to make it."[37] Indeed, she made it, only with help.

As the years rolled on, the delegate fund-raisers of the late 1940s, evolved into work parties. Pity the poor visitor who accidently dropped into the office when Potts was "getting out the *Smoke Signal*," though she never failed to acknowledge their assistance in the next issue. For decades, brigades of volunteers, including many grandchildren, worked the assembly line, collating, stapling, and stamping, then folding the paper in half again to be stapled closed, affixed with an adhesive address label, and bundled off to the post office to be carried across the state, across the nation, or sometimes overseas. Yet her own work, never seen by the public or most volunteers, was even more impressive: collecting stories, writing and typing copy, maintaining the printing equipment and supplies, recording longhand entries into an accounting ledger of subscriber names, addresses, and payments—siblings, cousins, Maidu kin, friends from her Greenville and Carlisle school days: Masons, Piazzonis, Peconums, Davises, and so many more from up and down the state who knew her only through the *Smoke Signal*. Evincing no cognizance of her pathbreaking role as a Native journalist, just a fierce dedication to her work, Potts reported her occupation in Sacramento's 1955 telephone directory as "maid."

A Newspaper of Her Own

The *Smoke Signal* breathed new life into Potts from the moment of its January 1948 inception. A vital member of the staff and publishing household, she played a prominent role in shaping its inaugural form and content, writing stories and columns that increased its appeal and circulation. When she took the formal reins in March 1949, long-dormant skills and sensibilities sprang all the more vigorously to life—and onto the newspaper's pages, where Carlisle's print and reading culture is firmly imprinted. The dedication and enthusiasm she demonstrated in these laborious and entirely voluntary roles as editor and publisher suggest that she may have looked with both envy and esteem upon her youthful peers who wrote and produced the *Arrow* while she was busy catching up to grade levels. Yet the *Smoke Signal* also bears evidence of her hard-won, post-Carlisle education.

The literary and journalistic sensibilities awakened in midlife were not those of the adolescent girl who followed Eli out to Pennsylvania, certain she could chart her own future. They were those of a mature woman schooled for three decades in a curriculum of inequality—gendered, racial, and economic. Her sentiments about the stereotypes and limited socioeconomic opportunities she experienced as a Mountain Maidu wife, mother, and domestic laborer also found their way into the *Smoke Signal*. Cleverly, she deployed Injun Louie to voice these biting critiques of white society and the federal government, oscillating between sharp-tongued sarcasm and insider humor. This division of editorial and authorial labor worked to her advantage in the gendered, patriarchal, and racialized world Native women inhabited at mid-century. Attributes readily identifiable in her youth still shine through. Her innate determination, gregarious personality, and inquisitive spirit fairly dance off the page in this "newspaper of her own." She found her passion. Calling fondly upon her literary education of old, she wrote and communicated on behalf of not only FIC and California Indian land claims but also Native California cultures more broadly—their shared histories, traditions, and rights. Just as the print culture of American Indian boarding schools was used to shape public perception of American Indians, federal assimilation policy, and the supposed virtues of detribalization, Potts used the *Smoke Signal* to build the bonds of California Indian diaspora, defining common experiences, traditions, and political concerns.[38] In the coming years, she would carry the *Smoke Signal* to new heights of purpose and circulation. And it would carry her to places she never dreamed of going. Three decades later, when the American Indian Press Association began to take shape, professionally trained, college-educated American Indian journalists gazed with awe upon this diminutive seventy-five-year old Mountain Maidu woman, a founding member, who had pioneered the Native press out of her humble abode in Sacramento.[39] In these early years, however, this expansive stage was still being set, as the FIC made its presence known in the city and across the state.

6

"Real Indians"

It is with this thought in mind that I urge our people to turn back the pages of history and review the romance, drama, and achievements of our past. In doing so we shall be reminded of the courage and indomitable spirit of those who built the foundations of this State, and gain the inspiration to guide California into an even greater century of progress still to come.

—Governor Earl Warren, January 1948

Many on-lookers for the first time saw real "Injuns" with feathers, and to their surprise they all spoke English fluently.

—Smoke Signal, June 1948

The duties of FIC publicity agent included more than *Smoke Signal* editorship. Between 1948 and the mid-1950s, FIC received numerous invitations to appear in public venues to mark historic and patriotic occasions ranging from Flag Day to California centennials of gold discovery, the gold rush, and statehood. The FIC exploited these invitations from the Sacramento mayor, the governor of California, veterans' groups, and small towns to its own advantage, fully cognizant of the irony involved in appearing as "Indians" at these settler celebrations. This was a price the group willingly paid to further its land claims agenda. This string of appearances began under Kitty's tenure in office, but the organizational labor was always spearheaded by her mother, chair of the Sacramento chapter. Potts exhausted herself organizing these parades and encampments yet also took great pride in winning monetary awards and newspaper publicity. The latter increased FIC visibility to Native people. The group attracted new members, both statewide and among Native communities indigenous to the region. This chapter tracks two parallel processes related to these appearances: those in which FIC members performed generic "Indian" identities for the public, and those where FIC members gathered to be themselves—contemporary descendants of ancestors whose lands were the subject of their ICC grievance. Potts's *Smoke Signal* coverage of these events—planning, reporting, and after-the-fact interpretation—reveals how exasperated she became with the demands made of them by host organizations and the onlooking public. She carried on despite this, cultivating sympathetic allies, political leverage, and a broader Native network. The Sacramento chapter became the FIC powerhouse during these years, developing an urban presence in the local and statewide press that positioned the group as something of a novelty. This was entirely the members' own doing and shows just how savvy they were about the role they occupied within the American imaginary.

Performing Indian Identities

An astonishing sight greeted bystanders along the route leading from 2727 Santa Clara Way to the state capitol on Friday, February 6, 1948: a runner in fringed and beaded buckskin. A hefty upright feather in his headband ensured that observers properly associated him with an American Indian identity. The young man, charged by Stewart with delivering a missive from Fuller to Governor Warren, drew plenty of attention on his three-and-a-half-mile journey. Photographers were poised for his arrival. So was Warren, who accepted a paper scroll from Pomo runner Tommy McWhinney, newly elected chairman of FIC's Sacramento chapter. His father, Archie or "Chief Golti," stood beside him, nearest the photographer. Chapter vice chairman, he wore a beaded buckskin vest and imposing feathered headdress. Clipping a newspaper article and photograph of this event to send friends, Stewart later explained that she too was there, "just back of the Indian runner."[1] The elder McWhinney's voluminous headdress literally and figuratively eclipsed her. This scene-stealing potential was entirely the point. "The Indians, in full tribal regalia, offered the traditional pipe of peace to symbolize good will of the tribes, although the Federated Indians have on file a claim action against the government for alleged confiscation and seizure of Indian land almost 100 years ago."[2]

Ironically, FIC organized on the cusp of California's three-year historical extravaganza celebrating settler colonial conquest of Indigenous peoples and lands—the stolen territory at stake in its ICC grievance. On May 31, 1947, Warren signed a bill creating a five-person California Centennial Commission and

Figure 10. Governor Earl Warren accepts an FIC invitation from Pomo
Tommy McWhinney and his father, Archie McWhinney, 1948.
Courtesy Marine family.

appropriating $250,000; counties were encouraged to apply for assistance in
financing historical celebrations.[3] Only two weeks before FIC's runner met him
at the capitol, Warren was in Coloma issuing a proclamation heralding the start
of centennial events:

> When James W. Marshall first found yellow metal on a bank of the Ameri-
> can River at Coloma, on January 24, 1848, he set off a chain of events which
> tremendously accelerated the early expansion of the west. As a result of
> his momentous discovery the sparsely populated territory of California
> developed at such a rapid pace that in less than 32 months it became a
> state. . . . Between now and September 9, 1950, when this observation will
> culminate in ceremonies marking the 100th anniversary of California's
> admission to the union, all of us will join in celebrating the glory of our
> state's romantic past.[4]

Settler nostalgia must have exasperated FIC officers, for whom these successive
celebrations of gold discovery (1848), the gold rush (1849), and statehood (1850)
marked anniversaries of ancestral encounters with genocidal militias, deadly
pathogens, enslavement, and theft of lands that had sustained Indians since

time immemorial.[5] Still, they recognized in these events a chance to advance their own agenda.[6]

Importantly, FIC's land claims grievance was against the federal government, not the state of California, whose authority and power the FIC continued to actively appropriate in the personages of Allen, Baker and all others they could recruit to help sideline Collett and Foster. When the opportunity to exploit the centennial craze presented itself, Stewart and Potts made a calculated and practical concession, choosing to defer their grievances with California settler injustice for the sake of bolstering their prospects with the more immediate concern of ICC. Sending an "Indian runner" to the capitol was about positioning Warren as a political ally in their case against the United States and in their competition with rival groups.[7] The photography and fanfare accompanying Warren's receipt of their hand-delivered invitation was the opening act in a spectacle that took place two days later, on Sunday, February 8, at the State Indian Museum (SIM). There, at Sutter's Fort, where one hundred years earlier James Marshall had announced his gold discovery at Sutter's Coloma Mill, Warren smoked with the FIC. He followed this symbolic gesture with an impassioned speech and display of paternalistic power, scolding "ambulance chasing" lawyers in Washington and the government that had rejected the California treaties a hundred years before. The *Bee* was on the scene:

> Governor Warren smoked the traditional "Pipe of Peace" and witnessed Indian rituals at the Indian Museum in Sutter's Fort yesterday while a crowd of nearly 1,000 braved the rain to take part in the "pow-wow" sponsored by the Federated Indians of California. The "peace pipe" ritual was the feature of the Federated Indians' tribal session, which closed at the courthouse last night. The ceremony was opened with an Indian prayer by Chief William Fuller of the Miwuk tribe, Tuloumne, head of the Federation. The prayer was interpreted for Governor Warren and the throng, which was liberally sprinkled with children, some of whom got their first glimpse of a real, "hones' Injun" Indian.[8]

FIC knew exactly how an "Indian" should look and told delegates coming to February's monthly meeting and "ritual" to show up looking like one. Members received preprinted postcards reading, "On February 8, 1948, I have scheduled a 'pow-wow' with, I hope, some noted official. It is hoped that this official will smoke the Pipe of Peace with the Delegates of the Federated Indians of California." Remarking on advantages to be had "if we could retain the old Indian traditions as far as dress is concerned," Kitty wrote, "we would appreciate your cooperation in bringing the regalia of the tribe you represent.... If a full traditional costume is not available, please bring some garment of your tribe."[9] Benjamin Hathaway, SIM curator and Potts family neighbor, supplied some of this on-site:

Taking part, in full Indian regalia furnished by the State Indian Museum, were Chief Fuller, Lawrence Burcell, Karok tribe, Siskiyou County, Archie McWhinney of Sacramento, Pomo tribe; his son Tommy McWhinney of Sacramento, Pomo tribe; Arthur Treppa, Pomo from Upper Lake; Dora Joseph, Pit River; Kitty Flores, Maidu tribe, William Graves, medicine man, Pomo tribe; Mrs. Bertha Stewart, Tolowa tribe (Smith River), and Marie Potts, Maidu, who stole the "show" carrying her grandson, two-month-old Michael Marine, in papoose style, strapped to her back.[10]

The next day Stewart reported, "I wore a Smith River Tribal Costume but had to keep my coat on, as it was cold and beads alone don't keep one very warm. Sam [Lopez] got mad at me because I didn't beat the drum or do a dance." The outfit came from SIM, but ambivalence at having to don it and perform an ancestral identity for journalists and public onlookers was all hers.[11]

Stewart and Lopez shared more than Tolowa ancestry. Both were subjects of ethnographic portraiture in younger years. Edward Curtis had photographed Lopez in a Jump Dance headdress and clamshell bead necklaces. Missionary-turned-anthropologist Pliny Earle Goddard had photographed Stewart alongside her mother, Lizzie Grimes, aunt Mary Grimes, and grandmother Clara La Fountain, all in ceremonial dress, at Burnt Ranch, Del Norte County.[12] Lopez was a young adult when he agreed to pose for the romantic portrait that brought him fame upon its 1923 publication, but three-year-old Bertha Grimes had no choice about whether or not to "beat the drum and dance" in 1903. Each understood the cultural and political currency embodied in such imagery, but for Stewart, even political stagecraft had limits. She was exhausted that day by her own admission: "[The Sacramento chapter] dance lasted until 3 A.M. last night and I very foolishly stayed until the end, but had a lot of fun."[13]

That there was serious fun to be had in this work, despite the circumstances, was undeniable. This may explain why Potts responded with such dedication to the flood of publicity opportunities that rained down following their February 1948 appearance. Kitty was the formal point of contact, but she was so quickly overwhelmed that she resigned as chapter recording secretary to manage duties with the "mother organization."[14] A year later she gave that up too, and Potts was already handling many of those responsibilities. As with the *Smoke Signal*, she had a natural affinity for this work and understood the bargain involved. Appropriating centennial publicity was a pragmatic form of resistance, a partial accommodation to settler expectations that furthered FIC goals.

Assessing the stakes, FIC officers and Sacramento chapter members held their noses and played the part scripted for them in this conquest pageant. They would be "Indians" to these ridiculous cowboys and gold rush settlers. The alternative was to watch white people inhabit that role, to be imagined as truly vanished, and to turn their backs on the symbolic and material gains to be had from starry-eyed settler celebrations. Publicity appearances in buckskin, beads, and feathers gave them an unparalleled platform from which to recruit new members and to generate a media presence that overshadowed rival entities, especially CCI, which announced the opening of a downtown Sacramento office the very day Tommy McWhinney made his capitol run. The *Smoke Signal* lampooned Foster and CCI's infiltration of FIC's Capital City stronghold. A man whose striking resemblance to Foster is confirmed by the label "ambulance chaser" worriedly wipes perspiration from his brow while gazing at a "Member-Ometer" at least as tall as he. Measuring FIC "Voluntary Membership," the mercury nears four thousand on this tube that tops out at twenty-four thousand, the total count of California Indians on the 1928 roll. "Boy, this is getting HOT!"[15]

The Freedom Train: A Publicity Stunt Produces an Iconic Image

Before long, everyone wanted "Indians" at their event. Belle Cooledge, Sacramento's first woman mayor, was coordinating the Freedom Train's March 20 Sacramento stopover. She arranged for Warren to speak at the opening ceremonies and invited FIC to send five representatives to join the welcoming committee. This was not a centennial event, but the ironies were no less pungent. The Freedom Train was a touring exhibit of archival documents pulled by a locomotive dubbed *Spirit of 1776*. The seven-car train traveled to more than 322 cities, accompanied by enough patriotic fanfare and publicity to light the night sky. Between September 1947, when it left Philadelphia, and January 1949, when it pulled into Washington, D.C., for Harry Truman's inauguration, it churned more than 3.5 million visitors— around nine thousand per day—through three rail cars featuring 133 archival documents that were broadly themed around "freedom." Although the project was substantially altered during development, credit for the original concept goes to William Coblenz, who was inspired by a National Archives exhibit on Nazi war propaganda. A former *Boston Post* journalist, veteran of both world wars, and Department of Justice public information officer, Coblenz shared with DOJ his vision for an exhibit that would juxtapose American and Nazi documents. From this kernel emerged the powerful American Heritage Foundation, assembled as a nonpartisan, nongovernmental vehicle for sponsoring and funding the exhibit.[16]

The day before the exhibit's arrival, the *Bee* explained, "The collection begins with a late Thirteenth Century manuscript copy of England's Magna Carta and the first printed letter by Columbus concerning his discovery of America. The copy was printed in Rome in 1493."[17] One wonders what Injun Louie would have said: a Columbus discovery letter but not a single unratified California treaty? An avid newspaper reader, Potts probably followed the train's journey from its Philadelphia launch. This was the city about which she had written with such enchantment after her YWCA excursion to see Billy Sunday, the Liberty Bell, Betsy Ross's House, and the university museum. Even so, she knew that the Freedom Train's propagandistic discourse of a unified "American Family" rang hollow. Stolen ancestral lands drove this point home, and so did criticism the exhibition garnered from those for whom freedom remained elusive. The National Urban League president worried that African Americans would face segregated lines, touring hours, or touring days in the forty-nine southern cities the train was scheduled to visit. Criticism during its East Coast tour had come mostly from political dissenters, "communists and contentious objectors."[18] J. Edgar Hoover surveilled protestors in every city and had some arrested, but the problem of segregation loomed.

As the locomotive decked out in red-and-white stripes chugged along the Eastern Seaboard, Langston Hughes penned the poignant verses to his poem "Freedom Train." Published in the *New Republic*, it began, "Down South in Dixie only train I see's / Got a Jim Crow car set aside for me. / I hope there ain't no Jim Crow on the Freedom Train, / No back door entrance to the Freedom Train, / No signs FOR COLORED on the Freedom Train, / No WHITE FOLKS ONLY on the Freedom Train."[19] The foundation disseminated a press release establishing anti-segregationist procedure to be followed at every stop. Memphis and Birmingham refused to comply and were stricken from the tour. Potts may not have read Hughes or the *New Republic*, but she read. The Advertising Council had done its job, flooding the press along the train's route with professional, enticing publicity. Even without an invitation to participate and enjoy a preopening private tour, sheer intellectual curiosity would have drawn her to downtown Sacramento; original documents of such antiquity were not to be missed.

On March 19, the *Bee* reported that twelve thousand people were expected to view the exhibit during its twelve-hour window, with fifty thousand more gathering to view the train's exterior and participate in opening ceremonies. Many were impelled to be on-site for culmination of the foundation's Rededication Week programming, designed to engage different sectors of the community in citizenship activities in the days preceding the train's arrival. Each sector adopted its own schedule. In Sacramento, Freedom of Religion Day fell on Sunday, followed by consecutive days dedicated to women, veterans, industry, labor, and schools, finally arriving at Saturday's Freedom Train Day. Orchestras played Irving Berlin's "Freedom Train," composed in honor of the exhibition; men, women, and children recited a "freedom pledge" and either signed a "freedom scroll" on-site or mailed a signed pledge directly to the National Archives. Feverish postwar patriotism permeated every corner of the city. Thousands queued up on the morning of March 20; a mother and her nine-year-old-son heading the line arrived at 1:00 A.M. Warren and Cooledge kicked off public viewing hours with emotional testimony. Cooledge proclaimed, "The contents of the Freedom Train represent a heritage that keeps us from tyranny, protects us from the inequalities of dictatorships, and preserves for all of us the liberties we have come to accept as a matter of course."[20] Photographs taken from the platform attest to the diverse crowd, including countless Japanese Americans who had been incarcerated in internment camps not even a decade before. The liberties Cooledge claimed Americans had "come to accept as a matter of course" clearly did not extend to them.

A last-minute scheduling conflict arose for Stewart, so Marie invited Gladys Mankins (Maidu/Paiute) to come down and take her place.[21] A *Bee* reporter chronicled FIC's presence, which grew to eight individuals as the day progressed: "The group includes two women and a papoose, and all are dressed in authentic tribal clothing, from ornate feathered headgear to moccasins. They were almost continually in demand as picture subjects. They posed willingly and autographed souvenir programs right and left—another symbol of America's dramatic history." Arrayed in clothing supplied by Hathaway and SIM, they were stationed in front of the speakers' platform draped in stars and stripes.[22] All three men were decked out in spectacular headdresses, two with trailers nearly dragging the ground. The candid expression on Mankins's face as she inspects Archie McWhinney's headdress is priceless (figure 11). Much of the men's attire was making a second publicity appearance: Fuller now sported Tommy McWhinney's buckskin suit—no worse for his capitol run, while Tommy appeared in the vest his father had modeled on the prior occasion. Mankins and Potts wore buckskin dresses, and everyone exchanged shoes for moccasins. Pansy's son, Michael, was star of the show, tucked away in a Plateau-style cradleboard on his grandmother's back.

As the city hoped, FIC added unique but uncritical texture to the Freedom Train's Sacramento stop. Spectators were not really challenged to think about colonial legacies, but FIC benefited by laying a cornerstone from which to begin narrating a counter-history. It would be mid-1949 before this came to full fruition. They were biding their time, building relationships with city officials, playing—for now—by the rules. They understood that dressing up in buckskin and feathers tapped into the multiple romantic currencies affiliated with "generic Indians."[23] The movie industry exploited popular cultural fantasies of Native people as national patrimony while turning a blind eye to violent histories and legacies. Contemporary theme parks continued this practice as sites of frontier imagination and reenactment. The Cherokee actor "White Eagle," hired to inhabit a generic "American Indian" persona for Knott's Berry Farm, dressed in Plateau

Figure 11. FIC Freedom Train publicity appearance, Sacramento, 1948. *Left to right*: William Fuller, Tommy McWhinney, Archie McWhinney, Gladys Mankins, Marie Potts, and Potts's grandson Michael Marine. All are dressed in clothing loaned by Benjamin Hathaway, State Indian Museum curator.
Courtesy Marine family.

beadwork and Plains Indian elements. The material heritage of his own tribe held too little purchase on the scale of settler nostalgia and imagination for him to inhabit his Cherokee identity. Native people learned to exploit the objectifying gaze of Euro-Americans to make a living as craft demonstrators in museums, Wild West shows and theatrical pageants, expositions, county fairs, and national parks, a tradition well established in northern California by the 1920s and 1930s. "Tabuce," or Maggie Howard, wore buckskin to demonstrate weaving in Yosemite National Park, like Selena LaMarr at Lassen National Park and a youthful Mabel McKay, whom newspapers described as an "aged weaver" when she appeared at Hathaway's state capitol exhibit precursor to SIM.[24] FIC members were not the first California Natives to assemble odd pastiches of "regalia" from museum repositories, photographers' trunks, or private collections to bring sociopolitical and cultural concerns into a public spotlight.[25]

Images of ancestors clothed in the material trappings of other Native nations, or no actual nation, sometimes evoke disappointment among contemporary descendants.[26] Yet this speaks directly to the conditions of domination these generations navigated, including limited avenues to ply their cause. Some lacked ready access to their own material heritage or lacked the time and money to sit side by side with a tribal authority or to study examples and produce likenesses.[27] Ceremony was sometimes tucked away, or hidden in plain sight, in routine forms that kept it alive right under the nose of those who sought to suppress and outlaw it. This was the case with Kwagiutl carver Ellen Neel, who kept her family's heritable totem and mask carving rights and tradition alive, in small scale, by moving to the city and adapting them to a commercial, tourist market during the period when potlatching and related spiritual practices were outlawed by the Indian Act (1884–1951).[28] Colonization ravaged the processes by which intergenerational transmission of ceremony and regalia were handed down; the same was true for everyday objects whose ongoing manufacture was inhibited by lack of a land base, time, and access to materials. In the same way that some parents refused to teach children Native tongues, others shed all references to old ways so that offspring would not suffer racism and scorn.

The politics of self-presentation in the first half of the twentieth century served an exhausting long game. These generations endured the onslaught of assimilationist policy, yet like those who came before them, they continued to define and preserve tradition. Recovery of ceremony, language, and expressive culture emerged in swift and desperate strokes during some generations, only to be secreted away for quiet and thoughtful elaboration by another. Rends were mended with whatever knowledge and material was at hand. Over time, culture keepers always deem some strands worthy adherences to the spirit of tradition and others not. Plucked out and summarily discarded by one generation, they may be recovered and cherished by another that gazes with awe and recognition at creative adaptations enabling cultural persistence. The ghostly presence of colonization impales itself upon the long arc of Indigenous histories and traditions but does not obliterate them. Losses and scars are slowly woven over, embellished by the Native artists, intellectuals, healers, political leaders, and everyday people whose lives form a variegated tapestry of indigeneity. Disenfranchised from their land base in whole or part, California Indian people continued to darn and suture their worlds at mid-century. However pragmatic and pained these fixes may have been, they were exercises in continuity and power.

The "Problem" of Modernity

Stewart and Potts understood that they were being invited to a very specific and frustrating mise-en-scène. Several years later, an *Oakland Tribune* writer perfectly articulated what misfits they were in an article titled "Paleface Wants Wampum, Heap Big Squabble Results."[29] Collett, the paleface in question, was still trying to push through legislation allowing him to claim $8,100 from K-344's award as retroactive payment for so-called lobbying efforts. The writer reports that Collett's residence is a "cream-plastered wigwam he rents from San Francisco's Hotel Manx" and then explains, "Collett, an elderly balding man who identifies himself as the founder, executive representative, and sole paid employee of an organization called 'Indians of California, Inc.' sent out smoke signals to the Bay Area Indians for a tribal pow-wow in his hotel suite." The subheading "Still 'Warlike'" hints at the account to follow: "About 20 showed up, half of them representative of a rival outfit, 'the Federated Indians of California.' The group looked more like a gathering at a neighborhood PTA than the descendants of Native tribesmen. Two hours after the session began, the first verbal tomahawk flew through the air. It came from Mrs. Bertha Stewart."

In fact, they *were* PTA members. This was their problem. They were *not* tomahawk-carrying, wigwam-inhabiting people. They were modern people doing modern things. That they could do these things and also be Indian people simply defied settler comprehension. They prided themselves on progressive values, ran a professional organization, and founded a newspaper published by and for California Indians. They kept detailed financial ledgers and submitted them for monthly audits; made use of affidavits, notary publics, and parliamentary procedure; recorded and archived meeting minutes; reserved dance halls, bought newspaper advertising, and dealt with the musician's local to hire dance bands and orchestras. And yes, they also traded their pillbox hats, hosiery, and smart woolen suits for moccasins and buckskin dresses to make sure things stayed on course for them in Washington. It was not enough to simply gesture toward their ancestral origins by reference to nonratified treaties and ICC; they had to shoehorn themselves into the "savage slot" ascribed them by the American imaginary.[30] And they were just getting started.

In late March 1948, Kitty sent press releases and the now iconic photograph from their recent Freedom Train appearance to newspapers across the state. Two of five FIC representatives were from the Plumas–Lassen area, so the *Chester Progressive* and *Lassen Advocate* predictably published the story. This was no stroke of luck. FIC knew this would advance their membership and credibility in a location Collett worked religiously.[31] On March 29, Fuller and Potts were up at Bald Rock, in Butte County, at Victor Brown's invitation. They explained FIC's land claims work to Maidu people and posed for photographs in SIM clothing.[32] Back in Sacramento, Marie ordered one hundred prints of their Freedom Train publicity photo, an investment of twenty-five dollars. The chapter intended to sell the prints for fifty cents apiece for the delegate fund. Picking them up on April 10, Marie headed right for the monthly benefit dance. The next day she recorded in the cash ledger proceeds from sale of thirty-nine photographs. This brief publicity stunt and Potts's decision to order and sell the photographic reproductions generated much-needed publicity and revenue, and the impression among many people today that FIC members wore this garb as their own. They did not; they were playing, with unrivaled success, to settler colonial fantasies.

Two days later Walter Woehlke, head of the California Indian Agency in downtown Sacramento, wrote an esteemed Berkeley historian. "My dear Professor Bolton," he began,

> May I suggest, unofficially, that the Film Advisory Board of the California Centennial Commission consider depicting the important though very passive role the Indians played in the colonization of California since 1769? . . . The books on the Donner party, involving the death of some thirty white persons, would fill a five-foot shelf. Some 40,000 to 50,000 California Indians died by bullet, knife, starvation, and disease in the decade from 1849 to 1859. If I am suggesting too sour a note for the Centennial celebrating, let's forget it.[33]

Woehlke had a front-row seat on FIC. Members were dressing in buckskin one week and filing into his office the next to hash out land claims issues and heirship paperwork and to comment on legislation that would abolish the BIA and U.S. treaty obligations right along with it. Gold rush and statehood centennials loomed over the next two years, and Woehlke was already dyspeptic over hagiographic treatments of John Sutter and early settlers. His suggestion that Native experiences of colonization ought to be truthfully dramatized in a series of official centennial documentaries was radical for its time.

Veteran Organizations Come Calling

Invitations flowed. The California chapter of the Grand Army of the Republic, a Civil War veterans' organization, was holding its annual encampment in Sacramento. It hoped FIC might send "Indian dancers" to its Grand Ball at Memorial Auditorium on May 20, where Warren and Cooledge were slated to speak.[34] Days later an invitation for Sacramento's Memorial Day Parade arrived. The *Bee* announced FIC's May 9 vote to accept it, along with an invitation from Louis Rahlin of the VFW Affiliated Council to participate in a Flag Day pageant at Sacramento Junior College's Hughes Stadium.[35]

FIC's Memorial Day float nudged the public toward recognizing California Indian people's wartime contributions and contemporaneity by juxtaposing American Indian tradition and modernity "arranged in two units on a 16-foot flatbed truck covered with banners, evergreens, and flowers. The theme represented Indians honoring the dead as it was done a century ago and as it is done today." The traditional scene featured a father grieving his warrior son alongside his daughter-in-law and grandchild. A war bonnet symbolized the fallen son. A soldier, sailor, and marine stood watch in the counterpart. Instead of a war bonnet, there was a white cross and a flag-draped coffin associated with Christian military burials. Lest the symbolism be too subtle, signs labeled each vignette: "1848—In Memory" and "1948—Honoring a Lost Comrade." The *Smoke Signal* reported that the entry was the talk of the parade.[36]

"Real Indians" at the Flag Day Pageant

Two weeks later, the Sacramento chapter paraded in nearby Folsom at a centennial event brought to its attention by an FIC patron who was familiar to *Smoke Signal* readers: "Mrs. Richard Codman spoke on the possibilities of taking part in a celebration in Folsom sometime this spring. She also introduced Mr. Rollins [sic], who spoke on the importance of publicity and the possibilities of having speakers talk before clubs, lodges, and other organizations."[37] Meeting minutes were more candid: "Mrs. Codman informed the organization that a celebration was being held in Folsom and that they wanted some real Indians to take part."[38]

"Real Indians" aptly named their condition. Folsom's parade was the day before the big Flag Day pageant, so the Sacramento chapter shifted into high gear to meet these two consecutive commitments. Its float "portrayed a group of Indians in costume, which was led by the colorful banner of the FIC and the American Flag." The eight thousand spectators who turned out to see "real Indians" caught a glimpse of more than a few Hukespem and Mariah descendants, including Pansy, Jeanne's son Marvin Potts, and Josephine's children, Aglaee, Claire, Bobby, and Nancy DuFresne, who came down from Virginia City. Marie and Kitty would have been there, but they were busy with FIC's monthly meeting in downtown Sacramento. Florence Beck, along with "Sunny," "Sissie," and mother Elizabeth Paddy, helped populate the float. Lawrence Burcell, from Fort Jones, carried FIC's banner, and Marjorie Olsen of San Francisco was color bearer.[39] It was July before the chapter learned it had won honorable mention. By then the chapter had two other awards.[40] Investment in an American flag, FIC banner, and set of side panels bearing the organization name paid dividends during these centennial years, when making its presence known and competing for cash awards funneled money into its treasury and social capital into the organization.

The Hughes Stadium Flag Day pageant was slated for newsreel coverage. Fuller had a place of honor on the VIP platform; others acted in a dramatic "tableau depicting the Indians in natural surroundings raising 'Old Glory,'" a role Rahlin scripted: "You are the original Americans and should be honored with the principal part on this great occasion."[41] Urging FIC members to show up, the *Smoke Signal* intoned, "Remember the date June 13 has been set for the next FIC meeting. Keep this date in mind and make plans to attend. Watch 'The Indians at Work.'"[42] This was pure Potts, punning on the name of John Collier's Indian Office publication.

FIC officer and delegate ranks swelled with world war veterans and defense industry employees, including Kitty. Patriotism and pride suffused their work. *Smoke Signal* coverage of the Flag Day pageant brimmed with this spirit of loyalty to "our great American Flag." Fuller led a procession of delegates, including Charles Putt, Mary Wright, Alfred Lorenzo, Lela Dunlap, Irma Bahnsen, Marjorie Olsen, Florence Beck, Marvin Potts, and Harrison Williams, as well as Potts and Stewart.[43] Patriotism did not compromise their intelligence: "Many on-lookers for the first time saw real 'Injuns' with feathers, and to their surprise they all spoke English fluently."[44]

1948 Indian Day Dance—Making California Indians Visible

Agreeing to show up and be "real Indians" directly challenged settler predilections for "playing Indian," a well-documented and institutionalized U.S. pastime.[45] The Sacramento chapter was not above renting the Improved Order of the Red Men's Hall for benefit dances, and members no doubt chuckled about raising funds for their land claims case in a fraternal hall dedicated to the amusing concept of an "improved" version of themselves.[46] Dances offered private spaces to be Native in the uncensored ways that are key to meaningful resistance because they provided places to assert autonomy and dignity.[47] The *Smoke Signal* certainly provided a discursive space for this, but it was benefit dances that served this purpose in the most literal sense—that is, until Indian Day got off the ground.

In September 1948, the Sacramento chapter hosted an Indian Day Dance at Governor's Hall on the grounds of the state fair. It was here that attention to revivifying and celebrating California's distinct tribal nations and traditions first emerged in the city. Anticipation mounted in August, and by September it was embodied in an intriguing front-page *Smoke Signal* illustration. A California Indian, so identified by the inscription on his rawhide shield, stretches his left arm eastward, in a salute beyond the rolling hills. There Lady Liberty, illuminated by the rising sun behind, holds a torch high in her right hand, mirroring the California Indian's gesture. Hand-printed lettering above captures FIC's sense of optimism: "Indian Day Marks New Era for California Indians." The lead column, "FIC Sponsors Indian Day Dance," followed below. They were rolling out the red carpet: "Buster Peart's twelve-piece orchestra will furnish the music for your dancing pleasure." John Hill, a Mission Indian Sacramento resident, and Marjorie Olsen, a young Pomo from San Francisco, planned solo and paired dances for intermission, and "several different groups are expected to present their tribal dances." Elaboration was offered in "Via the Grapevine":

> The Yurok Tribal Organization are very much interested in the Indian Day program and will no doubt come prepared with an outstanding number for the program. The Smith River Tribe is busy rehearsing one of their old-time ceremonial dances which has been witnessed but once in the past thirty years, and this may be the last time the dance will ever be performed in public. Everyone who can should attend the Indian Day program to see this dance.[48]

Injun Louie just happened to be hanging out in front of his teepee on the same acreage. Clutching a long microphone stand firmly planted in a box laughably labeled "soap," he holds forth in an earnest effort to lure members to Sacramento for the September 25 Indian Day Dance. Little Aloyitious sits at Louie's feet banging a drum. "Boom, Boom" rings the musical score carried aloft by two half notes. "Whoop-um up Aloyitious. Us gotta practice for Injun Day program in Sacramento City. Make-um heap big slam-bang good Injun jive."

An array of personal notices dotted the same page: the former president of the Pomo Athletic Club was now "making local history" managing the All-Indian Nine; the all-girls team on Banning home ground featured two Sherman alums; the Upper Lake Pomo were holding an FIC benefit dance on Collett's old collecting grounds—imagine his disappointment; Ora Evans of Susanville and Willie Spring of Alturas had passed; two new California Indian babies had been born, a bouncing boy and a sweet little girl. Sandwiched there, between the asterisks, was another inducement to join them: "If you want to meet old friends, schoolmates and classmates, you will find them at the Indian Day Dances. Carlisle, Haskell, Chemawa, Sherman and other will be represented."[49]

Stewart was Indian Day Dance committee chair and may have stretched the truth about the Tolowa dance possibly being their last, but ceremonies were in danger.[50] Ancestral songs and dances, long suppressed by missionaries and Indian Office policy, were threatened by the passing of elders who knew them firsthand. Even those with a collective land base and control over sacred sites knew that cultural tradition was perched on a precipice. It was being coaxed back to safety in some quarters, even as support for termination in others threatened the existence of tribal nations. Like many California Indians, Stewart was initially taken in by propaganda that Congress and the BIA used to convince Indian people to give up their lands and sovereignty, but loyalty to her people was never in question. Her correspondence with DNIWA reveals how exhausting it was to stage FIC publicity appearances while simultaneously acquiring resources, such as surplus housing and building materials, for Smith River tribal members. She worked overtime for improved housing, water, and sanitation while also pushing land claims forward. Writing DNIWA president Joseph Hostler in August, she reported that all attorney contracts were approved: FIC's with John Preston, Collett's group with Ernest Wilkinson, and CCI's (still called the Bay Area group), with Reginald Foster. Each now awaited word on whether they would count as an "identifiable group," terminology used along with "band" and "tribe" in ICCA. She told Hostler that Baker and several FIC delegates had recently met with Preston in Los Angeles and remarked how "lucky they were to have attorneys who considered the wishes of their client."[51] Finally she turned to Indian Day, explaining that they had scrapped plans for a daylong event in favor of a social dance that would feature tribal dances at intermission; she would "hate to see Smith River left out," telling them that FIC could cover room and board for three.

A formal and fairly detailed response to FIC's Indian Day Dance invitation came from DNIWA officer Sadie Gorbet. DNIWA met to discuss the matter. Sending dancers and singers was expensive, and as FIC was charging admission, DNIWA wanted FIC to cover gas. Sam Lopez argued that given the admission charges, dancers should be splitting proceeds with DNIWA's treasury; some would also be losing a day of work. Eventually they acknowledged that this was a fund-raiser. If FIC paid lodging and gas, they would come. Once Stewart confirmed, they would begin organizing a crew of singers and dancers, having already decided that at least eight, but no more than ten, should perform. Stewart was pleased and wrote multiple times, asking them to verify dates of arrival. Could they come a day early and be part of a parade? Was Robert Spott still bringing a Yurok group? Word was elusive. Competitive pride in ancestral tradition was mixed with fund-raising worries, "We are playing up the idea that the Smith River tribal dance may never be seen in public again so if they want to see it they will need to come to the program." The *Bee* wanted photos and program details. "The white people are sure interested in the program," Stewart coaxed. FIC certainly needed them to be. The Sacramento Musician's Union insisted that nothing short of a twelve-piece orchestra was suitable for Governor's Hall, "So, we shall have good music and plenty of it."[52] Two days later, anxious for confirmation, she exclaimed, "Boy! Even the Indians are excited about seeing the Smith River tribal dance." She could supply an extra Smith River costume from the museum or "a beautiful girl to go with the costume . . . after all, it might be the last dance (tribal) the Smith River Indians will ever put on and we can't let it be anything but the best."[53] Neither group came. Gas was being rationed due to an oil workers' strike; the dancers could not risk being stranded along the highway."[54]

The Tolowa dancers' absence tightened the focus on nearby tribal communities such as Auburn, Ione, Tuolumne, and Wilton, where traditional song, dance, and foodways were alive and reminded Potts of home. The dance opened with a grand march. Hill and Olsen danced at intermission. Ramona Burris played the piano, while Pansy, Kitty, and Olsen performed a pantomime of "Indian Love Call." Youngsters Sonny Paddy, Patricia Hurtado, and Larry Marine performed the Maidu Harvest Dance. Food was plentiful—"hot dogs, coffee, pop, and homemade cake"—but the real star was acorn soup courtesy of Mr. and Mrs. Henry Miller of Ione. Door prizes included a beaded belt and a Paiute baby basket.[55] Indian Day was barely over before Potts was planning for next year. Meanwhile, she had a full calendar of publicity appearances to organize.

'49ers Days and the Fair Oaks Fiesta

In 1949 Potts developed a close working relationship with Winnifred Codman, whose FIC patronage began out of a desire to quash Collett but was sustained by a sincere belief that Native California people had been dealt a dirty hand by the state and federal governments. Within the limits of her own paternalism, Codman supported an equitable remedy to this legacy of dishonesty and threw herself wholeheartedly into FIC's cause. Gladly accepting her mentorship and lead, Potts very quickly learned that she had met her match in Codman.

FIC entered 1949 worried about finances. Treasurer Miller reported a beginning balance of $149.06, although donations from members and regional chapters brought them solidly into the black by February's meeting, with a balance of $683.98.[56] Publicity was proving to be expensive. Trucks for floats were typically donated or borrowed, but transportation and parade entry fees were costly. Codman had long urged FIC to be more entrepreneurial, encouraging them as early as May 1948 to write the California State Automobile Association for a calendar of centennial events they could capitalize on. That month she mailed Stewart her March 1948 *Motorland*, where she had starred folk dance festivals, a sportsman's show in Oakland, Calaveras County's Jumping Frog Jubilee, and the Mountain Play in Mount Tamalpais. "Work in Indians??" she asked.[57] Drawing on decades of DAR and BIA experience, she wrapped a long note around the margins on the opposite page, suggesting they find California Indians to print recent publicity photographs: "Cost about 1 cent apiece that way, for postcard size prints, commercial price from 6 cents to 8 cents—W.R.C." Having illustrated countless DAR lectures with fieldwork photographs, she knew they would sell. The following year, Codman materialized this vision.

In March 1949 Codman invited FIC to participate in her hometown's Fair Oaks Centennial Fiesta, May 20–22. Letters flew between 2727 Santa Clara Way and Codman's three homes in Fair Oaks, Michigan Bluff, and South Lake Tahoe. Carbon-copying Potts and Fuller on all correspondence between herself and the fiesta committee, she finally solicited San Francisco's Kodak Studio to donate photographic postcards for FIC to vend. She appealed to the Pyramid Lake Women's Club and the manager of Carson Trading Post at Stewart Indian School for objects that FIC could sell, suggesting beaded tie slides, small baskets, and "any other small trinkets that would sell for from 50 cents to two or three dollars." She apparently made the same request of Pomo contacts; her Carson Trading Post letter reads, "The enclosed carbon copy of a letter I wrote to a famous Indian singer, William Graves, explains what we have in mind."[58] Writing the former Tuolumne County supervisor, whom she knew from her "Indian Service Work," she complimented their centennial booklet and asked him to send one to Fair Oaks centennial chairman Bob Massey. Finally, "Would you like to have Indians in your parade and an Indian concession during the Centennial? They are coming here for ours, and we hope they can make some money in the concession for their claims case expenses. They will have Indian singers and dancers in a stockade for admission charges, and also sell small Indian articles."[59]

In a feverish May 1 letter, Codman spilled out her thoughts regarding their immediate prospects at Fair Oaks and beyond. She had sent "postals to several places where they are going to have Centennials—Folsom, Auburn and Sonora. You might have a concession there also, as their dates are not conflicting—and since you have the set-up, make more money than just in one. Nearby Indians could maybe help out—as in Tuolumne. . . . Get enough postcard pictures for all the Centennials—they will come in handy"[60] Massey, the fiesta chairman, wanted to open the event with an Indian runner. Could they find some "young chap" to carry the FIC banner along with that of the fiesta? Suggesting unbleached muslin for posters an artist was painting for FIC, she cited prices and sources for fabric, explaining that they would more easily attach to the "stockade," or booth. "Good for decoration," she added, "would be an acorn soup setup—mortar, raw acorns, flour and finished soup in a jar, the baskets, stirring spoon and rocks in a cooking basket." They could use photographs from her DAR fieldwork—just "pin them on the inside of the canvas, along with baskets." She would handle publicity for the *Sacramento Bee, Sacramento Union*, and foothill newspapers. Over at 2727 Santa Clara Way, Potts's head must have been spinning.

Next Codman drafted an impassioned essay for FIC to distribute: "Centennial Celebrations in California and the History of the California Indians from 1850–1949: One Hundred Years of Waiting for Justice." A long condemnation masqueraded as a subtitle: "Can a Centennial in California be celebrated on stolen ground? It couldn't happen here? Read on, and let us see." Reviewing colonial violence and empty treaty promises for three single-spaced pages, she berated the U.S. government and chastised California pioneers. Moving on to CIJA's inadequacies and the loophole allowing its paltry court of claims award to be held "in trust," she ended: "Remember, we STILL owe them 0) million dollars, [the] balance due them for their rights of occupancy, and we celebrate "our" Centennial of the 1850 generation of squatters and claim-jumpers who stole this beautiful land of theirs, California. Some of us are descendants of those squatters and claim-jumpers. Let us try to right this century-long wrong by helping our Indian fellow citizens to recover what belonged to their ancestors—its value in our money."[61]

In early May she wrote Potts from Michigan Bluff. Enclosing her essay for mimeographing, she suggested that Potts add her former DAR titles to clarify that it was authored by a settler descendant, believing this would sway more minds. She was headed back to Fair Oaks by way of Lake Tahoe—"a long way around," she admitted, "but I want to get that rabbit blanket for display in your booth."[62]

The Fair Oaks Fiesta Committee issued a press release in mid-May. It ran under Bob Massey's name but was clearly Codman's work:

BIG INDIAN SHOW AT FAIR OAKS FIESTA. An Indian runner from Tuolumne will open the three-day Fair Oaks Centennial Fiesta when he arrives at the American River town at 10 A.M. next Friday morning. During the three-day Fiesta there will be a continuous Indian show and encampment. Indians, both children and adults, will be there in authentic ceremonial costumes, will display native arts and crafts, and demonstrate the tribal dances of the Tuolumne, Maidu, and Pomo Indians. The Maidu dances will be performed by a group of boys from Susanville, in Lassen County, who learned them from their grandmother. The Indian encampment has been arranged by Chief William Fuller of Tuolumne, president of the Federated Indians of California. The University of California Anthropology Department is expected to send graduate students to the Fair Oaks Fiesta, as they usually do when Pomo ceremonials are given in Lake County. Only 24,000 Indians are left in California, out of an estimated population of 200,000 a century ago.[63]

The local paper gave it front page billing: "Thousands Expected for Big Celebration."[64]

The promised "Indian runner" was Potts's eight-year-old grandson Larry Marine. Two younger boys, Fuller's great-grandson, Robert Cox, and Eugene Paddy, from Sacramento, accompanied him. Shirtless, they wore moccasins and fringed loincloths over shorts.[65] Potts described FIC's fiesta concession in the *Smoke Signal*. The centerpiece was an exhibit titled "The acorn from 'nuts to soup,'" with samples for tasting. A glimpse of natural sarcasm peeks through Potts's affable publicity agent veneer in reference to frustrating demands made of "real" Indians: "The dancers were given first aide by the Red Cross for blistered feet—*not from dancing but from parading on the hot pavement in their bare feet.*"[66] After hurling this one small salvo, she thanked Bob Massey for loaning them booth construction materials from the family orchard business and George Frazier for hosting their float on his flatbed truck. She sent thank-you letters to both men and to the editor of the *San Juan Record*, which gave them bountiful publicity. Massey and Frazier were treated to a bit of her ancestral tongue: "In the language of the Maidu tribe the translation of 'thank you' is 'yes, you have done so unto me.' (Maidu) *Cä äh tip nikee.*"[67]

Privately, Potts was increasingly exasperated by all this centennial ballyhoo. Adjacent to her *Smoke Signal* fiesta coverage, she asked, "What are we Celebrating? While the Californians are celebrating the Centennial of their admission into the Union, the Indians of California, in much puzzlement, are celebrating with them." Louie makes a timely appearance below. Holding out the "Treaty of 1852" to Uncle Sam, who strokes his beard in bewilderment, Louie asks pointedly, "Remember this, Uncle?"[68]

Three weeks later they were at it again at Auburn's centennial celebration, a three-day "Gold Rush Revival" with parade and concessions. Auburn Lumber Company donated booth materials; Fuller loaned baskets for display; Sacramento, Colfax, Weimar, and Auburn Natives demonstrated dancing; and, most importantly, FIC won "Best Individual Float" and a first-place trophy.[69] Potts thanked organizers and patrons for assisting. Unfailing polite, she expressed gratitude for "courtesies" and for proving that "the Indians of California do have a lot of friends." In correspondence with fellow editors, whom she knew were powerful gatekeepers and potential allies, she summarized contributions from individuals, companies, and community organizations. Her letter to the *Auburn Journal* reveals that she was attuned to its possible publication and the chance to clarify that they were not playing "cowboys and Indians": "The Federated Indians, through their association with the Auburn Gold Show Centennial have found that they have many friends who are willing to help them in their struggle for justice."[70]

Potts was spent by mid-June, but summer churned on. The Sacramento chapter took third place and a cash award in its Oak Park neighborhood Fourth of July parade. The next month, Potts was busy soliciting volunteers, exhibits, and costumes for the city of Roseville's centennial celebration.[71] Her *Smoke Signal* coverage extended special thanks to Reginald George for loaning baskets. Riding in "full regalia," he was accompanied by "Mrs. Irma G. Bahnsen of San Francisco and Shasta County, Mr. and Mrs. Clarence Taylor of San Francisco, Mrs. Marie Potts, Pansy Marine, and ALL her grandchildren. The float was decked with redwood boughs, corn stalks, 1 buck, 1 squaw, and a litter of papooses."[72] Humor continued to lift her up.

1949 Indian Day Picnic

Indian Day fell on September 24. After a vote at the August meeting to celebrate it with a picnic and dance at Oak Park, planning was turned over to the already busy Potts, who was long primed for another Indian Day.[73] Playful sarcasm enlivened her *Smoke Signal* announcement. She reminisced about traditional activities such as "old Indian football." Surely some "old-timers" could help coach and revive it, as "we would like to see as many of the old contest games as possible." Footraces were also on her mind. "In the old days women didn't wear spike heels and were always ready to take part. 'Ladies' bring your running shoes. This goes for the men, too. The first to grab the prize at the goal was the winner. Sometimes the first runner would miss the prize and the second runner got it; so you had to be good at running and grabbing." How about hand game? "Don't forget to bring your 'bones and stakes,' we'll be pulling for you." Leaving nothing to chance: "What's an Indian celebration without acorn soup?" Speaking of traditional food, "How about some of our sharp-eyed, sharp-shooting young bucks bringing in some 'buck-meat'? I don't mean shooting each other as we so often hear about in the papers these days during deer season, but wouldn't good old venison taste pretty good with acorn soup?" Injun Louie had to get in on this act: "Injun Louie so busy. Shine um up shoes for Indian Day. September 24, 1949. Jus aint no time to pose for picture." Indeed, the single-frame cartoon carries his words but no visage.[74]

Cooledge opened the day, the newly formed all-Indian VFW post's color guard marched, and FIC's Mother Lode Council sold twenty-five-cent buttons commemorating the occasion. A sense of exuberance pervades Potts's front-page recap. From Ione, the Millers brought their trademark acorn soup and biscuits: "They seem to be the only natives who haven't forgotten how to pick, store and prepare acorn. The rest of us natives just remember how to eat it." Stewart won the footrace in the grandmothers' division and Marvin Potts in the boys'. Nostalgic for the big times of her youth, Marie lamented that everyone forgot to bring bones: "This is one of the games that has always been the biggest attraction at all Indian

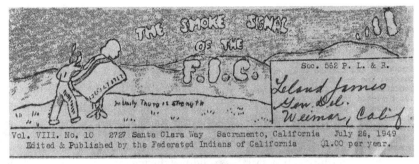

Figure 12. *Smoke Signal* masthead, July 26, 1949.
Courtesy of the author.

gatherings and it seems a shame that we do not keep this game alive." The Upper Lake Konocti Arrowhead Athletic Girl's Club challenged the men to softball. A dance group was "the main event" for Potts, who encouraged other groups and individuals to participate next time. The evening's entertainment was an amateur talent show, with admission fees going to the delegate fund. There were only two impromptu entrants. Betty Treppa twirled to Beryl Potts playing the drum. "The other entrant was the 'old gray mare in brown,' [Pansy] Marine as the forelegs and her mother as the horse's—hind legs."[75] She had come prepared with guest registers. One for boarding school alumni featured separate pages for Chilocco, Carson, Chemawa, Stewart, and Carlisle, with columns for years attended, name, and current address. She was actively archiving Native history, building political networks, and making Native urban space. The 1948 and 1949 Indian Day gatherings mark the earliest expressions of Native community-building in the city, but even Indian centennial appearances watered fertile seeds that blossomed into platforms for recuperating traditions suppressed by assimilation.[76]

Strategist and Bricoleur

At mid-century, FIC exploited settler colonial nostalgia by accepting invitations from a host of local and regional organizations that wanted "real Indians" at their historical and patriotic spectacles. FIC made these appearances serve their own ends, as "real" California Indians demanding compensation for stolen ancestral lands. Yet Potts's political investment in this work, as with the *Smoke Signal*, encompassed something far more lasting and powerful than monetary compensation. She was building and mobilizing Native networks on behalf of a cultural recovery movement yet to be envisioned and articulated as such. Her organizational skills and leadership qualities took center stage as she rallied family, friends—both Native and white—the mainstream press, and local businesses to her cause. She may have been "playing Indian" in front of the camera, but behind the scenes she was dropping Maidu language into her thank-you letters, reminiscing in the *Smoke Signal* about the Native sports and foodways of her youth, and exploiting Indian Day to strengthen bonds between herself and regional Indigenous communities.

Potts's friendship with Stewart was solidified during these years of rapid-fire publicity appearances and Indian Day celebrations, but she was also developing a relationship of mutual respect with Codman. Contemporaries, the two discovered common ground despite their obvious differences. Though married women, they were actively carving out independent lives and identities—Codman by sheer force of personality and Potts by necessity and design. Between the *Smoke Signal* and organizing FIC publicity appearances, it is easy to imagine that Potts had plumbed the depths of her creative talents and intellectual ambitions. As the next chapter shows, this was hardly the case.

California Indian Curator at the State Fair

> Everything we show comes from the homes of the Indian people
> and sometimes I borrow from my white friends when I can't find
> it any other way. Most of our Indian things have been sold to white
> collectors a long time ago.
>
> —*Marie Potts, 1952*

On March 6, 1950, the Marin County Board of Supervisors convened to take up its weekly business. On the agenda was an appeal from Potts, which began, "Dear Sirs: The Federated Indians of California, a non-profit organization, are sponsoring an all California Indian exhibit at the 1950 State Fair. This new exhibit will be in the Education Department and we plan to display art, and crafts, both old and modern, of every tribe of California, some of which are in your county. This is the first time in the history of California for an exhibit of this kind to be sponsored and planned by the Indians of this state."

The board sent a terse response that afternoon, "Gentlemen: Your letter of March 1, re: the above captioned subject was read at a regular meeting of the Board of Supervisors held this date. Please be advised that the Board has no legal authority to contribute to activities as outlined, so they are unable to comply with your request."[1]

The following morning, San Rafael's *Daily Independent* published a more accurate appraisal of the supervisors' meeting. The headline read, "Ain't No Indians in Marin, so County Won't Help Pay for State Fair Exhibit." The unattributed column dripped with sarcasm: "Marin county has no Indians, Marin county has nothing to offer in the way of an Indian exhibit at the coming state fair, . . . 'No Indians here,' said Supervisor James Kehoe of Inverness. 'We got nothing to display,' said Supervisor William Barr of San Rafael. 'It's against our policy,' opined Board Chairman Fred Bagshaw."

If the wholesale rebuff was based on historical ignorance versus discrimination, then the author's closing salvo hit its intended mark: "Actually, there were some 30 tribes of Indians in Marin when white men first set foot here. At its height, the San Rafael Mission hosted some 3,000 Indians. A reservation was established for them near Nicasio. The reservation went out of existence shortly after California became a part of the U.S.A."[2]

Allusion to this 1835 Mexican land grant was apropos as California entered its third and final centennial year. After American conquest and statehood in 1850, the Native population that once sheltered and labored on Rancho Nicasio met a now familiar fate: expulsion.[3] Today, travelers headed north on Highway 101 encounter the Lucas Valley Road exit just a few miles beyond San Rafael. Wending its way northwest for some twenty miles, this bucolic stretch leads to the tiny, unincorporated village of Nicasio. Home to George Lucas's Skywalker Ranch, this is Coast Miwok country from time immemorial.[4] Now—as in 1950—enormous stakes drive the ceaseless labor of historical forgetting.

Potts was not dissuaded. Her extraordinary work curating the 1950 state fair exhibit produced a bounty of correspondence—formal and polite letters, pleading letters, frantic and frustrated letters, confident letters, letters to whites, letters to California Indian people, and letters about her disappointment in one, the other, or both. Potts published calls for financial donations, object loans, and building materials in the *Smoke Signal*, but it was the missives she pounded out in multiple carbon copies on her little Underwood typewriter between January and August 1950 that brought this award-winning exhibit to fruition. Things were touch and go in the weeks leading up to the August 31 opening of FIC's All-California Indian Exhibit as Potts scrambled to secure objects, funding, and labor, but her hard work paid off. The inaugural exhibit was so popular among fairgoers and Native people alike that it was reprised for many years to come.

The All-California Indian Exhibit

Potts's pathbreaking curatorial work emerged from Codman's patronage. The 1949 Fair Oaks Fiesta was barely over when she dashed off a letter to Earl Warren's secretary, Helen McGregor. Opening with small talk, she reminded her that Warren had smoked with FIC at Sutter's Fort. She then moved on to "Judge Fred Baker (an old friend of the Governor's and yours) who is in Washington taking care of their claims case. How about squeezing them in a booth free of charge to them at the State Fair?"[5] McGregor routed the query to E. P. Green, head of the California State Agricultural Society. He agreed to meet, but an inter-office memorandum revealed "considerable doubt in his mind as to whether such a booth could even make expenses at the State Fair." It is unclear whether Codman managed a meeting. Back and forth between homes that July, she often left one place for the other, only to discover that missed correspondence had been forwarded to the house just departed.[6] Green's letter caught up to her in Forest Hill. She sent word to Fuller and Potts, but the timing was off.[7] FIC and Potts were exhausted, even if Codman was not. When the subject of a 1950 fair exhibit surfaced at November's meeting, it was tabled until officers were elected the next month. Potts was the sole nominee for publicity chair. She was already a hard act to follow and too busy executing the demanding duties of her office to attract intelligent competition.

The December 1949 *Smoke Signal* announced, "For the first time in California History, the California Indians are going to put on an ALL Indian exhibit at the California 1950 State Fair. This project is not for the Federated Indians alone, but ALL California Indians." A January front-page notice aimed to drum up interest and exhibit materials: "To date the response has been very slow, so let's all take inventory and find what we can contribute toward the display. The success of this project depends on *YOU*."[8] Worried when no one seemed to be coming forward, Potts, Kitty and Kesner Flores conferred with BIA area director James Stewart about the possibility of borrowing some California Indian dioramas. According to Kitty and Kesner, they were sitting in storage down in Bealer Hall at Sherman Institute. Writing Superintendent Myrthus Evans to see if they were available, Stewart also inquired about any California Indian arts and crafts FIC might borrow. In late January, they learned the dioramas were too deteriorated; they would have to look elsewhere.[9]

By March 1, Potts had a concept in mind. Rolling a mimeograph stencil into the typewriter, she entered a partial address: "County Board of Supervisors." Explaining the group's nonprofit status and financial challenges, she shrewdly asserted, "[S]ince the Indians of California are from every county, we felt certain that the counties would stand behind us in this most worthwhile project." Assuring supervisors that FIC and county Indians would be grateful for their generosity, she added, "We would also appreciate any information as to Indian leaders of your county that we might contact for exhibit material." Mimeographing multiple copies, she rolled each one back into the typewriter to enter county names and street addresses, signed all fifty-eight, and mailed them off.

Counties wrote back with every imaginable response. None was as curt and dismissive as Marin, but ambivalence and faint praise were in strong supply: "As far as we know, there are no Indians in Solano County; but the Board has directed that your communication be delivered to the several tribes and councils in the County."[10] It is difficult to imagine a more contradictory statement. From southern California came a lament about lack of funds or individuals to whom the letter might be forwarded, since there were "very few native Indians in Ventura County."[11] Alameda waited until late May to reply, not wanting to overlook any opportunity for "constructive publicity in the event that there were any Indians within the confines of ALAMEDA COUNTY." Moreover, "A very careful survey was made throughout the County to ascertain whether or not there were any remaining members of the old 'DIGGER TRIBE' who at one time inhabited an area in Southern Alameda County. Talking to residents in the area of Pleasanton and Sunol, no trace of any Indians could be found."[12] Were it not for Mendocino, the effort would have been a dismal failure. Deputy Clerk Edith Beck passed along the supervisors' decision:

> They directed the preparation of a county warrant for $100.00 towards the project which will be sent to you on April 3, the next allowance date. Mrs. Elsie Allen, of Ukiah, is one of our leading Indian citizens and it is suggested you consult her for material for your display as she has quite a lot of experience in this sort of thing, taking charge of local displays at county and district fairs, etc., and would know what would be required.[13]

Alice Ward, Ukiah Health Center's Indian field service nurse, also wrote. The Pomo Indian Women's Club was interested and would discuss the project at its next meeting.[14] Stanislaus County's letter ended up in the hands of Alton E. Wilder. Writing on his company stationary, Wilder Printing, he told Potts that he had read her letter with "much interest."[15] After three weeks of disappointing trips to the mailbox, Potts was primed for the next line: "Having once been chairman of the publicity for a convention of the California State Horsemen's Association, may I offer my condolences." Enthusiastic nonetheless, he strategized how Potts could gain county support.[16] Though she was frustrated with fund-raising, her network of statewide contacts was growing exponentially.

Sacramento County should have been the first to donate, but Potts's letter was shuffled along to County Manager Charles Deterding, who submitted it for *Bee* publication. Codman saw this and wrote Deterding a personal appeal:

I hope very much that Sacramento County can see its way clear to helping this very fine group of Indians in their efforts to do something for all the California Indians. Indians are colorful—and what is done to help them to help themselves will be repaid by the interest shown by the public in their exhibit—and so in other exhibits—at the State Fair. I recall years ago, one of my good friends who also does volunteer Indian work promoted for the Mendocino County exhibit an old Indian woman from Covelo who stayed in the booth all the time, weaving baskets—almost a lost art among California Indians. It is an art in the truest sense of the word, for the California Indians baskets are considered by scientists to be the finest examples of basketry in the world.[17]

Leaving no angle unworked, she ended, "I helped them organize in 1946—Bertha Stewart, their Secretary, is an old friend of mine, and she stayed here with us for about six weeks during that time. From a beginning of about thirty Indian leaders, their Federation has grown to about 5000 members.[18] Ringing the margin of a blind carbon copy was a hastily scribbled note: "Mrs. Potts: Now go after them again—you might get some money. How about sending a copy of the History plus a follow-up letter to the Boards of Supervisors? W. R. C."[19]

Exhibiting the "Progress of California Indians"

The 1950 state fair was billed as "California's 100th Birthday Party."[20] Fair officials were glad FIC could join the party. They knew that "Indians" epitomized history to settler descendants in a way that denim- and calico-clad "pioneers" bent over antique mining sluices and cast-iron kettles could never achieve. Codman's own language, "Indians are colorful," invoked this stale imaginary. Tired of playing this foil, Potts wanted to disrupt this narrative and show California Indian people as coeval. Finally she had sufficient autonomy and a publicity venue where she could challenge a settler colonial consciousness that positioned Indigenous society as counterpoint to the present.[21] California Natives were part of the social landscape in the 1850s, but so were they part of it in 1950. She settled on a theme that dovetailed with the fair's historical focus without imprisoning Native people in tintypes and sepia-tone time warps. Exhibiting the "Progress of California Indians" through "arts and crafts, both old and modern," allowed her to foreground contemporaneity. Superficial readings of the word "progress" might induce speculation that she had internalized assimilationist ideology and social evolutionism from her boarding school years, but this is the very same

woman who was monthly publishing cartoons caricaturing white society's pre-
dilection for racist stereotypes of Native Californians. Her correspondence, cited
at length below, leaves no doubt that other impulses and experiences informed
her theme. World's fairs and expositions had been cosmopolitan venues and
popular educational forums during her boarding school years. Greenville and
Carlisle had sent pupils and student work to them.[22] Now on the curatorial side
of cultural production, Potts held the reins of representation. She could claim
and exercise her insider authority. What does resonate with her Carlisle experience is her commitment to *all* California Indians. Her 1915 essay "A Trip to
Philadelphia" had voiced the disappointment that she and some of her YWCA
peers felt upon realizing that they were not among the tribal nations represented
in the University of Pennsylvania Museum exhibits. That erasure still loomed
large.

Seven pages into February's *Smoke Signal*, an eye-catching headline featuring
ponytailed Injun Louie animates the top third of the page. Two feathers nested in
the back of his headband flutter aloft as he sprints toward two bold, hand-lettered
words on the page's left side. Hugging a stack of newspapers under one arm, he
clutches the exclamation point in "Special Notice!" in his outstretched right hand.
Like an Olympic torch relay runner, Louie symbolized cooperation. "You Too
Can Help Your Community" introduced three stories. One reminded readers to
report deaths, name changes, and new addresses to the Sacramento-area office
pursuant to H.R. 1354, which had reopened the roll to out-of-state California
Indians denied enrollment in 1933 and facilitated $150 per capita payments from
CIJA.[23] Another column explained that area office director James Ring was home
from Washington, where he had learned about plans for withdrawal. He was now
traveling throughout California Indian Country to ascertain sentiment toward
termination. Readers were encouraged to speak up and be heard. Sandwiched
between was a third column: "State Fair Indian Exhibit Planned." Potts explained,
"[T]he process of gathering material will be the next step in which the cooperation
of all Indians is essential. Relics, art and crafts of the old mode of life as well as
modern handicrafts will be needed and any assistance will be welcomed. This is
the first time in the history of California that the Indians have attempted such
a project and the success of this enterprise depends entirely on the cooperation
of all Indians."[24] The project offered an opportunity to transcend divisive land
claims politics, but it was one thing to proclaim that the exhibit was nonpolitical
and another to convince individuals enrolled with rival organizations to support
FIC's exhibit.

Following up with county boards in late March, Potts focused on exhibit materials, especially from Indian-owned businesses. Stapled atop a copy of her earlier letter, a brief memo asked boards to forward her contact information to Native people in their county. April brought news from former BIA employee Edith Van Allen Murphey in Ukiah. Elsie Allen and Caroline Clarke had been over the night before. Allen and her mother, Annie Burke—both accomplished Pomo weavers—planned to arrive during the second week of the fair and stay through Admission Day. Murphey suggested that Potts get a notice published in *California Clubwoman*. Another update came in late April. If hop picking was over, Allen's son would drive her down, but Murphey wondered how baskets would be displayed. At the county fair in Petaluma, they had sat on a table. Wall displays were superior, Murphey insisted, revealing that it was her nephew Guy Redwine who had pushed for Mendocino County's one-hundred-dollar donation. The University of California Anthropology Museum had commissioned Murphey, who was well versed in ethnobotany, to develop a northern California basketry collection in the 1930s. Murphey and Potts shared a common friend in Codman. In March, when Codman wrote Deterding about FIC's exhibit, she gushed, "Well—this old Mary Major simply stole the show at the Fair that year. Crowds of people were constantly watching her weaving. I drove her and Mrs. Murphey back to Covelo. I believe she took orders for quite a lot of baskets—so helping her to support herself." Murphey recalled this in Major's 1958 obituary:

> It was my good fortune to take her to the State Fair in 1935 [*sic*], when I was state chairman of Indian Welfare. She sat in the Mendocino county booth and made baskets and was quite an attraction. The big silver cup Mendocino was awarded that year must have had at least one handle on it due to Mary Major as "the greatest human interest." . . . Mary's trip to Sacramento was a highlight in her life. She made many friends at the fair and many booths gave her sacks of beans, rice, etc. to take home. A Sacramento florist filled her big stone mortar with flowers daily, with a corsage for Mary every time.[25]

Mary Major (Lassik/Wylacki) traveled only once to the state fair, but she wove for the Mendocino County Fair for years. County fair participants naturally came to mind when Potts asked for exhibit assistance. BIA social worker Mildred Van Every passed along contact information for Josie Atwell, whose granddaughter was involved in the Kings County Fair. Writing her, Potts homed in on issues that would resonate with a contemporary: "Our main objective is to show the progress that we Indians have made so that they may better understand us and our problems." She also planted a subversive thought: "We do not have many relics that have not already been exhibited by collectors."[26]

At her typewriter daily from March through August, Potts followed up on literally every lead. Many heard versions of "Old relics are scarce among the Indians, so it has been hard to locate things that have not already been on exhibit by collectors."[27] In her commitment to inclusivity, she was learning about California's diverse Native nations. And she was becoming inventive. By mid-July she was telling correspondents that FIC was willing to serve as a vendor for arts and crafts sent for display and that she was planning a baby basket exhibit.[28] Earlier that month she had sent a desperate plea to Harrison Williams in Klamath. Did he have photos depicting his business? Perhaps some canned salmon with his label "would be good advertising." Old nets and tackle were also acceptable. Mostly, she needed dancers: "They insist on authentic California Indian garb and dances. Have you made any contacts with any of your people about the dance? I am very anxious to know as I will have to make a report to Fair officials soon."[29] The fair had already disseminated a press release promising demonstrations and dancing on the adjoining stage. The *Bee* waited to publish this story, but a southern California paper ran it immediately.[30]

Potts was a doer not a worrier, but one July night she was up in the wee hours of the morning pouring her heart out to the person responsible for her distress. The shortage of money, security, transportation, and commitment from others had worn her down. She was considering canceling the space. Codman replied immediately. Apologizing for having seemingly abandoned her, she offered potential solutions to the most vexing issues, including security for objects. She encouraged another appeal to county supervisors. Carbon-copying Stewart and Murphey, who "used to have lots of baskets," and also the Indian Office, which "surely ought to know people with collections," she added, "What about Chas. DeYoung Elkus? . . . He might get the Indian Defense Association to help. Tell him I suggested you write him. He is a most public-spirited man, and generous with his legal talent, which is the same as money to him."[31]

Potts had already recovered by the time Codman's letter arrived. Writing Valeria Navarro in San Jacinto, she quipped, "Fair officials want authentic California costumes. Up here where I live that would be no problem, as our people didn't go in for clothes, so if your people down south were like mine, fancy costumes wouldn't be necessary. There is one Mission man here that could help out as that is what he does for a past time, he used to do dancing and entertaining quite a lot and he could work right in with your group, that is if you wouldn't object."[32] Joking about her own people "not going in for clothes," much less fancy costumes, was a clever way to simultaneously underscore and critique the fair's insistence on "authentic" costumes. Her sarcasm playfully built rapport with fellow California Indians.

"That Injun Look"

On July 17, she was at her typewriter again. Determination to deliver on her exhibit vision is foregrounded in this set of correspondence, but so is her sociability and fierce work ethic. Exhibit layout and design elements were on her mind. A July 11 memorandum instructed exhibitors to submit a rough draft of their exhibit plans "at once," revealing that six awards would be given.[33] Her facility for strategically positioning Native people in relation to dominant society is evident in this correspondence, where whites are historical adversaries and relentless usurpers of California Indian material culture and authority.

Richard Barrington (Washoe), a Carlisle alumnus, owned a Sierraville mill. He was a Collett supporter, but she wrote anyway, asking him to donate cedar bark to conceal the fair cabinetry's modern design. Hoping a truck might be coming through Sacramento and able to drop off a few strips, she was also willing to use shorter ones that could be transported by car. She invited him to follow Abe Benner's lead and send eight-by-ten-inch photographs of his business and crew. If he identified locations and loggers' tribal affiliations, she would showcase his business, augmenting her depiction of modern Indian life. "We are making very good progress toward our exhibit through the cooperation of the many interested Indians. As we have said before, it is the Indians that are putting on this project, we do not have any white supervisors although we have had to get information from officials at the Fair ground."[34]

Two Mountain Maidu, Carl Salem and his stepmother, Rose, owned a ranch on the east side of Lake Almanor, near Hukespem's old camp. Potts had baskets from other places but was eager to show Maidu examples—especially some "burden (*Wall-lom*) baskets." Beadwork and buckskin would also be useful, she hinted. "We are exhibiting modern things that the Indians are doing too," she explained, suggesting they send photographs of their fishing business and pond. She was planning demonstrations of basket weaving, acorn soup making, and buckskin processing. Her long letter is peppered with provocative statements, offering an unfiltered glimpse into her sentiments about Natives and whites:

> This is the first time that Indians themselves are doing this. Always before, some white man is always the boss of such things. . . . Old Indian relics are

hard to get, so I'm having quite a time. . . . At the other booths every one brings their own exhibits and are glad to, but I think we have got in the habit of someone doing for us so we expect them to. I don't mean you and I, but a lot of these other Indians, especially those under the reorganization act. I find a lot of them won't do anything unless they are paid to. I'm sure learning about people since I've been working on this Fair business.[35]

Earlier correspondence revealed some exasperation, but here a litany of complaints spilled forth: "Always before, some white man is always the boss of such things." Yet California Indians were not stepping up either. Federally recognized groups were especially in her crosshairs. She was toiling night and day for free, with no budget, tribal infrastructure, or white supervisors, and this was not enough to stoke their generosity. Her lament about the difficulty of getting "old Indian relics" was aptly directed. "Rosie" Meadows Salem was an expert weaver, born in 1883. She and her older sister Daisy Baker had learned the craft from their mother, Kate Meadows McKinney.[36] The Meadows women produced superb specimens, demonstrating the highest level of Mountain Maidu artistry. "Let me hear from you, if you do not care to exhibit," Potts implored, "let me know so I won't be depending on it." In an afterthought: "At all the other exhibit booths people bring their own material, but I think we [Indians] have got in the habit of someone doing for us. Hope you can take part, but if not come and see our exhibit."

Her tone with John and Otie (Henry) Davis was humorous and relaxed, reflecting their longtime friendship.[37] She wanted deer hides "to give the walls that 'Injun look.'" She heard from their nephew Frank that hunters had abandoned some at their place.[38] No need for them to be dressed, but she hoped someone could wet and stretch them. Given her reputation as an expert hide tanner, she anticipated the curiosity this request would generate, explaining that there was no room to do this at her house. She inquired about exhibiting one of the "beautiful patchwork quilts" John's sister Freda had made. Apprising them of other inquiries she was making—with his brother-in-law Henry Jackson, for instance—she asked if they could suggest anyone else.[39] "Old Indian relics are the scarce article; we sure don't find any," she proclaimed. "Do you know of anyone with a yellow hammer head band?" Drawing slowly to a close, she conjured reminders of their boarding school years, wanting to show Otie a photograph she and cousin Rose had taken with Edward Ament just before he died in 1949. Their old friend Edna Calac still asked after Otie and remembered Maidu words Otie had taught her.[40] Leaving nostalgia behind, Potts sighed, "Sure working hard on this project. First time

Indians are doing anything like this without white man bossing them." A final note was directed to John, who was more than a decade her senior. Potts felt a deep kinship with his large extended family. Everyone had gotten "a kick" out of his recent *Smoke Signal* letter, she said, assuring him that there was no need for apologies over misspelled words; she did this "all the time."[41]

Writing Maidu friend Abe Benner, she explained, "I'm looking for more beadwork and old Indian relics. They really are scarce as the old timers used to burn them after death. The few that have them do not want to part with them." She was taking this seriously: "I just called an insurance company about having the things insured in case of fire or theft. There will be a guard stationed at the place where we exhibit from 10 P.M. till 10 A.M. . . . . During the day we will have to be alert and watch things. White people don't trust us so why should we trust them?"[42] White people had taken their things for more than a century. Some families had been forced to part with heirlooms to support fathers and mothers and children and grandchildren. So much Maidu culture was already in the custody of settlers—in private collections or museums. The connection between her own exhibit and this history of dispossession was not lost on her; families who still owned treasures needed to know they would be safe in her care.

Gladys Mankins was next. Potts wanted a photograph of her holding pheasants from their property and hoped that her mother, Kitty Joaquin, would help with acorn demonstrations.

All I have is a small mortar that I planned to use for exhibits. Any big flat stone would do, just so we could move it around. We have the use of a stage for the demonstrations, it adjoins our booth. Oh yea, the stone would be used for pounding the acorn so it would have to be thick enough to stand the pounding. You know what I mean, what am I wasting my fingers for. . . . I've been pecking steady all day on this typewriter. Someday I hope to learn to use it right. What about the Indian dress you were going to try and get for the exhibit? . . . We want tribe name and stuff like that. Ask your mother what kind of shelters (house) the real old timers had before the white people came. We are trying to make a group of them for display . . . that is what we want the cedar for. One of my nephews is going to help me. These things take a lot of time. Sure surprising how much time I've put into this thing."

Family finances were tight; she had delayed a trip back home, where she could approach people in person, but she was thinking of riding the bus to Reno. "If

you could come over I would go to Susanville and around and see what I could
see. I'm getting like Collett," she joked. "I just beg and beg."[43]

A final letter that day went to the "girls" at the Indian wing of the Weimar
Joint Sanatorium. Reginald George, who had been so helpful in the 1949 Placer
County Centennial Parade, connected her to this cohort of industrious women.[44]
In an April 5 letter, he told Potts he was having his aunt make a baby basket, was
scouting local baskets and beadwork, and needed an address where these should
be sent. Since then, contemporary beadwork from the Colfax/Weimar area had
been arriving from him and the women at "the San." Her July 17 letter included
funds from the early sale of earrings and pins, and buckskin scraps for moccasin
making. She was way ahead of the game in figuring out how to integrate their
presence into the booth: "I'm sure glad the girls took to the idea for the fair, it gives
us more for the exhibit as well as giving your girls a break. I thought of setting
it up as representing Indian patients; give it [a] big splash or something. Get the
sympathy of the public, you know what I mean?" She was a natural at publicity.
Native nurses staffed the Indian wing of this multi-county sanatorium developed
in the late 1930s, when tubercular California Indian people were often excluded
from local hospitals and sanatoriums due to widespread racism.[45] A display about
Native health-care professionals serving Native patients would garner sales for
the women and help quash stereotypes.

The next week she rode the bus to Reno with grandson Bobby DuFresne.
Gladys picked her up. The local press covered her visit in a brief front-page col-
umn, "Indian Relics Sought Here for State Fair," explaining that she was chair of
FIC's All-California Indian Exhibit and was gathering material in Plumas and
Lassen Counties for display.[46] This trip was nothing short of transformational.
Not only did she negotiate multiple exhibit loans, but she was emotionally moved
by encounters with the rich material world of her Mountain Maidu ancestors.
The affective force of their tangible presence in her modern life—the milieu she
was earlier so intent on evoking through contemporary arts and industry—was
evident in letters penned the following week. They mixed gratitude for objects
from her homeland with continuing calls from other tribal groups.[47] When she
sat down to write DNIWA's Thelma McVay, the wonder was still fresh. Dazzled
by the objects and chance to exhibit these ancestral things, she wrote,

> I just got back from Lassen and Plumas counties, collecting a few things
> for the Fair, in fact I got much more than I anticipated. I was surprised that
> they would trust me with some of their prized possessions. I had wonderful

cooperation and had I more time I think I could have gotten more learning about Indian things as I could stand a lot of that particular kind of educating. They are going to make a few other things that I do not have that were essential to the use of their daily living. I think we are going to have a pretty good exhibit. . . . I am learning so much myself that I am more enthused every day. It's a lot of work and one of my friends said the Indians just don't appreciate what we do for them but I am happy in doing it anyway. Are you giving the news items about the exhibit to the papers? The *Lassen Advocate* had a very nice write up for me about the collection and the exhibit. I think that is what stirs their interest more. Indian tell them something, they won't believe it, let a white man write as news and no matter how wrong he is, they will believe it, at least that has been the way here.[48]

Realizing she had gone off the rails, Potts rolled her letter back into the typewriter and squeezed in a couple crooked lines: "Hope you don't read this to your group. It sounds awful now that I have gone over it. Oh well! They probably like to hear a good honest gripe. Let me hear from you again. . . . I'm not drunk, just crazy."[49]

In this "honest gripe," Potts reveals the distinctive contours of her own subjectivity. At that moment, she cannot relate to either whites or Indian people. After months of trying to rally everyone from county boards to Native friends, all it took was one mainstream newspaper article to convince them of the project's importance. She also acknowledged a cultural deficit: she could stand a lot of educating about many "Indian things." The trip home brought her into spheres of traditional knowledge that sharpened her sense of distinction from older generations. The circumscribed nature of her Carlisle education was suddenly crystal clear. She longed for access to this other world, so tangibly embodied in these "prized possessions." Her emotional response is a poignant index of loss. At the same time, she is exhilarated with this exhausting and frustrating work. She is "learning so much."

Potts kept up this pattern of writing and cajoling until the end of August, needing money, demonstrators, and booth attendants. She obtained courtesy passes for Allen and her mother. Van Every agreed to host and ferry them back and forth to the fair daily. Writing with this update, she added, "I would so much like to show some Pomo baskets . . . also a baby basket of that tribe. . . . The Indians are very slow to respond. Maybe next year after they see what we are doing, they may show more interest."[50] Allen's response was disappointing. She talked up the exhibit among her Pomo friends, but they would not show their baskets without remuneration, as was the county fair custom.[51] There was more. Burke was worried about Sacramento's blistering heat and could not be left home alone. They would try to make a day trip.[52]

A week away from opening, she was without weaving demonstrators. The much-wanted Mountain Maidu baby basket also remained elusive. Wagering that Lilly Baker, a fourth-generation weaver, would share her cultural pride, she followed up on their mid-July meeting: "I sure hope you can come down. I haven't found anyone else so please don't let me down. I thought if you couldn't come at the last minute, I could find someone but they are all so funny about things. Other Indians aren't like us, they are funny people. . . . Bring some of the baskets that you have made, the unfinished one, our kind and [the] hat creek basket so that you can demonstrate both of them." Only then did she ask, "How are your Grandma and Mother? I hope they are all right. I sure hate to see anything happen right now and as far as that goes, any other time. I did sound kind of selfish, didn't I?"[53] She knew she sounded desperate, but she wanted their art and culture to shine.

Two days later Thelma McVay and Sylvia Hostler confirmed that they were headed down with Audree Bowen. Potts's relief was profound.[54] Here were three kindred spirits, riding a bus from far northwestern California to share in this groundbreaking exhibit opportunity. They would stay the week, maybe two, and hand-carry their objects back, but only if money held out and they could "stand the heat." They were counting on Potts to meet their bus: "Look for two or 3 scared injuns—that's us—we've been told we'd better take a bucket of fog to cool off Sacramento with."[55]

In mid-August Potts hustled for funding. A visit to city and county supervisors in San Francisco proved they knew nothing of her March letter. Preparing a last round of appeals, she generated an estimated budget: $768 was devoted to "maintenance for personnel and demonstrators, 8 persons for 12 days @ $8.00 per day."[56] Transportation, building supplies, publicity, and miscellany brought the total to $1,568. Printed on FIC's new letterhead, the budget accompanied a final flurry of mid-August letters to prospective San Francisco patrons, including automobile dealerships, women's professional associations, and pioneer/western service organizations. In the latter category, she chose groups that in either name or action affiliated themselves with Native America and the West.[57] These ran the gamut from the Improved Order of Red Men to Native Daughters of the Golden West. She was clearly struck by the contradictions embodied in the concept of the latter, ending her letter to these settler women, "This appeal comes from a native daughter of many generations of native daughters and is meant in all sincerity."[58] She was whistling into the wind.

Despite her persistence, Mendocino County's one-hundred-dollar gift was the only substantial donation.[59] With only $160, she pressed FIC members and friends into action. John Porter drove his truck from Ione to the Sacramento Greyhound station to deliver artifact shipments to the fairgrounds and used his vacation days to man the booth. Viola Wessell brought exhibit items from Tuolumne. Reginald George arrived with his baskets, beadwork, a yellowhammer headband, and fancywork and other objects collected from lenders (such as Lizzie Enos) in Colfax and surrounds. Nurse Florence McClintock came from Modoc County's Fort Bidwell Indian Community, staying all day to help install her cargo, and three Smith River women arrived by bus, working nonstop to get their objects arranged. California Cedar Producers donated the much-coveted bark, and Mrs. W. H. Goodman Jr. made a 160-mile round-trip from San Francisco to the foothills town of Pioneer to retrieve it. Bill Barber, Ben Johns, and Kenneth and Mabel Strong labored on booth construction and exhibit installation.[60] Their installation window was tight. They could not begin until the morning of August 30 and had to be out by 5:00 P.M. They left, exhausted, at 8:00 P.M.

The educational exhibit area was partitioned into thirty-two booths, sixteen feet square and open on one side, with some exhibitors, such as FIC, occupying two booths. The outdoor stage was on the far end of the rectangular enclosure, opposite the visitor entrance. FIC adjoined it on one side and the Amateur Radio Club on the other. Booths lined the perimeter and formed a center island with exhibitors back to back. A pedestrian path looped in front of the stage. FIC was hard to miss.[61] Once Potts had worried that there would be nothing to display, but that final week she realized she was short on exhibit space [62] The last-minute loan of glass cases from the fair's education department saved the day, tripling her capacity to secure fancywork and rare "relics." She had exhibit donors prepare cards giving stories or other identification for their materials and used them as ready-made labels. Many are visible in surviving photographs. While FIC volunteers labored in the sweltering summer heat, the *Bee* heralded their work:

The exhibit, under the direction of Mrs. Marie Potts of Sacramento, and built around a centennial theme, will show tools and methods of preparing food in use when the first white man entered the state and examples of the work of Indians today, including printing, saddle making and tailoring. Indian baskets and beadwork will present a distinct contrast to the many

articles of fancy work now made by Indian women. Demonstrations **in**
various crafts will be given on the stage near the exhibit and there will be
dancing and other entertainment. Indians will don full regalia and perform
the ancient tribal dances to the beating of tom toms.[63]

Representing fifty-two California tribes, FIC promised displays of "Pomo, Miwuk,
Karok, Yurok, Tolowa, Wintun, Maidu, Hat Creek and Pit River tribes" and
"products of the Paiutes, Missions and Yokuts."[64]

Opening Day and Beyond

California Indians showed up in droves. They worked as cultural performers—not
in a county booth but in their own. Chris Brown ("Chief Lee-mee") brought his
Miwok Dancers from Yosemite to grace the adjoining stage.[65] Basketry demonstrations continued all day, amid displays of bracken and maidenhair fern. Acorn was
processed. Stick games were played. The Smith River women modeled Tolowa
dresses three times a day. Visitors signed artful guest registers organized by
alphabetic county groupings, bound with leather cords. County borders drawn
with colored pencil decorated their manila covers, and tabs made it easy for
visitors to locate their home county's page.[66] Used from 1950 to 1952, with new
versions in 1953 and 1954, these registers are visible on countertops in several
photographs. They document hundreds of visitors, including California Indians:
Konkow artist Frank Day and his wife; the Fullers and Wessells of Tuolumne;
David Risling Jr. of Humboldt; the Lorenzos of Arbuckle; the Barringtons of
Sierraville; Marvin Benner, Leona Morales, and Ronnie Morales of Susanville. In
1950 OIA directors and field service personnel visited, and former SIM curators
came by. An out-of-state register documented visitors from Brazil, Switzerland,
Finland, China, Poland, Germany, Canada, Indonesia, Japan, and nearly every
U.S. state. Off-reservation boarding school alumni registered in three-ring loose-
leaf binders. Hand-lettered and -illustrated covers identity one for "Sherman
and Other Visitors" and another for "Carlisle, Chemawa, Haskell, Phoenix, and
Stewart."[67] An improvised Chilocco tab was added in 1954. Columns for years of
attendance, names, and addresses ensured ongoing communication, including
local reunions. "Marie Mason Potts" is the first of three names entered for Carlisle,
perhaps the only preserved example of her handwritten signature including
maiden and married names. Not all Carlisle alums found their way to the dedicated
register. Potts's Carlisle classmate Harry Bonser signed on Sacramento County's
page.[68]

Generosity of friends and kin back home ensured that Mountain Maidu and neighboring material culture was well represented. Dr. Fred J. Davis Jr.'s family loaned seventeen items and prize-winning paintings by his mother.[69] Rose Salem loaned a fish basket by her mother, Kate McKinney, and a sifter from her grandmother Jennie Meadows. Hazel Sanchez loaned beaded belts and buckskin accessories. Leona Morales displayed a beaded bottle and a white tanned buckskin. Her mother, Roxie Peconum, was represented by her three-piece buckskin dress and a utility basket. Inez Pozzi (another of Roxie's daughters) contributed buckskin to help with "that Injun look." Besides supplying pine needles, acorn mortars, and the like, Gladys Mankins exhibited a Paiute baby basket, beaded buttons, and a willow basket. Potts's pride was evident in her *Smoke Signal* description, partially reproduced here:

> The All Indian Exhibit at the 1950 State Fair in Sacramento, California won an award for "Outstanding Non-profit Exhibit." This is the first time in the History of California that the Indians themselves have put on an exhibit of this kind. One entire table was devoted to the Indians of Del Norte Co., where both antique and modern crafts were on display as well as food of yesteryear and today. Ferns, greens, moss and redwood bark from Del Norte County were in evidence as decoration. As unusual item was a handmade violin inlaid with abalone shell. . . . A feathered basket worked on by four generations was displayed by Lela Dunlap. A shoe case filled with bead work and buckskin articles was very interesting. Sections were devoted to beadwork from Ft. Yuma, Calif., Modoc and Placer Counties. In the Hobby section were model planes, plastic work, brass plates and beautiful ceremonial headdresses. Oil paintings were in evidence, which proves that Indians are natural artists. Sewing and fancy work were plentiful and some canned goods. In the business line were printing matter, tailoring and saddle work. Two World War II service flags were on display from Modoc and Amador Co., and the most modern at the exhibit was the flag of the State's first All Indian V.F.W. Post 9054, chartered July 29, 1950.[70]

DNIWA funded transportation, meals, and housing for its crew. Potts showed her gratitude for the contribution in her choice of a photograph to be printed as a postcard acknowledgment mailed to exhibit donors. (See figure 13.) Booth attendants worked fifteen-hour days. Among many others, Potts thanked Irma Bahnsen, who "came early and stayed late, 8:00 AM to 10:30 PM." A paid attendant, Bahnsen later became a favorite travel companion. The hard work of Potts, who had once worried that she would have to abandon her plans entirely, culminated in an unrivaled show of success, as help finally came from many quarters in a wellspring of cultural pride and cooperation, earning FIC the Outstanding Educational Exhibit honor. (See figure 14.)[71]

A Turning Point and New Tradition

This curatorial experience recalibrated Potts's cultural compass, fostering a deep longing to know and preserve the sweet traces of her ancestral past. It elevated and expanded her Maidu and Native presence in the city. She sailed onto the radar of regional anthropologists, schoolteachers, policy makers, and nearby Native communities who valued and supported the revival of traditional dance, basket weaving, and regalia making—and with whom she later formed a lively circle of teaching and learning. These are important effects illuminated by the passage of time and discussed in later chapters. Did she recognize any of these

Figure 13. State fair postcard highlighting Tolowa participants and regalia, 1950. *Left to right*: Bertha Stewart's daughter, Barbara, and unidentified man in a Jump Dance headdress. Verso inscription: "Dear Friend: The 'All Indian Exhibit' at the 1950 State Fair won an award of 'Outstanding Non-Profit Exhibit.' In behalf of the Federated Indians of California I wish to convey to you our appreciation and thanks for your contribution in making this exhibit a big success—State Fair Indian Committee."
Courtesy Marine family.

Figure 14. Marie Potts (*far right*) in the 1950 All-California
Indian Exhibit booth at the state fair.
Courtesy Marine family.

possibilities in the moment? How did she apprehend and articulate the exhibit's value in these early years? Her correspondence shows that she was driven from the start by the project's historical significance and that she relentlessly pressed others to be equally compelled by this opportunity to engage in self-representation. Her letters document an awakening to cultural dispossession reflected by the dearth of traditional objects in Native hands and the wealth in museums and in collectors' hands. No wonder Plains headdresses saw so much light of day in mid-century California.

One index of value is in her annual reprisal of this labor-intensive project, but others emerge from her own voice and words. In 1951 fair officials asked exhibitors for "first-hand information on the various ways in which exhibitors in the Educational Area have benefitted by the opportunity to present their non-profit's function to fairgoers." Potts's detailed response was organized around five themes: "Object," "Recognition," "Overall Interest," "Social Relations," and "Indian Service." A long paragraph addressing "Social Relations" explains: "[P]romotion of mutual interest in cultural habits, arts, and crafts is one of the greatest factors in social relations."[72] She was well practiced in speaking with and to authority to foster public support for Native people and programs. Elsewhere, as in this excerpt from correspondence with an exhibit lender, she drifts into candid and contemplative territory, offering a rich portrait of her interiority:

> Everything we show comes from the homes of the Indian people and some-times I borrow from my white friends when I can't find it any other way. Most of our Indian things have been sold to white collectors a long time ago. We have a few, very few, young people who are actually interested in making the Indian things. They want to learn. One boy who just came back from Germany is very interested. In going among the Indians, I learn a lot about them, custom, habits, religion, ceremonies and all things like that. I went to an Indian school when I was quite young and got away from all these things so I am quite ignorant except for what I have picked up since my contact with them recently. For a few years, I was with my mother after my school days and some things I learned from her, but that would be only my tribe. They were very few in number so didn't have the ceremonies and other affairs that big tribes had. Next year, we plan on having a class of basket weavers, the girls already consented to take part and if we cannot get someone to teach them, I can always play second fiddle. I'm no expert but I know how and know enough to instruct them. Basket weaving is like anything else, practice makes perfection. I haven't made a basket in 20 years. . . . This year I taught one of the girls to do beadwork.[73]

After 1950, the annual state fair cycle was always bittersweet—a seesaw of grief tempered by warm anticipation of seeing old friends again. Kitty died in an automobile accident on April 1, 1951. Somehow Potts pushed through the shock and pain to install the exhibit. Pansy and her children helped out, and the DuFresne grandchildren kept her company in the booth. Two decades later she was confident in the exhibit's value but weary of carrying the weight. The fair moved to new facilities in 1968. She lobbied unsuccessfully for the site to include a California Indian cultural center and permanent exhibition. She could no longer walk to the fairgrounds. Almost an octogenarian, she reminisced: "For the second time since 1950, the Indians of California are not having an exhibit at Cal Expo much to the disappointment of the Indians and the public. The Indian exhibit has been a big attraction at the fairs. During the years the Indians exhibit has won four plaques. . . . At Cal Expo, the exhibitors were hindered by the people riding in the sky gliders throwing trash, cigarettes and spitting down on them. How rude can they be?"[74]

Potts's health was declining. Traditions fostered at the fair were thriving elsewhere. She was comforted by this but mourned the end of this one.

Ahead of Her Time

Potts's work curating the first All-California Indian Exhibit stands today as an unprecedented instance of California Indian cultural self-representation. Remarkably, she understood this significance well ahead of the scholarly curve, noting it over and over again in her letters to both Native and non-Native people.[75] Once again, she proved to have an enviable reserve of energy and dedication. The logistical coordination and physical labor were demanding, but the emotional work was more significant. This was a watershed moment. At fifty-five years old, she was forced to confront the limitations of her boarding school education and the sacrifices it had entailed. Searching out Mountain Maidu material culture, she encountered an ancestral realm almost lost to her by time spent away at school, by private collectors and museums, and by the modernity she initially thought to foreground. At the same time, her boarding school education, travel, and Philadelphia museum experience was the fuel that pushed her through barriers: lack of funding, ambivalence, scarcity of traditional objects, and the guardedness of those still in possession of them. Suppressed and long simmering, her intellectual ambition to be certain that California Indian people showed up in exhibits came rushing to the fore with a vengeance. County supervisor claims of "We have no Indians" merely amplified her commitment to making them visible.[76] She was venturing into new, educational terrain. Her networks of government agency, civic, and social workers expanded. So did her network of Native people—cultural leaders, weavers, and dancers. Her admiration for them was apparent; soon she would join their ranks.

8

Encountering Anthropology

Maidu Cultural Consultant

> Mrs. Potts was an unusual informant. . . . Although she did not
> attempt to guide the questioning, it was felt from time to time
> that she could have asked the questions better than could the
> interviewer.
>
> —*Robert Littlewood, 1957*

Beneath a canopy of sprawling oaks, Potts described how Americans confiscated Indigenous land and brutalized its owners: "They burned down their storage places, they killed the Indians right and left, murdered them, and had a bounty on their heads." Pausing for effect, she remarked, "That law is still in existence; you can get $60 for my head if you want." Nervous murmurs echoed across the lawn where anthropology students were gathered to hear from this septuagenarian. It was October 1971. They were gathered at Sacramento Junior College (SJC), where Marie's land claims career had launched in 1947. When she met with other California Indians on that crisp January morning to discuss K-344 and ICCA, the possibility that her future would involve Maidu cultural consulting for museums and anthropologists could not have been more remote.[1] Yet this is precisely what happened. A new historical consciousness emerged. She began to recognize the cascading effects of land theft—loss of livelihoods, ceremonies, expressive arts, and language—and she yearned to immerse herself in these realms of ancestral knowledge. The mid-century cityscape, so remote in time and place from her Big Meadow childhood, yielded unexpected opportunities to do so.

This chapter elaborates the process by which Potts gained access to venues, projects, and people who appreciated and sought out her Mountain Maidu knowledge during the 1950s and 1960s. On the surface, this might seem a logical development: she gained public notice in the late 1940s through her *Smoke Signal* work and FIC publicity appearances, and the 1950 California State Fair exhibit established her presence as an interpreter of California Indian culture. The reality is more impressive. Potts moved to Sacramento in time to witness and participate in the professionalization of museums and academic anthropology. Through an unlikely convergence of amateur enthusiasts, junior college students, and their professors—all trained in other disciplines—Potts soon became a familiar name and figure among a circle of anthropologists affiliated with the University of California–Berkeley. This brought employment that did not entail domestic labor. Exercising the cultural authority embodied in her Mountain Maidu identity, she was able to translate the traditions of her forebears in new contexts and mediums.

From Generic "Indian" to Maidu Woman

Potts's first public opportunity to distinguish herself as Maidu came in 1949, when the Northern California Council of DAR met in Sacramento and invited Potts to present a program. For decades, women such as Sarah Winnemucca, Mourning Dove, and Zitkála-Šá had delivered cultural and political lectures that were billed in the language of theatrical performance because their Native identities conjured romance and exoticism.[2] As an American Indian woman, Potts was viewed through this same lens, with the organizers promising that she would appear "in costume." Potts used the occasion to showcase her language and culture, performing several "songs and dances: Indian Lullaby, Young Peoples Dance, and The Hand Game of Fortune."[3] Publicity photos show the state regent and the state chairman of DAR Indian Affairs posing with Potts at the microphone. Her wardrobe—the now familiar buckskin dress and a beaded hair band tied fashionably at the nape of her neck—is understated in comparison to earlier publicity appearances. Her performance of Maidu expressive culture was well received, but her articulate command of political concerns was even more impressive.[4] A year later, DAR's state vice chairman on American Indians wrote for advice pertaining to "educational work for the Indians in the northern section of this state."[5] Respected for her intellect as much as her Native identity, Potts was courted throughout the 1950s for both. When the Sacramento World Affairs Council invited her to speak in April 1954, its press release indicated that she would discuss political matters and "display products of arts and crafts made by members of the Maidu tribe."[6] Her Maidu belonging and status as a Native leader were underscored in May 1954 when the press reported her departure for "a combined convention of the American Friends Service Committee . . . and reservation Indians in California," and again in October when her lecture for DAR's Sutter chapter was announced.[7]

In 1955 Potts embarked on an interdenominational study tour sponsored by the Northern California–Nevada Council of United Church Women (UCW), traveling to Santa Cruz on September 14, Reno on October 13, Humboldt on October 25, Santa Rosa on October 28, Sebastopol on October 31, and Madera in March 1956.[8] She titled her contribution to this lecture circuit "Indian Americans." Her fellow speakers were all white women talking about American missions. The Santa Rosa press announced her upcoming appearance:

> Mrs. Marie Potts is of the Maidu Tribe, Plumas Co., and has been in Sac-
> ramento since 1942; was educated at Government schools, her first years
> being spent at Greenville, Plumas Co., and later going to Carlisle, Penn.
> She graduated in 1915. Mrs. Potts is editor of "The Smoke Signal," a paper
> promoted by the Federated Indians of California. It is a publication of
> information about legislation (state and national) and any other news of
> interest to Indians of California. The California organization is also helping
> Indians in other states to promote legislation that is to the interest and
> betterment of Indians.[9]

These words were drawn nearly verbatim from Potts's earliest autobiographical sketch. Titled "Mrs. Marie Potts," it is written in first person throughout: "I am of the Maidu tribe of Plumas County. . . . I was educated at Government schools," and so forth. A final paragraph addressed FIC: "Our organization is also helping Indians in other states to promote or block legislation that is to their interest." Interestingly, UCW removed "or block" altogether rather correct her minor grammatical error. Perhaps blocking legislation was too subversive for its white Christian audience.[10]

This sketch is illuminating for what it tells us about her sense of self at sixty years old. It highlights her Maidu ancestry, boarding school affiliations, Carlisle graduation, editorship, and FIC activism, but her religious affiliation is notably absent. She was not touring to promote Christianity. The indoctrination that had suffused her boarding school education and led her to imagine that her daughters were welcome in Greenville Sunday schools had dissipated. No longer in its spiritual grip, if ever she was, she occasionally wrote brief prayers to the

Great Spirit for the *Smoke Signal*, as in the 1950 Memorial Day issue, where she asked for "courage and strength to carry on so that we may do and say what is best for our people."[11] Christianity was an intellectual tool that she used to navigate ecumenical settings where non-Natives needed to learn about California Indian people. Her own faith was vested in the same Creator her grandparents knew.[12]

Anthropological Lineages: From Boas to Kroeber and Barrett—Situating Potts

In August 1960, Marie dug out her UCW biographical sketch and penned in long-hand several addenda, including, "I work as an informant about Maidu Indians with the Sacramento State College and the California State Indian Museum." She was about to make her debut at Berkeley's Lowie Museum, now the Phoebe A. Hearst Museum of Anthropology (PAHMA). Theatrical allusions are not entirely poetic; this was a performance of sorts—demonstrating acorn cooking on the museum patio. A dozen years earlier, her dramatic entrance into the public sphere as an "Indian" at the peace pipe ceremonial and Freedom Train was facilitated by clothing and accoutrements loaned by SIM. Over the years intervening, two transformations occurred in tandem, one in Potts's public persona and the other in Sacramento's museum and academic landscape. The latter, although late in coming, followed a well-known pattern. Potts lived in Sacramento when this shift occurred. She not only witnessed it; she actively furthered it.

Anthropology's first institutional home was the museum, not the academy. Franz Boas, the German-born progenitor of American anthropology, tried to do anthropology in this context, developing collections and exhibitions for world's fairs and museums, including the Field Museum, the American Museum of Natural History (AMNH), and the Smithsonian. However, he quickly grew disenchanted with these institutions as forums for producing and disseminating scholarly knowledge.[13] Wrestling with the limitations imposed by old-school "museum men," Boas sought a university home for the discipline, where he could further the work he deemed most vital: collecting oral histories, languages, and other forms of expressive culture that did not lend themselves to culture-as-object modes of inquiry and display common to turn-of-the-century museums.[14] Appointed professor of anthropology at Columbia in 1899, Boas dedicated himself to establishing anthropology's scientific legitimacy and anchoring its reproduction in the academy. Museum anthropologists, whose positions had once connoted scholarly authority, were now marked as peripheral to the discipline's currency and future. Columbia's newly minted doctoral graduates maintained this posture even when they later accepted museum employment or university appointments (still rare in those days) requiring them to develop museum collections. This was the case for California's most famous anthropologist, Alfred L. Kroeber, Boas's first doctoral graduate at Columbia.

Kroeber came to California in 1900. Following a brief stint at the California Academy of Sciences and a return to New York to complete his dissertation, he was hired at UC Berkeley under the patronage of Phoebe Hearst. A founding member of Berkeley's Anthropology Department, he was a diligent gatekeeper kept exceptionally busy by virtue of the discipline's embryonic West Coast presence.[15] A fledgling university presence was to be expected, but even museums lacked scholarly gravitas remotely on par with the East Coast institutions where Boas made his curatorial mark. This was not for lack of interested amateurs. California had collectors aplenty, of both modest and wealthy means. Some opened their private homes and collections to the public; others aimed to preserve their collections in museums of their own founding. This group included Benjamin Hathaway, SIM's inaugural curator, who represented everything Kroeber aimed to quash.[16]

Sheer serendipity brought Potts and Hathaway together. He lived across the street and one door down from the Potts clan, at 2732 Santa Clara Way. Surprised when they moved in, he was surely euphoric when FIC became headquartered there in 1947. Indian people were coming and going seven days a week. He quickly befriended them, and they became beneficiaries of eye-catching regalia featured in early publicity photos. SIM was substantially comprised of Hathaway's private collection, which only partially explains how he could hold a curatorial position with only an eighth-grade education. Hathaway represented proto-anthropological authority in Sacramento because the city had no department of anthropology nor any instructors who held degrees in the discipline. Rather there were generalists whose personal experience, coupled with academic training in parallel fields, led them to develop and teach anthropology courses at the city's only institution of higher learning: SJC.

The department and museum Kroeber founded was undergoing its own transition when Potts arrived to demonstrate acorn cooking in September 1960. Kroeber was away in Paris, where he died on October 5. Archaeologist and ethnohistorian Robert Heizer, who shared Kroeber's interest in California Indian history and culture, was also in Paris, conducting yearlong research at Musée de l'Homme. Edward Gifford, retired from his longtime position as museum director, had passed away just months earlier. California Indian society was no longer UC Berkeley's primary focus; a new generation of anthropologists gazed further afield. The salvage ethnography that occupied Boas and drove Kroeber's early California work was now out of fashion. Most ethnographers felt that the window for this work had gone with a generation of elders like Hukespem, born before American invasion. Cora Du Bois, who earned her doctorate in 1932 under Kroeber's supervision, later reflected on her California field experiences, giving us insight into the anthropological sensibilities that built Berkeley's reputation and museum collections:

> I am writing in the State Guest House of Bhubaneswar [Indonesia]. It is a very comfortable hostel, and the various rooms I have occupied here intermittently for six years have been large and airy. There is electric light, an overhead fan, modern plumbing, and excellent service. I realize how vastly different from other field experiences this has been. It has little relation to my first field jaunts in the early 1930's among the Indians of California. There I was tied to a dilapidated car and stayed in roadside cabins on a minimal living and travel allowance. My task was largely salvage ethnography, and I never really left my own culture except by an act of imagination.[17]

This "act of imagination" was necessary not only because her field work was at "home," in a domestic colonial setting, but also because American anthropology's romantic inclinations were only a smidgen removed from those of mainstream society, for whom FIC donned feathered headdresses to make themselves legible as Indian people. Determined to find old ones who remembered a time before "Indian hunting-guide" gigs, made-for-market baskets, cars, studio portraits, bilingualism, and literacy pervaded Native communities, salvage ethnographers saw modernity's trappings as proof that indigeneity was vanishing, not enduring. Striking out from "roadside cabins" in "dilapidated cars," they combed the countryside for aged embodiments of a mythical and "authentic" past that existed before colonization—before anthropologists—knowing full well that language, kinship, intermarriage, technology, ceremony, and expressive culture were never circumscribed by invisible force fields.[18] Marie knew of these characters: Roland Dixon, C. Hart Merriam, and more than a few graduate students. They had been traipsing through northern Maidu territory since before she "rolled out onto the pine needles," recording languages, place-names, histories, and religious movements.[19]

Potts's Berkeley appearance emerged through her work with two anthropologists: Francis "Fritz" Riddell and Samuel Barrett, both UC Berkeley alumni. Barrett's standing was unique. He was the first PhD Kroeber produced, the first anthropology doctorate west of the Mississippi. Starting undergraduate work in 1901, Barrett completed his BA in 1905 and his doctorate in 1908. His dissertation, "Pomo Indian Basketry," grew out of high school years in Ukiah, where his father ran a store and bartered dry goods for basketry. He had retired from his position as the Milwaukee Public Museum director in 1939. Now life in and around his northern California home kept his interest in Native culture fresh. In a 1960 National Science Foundation grant application, he reported observing many "cultural residues" or "vestiges" of old ways. Barrett aimed to produce a visual record of California Indian people engaging in these cultural traditions, "as their forefathers did, perhaps with some modification to be sure, but still with reasonable attention to the ways of their elders."[20] Articulating the project's value in the language of salvage ethnography, he explained, "Direct observation by the student out in the field has become almost impossible . . . by reconstructing from the memories of the older tribesmen such arts, crafts, and procedures as even they had only seen practiced by their elders, and by having these specially re-enacted with fidelity by Indians before the camera, we could project our laboratory at least a generation or two farther back." Drilling down, beneath modern time, promised to yield a core rich in cultural depositions laid down before colonization. Potts, whose memories of her grandparents' lives made her precisely the sort of individual he sought, came to Barrett's attention through Berkeley alumnus Fritz Riddell. Riddell was SIM curator when he introduced these two, but he had known Marie for many years prior.

Potts and the Sacramento Anthropological Society: Encountering Fritz Riddell

Potts's ancestors were searched out in the field, but she was already engaged in cultural interpretation when local academics "discovered" her. Five weeks after the 1950 fair closed, the *Bee* announced formation of the Sacramento Anthropological Society (SAS) and revealed that Marie held one of five board positions. SAS members planned "to create a better understanding and sympathy for the culture of California, attend lectures and prepare papers on the general subject of anthropology, and publish a paper at regular intervals on subjects of interest locally in connection with anthropology."[21] Potts's standing as a peer versus an ethnographic subject is remarkable for the time, though she arguably embodied more intercultural expertise than her fellow SAS founders.

The inaugural meeting, held in SJC's Lillard Museum in fall 1950, hosted community practitioners, students, and faculty from both SJC and Sacramento

State College (SSC), a new four-year institution founded in 1947 but housed on SJC's campus until 1953.[22] SJC had earlier made several truncated strides toward a professional anthropology program. These efforts originated with Anthony G. Zallio, an Italian immigrant originally hired to teach fencing and Italian. Becoming enamored of Berkeley's anthropology program while earning his MA in Italian, he began auditing courses on California Indians taught by Edward Gifford. Completing his Italian degree in 1926, he returned for three consecutive summers, taking seminars with Bronislaw Malinowski, Leslie Spier, and Faye Cooper Cole.[23] In 1929, the same year Hathaway's collection debuted as a state capitol exhibit—SIM's precursor—Zallio taught SJC's first anthropology classes: California Indians and General Anthropology.[24] Course offerings expanded, and in the late 1930s, SJC enjoyed brief disciplinary fame when college president Jeremiah Lillard emerged as a patron and practitioner of central California archaeology.[25] He was initially an amateur enthusiast like Zallio. In 1931, when these two began developing SJC's museum collection, it was Hathaway who penned Lillard's letter of entrée to dealers, collectors, and diggers.[26] Lillard turned the corner, but Zallio remained a recalcitrant old-time pot hunter. Unable to marshal appreciation for the controlled excavation methods emerging in his midst, he was ostracized from the program he originated.[27]

Lillard's influence on several anthropologists with whom Potts later worked is the stuff of folklore. Heizer, a student from 1932 to 1934, recalled: "Along the [registration] line, when someone noted that I wanted to be an archaeologist, I was pulled out of line and escorted to meet the president. . . . Lillard, untrained and uninformed, was at the same time extraordinarily perceptive and energetic, and he saw in some fashion which I could not, and can never divine, that one could recover the story of the Indian past by digging and studying the materials recovered. He was absolutely indefatigable and on Saturdays we would go dig for Indian relics . . . this was pot-hunting, pure and simple."[28]

After entering graduate school at Berkeley, Heizer returned to supervise Central Valley excavations and to tutor his former mentor. By now, two brothers from Potts's ancestral territory were there. Lately of Susanville, brothers Harry and Fritz Riddell moved to Sacramento in 1936, enrolling together at SJC in 1938. Learning of their archaeological ambitions, Lillard introduced them to stratigraphy and controlled excavation in his summer field program. Deceased by the time SAS formed—and SJC's archaeological ambitions expired along with him—Lillard left a void not filled until SJC professor Richard Reeve gravitated toward the discipline.

Reeve was SAS founder and president. Recently appointed to the faculty of the new four-year college (SSC), where he became founding chair of the joint Department of Anthropology, English, and Speech, Reeve held a doctorate in English when SJC hired him in 1933.[29] Charles Packard, Hathaway's successor at SIM, was vice president; Phillip Onstott, SJC sociology and anthropology instructor, was secretary; and Packard's wife, Lolita, was treasurer. Potts's fellow members of the board were SJC geography instructor George Kimber and students William T. Douglass, Mae Hopkins, and Harley C. Baker. At monthly meetings, the group hosted experts in topics ranging from Pakistani dance to Mesoamerican archaeology. Potts eventually took her turn at the podium, exhibiting "Current California Indian Handicrafts" and taking orders on behalf of local artists.[30]

During its first year, SAS hosted two speakers with whom Potts formed lasting ties. One was British-born Jack Dyson, an "Indian hobbyist" from his days as a Boy Scout in Oakland. Dyson held an undergraduate anthropology degree and succeeded Packard as SIM curator. He presented "Songs and Dances of the Southwest Indians" to SAS in December 1951.[31] This talk gained him entrée into the heart of FIC's Sacramento chapter, where he taught these dances to Native youths, including several Potts grandsons.[32] Earlier that year, SAS hosted the man who later succeeded Dyson at SIM. The *Smoke Signal* reported: "Francis Riddell, a non-Indian, University of California graduate student spoke on primitive arts, song and dances which were halted by the arrival of the white men. Slides were shown of Indians and the round house. Recordings of songs were played. Bill Graves, of Upper Lake was the singer in the recordings. He is a member of the FIC. Riddell showed the different parts of the costumes used in the dances. His report was based on the study of the Pomo Indians of Lake County."[33]

After his SAS talk, Riddell returned to his Berkeley studies, including fieldwork in Peru and Alaska, writing his MA thesis in 1954.[34] When Dyson was promoted to assistant state historian in 1956, this left a vacancy at SIM for which Riddell was eminently suited. The timing was a blessing. Riddell's path toward the doctorate was grueling. He began to doubt the reward was worth the struggle, later confessing that the German language requirement got the best of him.[35] SIM job in hand, he left grad school with more elation than angst.

Although born in Redding, Riddell grew up in Lassen County, where proximity to a substantial Indigenous population and his father's work as irrigation district surveyor cultivated an early interest in Native life. After accepting SIM's directorship, Riddell wrote former Berkeley compatriot Clem Meighan, a UCLA assistant professor, to withdraw his application for a temporary position. Meighan's hearty congratulations included a felicitous reminder that Riddell was now positioned to conduct research without the heavy hand of graduate supervisors. In a thinly veiled reference to Heizer he joked, "About the time you start digging some of the delta sites, I believe I will be able to hear the Berkeley ulcers perforating." He was correct.

Riddell was booked for a second SAS talk after his SIM appointment. He remembered Potts and Pansy arriving together, that fall of 1956, with Pansy's youngest child strapped into a cradleboard. "Her feet were sticking out about a foot but she couldn't go to sleep any other way" he recalled. "[Pansy] told me, 'I had to come see who this guy was from back home.'" Contemporaries and schoolmates at one point, they had vague knowledge of one another. Marie, on the other hand, was the object of fond boyhood memories for Riddell. Spaulding's soda fountain, where Potts worked for a while, was a regular stop for Fritz and Harry. "I knew who she was," he said, recalling these Susanville encounters. "She knew how to talk to kids . . . she was a young woman, probably early 30s . . . vibrant and bubbly." Riddell's SAS talk included discussion of an excavation begun in the summer of 1940, following his and Harry's SJC graduation. After World War II and three years of Marine Corps service, Riddell completed the excavation under the auspices of the California Archeological Survey, dubbing this Lassen County site Tommy Tucker Cave.[36] Imagine his surprise when Potts strolled to the podium afterward to report that Tommy Tucker was her cousin.

Apprentice Anthropologists

Marie's cultural consulting began when three UCLA students in Professor William Lessa's yearlong ethnographic methods seminar decided to conduct fieldwork in northern California.[37] Lessa's junior colleague, Meighan, sent them to Riddell. On January 19, 1957, Robert Littlewood, Benjamin Swartz, and Joan Seibert—a doctoral, master's, and undergraduate student, respectively—arrived at SIM.[38] Riddell escorted them to bars on "skid row" that evening (now Old Sacramento State Historic Park) to meet with "itinerant Indians."[39] The next morning they stopped by Clear Lake to get Barrett. After visiting Big Valley Rancheria, they drove to Upper Lake, staying the night, while Bill Graves sang for them and discussed curing techniques. The following day they photographed the Big Valley round house before heading to Sulphur Bank Rancheria (now Elem Colony). Barrett showed them an earthen depression, the only remaining feature of the semi-subterranean round house where he had first witnessed dance ceremonies.

After photographing the site, they returned to Sacramento on January 22, via Middletown Rancheria.

Potts met the group that evening and spent two more days indulging their every query regarding Mountain Maidu weaving and acorn use. On Friday, Elmer and Eva (Martin) Smith met them at SIM and offered to show them Eva's mother's baskets, arranging a visit for later that week. The next morning they left on another excursion. With Potts, Barrett, and Riddell in tow, they headed to Grindstone Rancheria, in Colusa County, for a religious ceremony called the Bole-Maru, a mid-century incarnation of the Ghost Dance revitalization movement that Cora Du Bois had documented for Kroeber in the 1930s. Pomos from Lake County—Sulphur Bank and Big Valley Rancherias—had arrived earlier to join their Wintu friends. The Maru was in progress when the Sacramento entourage arrived. Paying the dance captain fifty cents a head, they gained entrance to the dance house. Throughout the long ceremony and night, they observed interactions between Red and White Bighead dancers, a Flathead dancer, singers, a clown, and spectator-participants, both children and adults.[40]

In the morning, part of a wall collapsed. Several women were partially buried under debris but were extricated uninjured, giving the observers yet another experience to mull over on the drive home. Riddell, Barrett, and Potts rode together. The only California Native among this like-minded coterie, Potts brought unique cross-cultural knowledge and texture to their lively conversation. This was an unexpected delight for Barrett, who joined the students at SIM during the next two days while they continued interviews and observations with Potts. On January 30, Littlewood and Swartz spent the day in Oroville with Elmer's father, Hood Smith; Selena (Davis) Jackson, Eva Smith's maternal aunt; and Herb Young. After photographing Selena's baskets, they returned that night to SIM.[41] Potts and Seibert joined them the following day. In Oroville, they picked up Elmer and Eva Smith, who escorted them to Feather Falls to meet Ina (Davis) Jackson, Selena's sister and Eva's mother. They photographed and measured Ina's baskets, interviewed her, and returned to Sacramento. Barrett toured the students through Berkeley's basket collection, a last stop, before waving them off to UCLA. They spent the semester analyzing and writing up their findings.

They were not the only ones contemplating these experiences. Two weeks as a teacher and student fostered a new sense of purpose in Potts: writing herself and her Mountain Maidu knowledge into the formal ethnographic record. She reveled in speaking her language; identifying Maidu terms for basketry-related plants, tools, and techniques; demonstrating twining and coiling; and recounting how Big Meadow people went to Indian Valley to harvest black oak acorn or downriver to Caribou for the live oak variety. She recalled their annual return to the same trees "that were pruned and bore better," hauling the harvest to Big Meadow in burden baskets. She described the drying processes, winter storage arrangements, pounding, leaching, cooking, and so forth. This work sparked place-based nodes of memory tethered to her Big Meadow girlhood. The Maidu world of her ancestors and birth rushed to the fore.

The papers resulting from this fieldwork are valuable for what they tell us about Potts. Littlewood's fieldwork focused on acorn consumption. Subsistence was often arduous, he reported, and Big Meadow's high altitude necessitated journeying to lower climes to procure acorns. Potts remembered being hungry, and the high value placed on every last bit of acorn meal, even if moldy. Realizing he had failed to follow up on the last two issues, Littlewood wondered if these were functions of colonization or long winters. Pressed about practices of winter storage and acorn use, Potts recalled each family having its own pine needle–lined storage pit, ringed with a drainage channel to ensure that this precious staple remained dry. "The supplies were never shared with another family, but if some families had not fared well during the winter, the informant reports that her grandfather would take food around with him on his visits."[42] Potts also embraced this practice, first as a young mother in Engelmine and Chester, and later in Sacramento. The Native people Littlefield met on Sacramento's skid row his first night were beneficiaries of Hukespem's teachings. Having absorbed her grandfather's values, Marie carried this Maidu orientation into modern, urban worlds. Asked about acorn's role within the larger diet, she reported that it was the staple for two daily meals, supplemented by "jerky, berries, fish, roots, greens, and other nuts." Maple, oak, or sunflower leaves comprised the wrapping for acorn loaves baked in ash pits. "Cooking leaves," green and/or water-soaked, were always at the ready of the well-prepared cook, who placed them to create quilt-like barriers between different foods layered in the same roasting pit. An expedient version of the looped tool used to remove cooking rocks from fire was sometimes fashioned by binding together two prongs of a forked serviceberry branch. These customs had been nestled for decades in the recesses of her mind, becoming couriers for other facts that spilled forth and into Littlewood's field notes.

Curating her annual fair exhibit brought Potts into regular engagement with Swartz's subject: basketry. Her collaboration with Swartz culminated in a term paper, a December 1957 conference presentation, and the article "A Study of the Material Aspects of Northeastern Maidu Basketry."[43] Like Littlewood, Swartz identified Potts as his "chief informant," a cultural consultant in contemporary parlance. She was paid for this work, acknowledging that her time and knowledge as a Mountain Maidu culture bearer held value. Swartz developed a typology of basket forms and functions featuring photographs of Maidu baskets. Two were Big Meadow baskets belonging to Marie, four were photographed in Oroville and Feather Falls (made by "Old Ann," Ina Jackson, Daisy Baker, and Marie Davis), and three were Berkeley specimens.

Riddell was no bystander during these weeks. On January 27, while Barrett and the students looked on, Marie demonstrated milling. First, she used a *walákum* (roller) on a flat stone, showing how seeds were traditionally turned to meal and the pulping process used with several plants "in the Queen Elizabeth Lace family (*papám, pulútim, sakómin*)" and "root medicines, leaves and camas (*poyóm*)." This demonstration caused her to remember and describe Josie's *walákum* and grinding rock, though the Maidu term for metate, later added by Riddell as *áhleh*, eluded her. Next she demonstrated how a bar-shaped or rectangular *walákum* was employed. Riddell recorded detailed notes on the biomechanics of grinding. The next day, responding to a colleague who had borrowed the 8-mm film he made of Kitty Joaquin and Roxie Peconum similarly engaged in Susanville, Riddell shared this new data and extolled Potts's knowledge: "Probably the most complete exposition of Mountain Maidu grinding techniques was given me yesterday."[44]

Potts gave it her all. A candid photograph shows her sitting perfectly upright, almost at attention, a coiled basket in progress on her lap. Mid-stitch, a strand of weaving material raised in her hand trails delicately out of focus and frame. Her attention is concentrated on her interlocutor on the photographer's right; she is fully absorbed in the work of teaching and translating her heritage. A portrait of keen awareness and intellectual acuity, she exudes confidence in the rich repository of Maidu knowledge still within her mental, physical, and linguistic grasp. Swartz later consulted Berkeley graduate student William Shipley for help translating Mountain Maidu words he documented during their interviews, using an asterisk in his publication to mark new contributions. Littlewood claimed less confidence in his ability to take down these words, remarking, "Although the informant was well-versed in the language of her people, I definitely feel that my linguistic techniques were inadequate to make even reasonably accurate transcriptions of the words. However, I did make every effort to transcribe as much as possible in my own strange and wonderful gloss."[45] The sole doctoral student in the group, Littlewood offered a critique of his fieldwork and analysis. The Maru ceremony posed many challenges, including a language barrier, interior darkness, recording prohibitions, lack of preliminary research, and simple endurance throughout the long night and multi-phase dance. He felt that brevity of time prohibited him from establishing sufficient rapport with the Smiths, Jackson sisters, and Young. All were praised as cooperative, even expansive, despite difficulty in some areas of recall and a tendency to lose interest in basketry and acorn talk.

Potts presented an altogether different "problem." Both men labeled her a "sophisticated informant." They established rapport with ease, finding her enthusiastic and knowledgeable. But she was atypical, Littlewood wrote:

> Mrs. Potts was an unusual informant. She was already accustomed to interviews and had, over the years, cultivated considerable objectivity towards her subject. Although she did not attempt to guide the questioning, it was felt from time to time that she could have asked the questions better than could the interviewer. This is not to say that she was prepared with the answer to all the questions. In fact there were many instances where the framework of the interview elicited recall of items which she had not had occasion to think about for some time. Another problem was the distance in time removed from the tribal setting. During the intervening years, her sophisticated interest in tribal matters had led her to many ethnographic sources, and, although the honesty of her responses was beyond doubt, it is not possible to determine how much these sources had influenced her reminiscences. Since her recollections were of a period (1895–1910) when considerable tribal disorientation had already taken place under the effects of white contact, there was the added difficulty of reconstructing the true aboriginal patterns.

He had regrets. He could have taken advantage of her intelligence and experience to probe more complex issues. Swartz made similar observations: "Mrs. Potts is highly sophisticated and is acquainted with some anthropological literature on the Maidu. Due to the scarcity of literature on Maidu basketry I doubt if appreciable bias was caused by reinterpretation of written ethnographic accounts. However, some effect was noted, e.g. her account of the procedure of splitting willow coincides closely with that of Dixon (1905)."

The "problem," then, was her literacy. She could—and did—read from precisely the same corpus of anthropological work they did. And why not? As both authors note in a dispassionate tone and language that utterly fails to capture a fate far from random and impersonal, the Maidu experienced "accelerated change after white contact." Marie's grandparents endured this invasion but were long deceased. She was a reader, a writer—a thinker. How natural it was to ferret out and consume any texts that shed light on the contingencies of her ancestors' lives and world. At the very least, she could plot intercultural encounters and temporalities. The likeness between Dixon's drawing of a Maidu Feather Dance cape and the one worn by Hukespem surely captured her imagination. (See figure 1.) In August 1899, weeks after Marie was hustled off to Greenville, Dixon was nearing the last leg of his initial collecting expedition when he checked into Quincy's Plumas House.[46] He would traipse through Maidu territory for four field seasons, making field notes and acquisitions for Boas, his mentor and employer at the AMNH.

Using AMNH accession records, one scholar reconstructed Dixon's itinerary and collecting techniques, which turned with each passing season away from objects and toward texts. During his initial foray, in the summer of 1899, Dixon purchased more than 116 Maidu objects, "including baskets from Genesee, Quincy, Indian Valley, Big Meadows, Chico, Mooretown, and Round Valley . . . 27 objects from Round Valley, 36 from the Concow at Chico and Mooretown, and 29 from the Mountain Maidu."[47] Dixon, Frederick Ward Putnam's doctoral student, took his doctorate from Harvard in 1900 while still engrossed in what some have called the first systematic collection produced by a professionally trained ethnographer or museum curator.[48] Putnam's expertise was archaeological, so he sent Dixon to Boas for linguistic and ethnographic tutelage. The latter's influence on Dixon is crystallized in an acquisition he described to Boas in correspondence sent from Harvard in October 1902: "I have obtained some thirty tales (some 15–16 pages of closely written English) aggregating over 100 pages in all." In 1903 he returned for more. Many came from an Atsugewi/Mountain Maidu intellectual named Tom Young, or Hanc'ibyjim. This was precisely the class of material that Boas argued should supplant material objects as the principal data for cultural analysis. Herb Young, whom the UCLA students met in Oroville, was Tom's son.

Anthropological Texts as Ancestral Testimony— The Indian Claims Commission

To read Dixon was to encounter her own ancestors. Mountain Maidu histories— spoken, sung, dance, and prayed—were cultural texts. They did not materialize on the horizon with settler wagons, mission schools, Indian agents, or ethnographers. The stronghold and archival repository of Maidu histories and beliefs is Maidu people. Although Marie had memories of orators and wise ones, their role as traditional knowledge keepers was threatened. Land expropriation, capitalism, and boarding school policy frayed kinship bonds, seasonal work cycles, and ceremonial calendars governing oral, intergenerational transmission of Maidu histories. The same colonial machinery that fostered anthropology's growth foreclosed on the legitimacy of sung, danced, and spoken words. These reverberations shook the lives of Doaksum et al. as legal contracts and signatures trumped verbal covenants.

This was plainly in evidence at ICC hearings. The printed word was front and center, the legitimate source of knowledge over and above any testimony to be extracted contemporaneously from descendants of those whose livelihoods, burial traditions, technologies, and myths comprised the anthropological record. Indigenous "word" carried meaning, not inherently but because it was anthropologically transmuted by the archaeological or ethnographic hand. Fixed in field notes, interpreted, and published, it formed the mountain of evidence on which California Indian claims rested. Still fresh from these hearings, Potts had every reason to institutionalize her knowledge in the formal ethnographic record. Her descendants' future under U.S. domination was unpredictable.

In the mid-1950s, as ICC hearings approached, Potts was busy with ruled paper and pencil, preparing *Smoke Signal* copy, most likely in the California State Library. A seemingly mundane archival document from this moment survives to instantiate her remarkable intellect and activist labor. In her impeccable longhand, she recorded the dates, locations, and names of the negotiating commissioners for each California treaty. When her task was complete, she inscribed a note to herself on the last two lines: "The secret of success is constancy to purpose—Benjamin Disraeli." Sitting in Boalt Hall on the UC Berkeley campus, in June and July 1954, looking thoroughly composed, Potts was anything but. Galled, transfixed, and cautiously hopeful, she exhibited that constancy, weathering long days of ICC proceedings with FIC stalwarts Stewart, Bahnsen, and Lela Dunlap.

Harold Driver and Ralph Beals, anthropologists for the Department of Justice (DOJ), argued that California Indian people used only a fraction of land for subsistence. Kroeber, Heizer, Gifford, and Barrett proffered evidence to the contrary for California Indian plaintiffs. Earlier that year, acting on a DOJ petition, ICC consolidated Docket 31 (representing ICI and FIC, via an amended petition filed on April 28, 1949), CCI's Docket 37 (filed on September 14, 1948), and thirteen separate suits filed by California tribes and bands into a single claim.[49] Eight years of saber rattling, ad hominem attacks, and staking out superior legal or moral high ground ended with these adversaries sharing the same stakes and set of cold, hard auditorium chairs.[50] The news media was on the scene daily. Relating a Klamath narrative about the precarious fate of souls carried by canoe on a riparian passage to the afterlife, an *Oakland Tribune* reporter explained, "Kroeber cited this bit of folklore in a continuing effort to prove 'beyond all question of a doubt,' that the Indians had possession of California for from 1,000 to 3,000 years, during which time they developed a thriving civilization, languages, customs and folklore."[51] Indeed, Young confirmed this Mountain Maidu reality for Dixon, and for Kroeber by extension.

It was tough being a spectator at hearings where one's ancestors' lives and traditions were hashed and rehashed. For all their own knowledge and intelligence, their fate was at the mercy of anthropologists and motley precursors, such as self-taught ethnographer Stephen Powers. A midwestern farmer, Powers trekked and wrote his way through California in 1871–1872. In 1875 the Bureau of American Ethnology (BAE) hired him to collect objects from tribes along the Sierra's eastern slope for Philadelphia's Centennial Exposition of 1876, the first U.S. world's fair. During this spate of fieldwork, he found himself in Susanville recording the appellation Marie's people used for themselves, Ná-kum.[52] Powers's early writings, subsequently incorporated into *Tribes of California*, laid a foundation for professional ethnographers like Dixon and Kroeber. A contrasting portrait of these two emerges from their visits to Chico's Maidu community. Dixon, dressed in rustic attire, was at home in the Mechoopda village eating Maidu foods, while dapper Kroeber overnighted at Bidwell Mansion, dining on fine china.[53] Whatever Native Californians first thought of Kroeber, his ICC testimony bought a moment of redemption. Mary Gist Dornback, CCI executive secretary, sang his praise: "Very few people came to see us when there were no roads, as I remember seeing Dr. Alfred L. Kroeber, our expert witness in our Claims Case, doing in early days—walking, riding horseback or in a canoe."[54]

One or two disciplinary generations earlier, Potts would have been dismissed as a modern, acculturated woman.[55] After all, Kroeber was so enamored of Ishi because he represented an ethnographic fantasy and archetype—the quintessentially "wild" or "real" Indian, unpolluted by the modernity that crashed ashore in the tide of human greed that engulfed his kinsmen and swallowed up his future. When Young shared his voice and stories with Dixon, Ishi was still self-sequestered a stone's throw from Big Meadow. Marie later professed that her family was intermarried with Ishi's.[56] Incorrigibly, she had continued to read, including Theodora Kroeber's *Ishi in Two Worlds*. She was not blind to the tyranny that anthropological knowledge wielded over Native lives in federal and juridical spheres. Oral tradition unmediated by anthropological imprimatur was classed as "unreliable folklore." She knew and read Vine Deloria Jr., who gave voice to many shared sentiments in the genre of which she was also master and connoisseur: acerbic wit and sarcastic humor. She engaged the discipline because she was an educator at heart and it provided another platform for her work. It put food in her grandchildren's mouths. And as Deborah Miranda asserts in relation to Rumsen Ohlone speaker Isabel Meadows' collaboration with Smithsonian linguist and salvage ethnographer J. P. Harrington, Potts knew it would nourish Maidu descendants.[57]

She moved between worlds and people with ease: Native and white, traditional and acculturated, urban and rural, youths and adults, federal politicians and grassroots activists. She also collapsed the classic binary between Native and ethnographer, inhabiting both subjectivities with absolute ease. Her abiding interest in other people and cultures can be traced back to Carlisle, where she counted among her friends an array of students from every imaginable background. Asked about this scenario in the mid-1950s, she revealed her analytic propensity:

> Some of the kids there were grown men and women. Now when we graduated, our class, there was one person that was 40 years old. And some of them—we called it, instead of a kindergarten class, we called it a normal class. And some members of that class, would be young men and young women that were in their 20s. Some would be much older than 20, particularly those that came from Oklahoma, where all of the money was. And they came in with their nice suits of clothes on, and their diamond rings and diamond pins and just learning their ABCs. It was kind of—in a way, it was kind of pitiful. It kind of showed, too, that they weren't too proud to come to school regardless of how old they were.[58]

Pressed for any Carlisle regrets, she replied, "Maybe I was just a little different. I felt comfortable no matter where I went."[59] This was decidedly the case.

Her eagerness to witness Grindstone's Maru dance was predictable, but she was not alone in transgressing disciplinary boundaries between ethnographic investigator and cultural consultant. Ella Cara Deloria, Zora Neale Hurston, and Bea Medicine—whom Potts met in the 1960s—are among many female intellectuals who gravitated toward cultural analysis. Frank Day traversed similar divides. Among the young students Marie tutored at Greenville in 1911–1912, Day was the son of a Konkow headman and traditionalist. Day left his Butte County home several years after the 1922 death of his father, Billy Day. Traveling the countryside for nearly a decade, he immersed himself in the variegated contours of Native worlds, from Utah to Oklahoma, before returning to California and a prosaic life, though one fraught with unfortunate travails brought on by his share of human

foibles. Over time, Day increasingly appreciated his father's teachings and Maidu
world as expressions of indigeneity equal to those encountered during his travels.
He alerted Berkeley anthropologists of his wish to preserve this knowledge, and
they dispatched a student in March 1952. Day sang in his native tongue and
escorted the student on a photographic junket across a Maidu landscape rich
in meaning. That summer, he visited Marie at the fair, where Maidu art and
technology were center stage.[60]

A self-taught artist, Day began committing Maidu stories to cardboard, canvas,
and his own tape recorder, an incomparable self-archiving project.[61] In August 1961,
Potts and Riddell worked out a plan for Day to combine ethnographic consulting
for Riddell with cultural demonstrations at the fair. Marie would locate an overnight host if he would paint and produce examples of traditional men's technology,
such as flint knapping and net making, at the exhibit.[62] It seems this never came
to pass. However, the Sacramento County Fair booked Day as a demonstrator
of "Indian painting" in 1963, and the following summer, Potts exhibited four of
his paintings, telling *Smoke Signal* readers that he was a self-taught artist whose
paintings depicted "Indian legends." In 1966, she showed *Test of Strength*, which
rendered one of these legends in pastel hues of yellow, blue, and green, to hundreds
of fairgoers. One was a *Bee* writer, whose headline, "Maidu Tribe Shows Dying
Ways at Fair," echoed a familiar trope.[63] These were important times for California
Indian people. An intense period dedicated to recovering and revivifying Native
tradition and ceremony—from basket weaving to regalia making to song and
dance—was about to burst onto the horizon. On the early cusp of this dawning,
Potts and Day authored cultural texts in new mediums, engaging in ethnographic
self-representations that pollinated these efforts.

America Indian Films Project

In 1958 Riddell hired Marie as a part-time cultural consultant and SIM demonstrator. She wove baskets on-site, fabricated Pomo-style clapper sticks like
those used at Grindstone, fashioned a shredded tule skirt, replicated a model
tule canoe, and, in the museum's side yard, constructed a domed "Central Valley
type" tule hut and a conical cedar bark house like the one she had inhabited in
Big Meadow.[64] These were props for a preliminary phase of the visual salvage
ethnography project Barrett and Kroeber intended to propose for NSF funding.
In Barrett's words, he had dusted off his old Cine-Kodak, "secured some rolls
of color film and started off on a 'voyage of discovery'—to see how much he
could find and how far back the clock could be turned. This first voyage yielded

results beyond our expectations."[65] Barrett cast Marie and her grandchildren in several of these films. During January 1957 field excursions, and in years that followed, Marie developed deep respect for Barrett and he for her, not simply as a repository of Native knowledge but as a tireless advocate for California Indian people.

Their collaboration began immediately. Barrett wrote Riddell in June 1957 to finalize arrangements for film prototypes already in the works. He was shooting a Brush Dance the next month with Grover Allred and their Hupa contact, David Risling, and was bound for Klamath Lake immediately after. Another project slated for Pomo country would feature eighty-year-old Harry Holmes fabricating a tule canoe. Film and audiotape orders were made; Barrett was raring to go: "Also, have you heard anything new on the Clear Lake balsa deal or any of the work in which Mrs. Potts is concerned?"[66] Shot in 1957 and produced the following year, *Pomo Tule Balsa* accompanied the NSF grant proposal. It opens with a scene of two boys, Marie's grandsons Larry and Marvin Lee Marine, paddling the newly made vessel on Folsom Lake.[67] With never a dull moment in these years, the

Figure 15. Coiling a basket at SIM, 1959. The basket was featured in a 1975 exhibit in Governor Jerry Brown's office. The exhibit catalog, *I Am These People*, includes a photograph of Brown in front of the glass case where the completed basket was displayed.
Courtesy California State Parks, 090-P60134.

Smoke Signal sometimes simmered on the back burner. In October 1958, Barrett trained his lens on Lizzie Enos and Marie processing acorns. They cracked and hulled, pounded and leached, heated cooking rocks, and stirred mush in one of Marie's Big Meadow baskets.[68]

Marie built acorn caches and cedar bark huts in Maidu country and fashioned objects and film props that PAHMA later accessioned. In May 1957 she prepared bear grass weft and coils of split maple for a Lake Almanor basket weaving shoot, where she was filmed twining a small burden basket. In September 1962 she fashioned two buckskin and shredded maple bark dolls with clamshell-bead eyes, each varying slightly in style and composition but mirroring the Maidu

Figure 16. Marie Potts and Lizzie Enos process acorns in Clipper
Gap for Samuel Barrett's American Indian film project.
Courtesy California State Parks, Album 31, H-47.

Figure 17. Marie Potts tests the readiness of her acorn mush.
Courtesy California State Parks, Album 31-H-50.

dolls she played with as a child and that Elsie Bidwell glimpsed inside the cedar bark dollhouses pupils built in the woods behind Greenville school. A longer Barrett film depicting Yahi culture was staged partly in Humboldt County. Marie dug bulbs and several grandchildren are shown "soaking basket materials . . . cooking meat and fish over fire, winnowing seeds, playing grass game, spinning tops, receiving instruction in pressure flaking arrow points and basketmaking." Additional footage of granddaughters playing along the riverbank and a grandson using a fire drill was shot on the Bear River near Colfax.[69]

Another batch of accessioned materials—a bundle of redwood bark basketry material and samples of acorn flour—was requisitioned from Potts for the sum of $150, remuneration for her stint as a cultural demonstrator in 1960. The acorn was jarred in three states: "meats shelled and rolled to remove fuzz, acorn chunks separated from meal for regrinding, acorn after final grinding."[70] Spectators and the news media came in throngs to watch her work from one to five every afternoon, September 13–18. Images of Marie laboring on the patio in her shirtwaist dress and heels are juxtaposed with her pithy remarks about white people starving during the cold winters without Indian people's help. Reporters were not to be outdone: "A full-blooded Maidu Indian and true connoisseur of acorniana has been demonstrating how modern man can survive an atomic holocaust"; "One museum aide cannot wait to get to her stove to try the dish"; "Despite the popularity of the show, there has been no noticeable rush at campus dining spots for inclusion of any acorn by-products on the menu."[71]

Before leaving for her Berkeley appearance, Potts wrote Fred Baker. Mentioning her museum engagement, she promised to visit if time allowed, musing, "The State Fair is in full swing, the weather is wonderful, very cool nights." Contentment was tempered by disappointment over land claims, "I do not have much faith in the Department [of Interior] doing anything. I feel their letter was just to appease our group. I could be wrong. I will be attending the hearing September 8." She was a consummate juggler. The fair exhibit, BIA hearings, and Berkeley commitments ran end to end for three weeks straight and she never missed a beat.

Barrett died on March 9, 1965. The loss hit Potts hard. She was nearing her seventieth birthday. Pansy was hospitalized and Marie would soon be writing her obituary. She had mourned Kitty in the *Smoke Signal*, and her tribute to Barrett was equally poignant. Sixteen years her senior, he had recognized that her generation of California Indians was modern, but Indigenous nonetheless. Memorializing him in verses that evoked the sense of urgency many California Indian people felt as their own elders passed on, Potts concluded her tribute with a brief biography:

FAREWELL TO OLD FRIENDS

He was here yesterday and the day before and the day before that. We did many chores together. We saw many things together. We saw the beauty of the earth, the plants, the animals, and heard the singing of the birds together.

Now he has finished his life here and gone on a journey to never return. The work he did here will remain. It is a symbol of why he was given life, to DO and this he DID. He is gone but the work he did here will be everlasting.

Others will see it and use it so his work continues to live and memory lingers on.

Funeral services were held last month for Dr. Samuel Barrett in Sonoma, his hometown. At the graveside service, Rev. George Effman gave a final farewell from the American Indians. Dr. Barrett, an ethnographer, was reared in the Ukiah area among Pomo Indians. He wrote many articles on the Pomos and Mewuks while he was the Director of the Milwaukee Museum. . . . A few years ago he made a moving picture of the Maidu Indian ceremony, known as the "Bear Dance" in Janesville. Indians and non-Indians who worked with Dr. Barrett will miss seeing him around with all his paraphernalia. In his last few years, he worked under a great handicap. He is now relieved of all the strenuous duties. We are relieved to know he is resting in peace.[72]

As this latter passage shows, filming and revivification of the Bear Dance, at the Mankinses' ranch on June 9–10, 1962, was especially important to Potts. A swarm of Maidu worker bees in Plumas and Lassen Counties, including Gladys Mankins, Herb Young, Tom Epperson, and Elmer Smith, made this happen, as months of correspondence between them, Riddell, and Barrett reveal. Two years earlier, several Maidu cultural consultants attended the March 5, 1960, dedication ceremonies for Kroeber Hall. The building's namesake was speaking, and Maidu people were contributors to the exhibit *Indians of Western North America*, inaugurating the new quarters. Epperson and Ole Salem, another Mountain Maidu consultant, stopped in Sacramento to pick up Potts and Riddell before heading to Berkeley. Perhaps the concept for a Bear Dance originated over the course of this evening spent with Barrett.[73]

Ethnographic Interventions

Potts's SAS board membership was a direct outgrowth of her work curating the 1950 state fair exhibit. Her engagement in both settings comprised active intervention in domains of cultural production closed off to her grandparents' generation, whose transfer of knowledge to salvage ethnographers, from Dixon to Kroeber, literally underwrote the emergence of professional anthropology in northern California. Potts stepped into these shoes and spheres without a second thought, bringing cultural authority and legitimacy to work still dominated, in Sacramento, by amateur enthusiasts like Zallio, Hathaway, and Lillard. Her introduction to anthropologists with whom she would later collaborate emerged from this context of emergent anthropology at SJC.

Like all knowledge, Potts's consulting work with Riddell and Barrett was situated and contingent. It was labor—labor for which she was paid and equally a labor of love. Reading her ancestors' contributions to salvage ethnography tethered her work and world to theirs. Most scholars now concede that salvage ethnography produced a corpus of material that documents settler colonial subjectivity at least as much as Native language and culture. Today a new generation of Native and non-Native scholars confronts the archive of that subjectivity, peeling back its layers to interrogate ancestral silences, obfuscations, and illuminations coded for descendant generations.[74] Potts would appreciate these projects. They are contemporary iterations of her own engagement with ethnography—natural progressions of Native scholarship, whether in Native studies or in allied disciplines. Mohawk anthropologist Audra Simpson's work on Indigenous refusal—political, ethnographic, and otherwise—is worth considering in relation to Potts, whose ethnographic consent, indeed excitement, cannot be understood apart from her unprecedented exercise of political voice and cultural authority in the *Smoke Signal* and the All-California Indian Exhibit.[75] Her status as a boarding school alumna and urban-dwelling Indian, attributes that marked her to some as acculturated, surely sweetened these opportunities to indulge ancestral memories and to accentuate her Native belonging. More significant still were her experiences of 1954 and 1955, at hearings before the ICC, the court of colonial power. Here she witnessed contemporary claims to ancestral lands adjudicated through anthropological field notes, journals, and publications—ancestral voices and lives transmogrified into legal evidence establishing aboriginal possession since time immemorial. As with the shape-shifting presence of settler colonial power, Potts witnessed ancestral ethnographic consent mobilized both for and against land claims.

Finally, as Abenaki anthropologist Margaret Bruchac reminds us, Native people are also drawn to cultural inquiry and analysis—and are often better at it, as was the case with the fascinating figure of Bertha Parker Pallan (Seneca), who was working among the neighboring Mechoopda Maidu while Potts was in Chester, struggling to keep house and home together.[76] When her own opportunity to read, study, and contribute to the ethnographic record of California Indian and northern Maidu culture arose, Potts jumped at the chance.[77] All else aside, it fed the intellectual curiosity and adventurous sensibility that carried her out to Carlisle and that she continued to cultivate at every possible turn.

9

"A Grand, Wise Lady"

National Activism

After the meeting, I was asked if I would go to Washington, D.C., and help in the office of the National Congress of American Indians. Being a blue-blooded Indian I couldn't refuse.

—*Marie Potts, July 1961*

Potts loved to travel, and activism opened new vistas for this ceaseless passion. During her Carlisle years she mastered the art of getting around on a modest budget. No destination was too distant or daunting. When her daughters were boarding at Stewart Indian School and Sherman Institute, she would hop on a bus to be there for Mother's Day teas, musical performances, and plays. In the late 1940s, she volunteered for FIC fieldwork, recruiting new members and keeping track of rival group activity. Touring with UCW, she transformed their religious lecture circuit into a forum for promoting FIC's land claims and legislative lobbying. Like the Sacramento World Affairs Council, for whom she was guest speaker in April 1954, UCW sought her out after the mainstream press covered her recent FIC delegate trips to Washington. This was important work, but the most rewarding returns were yet to be realized. These excursions brought her onto the radar and into the orbit of key members of the NCAI. Before the decade was out, Potts was propelled onto the national stage of American Indian activism, where she made significant contributions to NCAI, the American Indian Chicago Conference (AICC), and the American Indian Press Association (AIPA). This chapter opens with a chronicle of her first FIC delegate trip.

FIC Delegate

In the summer of 1953, Potts and Stewart traveled to Washington, D.C., as FIC delegates to testify before ICC.[1] These creative and hardworking friends crafted an itinerary that mixed business with plenty of sightseeing. They managed their monthlong excursion so inexpensively that it became legendary in the annals of NCAI, one of many stops along the way.[2] A July 11, San Francisco red-eye deposited them in D.C. on the afternoon of July 12. A month later, they hopscotched their way home by bus and train, zigzagging across the country on social and professional stops. Their expenses totaled $1,005.67, a sum raised entirely through member donations.[3] To say they had a grand old time is an understatement in the extreme, but work was the breath of life for these two. Visitor passes to the House of Representatives and the Senate chamber on July 17, 1953, are among the ephemera that Potts archived as mementos of her delegate experience. Professional contacts from this trip snowballed into new political opportunities, but immediate gains were equally plentiful, as the delegates reported at FIC's August meeting in the county courthouse. Members scattered farther afield read about their trip in two successive *Smoke Signals.* Potts documented their legislative and ICC meetings in August and ancillary activities in September. Narrated as a series of anecdotes—for instance, about visiting northern California Indians living in Virginia—this column recognized and thanked their many hosts. Today it comprises a valuable record of the circumstances in which political networks began to take shape. For instance, midway through the column, she proclaimed in her humorous and self-deprecating style, "A pleasant day was spent with Mrs. Ruth Muskrat Bronson in her home where for once, after the trying days and terrible heat, one of the delegates fell down on the job and slept all afternoon." Shifting the typewriter carriage to the next line purely for effect, she added, "A very enjoyable afternoon!"[4] Despite her jocular recounting of this episode, she had truly fallen asleep on the job.

Bronson's Georgetown home was NCAI's first headquarters and remained its center of gravity long after it leased a Dupont Circle office. Bronson was the younger sister of Harvey Muskrat, whom Potts knew from Sacramento's California Indian Agency. Though involved in NCAI's formation, Bronson could not attend the 1944 charter convention in Denver. Nonetheless, she immediately set to work, mostly on her own dime, translating her political expertise and activist energy into a vital legislative news and legal aid service for the embryonic organization.[5] Her role rapidly expanded to that of executive secretary, a position partially paid by her own fund-raising and heavily dependent on volunteer assistance. Potts carried out her work under nearly identical conditions. Bronson resigned this NCAI position in 1949 but was regularly there to save the day as the men who succeeded her resigned.[6] Though land claims hearings occasioned their meeting, Bronson used this visit to instill a critical view of termination, which paid near-instant dividends in the press. In Manhattan, on the first leg of their journey home, Potts and Stewart made several publicity calls. One resulted in a *New York Times* interview. Asked about withdrawal, they expressed circumspection regarding the overly hasty timeline of the Department of Interior (DOI).[7] Before leaving, they took the ferry to Ellis Island, cruised around Manhattan, admired its skyline from the Empire State Building observation deck, watched an NBC taping of the Morey Amsterdam TV show *Breakfast with Music*, and witnessed a United Nations session.

From there they traveled to Carlisle, Pennsylvania, where her old campus, which had reverted to its former status as an army post, was so transformed that Potts was momentarily lost. Carlisle Barracks officers gave them a tour, opening the old Hessian Guard House. Briefly used as an alumni center, it was now a forlorn museum. Marie was amazed to find her 1915 class pennant bearing the slogan "Fidelity" among the few items displayed.[8] Their tour guides mailed her a newspaper story published after their departure. After describing their delegate work, it recorded their nostalgia:

> Mrs. Potts, who was Marie Mason in her school days, said she hardly recognized the grounds, adding that she wished some of her school chums might see it also. "It's nice to be back. This is the first time I've been here since I graduated," she added. During their stay, Mrs. Potts and Mrs. Stuart [*sic*] leafed through old newspapers and photographs recalling old friends. Viewing a clipping of a Carlisle victory over Harvard, Mrs. Potts said, "We always used to skunk them." Mrs. Stuart [*sic*] recognized pictures of acquaintances she met at Chemawa School when some of the students of the Carlisle School were transferred there after it was closed in 1918.... As the women left for their California homes, Mrs. Potts remarked, "I had some of my happiest moments here."[9]

In Canton, Ohio, they visited Marie's friend Peter Calac, a former Carlisle football player and first cousin of Saturino Calac, president of FIC's Mission Indian chapter of NCAI. In Massillon, Ohio, Potts reunited with Carlisle alumna and Maidu friend Lena Watson Holloway. Hopping a train to Kansas, they toured Haskell Institute, discovering many friends in common among students and

teachers. Bronson had worked at Haskell from 1925 to 1930, and she had undoubtedly wired ahead to ensure their VIP treatment, because the students presented
them with personalized souvenirs. Using hers to sign Christmas cards a decade
later, Stewart asked, "Marie, remember the metal name plates they made for us
at Haskell?"[10] Potts's ebullient tone carried readers to a final stop. Though it was
seemingly insignificant, history proves it otherwise. "In Denver, Mrs. Stewart
and Mrs. Potts met with D'Arcy McNickle and Helen Peterson, Director, Mayor's
Committee on Human Relations and discussed Indian welfare and the possibility
of a workshop in California in the near future. A visit was made to the Indian
Development Project where information was gained." Without skipping a beat,
she ended, "Send *Smoke Signals* for Christmas gifts!"[11]

Always on the lookout for stories about Native pathbreakers, Potts had first
introduced readers to McNickle in a May 1952 NCAI *Bulletin* excerpt.[12] Six months
shy of their delegate work, she met him at the California Federation for Civic Unity
(CFCU) conference, held on December 20, 1952, in Asilomar, on the central coast.
Chaired by wealthy Bay Area Quaker Josephine Whitney Duveneck, the confer-
ence featured speakers Frederic Baker, Charles Elkus of the Northern California
Indian Defense Association, and two Sacramento Indian Office staffers. Joining
Stewart and Potts were tribal leaders Steve Ponchetti and Juanita Ortega from
San Diego County, Gilbert Marshall and David Risling from Hoopa, and Frank
Treppa and Lila Dunlap of Lake County. They passed a resolution imploring the
governor to include Native representatives in termination-related meetings and
to appropriate funds enabling their participation.[13]

Potts and Stewart knew McNickle from CFCU, but their introduction to
Peterson (Cheyenne/Oglala) came in Denver, where she was in her fifth year
as inaugural director of the Denver Mayor's Commission on Human Relations
(DMCHR). This was a fortuitous meeting for Potts, as Peterson was soon to
become a friend, mentor, and admirer. Bronson and McNickle had deep respect for
Peterson's intelligence and political savvy.[14] In 1948, when NCAI began to pursue
a coherent public relations plan, Peterson was named to the inaugural standing
committee on publicity.[15] She traveled widely for work, and her correspondence
shows she was adept at integrating NCAI publicity duties with opportunities
arising from her DMCHR job. The reverse was true as well. Insight into the
contours and problems of human relations cultivated through NCAI benefited
her commission work. The warm friendship the two women shared was matched
by the parallel passions and worlds of Peterson and McNickle. Both international
travelers, they were oriented to hemispheric definitions of American indigeneity

and attuned to looking to other societies and nations for solutions to problems at home. Their paths crossed frequently, as during the Second Inter-American Indian Conference in 1949 in Cuzco, where Peterson bought Bronson a beautiful handwoven textile, handing it off to McNickle to carry home to Washington for delivery.[16]

Bronson routed Potts and Stewart through Denver to benefit NCAI. For months, she and McNickle had spearheaded Peterson's recruitment to NCAI's executive directorship. An astute negotiator, Peterson was reticent to leave DMCHR, where she accomplished important work and was assured an adequate and dependable paycheck. A single mother, she insisted on the equivalent from NCAI and was still negotiating when Potts and Stewart arrived. Days before, she laid out her terms to President W. W. Short: "My salary and necessary travel expense must be guaranteed, because I feel that no person can do a good personal job if he has to worry about his next pay check."[17] NCAI was in dire fiscal straits. Tribal membership dues, once envisioned as a dependable revenue stream, were inadequate. Expanding tribal membership was predicated on field contact and publicity, costly work burdening a budget already suffering shortfalls from annual conventions and congressional lobbying. With the organization approaching its tenth anniversary, promises of self-sufficiency were wearing thin. The Robert Marshall Civil Liberties Trust renewed NCAI's grant contingent upon its hiring an executive director, whose job would be to grow tribal membership. Bronson knew that Peterson needed California Indian contacts. Potts became one, and so much more.

Potts arrived back in Sacramento two weeks before the state fair opened. She hustled to design and install FIC's exhibit while preparing her delegate report for an August 23 meeting. Members farther afield awaited coverage in the *Smoke Signal*. Pansy, as "pinch editor," got the paper out. After winning an Outstanding Educational Exhibit award at the fair, dismantling the booth, and getting all the loaned materials safely back to owners, Potts settled in to write the second installment of the delegate report. November 6–8 she attended CFCU's annual conference, where termination was discussed.[18] The theme "Nineteen Fifty-Forward for Better Relations Among all Races, Creeds, Colors" set the tone. Duveneck, representing AFSC and newly named to CFCU's board of directors, hosted Potts and Stewart at her Los Altos Hills estate, Hidden Villa Ranch.[19] CFCU determined that a "program for a specialized education of California Indians" was needed. "The council wants to teach Indians about water rights, how to register for voting and the theory and mechanics of taxation."[20] This was predictable. Termination under

House Concurrent Resolution 108 (HCR 108) was believed a fait accompli.[21] The "Freedom from the Bureau" rallying cry of the Eighty-Third U.S. Congress masked termination's real beneficiary: the federal government. Education was the cure-all hyped by withdrawal advocates. At CFCU, California Indian people argued that the magnitude of the task was unfathomable and would take years to achieve.

In late February 1954, Potts and Stewart flew back to Washington. Congress was licking its chops, and Peterson feared that lawmakers would pounce before tribal peoples fully awakened to their status as prey rather than "freed Americans."[22] Joint hearings on S. 2749 and H.R. 7322 (pursuant to HCR 108), were about to begin when NCAI called an emergency meeting of tribal delegates.[23] This time Stewart and Potts had Arthur Treppa in tow.[24] With its modest budget, FIC would have been extravagant to fund three delegates, but they arrived at an ingenious solution. In exchange for assistance with delegation expenses, they would read statements into the record or deliver affidavits for FIC-affiliated tribes that could not afford to send their own representatives. On March 4 Stewart spoke for FIC and read statements from DNIWA, the Howonquet Indian Council of Smith River Rancheria, and the Elk Valley Rancheria of Crescent City. Potts represented the interests of Fort Bidwell Indians, and Treppa spoke for his tribe. In coordination with their legal firm, Wilkinson, Cragun and Barker, Peterson organized publicity statements and photographs. The three FIC delegates, with Lowana Brantner (Yurok) and Nellie Winton (Yurok), posed with California congressman Hubert B. Scudder on the Capitol steps. Northern California newspapers ran the photograph and a caption, explaining they had "come to town for hearings on Indian problems."[25] At their request, Peterson offered a brief NCAI statement concurring with their termination concerns, but she was still struggling to assess California's tribal landscape.[26]

FIC Withdraws Docket 12, Joins Docket 31

Bronson, now NCAI treasurer, helped Peterson sort out the bewildering history and politics of California land claims. During NCAI's early years, she fielded constant queries about the CIJA judgment fund and Collett-related factionalism. She worked assiduously to safeguard ICC from the barrage of conservative bills designed to extinguish it. NCAI recognized that ICC and termination were conjoined efforts to disclaim and end federal responsibility for treaties and tribal peoples. They hoped to benefit from the first while forestalling the second.[27] A vigorous NCAI presence was critical to these efforts, and California was virtually untapped territory in 1946 when George LaMotte wrote Stewart; it was Bronson who had given him Codman's name. LaMotte's Los Angeles location was advanta-geous for Mission tribal recruitment. The Agua Caliente Band of Mission Indians was the first California nation to join, and tribal chair Vyola Olinger lent an early California presence to NCAI's formal ranks. Saturino Calac (Luiseño) of Rincon Reservation responded to LaMotte's campaign, hoping to counter the influence of Collett and MIF.[28] On January 6, 1948, he wrote Bronson about progress recruiting new members, alerting her to the imminent arrival of FIC delegates.[29]

Stewart and Edna Calac, Saturino's wife, with Potts as alternate, were the first delegates elected to serve FIC at commission hearings. Bronson awaited their arrival in vain. The trip was postponed while the court of claims deliberated whether or not any of the three rival California entities comprised an "identifiable group" under ICCA. On March 21, a preliminary ruling argued that FIC and ICI could not move forward representing the same plaintiff: "Indians of Cali-fornia." In April 1949, following attorney deliberations, FIC agreed to withdraw Docket 12 and join Docket 31, whose attorneys were practiced land claims litigants. Together they filed an amended petition for Docket 31. Then, in December 1950, ICC ruled that "Indians of California" were not an "identifiable group." Attorneys appealed this ruling to the court of claims. Meanwhile, in May 1951, Representative Clair Engle introduced H.R. 3979 designating them as identifiable within ICCA's meaning. The five-year deadline for filing ICC petitions approached, so bills extending the commission's life had to be argued and passed. The summer 1953 delegate trip to appear before ICC marked Potts's first face-to-face interaction with ICC or NCAI. Docket 31 finally got the greenlight at the end of 1953.[30]

Peterson Comes to California

In mid-May, Peterson sent a follow-up memo to the 1954 joint hearings, addressed to "The California Indian Groups: (Siva, Winton, Brantner, Stewart, Mazzetti, Treppa, Forrest, Lavato and [NCAI president] Garry)." In a declaration of brutal honesty, she confessed, "I want to tell you what I know and understand about the California Termination Bill—which is practically nothing. I also want to ask you what is going on there and what the feelings are of the tribes you work with."[31] March testimony revealed that termination sentiment varied widely. Counseling delegates how to communicate their desires in the clearest terms possible, she appended three form letters—for representatives, senators, and Indian Affairs Subcommittee members. Each gave terms of address and boilerplate language that was respectfully assertive while underscoring the signatories' status as constituents and voters.

Potts, Stewart, and Erin Forrest spent May 28–30, 1954, at an AFSC conference at the Duvenecks' estate. FIC member Forrest (Pit River/Modoc) represented XL-Ranch at the joint hearings.[32] The Duvenecks, recently returned from touring northern California reservations and rancherias to discuss termination concerns, gathered an expert panel on law, water rights, taxation, social work, and education. Attendees posed direct questions to speakers and left concerned. Out of this forum and earlier NCAI consultation came the concept for a California tribal coalition. Forrest returned to Alturas, penned a letter of invitation listing seven benefits that intertribal organization would provide, and mailed it to every federally recognized California tribe. A June 19 meeting was set.[33] That weekend 117 tribes, many with FIC members in their ranks, formed the California Indians Congress (CIC). Forrest was elected president; in fact, every officer elected had attended the joint hearings.[34] Quickly reaching a common mind, they forwarded to California's senator William Knowland a resolution outlining their now fervent anti-termination stance, asking him to append it to the March 4–5 joint hearings record.[35] Naturally, the *Smoke Signal* carried this news.

That summer, Peterson came to California on a round of western states fieldwork dedicated to tribal recruitment and fund-raising. From late August to early September, her brother's Presidio Park apartment served as NCAI's ad hoc field office. This was a painfully productive moment to come to the Bay Area. June and July's ICC hearings were fresh in all minds. Dockets were consolidated, but animus lingered. Vitriol generated by now irrelevant ideological and procedural differences could hardly dissipate overnight, and each group clung resolutely to distinct affiliations. Self-righteousness was partly to blame, but so were practical considerations. Each group comprised a sociopolitical network and trusted channel of communication. Sparring and character assassination continued. Peterson trained her focus on helping each organization achieve an accurate understanding of legislation, regardless of intergroup squabbling. Behind the scenes, she made judgment aplenty.

Potts was busy organizing FIC's state fair booth when Peterson arrived in California, but the first week in September, Stewart accompanied their mutual friend to Sacramento. Peterson was impressed with Potts's exhibit and spent considerable time talking with her.[36] She also joined FIC and CIC representatives meeting with Senator Dale C. Williams of the California Senate Interim Committee on Indian Affairs, reporting, "It seemed to me they have the soundest approach of any state group I've seen; now that the Committee has been formed and is looking into facts, they are dead opposed to the bill presented last session."[37] In San Francisco,

Stewart and Peterson met with Raymond Armsby, IDA president. Peterson came away disturbed: "Frankly, I think the Elkus group isn't doing Indians any good and the fact that they seem to be looked to and respected makes it even worse." She praised the American War Mother's Club, which agreed to fund-raise on their behalf. "We asked for a minimum of $100 to strengthen Marie Potts' and Bertha's efforts on the *Smoke Signal*; $100 for field work to help Indians prepare for these hearings; and $500 to hold a state meeting of California Indians . . . to prepare for their stand on termination legislation."[38] Potts reported additional details of Peterson's visit: "While in Sacramento, she met with a group of Indians from Sacramento and Ione, at the home of Mrs. Sam Tripp. Mrs. Nancy Landuk entertained her at a dinner party."[39]

NCAI Volunteer

Peterson's California fieldwork convinced FIC members that NCAI had something to offer. In October they elected Stewart as their delegate to the December 1954 Omaha convention. Naturally, Potts went along.[40] By the 1957 convention in Claremore, Oklahoma, Marie had earned her NCAI stripes. The *Bulletin*'s "Pictorial Highlights," showcasing convention speakers, events, and resolutions, features a headshot cropped from FIC's 1954 publicity photograph with Chief Justice Warren. Centered on the page, her picture was ringed by portraits of male speakers and tribal leaders: "Marie Potts in Sacramento, California edits one of the brightest, best Indian publications coming out of Indian Country. In times past, she and her good friend Bertha Stewart from Smith River, California have practically hitch-hiked to the Nation's Capital to fight for Indians' interests. At Claremore, Marie worked hard at the convention on the regular things, and in addition she sold Oklahoma Centennial ties and coins to raise money for NCAI."[41]

This caption highlighted what Peterson most admired in Potts: her *Smoke Signal* editorship, tireless work ethic, and facility for getting herself wherever she was needed, regardless of limited financial means. This is how she got to Phoenix in 1959, to Denver in 1960, and to nearly every NCAI convention for three decades. In February 1958, when NCAI was organizing a trip to take a select group of leaders from across Indian Country to Puerto Rico to study Operation Bootstrap, Peterson wanted Potts and Stewart to go. Appealing to Elkus to sponsor them, she explained, "There is so much to learn about community planning and development, public relations, self-help programs, economic development, co-operative enterprises, housing that we feel some California Indian representative or representatives should go. Of course, Marie Potts with her publication could do much to report and interpret the experience."[42] Proving that Peterson had perfectly pegged IDA's politics during her 1954 fieldwork, Elkus acknowledged that she had "picked two fine outstanding persons" but opined that their budget was "too tight at this time for indulgence in such an experiment, even if we were convinced of its validity."[43]

Invitation to Chicago

In early March 1961, Potts found an envelope from the University of Chicago tucked among the usual FIC queries and renewals addressed to Injun Louie. "Dear Mrs. Potts,"

> The attached press release will tell you about a meeting in Chicago, February 10–14, at which plans crystallized for organizing regional discussions of Indian problems. D'Arcy McNickle was elected Acting Chairman of a Steering Committee, which—I presume—will meet to elect a permanent Chairman. At the same time, you were chosen as the best person to take leadership in organizing discussion in your region. You will therefore probably hear from D'Arcy McNickle, and I shall not write more about this.... Time is, of course, short; I hope things work out well. With all the best wishes—Sol Tax, AICC Coordinator.[44]

Known for "action anthropology," Sol Tax had been the Claremore keynote speaker and had appeared in the "Pictorial Highlights" issue showcasing Potts's volunteerism.[45] Both attended the 1960 Denver convention. A publicity photo identifies Potts and her road-tripping sidekick Irma Bahnsen, "California Indian Delegates," seated at a banquet table with Vice President Leo Vocu (Oglala) and Treasurer John Ranier (Taos), along with several NCAI guests. (See figure 18.) Peterson was courting academics working in western states, trying to develop collaborative partnerships and resource sharing to NCAI's benefit. It was here that Tax proposed the AICC, and McNickle's Resolution 11 was passed in support of it.[46] Immediately embracing her regional organizer duties, Potts published most of the enclosed press release:

> An American Indian Steering Committee has been created to prepare at the grassroots level a "declaration of Indian purpose" to be presented in June to a national conference at the University of Chicago. This conference will consider and act on the "Declaration of Purpose" as a guide to official and private organizations concerned with Indian Affairs. President Kennedy will be invited to receive this document, if adopted, on behalf of American

people. D'Arcy McNickle of the Flathead tribe, acting chairman of the new steering committee, pointed out that "this is the most intensive effort ever made to get the view of Indians in every part of the U.S., including many groups not now officially recognized as Indians by the Federal government." The 16 Indian participants in the 5-day conference have all expressed sincere appreciation that the University of Chicago is making possible this study and discussion, which will produce a statement on Indian plans for the "New Frontier."

At a meeting of the Indian Advisory Committee February 10–14 in Chicago, the U.S. was divided into nine areas, each to form a sub-committee. The California area representatives selected were Mrs. Marie Potts, organizing chairman; Erin Forrest, drafting committee; Bertha Stewart, rules committee; Harry Hopkins, program arrangement committee, and Max Mazzetti, public relations committee.

Each of the nine area sub-committees are to meet and discuss with other Indians, to take part in the decisions that make for policy and operating programs. The purpose of these meetings is to give every Indian a chance to participate, personally or through his representative, a chance to say what should go into the Indian Statement of Purpose, and present it to the General Council to be held June 13–20, 1961.[47]

It might be tempting to assume that her inclusion was based purely on friendship with Peterson, but this would discount the attributes and intellectual resources she brought to the table. Regular presence at NCAI conventions affirmed an activist commitment all the more impressive given her lack of tribal delegate status. Tax was attentive to this latter condition, actively seeking to incorporate non-trust-status Indians into AICC. Interim study group member Benjamin Bearskin was vocal about the life lens urban residence brought to Native experience. Furthermore, Peterson, the only Native woman at the February planning meeting, would have been sharply attuned to gender disparities.[48] Her 1954 correspondence with Bronson affirms Peterson's high regard for the *Smoke Signal*'s editor, and as a Native journalist, Potts was uniquely positioned to disseminate and report conference news at a grassroots level.

Regional meetings were the primary vehicles for Native people to make their voices heard in Chicago. Tax assured Potts that it was not her responsibility to book a regional meeting site. Nancy Lurie, assistant coordinator, was scouting options, including Reno, where Mary Sellers, University of Nevada–Reno (UNR),

Figure 18. NCAI Convention banquet, Denver, Colorado, 1960. *Clockwise from lower left*: Treasurer John Ranier; Amy Stearns; Dr. Robert L. Stearns (former University of Colorado president); Lorena Berger, Denver civic leader; Marie Potts; Irma Bahnsen; Vice President Leo Vocu; Loretta Vocu.
National Museum of the American Indian, Smithsonian Institution, NCAI 010.

had tentative departmental support. Lurie also awaited news from other contacts: "In California proper, there are a number of people at Berkeley. Dr. Samuel Barrett, former director of the Milwaukee Public Museum has retired to California and can be reached through the Anthro. Museum on the Berkeley campus or the Anthro. Dept."[49] She emphasized confidence in Sellers and Barrett by underlining their typescript names in thick black ink. Marginalia adjacent to Barrett's name cites a "nice letter" from him. In fact, his February response to her request for help in reaching California Indian communities was decidedly unhelpful, but she was glad to hear from him. Busy with his film project, Barrett was embarking on a southern California "reconnaissance mission." Assuring her that this fieldwork would benefit AICC, he postponed responding to her queries. While the urgency of her request eluded him, nostalgia for old times at the University of Wisconsin–Milwaukee, where her father was an engineering professor and colleague, did not. "On the margin of this I find your accusing finger pointing at me for having started you on this road to anthropology many years ago in Milwaukee," he teased.

"I must plead guilty for I remember how your father used to bring you when you [were] about knee-high to my office and I presume it was the after-effect of those visits that led you into the craft."[50] Off he went to southern California.

Meanwhile, President Kennedy was moving on campaign promises, nominating Stewart Udall as DOI secretary in December. Following his January 1961 confirmation, Udall appointed John Old Crow (Cherokee) as acting commissioner of Indian affairs and commissioned a task force led by W. W. Keeler, principal chief of the Cherokee Nation of Oklahoma, to "look into the organization and program of the entire Department, insofar as they bear on the Department's mission and responsibilities with respect to Indian Affairs."[51] Meetings were planned throughout Indian Country. The first was slated for Oklahoma City, March 20–21, and the last for Reno, where California, Nevada, and southern Utah tribal delegates would congregate on April 13–14. Since many California leaders would already be in Reno, AICC asked Sellers to host the California–Nevada regional meeting on April 15–16, heel to toe with the task force hearings.[52] No Nevada tribes were represented on the regional committee. McNickle knew that Sellers could disseminate information, but neither she nor the regional committee could mobilize tribal participation. That required a Native Nevadan.

AICC had grown too many legs for McNickle to micromanage. While he stamped "Indian Steering Committee chair" on letterhead adjacent to the coordinators' names and titles, his was a more intimate commitment: embodying Native leadership and a vision of AICC's ability to further self-determination. By late February, suspicions about AICC's origins and intentions—some plausible, others wildly off base—were sweeping across Indian Country. Cherokee attorney Earl Boyd Pierce suspected that Tax and AICC represented the leading edge of communist infiltration aiming to incubate Soviet conquest on Native reservations. One scholar traces this extreme expression of Pierce's Cold War conservatism and vigorous patriotism to a story Keeler related after a trip to the Soviet Union, where he was flabbergasted to have several Russians approach him, promising their support in helping to free Native Americans from federal imprisonment by establishing "Indian Republics" in the United States. Their aspirations to liberate Native people, and their vivid impressions of imprisonment, were derived from University of Chicago scholarship.[53] Pierce showed up to February's advisory group meeting discursively wrapped in Old Glory. NCAI was prepared to encounter political resistance to AICC, but this level of absurdity embarrassed them and made planning infinitely more difficult.

McNickle's early conviction that attending regional meetings offered a means to extinguish more plausibly based brushfires, of which there were many, dissolved into thin air as meetings began to be concurrently scheduled. On March 25, he bemoaned having to miss the Northwest regional meeting, where personal stakes were tied to his Flathead citizenship. As rumors about AICC continued to swirl, he strategized to Tax: "What I might do is go out to Sacramento and spend enough time with Marie Potts and Bertha Stewart, perhaps take in one or two local meetings with them, to get them indoctrinated. They work together and often travel together. On the way out, I would visit with Walter Voorhees [NCAI Phoenix-area vice president] in Nevada and get him working in the state (he might be able to carry his own expenses).[54] This never came to pass.

Potts was largely oblivious to these machinations though they might have seemed familiar—even inspiring—given her land claims experience. In mid-March Tax informed her that UNR was the regional meeting site and that the meeting was scheduled to abut the task force hearings. The latter were worthy *Smoke Signal* fodder. Potts undoubtedly looked forward to seeing her DuFresne grandchildren who lived nearby, but she needed no additional motivation to do her job. The "Voice of the California Indian" tagline, emblazoned since 1955 on *Smoke Signal* letterhead, articulated her journalistic vision. Apologizing for his upcoming absence at the Reno meeting, Tax explained that all attendees would find his letter of welcome in their packets. "I want to thank you for your work and of course I pray for your success."[55]

After months in the field, Barrett was home. On April 4, he sent Lurie a descriptive list of fourteen southern California "Reservations and Representatives." This dry, unenlightening by-product of recent fieldwork was appended to a three-page, richly detailed letter commenting on nine northern California communities enumerated in her early January list. Scanning the list, Lurie encountered a familiar name:

> 19. Maidu. You have in your more recent literature listed Mrs. Marie Potts, Santa Clara Way, Sacramento, as the representative. This is very good. I have known Mrs. Potts for years and what she puts her shoulder to usually goes through. If she will undertake [it], I am sure she can organize those people over there to really do something. The trouble with Mrs. Potts is that she gets so enthusiastic over something of this sort that she works to the betterment of the group to her own disadvantage and if there is any way

there could be some remuneration for her efforts this would be welcome and most needed.[56]

Although late coming, this was a worthy endorsement.

The task force convened its ninth and final meeting in downtown Reno. Some 250 tribal delegates from Utah, Nevada, and California streamed into the State Building civic auditorium on April 13 and 14 to spill forth disappointment and frustration over DOI's failure to competently execute its administrative and fiduciary obligations. The poverty and disease beleaguering Indian Country struck a chord with Kennedy on the campaign trail, and Udall highlighted this in Chairman W. W. Keeler's letter of appointment.[57] Damning testimony on this front and many others came from every quarter, and right on its heels angry and poignant pleas. California delegate Sidney Parrish (Pomo), representing Stewart's Point Rancheria, echoed many northern California tribal concerns when he described the rocky and arid land on which his people subsisted, imploring, "We need water and a school!" Frustrated that BIA was withholding a $55,000 allocation that would bring running water to the rancheria, he called out the hypocrisy involved in teaching young Indians white society's hygienic standards while denying them access to water. Forrest focused on BIA's personnel reduction, dropout rates among Native pupils, and problems arising from PL-280.[58] Calls came for greater authority to be vested in local agents, for academic and vocational education, and for housing and sanitation improvement on rancherias and reservations. Potts registered her concerns for California Indian people, including appeals for improved vocational and academic education for youths and adults, including dental and nutritional instruction.[59]

AICC Regional Meeting, University of Nevada–Reno, April 15–16

The UNR campus was a welcome retreat after two days of emotional testimony. Like everyone else, Potts looked forward to a more relaxing venue and the opportunity to socialize with peers. Voorhees and a contingent of Nevada tribal representatives worked with Sellers and other community representatives to plan the opening ceremony for this historic gathering.[60] The evening of April 14 was filled with pomp and oratory befitting the hosting of California Indian peoples by Nevada tribes and the welcoming of American Indians to the university, the city of Reno, and the state of Nevada. The regional conference and patriotic pageantry commenced at 8:00 P.M. in the Education Building's auditorium. An all-Indian Boy Scout troop from the Reno-Sparks Colony Christian Center presented the color guard, followed by an invocation and suite of welcome speeches.[61] State comptroller Keith Lee represented the governor's office, followed by Kenneth Young, UNR vice president, and Reno attorney Leslie B. Gray of the Nevada and U.S. Civil Rights Commissions. Forrest, NCAI's Sacramento-area regional vice president, delivered the keynote address, setting the tone for two days of discussion and collaboration. Sellers wrapped up the evening speeches by reading Tax's welcome message and reviewing AICC's origins and aims. A social hour in the student union gave delegates time to visit and relax before AICC meetings began the next morning at 9:00 A.M. The conference agenda delineated a set of discussion sessions for each day. On Saturday, they addressed education, health, general welfare, housing, employment and social conditions. Respite from these weighty deliberations came that evening, courtesy of Stewart Indian School. Situated in nearby Carson City, Stewart served a wide swath of western states and had begun admitting pupils from Arizona and New Mexico in 1958. A cohort from these southwestern states comprised a portion of the forty or so pupils who performed ancestral Apache and Hopi dances. The local community crowded into the UNR gym alongside AICC participants to enjoy the program.[62]

On Sunday they delved into problems of federal administration, termination, relocation, and management and economic development of trust lands. The conference ended at 4:30 P.M., but the work was just beginning for Potts, Forrest, Stewart, Voorhees, Tom Brown (Flathead, Bay Area Council), John Dressler (Washoe), and Harold Rupert (Washoe). This organizing committee spent four hours reviewing discussion notes and crafting proposals to forward to Tax and McNickle.[63] Potts's dual role as regional organizer obligated her to observe, as well as contribute to the dialogue. She was practiced at this. Trudging up and down the state to hear Collett pontificate, testifying at and reporting upon legislative hearings, and synthesizing policy and opinion were her fortes. She knew to listen for piercing silences and how to winnow down a cacophonous chorus into a matter-of-fact column. With Voorhees chairing sessions, she focused on the complex dynamics between varied constituents, with their distinct and crosscutting concerns: California versus Nevada Indians, federally acknowledged tribes versus non-status communities, urban versus rural-dwelling peoples, acculturated versus traditional. The Pyramid Lake Paiute responded early and enthusiastically to Sellers's invitation. Mobilizing for both the task force and AICC regional meetings, the tribe generated input at council and tribal levels to produce a report with thirty-eight recommendations. According to Potts—and for better or worse where California, urban, and non–federally recognized Natives were concerned—the tribe's list set the agenda for the task force meeting and much AICC regional discussion.[64]

Fifteen headings structured the committee's three-page report: Education, Economic Development, Housing and Sanitation, Health and Welfare, Technicians and Technical Services, Termination, Relocation Policy, Eligibility, Law and Order, Trust Land, Tribal Organization, Communications, Advisory Committee, Area Offices, and Youth Conservation Corps. Education was accorded the most substantial attention. Everyone concurred that California Indian educational issues were dire, though recommendations were equally applicable to Nevada: "Many Indians are not adapted to a public-school education. This results in staggering dropout rates. It was recommended that Indian schools in the West be restored to full curriculum; that serious consideration be given to advancing Indian schools to Junior College level; that these schools be reopened to use by western Indians; i.e., California and Nevada Indians," the latter a clear reference to Sherman and Stewart. "It was pointed out that many Indian children would benefit more by a complete vocational training program,"[65] which should be open to all Indians whether or not they live on reservations. Native Nevadans opposed PL-280. Citing jurisdictional complications in California and lost hunting and fishing rights restored only by lobbying for special legislation, representatives from both sides of the state line called for its California repeal. Everyone complained about subpar communication from the bureau and about understaffed local agencies. Nevada tribes wanted more authority placed in the hands of local superintendents and more responsive sub-agencies. They supported a nine-member DOI advisory committee comprising one representative from each AICC region, with a minimum of five Native members to guarantee its BIA watchdog function.

Chicago Steering Committee Meeting, April 26–30

Potts left for Chicago the next week. Most steering committee members were citizens of Native nations, and AICC hoped their tribes would defray transportation and lodging costs. Potts lacked tribal citizenship, and while FIC and *Smoke Signal* were valuable markers of Native identity, these were financially strapped operations fully contingent upon her considerable volunteer labor. Tax insisted it was absolutely critical that steering committee members and regional organizers—and she was both—make April's meeting. In March he confirmed that AICC would cover International House room and board. Then, in language astutely crafted to preclude embarrassment, he continued, "I am asking the people not being sent by an organization to kindly tell me the way they will travel and how much it will cost." Potts researched rail fares, and in mid-April Tax forwarded a tax exemption certificate and a $125 check covering round-trip fare on Western Pacific, promising to reimburse expenses incurred en route. A Chicago Indian Center member greeted her train on April 25.

International House overflowed with Native people. Members of the drafting and steering committee, as well as regional organizers, were all on-site. Three subcommittees were formed to process the voluminous regional findings: community development; health, education, and welfare; and law and jurisdiction. Potts sat on the second with Howard McKinley (Navajo), Helen Miner Miller (Winnebago, voted onto the steering committee on-site), John Ranier (Taos), and Frank Takes Gun (Crow but representing the Native American Church). Handwritten notes summarize contributions from Ranier, Potts, McKinley, and Takes Gun. Potts emphasized difficulties that non–tribally affiliated Natives suffered in accessing health care and reported that Nevada Indians wanted more clinics to help their widely dispersed rural population.[66] Several observers attended the meetings, including Lurie, who got along famously with Potts. Apologizing for her tardy response, she told Barrett in May, "However, while at Chicago, I had the good fortune to get to know another Sam Barrett fan, Mrs. Marie Potts. She is a grand, wise lady and we had some grand chats. I wish we could, as you suggest, make some remuneration for her but the best we have been able to do in any case is pay travel and living expenses of the steering committee while at the meeting in Chicago this last April."[67] The two women had plenty to talk about beyond their mutual acquaintance with Barrett, but dramatic gender disparities surely fostered companionship. Prior to the on-site seating of Miller, only three women populated the fifteen-person steering committee: Potts, Peterson and Georgeann Robinson (Osage).

Potts to the Rescue: Sojourn at NCAI

Potts originally planned to go home when the meeting adjourned. Instead she flew to Washington, D.C., with Peterson, who needed help digging out from under an avalanche of NCAI work. She was due back in Chicago in early June, and her Washington stay eliminated cross-country trips.[68] NCAI was always desperately understaffed, as Peterson knew when recruited to the executive directorship. Careful to negotiate a dependable salary, she underestimated the challenges involved in maintaining support staff equal to NCAI's growing needs. In May 1956, she told President Joseph Garry that she had another job offer and laid her cards on the table. "I regard our inability to train people and expand our staff

Figure 19. AICC steering committee meeting, International House,
University of Chicago, April 1961. Seated at table (*left to right*): unknown,
Marie Potts, Howard McKinley, D'Arcy McNickle (*at head of table*). Seated
behind (*left to right*): Al Wahraftig, Nancy Lurie, and Sol Tax.
National Anthropological Archives, Smithsonian Institution.

as a crisis. I have tried for a year now to find outside funds to bring from one
to three Indian persons to Washington for 'on-the-job' training in this office. It
is a disservice to the organization," she admonished, "and whomever you may
employ as your director not to find the means at once to select, train and break in
at least two professional staff members, not only to give minimal service, but also
to assure continuing and uniform administration of NCAI in the event of loss
of a staff member. Such things as regular publication of your bulletin, sufficient
work on legislation and at least annual field visits to the major tribes are totally
impossible with our present staff and yet these should constitute the minimum
contact and service we should be giving."

Lobbying activity precluded NCAI's qualification for nonprofit status. An
earlier NCAI Trust (renamed Arrow, Inc.) was no longer affiliated, so Peterson
was unable to tap the philanthropic resources sustaining other Indian rights
organizations. For years, private donors gave small sums without the benefit of
tax deductibility, hinting that tax-exempt status would enhance their generosity.
Staffing solutions lay just out of reach, so in collaboration with NCAI attorneys,

Peterson inaugurated the NCAI Fund.[69] Soliciting donations from charitable foundations, granting agencies, and Hollywood celebrities such as Jane Russell, she told one donor, "One of the really fine things we can do under this fund is to train promising young people in national Indian affairs. One of our greatest needs is for staff. And yet it takes two or three years for a person, even with good educational background and some experience, to become proficient in here."[70] Peterson was straightforward with recruits about their value to NCAI:

> There is no office in existence where one can get as much variety of experi-ence, national Indian thinking and see the tribal Indian picture as much as in this headquarters office of the NCAI. Naturally, we would encourage and assist you in seeing Washington points of interest, including the working of the Indian Subcommittees in both houses of Congress, as well as the Bureau of Indian Affairs and Division of Indian Health, U.S Public Health Service. From your point of view, the work would be hard work and I wouldn't want to mislead you about this. However . . . I sincerely believe you would find it to be the most concentrated, valuable opportunity for an over-view of Indian affairs that you would find anywhere.[71]

In March 1960, just as Peterson's on-the-job training program was starting to pay off, NCAI's office manager resigned. Despite adages to the contrary, some employees are irreplaceable. Hilda Henderson Cragun was one. "I hate to sound like a broken record," Peterson later groused to attorney Earl Boyd Pierce. "After five years, I'm sure you will understand, she had taken on many, many things which I never even had to review. In trying to find a replacement for her, we tried four different people only to find that they would not do. This not only took my time to recruit and supervise, but in the meantime, I had to let my own work go. This has caused a dearth of publications and correspondence to pile up. It also kept us from field work and promotion, which cut into our income."[72] On-the-job trainees were Native youths who earned a monthly wage in temporary staff positions. The first, Miles Brandon (Alaska Native), worked part-time while a high school senior (1954–55). Helen Maynor (Lumbee) came on board in August 1958 as the first full-time trainee, leaving in December 1959, three months' shy of Cragun's departure. Maynor overlapped with Bernadine Eschief (Shoshone-Bannock) from Fort Hall, who arrived in May 1959 for a two-year stint. She joined Rose Marie Mandan (Mandan), who had come from the Chicago Indian Center on a cost-sharing loan a month prior. Mandan was so accomplished that two weeks in, Peterson already envisioned her as Cragun's replacement. When Mandan could not even extend her six-week leave of absence, Peterson was devastated: "[I]t is overwhelming in here and to have lost both little Helen and Hilda is crippling. We tried one woman who looked good enough, and I had to tell her at the end of the first week we couldn't use her. Her handwriting was worse than a child's; she was messy and sloppy in every bit of work she did; she couldn't spell; she was an 8-to-5-er, with coffee breaks and long lunch hours; and her personality was wrong."[73]

NCAI *Bulletin* Guest Editor and Indian Leader Observer-Trainee

Into this chaotic scene strolled Potts, editor and activist—anything but "an 8-to-5-er." Peterson hosted Potts in her home and originated a new title befitting her status: Indian *leader* observer-trainee. Previously, observer-trainees were college students whose tribes sponsored them for brief, mostly summer stints.[74] Peterson's first NCAI Fund report showcased Potts at work in the office. Though two thousand miles from California, she was never more at home. Here was a national version of Santa Clara Way, where the work was endless, Native people came and went, and volunteers worked around the clock. Washington was familiar territory; prior trips to the city and Capitol meant that she knew her way around. She guided tribal delegates to their destinations, couriered paperwork back and forth to the Hill, and occasionally stood in for Peterson, as when she presented Congressman Wayne Aspinall with a beaded gavel from Fort Hall—a token of appreciation for his parliamentary procedure workshop given at an executive council meeting. True to the observer-trainee component of the position, a reciprocal benefit involved gaining greater familiarity with the federal government in relation to Indian affairs. Potts sat in on House and Senate hearings, observed Interior Department functions, met with every California congressman, and used her NCAI status to write California Senate and Assembly members for updates on legislation related to Native Californians. California Indian claims were not on the commission's agenda during her Washington sojourn, so she observed the Warm Springs court of claims proceedings and caught up on the status of California Indian claims by visiting their attorneys' offices. Potts's extensive FIC experience meant that Peterson could trust her to handle administrative duties: invoicing tribes for membership dues, writing legislative reports, and checking on the status of land claims cases for correspondents who sent queries to NCAI.[75] Without doubt, her greatest contribution was editorial.

NCAI's *Bulletin* began as a monthly, but years of waging war against the congressional forces of termination had wreaked havoc on already meager resources. Two years had elapsed since its last appearance, in mid-1959, and Peterson was determined to resuscitate it. Communication with member tribes was especially critical at this moment, since many had accepted or bellicosely refused AICC's invitation to participate in regional meetings. Rumors swirled in all directions about NCAI's role in the event: they were in bed with the BIA; they were plotting to overthrow the BIA. Speculation ran amok.[76] News from the 1960 convention, plans for the 1961 Lewiston convention, transitions in federal and NCAI presidential administrations, DOI task force activity, unforeseen impacts of the Menominee vote for termination, upcoming legislation about fractionated heirship—all awaited coverage. As Peterson observed in her column, titled "Marie Potts Guest Editor This Issue," Potts was a godsend, bringing to the task more than a decade of experience identifying, authoring, and editing *Smoke Signal* news.

The May 1961 *Bulletin* rolled off the press as an eight-page compact tabloid, lavishly illustrated with twenty-seven black-and-white photographs ranging from head shots and group portraits to publicity images of tribal floats featured in Kennedy's inaugural parade.[77] A portrait of Potts holding California Indian baskets accompanies her byline and Maidu affiliation on an eloquent and in-depth article about April's AICC steering committee meeting. Subsuming three-quarters of the page, it lays bare the disappointments, fears, and dreams of committee members, regional meeting participants, and Indian people everywhere in the wake of Kennedy's election. Damaging stereotypes escaped neither steering committee discussion nor Potts's pen. "The general public seems to have an idea that Indians are 'taken care of' by the federal government, even that Indians receive some kind of monthly check from the government!" she wrote with exasperation and personal knowledge that nothing could be further from the truth. "Another prevalent idea is that Indian reservations are 'concentration camps'; that Indians ought, somehow, to be 'gotten off the reservations'; that Indian communities or reservations are 'rural slums.' The Indians ceded vast tracts of land, often against their wishes in return for guarantees that they might live forever, unmolested, upon the remaining lands."

California's rejected treaties must have loomed large in Chicago and Washington, where she mingled with tribal people whose treaty rights, reservations, and federally acknowledged status were the antithesis of her own experience. Even so, this did not obscure their common ground; she knew her ancestral lands and addressed this topic with passion and authority.

The Indian's view of the land is different from that of the non-Indian. Indians feel a *social* relationship to the land while the non-Indian regards the land in commercial terms. Indians are concerned about the development of their human and natural resources and cannot see why people must be dispossessed of their land or other natural resources to help them "get on their feet." Their lands—even to most Indian people who have departed their reservations—are revered lands, and their last remaining hold upon a continent that was once theirs. It is the base of their existence, of tribal organization and of Indian identity.

In closing, she summarized steering committee sentiments that non-Indians needed to know:

the non-material cultural values of Indians, the high value placed upon generosity and sharing; the tolerance of others' weaknesses, or their abuses; their patience with the faults of their own or other human beings, their inclusion of everybody in whatever they may do or the sharing of whatever they may have; their lack of aggressiveness or greed (often viewed by others as a detriment to "progress"); their love of beauty; their appreciation of the present as different from an obsession for the future; their dignity, calm, deliberateness, their love of the uncomplicated; and their marvelous sense of humor.

With no line item covering publication costs in her budget, Peterson was gambling on long-term dividends with the May 1961 *Bulletin*.[78] The handful of ads sold at $5 per column-inch barely dented the $1,089 production cost. Yet without a current *Bulletin*, NCAI's ability to court new member tribes, compete for educational grants, and attract philanthropic donations at AICC was vastly diminished. The two women peddled the *Bulletin* locally at twenty-five cents per copy, a dime over cost. "Mrs. Potts and I sold $6.50 worth of copies in the Bureau of Indian Affairs the other day in less than an hour," Peterson reported, "and especially the Indian people there were very glad to pay for the copies."[79] Potts later sold copies at the state fair, mailing proceeds to NCAI in mid-September.[80]

Manhattan and Seven Springs

In mid-May, Peterson announced that she had appointments with Manhattan scholarship foundations and invited Potts and Eschief to join her. What better way to demonstrate the value of the NCAI Fund than to showcase the *Bulletin*'s California Indian guest editor and her youthful counterpart, a Shoshone-Bannock college graduate? Off they went in Peterson's car. On their first evening in Manhattan,

California advertising whiz, satirist, and radio personality Stan Freberg made an appearance on Jack Paar's *Tonight Show* to promote his new and controversial "Broadway revue." Released in LP form and denied airtime by major broadcasters, *Stan Freberg Presents the United States of America, Vol.1—The Early Years* was banned in Arizona and New Mexico.[81] That evening, Freberg sang his original composition "Take an Indian to Lunch This Week," written for his tongue-in-cheek history. After his performance, Paar grilled him, "Are you a hypocrite? How often do you yourself take Indians to lunch?" Caught off guard, the satirist sputtered cavalierly that such a prospect had never presented itself, but if any Indians showed up to his hotel the next day at noon, he would do just that. The audience was already on its feet applauding, but the punch line was yet to come. When Paar demanded the hotel name, Freberg proclaimed: "The Algonquin!"

The next day, Potts, Peterson, and Eschief joined twenty-three American Indians in the hotel lobby.[82] Potts recalled, "So we were there and waiting and he didn't show up, and this friends of ours, she called NBC and told them that there was a whole bunch of Indians here waiting to be taken to lunch. So we all waited around that hotel until he came and he brought photographers and newspapermen and everybody, you know, with him. So we got quite a write up and we got a lot of pictures taken too."[83] Peterson was interviewed and quoted widely in the press: "We commend the use of political satire to tell the Indian story and to promote respect and appreciation for all men's values and aspirations." Naturally, Paar claimed credit for this implausible gathering and shared the photographic evidence on his show. Years later, Freberg joked about the reaction of the "ancient and very crabby" maître d' who managed Algonquin's sophisticated Rose Room: "This was sixties, remember. *What the hell is this?* his face said. *Some new militant group demonstrating? Some wacko protest march in off the street? Not in my dining room!* . . . 'Table for TWENTY-EIGHT?' I shouted."[84] A dozen years later, Potts still marveled at the coincidence of timing behind this remarkable experience.

Freberg was right—it *was* the sixties! Self-determination and new forms of American Indian protest were emerging. In a few weeks, Potts would witness these stirrings at AICC. Meanwhile, copies of the *Bulletin* in hand, she was off to another destination. True to the spirit of the observer-trainee premise, and perhaps also to keep an eye on two traditionalist speakers who held NCAI in the lowest possible regard, Peterson sent Potts to a seminar on American Indian history, on June 2–4 at Pennsylvania's Seven Springs Resort. The intimate setting brought attendees and speakers—tribal representatives, academics, and BIA personnel—together for meals and conversation around regional Native histories and contemporary issues.[85] Two seminar speakers had posed challenges at AICC regional and steering committee meetings with their animosity toward DOI and NCAI. Potts gained a new perspective on their political sensibilities at Seven Springs, witnessing their profound skepticism and distrust in relation to Six Nations land expropriation. Opening speaker Reva Barse (Seneca Nation) addressed the Kinzua Dam, conceived in 1938 to protect Pittsburgh and other downriver cities from the unpredictable Alleghany River. The Army Corps of Engineers planned to displace more than 145 households and upward of six hundred tribal members for reservoir construction. Barse's accounting of court battles, congressional lobbying, alternative impoundment site proposals, and a failed appeal to Kennedy was laced with anger and despair. Imminent destruction of a longhouse, cemeteries, churches, general stores, and ten thousand acres of rich bottomlands farmed for generations prior to the 1794 Treaty of Canandaigua represented more than material losses.

On the final day, William Rickard reviewed the Tuscarora's opposition to the New York State Power Authority's plan to commandeer one-fifth of their land base for hydroelectric works. In *Federal Power Commission v. Tuscarora Indian Nation*, the Supreme Court had found in favor of FPC, and the Tuscarora were dispossessed of 550 acres at $1,500 per acre. While acreage targeted for condemnation was reduced, exercise of imminent domain was a harsh slap in the face of sovereignty and self-determination. These were compelling scenarios for Potts, whose personal frame of reference for such devastating loss was inundation of Big Meadow. Potts returned to Washington with an enlarged understanding of treaty rights and tribal sovereignty. Seven Springs left a lasting impression. In 1963 she penned the *Smoke Signal* story "Operation 'Dam' Rush." Labeling the Army Corps "Beavers," she griped that first came the gold rush, then the homestead rush, "and now it's the 'Dam' rush that is pushing Indian lands right out from under them." Ticking off a list of reservoir projects and flooded Indian lands, she remarked on loss of place, both tangible and intangible, joking with sarcastic resignation that surfboards had supplanted canoes. That she missed Big Meadow and the Maidu canoes of her childhood was evident.[86] When Seven Springs seminar chair Edward Stachowiak relocated his medical practice to Salinas General Hospital in 1970, Potts introduced him as a faithful subscriber since 1961, publishing his essay "America Still Has Not Learned to Say 'Thank You.'"[87]

AICC

Potts and Peterson returned to Chicago for a final steering committee meeting, June 10–12. Procedural concerns dominated the agenda. They determined that the conference chair would rotate daily, six general assemblies would be held, and small discussion groups would select their own chairs. Ten steering committee members were assigned as placeholders, including Potts, who stayed with health, education, and welfare issues. Several April recommendations were reviewed and retained. Ballots would be weighted 60/40, privileging federally recognized tribal delegate votes. In the 40 percent category were "non-federally recognized tribes or bands, organized urban groups recognized as such if in existence for at least a year, individuals not associated with any of the above each to be accorded one vote."[88] Keying off concerns that Keeler and other Five Tribes leaders expressed in their April regional report—that the non–federally recognized Oklahoma Indians AICC was courting might outvote or misrepresent their status—a credentials committee was suggested.[89] It was populated at this meeting with thirteen people, including Potts and Harry Hopkins (Torres-Martinez Band of Mission Indians).[90]

Potts had worked credential committees for NCAI conventions, but this was different. The committee became the locus of a long-simmering NCAI battle between wealthy, politically powerful Oklahoma tribes and leaders such as Keeler, whose recent task force appointment spotlighted their outsize influence on federal Indian policy, and western tribes whose values, resource bases, and concerns were starkly different. Some have parsed this as a mixed versus full-blood battle, but this gloss masks deeper complexity and crosscutting ties.[91] These troubles boiled to the surface at AICC, setting the stage for the 1961 convention, where a landslide election installed Walter Wetzel (Blackfoot) as NCAI president and led to Peterson's resignation.[92]

Potts had a front-row seat on the opening act of this drama. On one side was an older guard that had birthed NCAI and nurtured its growth while trying to track and arrest the sinuous congressional machinations that had culminated in HCR 108, the most sinister piece of legislation to come from these "barren years."[93] In the other camp was a fiercely traditionalist, new, and largely younger guard champing to take control and loose the hounds of hell on Congress and the colonial power structure. Potts witnessed the electric energy rumbling through Chicago's corridors in the form of the lively contingent of American Indian Development workshop students McNickle had brought to AICC for an immersive, baptism-by-fire introduction to intertribal leadership and politics.[94] Encouraged to share their experiences and insights in discussion sessions, some later argued that they felt shut out of conversations and invisible, particularly in larger assemblies. Though not a hint of rebelliousness or elder disparagement found its way into any of the abundant archival correspondence between Lurie, Tax, Peterson, and McNickle, Clyde Warrior later argued that AICC kindled formation of the National Indian Youth Council (NIYC).[95] Historian Bradley Shreve's meticulous chronology of NIYC documents the range of AICC influence, not all negative, on the coalescence of young attendees who by August 10 self-identified as the Chicago Conference Youth Council.[96] Potts knew and admired a number of them, including Eschief and Mary White Eagle Natani, who worked with her at NCAI. Warrior she had known since 1957, when he had entertained banquet-goers with his fancy dance artistry and skill at the Claremore convention. Youthful political engagement filled her with hope for the world in which her grandchildren were coming of age. After AICC she received updates from Boulder and followed these young people for years.[97] In 1965 she announced the tenth-anniversary workshop dates, urging California Indians to apply.[98] The next issue announced Gerald Brown's election to NIYC's presidency. His San Francisco Indian Center affiliation brought them into shared circles, and she rallied to his cause: "He needs everyone's help. He can't do it alone." A subscriber to NIYC's *ABC* (*Americans before Columbus*), she printed its "Indian Glossary" immediately below, offering an original addition: "Vista Volunteer: A youngster sent out to teach Indians how to live but ends up learning how to live the Indian way of life."[99]

AICC politics did not eclipse pleasures. Ceremony, sightseeing, and entertainment were high on Potts's list any day of the week. Chicago did not disappoint. AICC opened June 14 with a Calumet peace pipe ceremony. A photo of Forrest sharing the pipe with Ho-Chunk chief Whirling Thunder made papers across the country.[100] The University of Chicago's Stagg Field was the site of a welcoming feast, where "whole steers were roasted over open-pit fires."[101] Sacred ceremonies continued across campus during the week, and McNickle's skit "Bureau of White Man's Affairs" was a smash hit.[102] Though AICC attendance figures vary widely, organizers cited 460 registrants representing ninety tribes, acknowledging that many more participated unofficially. The AP heralded AICC as the largest intertribal gathering in history, bringing "some 1,000 representatives from several hundred tribes, from the Aleuts of Alaska, to the Seminoles of Florida" to Chicago.[103]

After the convention, Rickard rendered a blistering six-page report portraying AICC as a puppet show run by NCAI assimilationists buttoned into the hip pocket of the BIA. Accusing committee chairs of silencing non-recognized eastern

Indians, he was disturbed to witness the floor and respect accorded to Native people who could not speak their languages and did not know their tribal history, while the ideas of "federally unrecognized Eastern Indians" were summarily dismissed.[104] Loyalty to Peterson did not blind Potts to Rickard's recognition of inequities she had faced her entire life, as a landless, now urban-dwelling California Native. Yet she knew AICC furthered self-determination. When Pierce wrote Potts for a "full and frank assessment (brick bats and all) concerning the Indian Conference at Chicago," wanting it for the interior secretary, she begged off as too busy, sending a *Smoke Signal* instead. Chuckling to herself, she wrote Peterson, "Thought this bit of information might amuse you."[105]

"A Blue-Blooded Indian"

Potts returned to Sacramento weary and exhilarated from her six-week sojourn in Chicago and Washington, D.C. A tower of mail awaited her, including numerous *Smoke Signal*–related queries and complaints about not receiving the paper. She grew increasingly agitated the longer she pored over them. Many correspondents had not renewed their subscriptions in years. Potts had kept them on the mailing list out of courtesy and her own devotion to political engagement. Some editors might have published an inconspicuous apology in the next paper. Not Potts. Sitting down at the typewriter, she pounded out a missive detailing the many activities and commitments that had interfered with her ability to publish the paper on its regular schedule. Outwardly apologetic, her tone of jubilance and wonder countered words of contrition as she reviewed her summer's whirlwind schedule:

> After the [April steering committee] meeting, I was asked if I would go to Washington, D.C., and help in the office of the National Congress of American Indians. Being a blue-blooded Indian I couldn't refuse.... I was in Washington from May 1st until June 8 and most of their time was spent working in the office of NCAI. The girls who worked in the NCAI office are not clock punchers so you often found them working very late at night. They were dedicated to their work. The Executive Director never left the office before 12:00 midnight except for a business engagement. During the time the NCAI Bulletins were being mailed, volunteers came into to help after their working hours. Thousands of Bulletins were mailed. I enjoyed the experience I had there. To appreciate what the responsibilities of the NCAI are, one must be there and watch it in operation. It's the only way.

Gently scolding readers who took her labor for granted, she reminded them that she was a volunteer newswoman whose own material needs were seldom met: "I arrived home on June 25th and have been canning fruit and trying to catch up with all the correspondence that has piled up since my departure. I get pretty hungry sometimes, and so do my grandchildren so we have to put away for a stormy day." Confronting a six-week stack of accumulated work, she knew the mountain Peterson faced in her Dupont Circle office was much higher. In this now fast friend, she recognized a version of herself, a Native woman navigating life on her own, a mother caring for extended kin, a tireless advocate drawing upon personal resources for community betterment.

Allegiance to NCAI choreographed Potts's travel and sightseeing for the better part of two decades and always entailed volunteerism (figure 20). In September 1961, she and Bahnsen rode the bus to Lewiston, Idaho, for the eighteenth annual convention. A *Lewiston Morning Tribune* photograph captioned "California Delegation" shows them with Erin and Stella Forrest and grandson Poco.[106] Here Potts was elected NCAI area vice president and appointed by Walter Wetzel to an ad hoc committee to study problems of off-reservation Indians, joining Lucy Covington, Helen Miller, and George Pierre. The November 1961 *Bulletin*, published just before Peterson left Washington, was substantially *Tribune* convention coverage. Two of twelve pages were NCAI-authored. Paschal Sherman reminisced about Peterson's eight years of service and the personalities who animated NCAI, including "Marie, the Happy Warrior." This image of her as affable and industrious, first chronicled in 1900 by Emma Trubody for the *Indian's Friend* and then in the *Arrow* from 1912 to 1915, was further affirmed by Peterson's introduction of the May *Bulletin* guest editor: "Great Grandmother Marie Potts, *Maidu*, is still one of the most courageous, independent, happy warriors among the Indian people! Always reasonable, considerate, and good natured, at the same time she demands fairness and justice."

American Indian Press Association

In 1969, when Charles Trimble (Oglala Lakota), *Denver Indian Times* editor, began assembling Native journalists who were making their mark in Indian Country, Potts was among the first he contacted to help found the AIPA.[107] Peterson, also working in Denver, put him in touch with her. A new crop of young, professionally trained, and college-educated journalists was on the rise. And they were writing beyond Alcatraz. They were paying attention to the raft of local and national issues eclipsed in the mainstream mass media by sensationalistic coverage of

Figure 20. Registration table, NCAI Convention, Lewiston, Idaho, 1961. *Left to right*: Irma Bahnsen, Bernadine Eschief, Ann Tussing, Earl Gould, Marie Potts, Helen Peterson, John Ranier, Mary Natani, and Elizabeth Roe Cloud.
National Museum of the American Indian, Smithsonian Institution, NCAI 010.

Alcatraz: the Pit River Indian occupation of ancestral lands held by Pacific Gas and Electric, Pyramid Lake Paiute struggles for water rights sovereignty, and Taos Pueblo's fight to regain possession of its sacred Blue Lake. And yes, they were also covering Alcatraz, but they were focused on *why* it was happening, rooting the occupation in the centuries of inequity that had culminated in this action.

AIPA quenched Potts's wanderlust. A July 1970 planning meeting was held in Spokane. Off she went with daughters Jeanne and Beryl, who reunited with their "friends, uncle [John Mason] and cousins whom they had not seen in forty years."[108] In late September, AIPA held its inaugural conference in Durango. Beryl went along. Potts chronicled their grand excursion with the same aura of cosmopolitan desire that had permeated her 1915 "Trip to Philadelphia."

> We drove the little red and rustier Volvo through Nevada, Utah and into Colorado. We missed the road a time or two but that gave us a chance to see more beautiful country. To me, that is the best way to travel, get lost! You see country that is never advertised, and generally, most beautiful. We went

into Colorado down the Million Dollar Highway. I wondered if I should wash the little red, rustier, and dirty by this time, Volvo before attempting the Million Dollar Highway. It turned out okay. The little red, rusty, dirty Volvo went zooming down the Million Dollar Highway like it owned it, over the eleven thousand feet mountains. What a breeze! On our way back . . . we visited the Aztec Ruins in New Mexico, circled around Shiprock and to the Mesa Verde Monument. What a sight! That was an all-day sight-seeing trip. We visited the Ute Reservation near Cortez . . . a very interesting place was the school in Many Farms in Arizona.[109]

On they went to Tuba City, Glen Canyon Dam, the Grand Canyon, Boulder Dam, Las Vegas, and "across the hills to Lone Pine and Tioga Pass." There was no stopping Potts. She always had someplace to be. Later reminiscing about her travel and her truly wondrous life, she admitted that Europe held no real draw, as there was so much beauty at home. She had climbed to the summit of Mount Lassen three or four times and hiked every winding trail into the damp depths of Carlsbad Caverns. Then, after a ponderous moment or two, she proclaimed that she *would* like to see a bullfight.[110]

AIPA opened new doors. On October 31, 1970, the "First General Assembly" of the National Indian Women's Action Corps met in San Francisco's American Indian Center. Potts was slated to lead a Communication and Publicity workshop in the afternoon but had an important role to play that morning. At Indian Day in 1949, she had deemed herself unqualified to deliver the opening prayer; here it was her honor to do so. A few weeks later she flew to Alaska with Beryl. One of three AIPA delegates to NCAI's Anchorage convention, Potts occupied AIPA's booth for the duration, distributing brochures about the agency's clipping and press release services. Her diligence was rewarded when she won two fur parkas raffled at the banquet. She put them to immediate use when British Petroleum flew her and forty-one other Natives up to Prudhoe Bay on Alaska's North Slope. "We were bussed around to all the oil wells and finally embarked on the shore of the Arctic Ocean where we walked out on the ice and had our pictures taken. Before returning, we were given lunch fit for a king. We had a wonderful trip flying over the snow-covered mountains, looking Mt. McKinley right in the face."[111] When the American Indian Historical Society designated her an honored Indian historian the next month, fellow Native journalist Bill Jennings claimed it was long overdue: "Marie has never wavered in her belief that Indians do better when they work together. At long last the grandmotherly Marie is beginning to get some of the rewards her ceaseless and selfless service to her people should have earned her long ago."[112] "Grandmotherly" Marie impressed a new generation of activists, but they also inspired her.[113]

There was nothing like a road trip through the Rockies, and in 1972 Potts made two. The first was to an Indian Ecumenical Conference at Morley Park, Alberta, where she filled in for George Effman.[114] Then, in November, she and Beryl drove to Denver for AIPA. Another honor awaited her: presenting the first Marie Potts Award for Journalism Achievement to Jerry Gambill, or Rarihokwats, *Akwesasne Notes* editor in chief, on November 16 at the Denver Indian Center (figure 21). The local press reported, "The award includes a $500 prize and is the AIPA equivalent of the Pulitzer Prize."[115]

Figure 21. Marie Potts prepares to present AIPA's Marie Potts Journalism Achievement Award to Jerry Gambill, editor of *Akwesasne Notes*, November 16, 1972.
Courtesy Marine family.

Called to Activism

National activism brought Potts new opportunities to advocate for California Indian people. Although she lacked tribal citizenship, she never questioned her duty to represent Native California people at NCAI, believing that her Mountain Maidu heritage endowed her with this responsibility. The "blue-bloodedness" that compelled her to volunteer her time and talents to NCAI was her inheritance from Hukespem. As his direct descendant, she was honored and obliged to carry forward his Mountain Maidu values of generosity and assistance to those in need. No doubt she admired young women like Vyola Olinger, who chaired the Agua Caliente Tribal Council, breaking new ground within her nation and at NCAI, but Potts forged her own path in the organization as an individual member.[116] Her election as NCAI regional vice president demonstrates how adept she was at carving out a space for herself, carrying out the responsibilities of her Maidu birthright, and plying her political passions in a national forum. In fact, her American Indian identity and belonging were never more affirmed than through her AICC, NCAI, and AIPA participation. Annual conventions offered an outlet for her adventurous spirit and a community that recalled Carlisle's intertribal milieu.

National engagement also enhanced her state and local activism, giving the *Smoke Signal* additional heft, especially during the 1960s as the early stirrings that later culminated in Red Power gained momentum. It elevated her image back home and perhaps her sense of authority and self-importance, although never is there any hint of this in her *Smoke Signal* commentary or activist correspondence. In fact, just the opposite appears in her apology to readers. After indulging a moment of frustration that her uncompensated *Smoke Signal* work and struggle to feed her own grandchildren were taken entirely for granted, she expressed gratitude to the NCAI staff for their labor and the chance to represent California interests in Chicago and Washington. Barrett had warned Lurie that this was her tendency. She could never be cured of this affliction, and it accelerated at a dizzying pace in her final years. When AIPA came along in 1969, she dove right in, headfirst, exhilarated to have colleagues who understood her commitment to Native news.

10

Being California Indian in the City

Cultivating Native Presence and Place in Sacramento

I don't think I'll fool with him anymore. Reagan's not for us. He's
scared. He's afraid of too many Indians coming together at once.
After all, how many did he kill in the movies?

—*Marie Potts, 1974*

In March 1961, before departing for Chicago and AICC, Potts hosted a Tule
student delegation, set to arrive the evening of Thursday, March 23, for Friday
visits to the governor's office, State Indian Museum, and Sutter's Fort. Potts rallied
support through the *Smoke Signal*: "A potluck dinner will be served at the Clunie
Club House, Alhambra & F, at 6:00 P.M. You are invited to bring a prepared dish
and join the group. Let's give these students a warm reception. Okay? Okay!"[1]
The spectacular enthusiasm and generosity Potts exhibited as the city's and the
capitol's de facto Native ambassador was legendary. Upon her return from Chicago,
the California League for American Indians (CLAI) offered her employment as a
fieldworker. She was eager to accept but did not yet drive. In Washington, Helen
Peterson's ninety-year-old mother had ferried her hither and yon. A youngster
by comparison, Potts took the plunge. Twice failing the local driving exam, she
headed up to Plumas County and passed with flying colors. Home she came and
off she went: to the fifteenth annual National Association of Intergroup Relations
Officials Conference in San Francisco in November 1961; south to Big Sandy
Rancheria at Auberry, where she counseled them on land claims progress; down
to Tule River Reservation in Porterville, where she spent three weeks teaching

beadwork, attending council meetings, and watching girls' softball and basketball games. After a quick stop at Santa Rosa Rancheria, she headed home. She was at it again when summer rolled around. After teaching basket weaving and beadwork at a Hidden Villa children's camp, she headed off to northern California rancherias, documenting long waits for public health service from the far northwest down to Ukiah. Where was the flurry of development BIA had promised as a condition of termination? Where were the improvements to sanitation and irrigation systems, or to housing, which had to be brought up to state and local code?[2] She was already familiar to many as the *Smoke Signal* editor, and California Indians welcomed a Native fieldworker who knew the legislative players and landscape.[3] She had played this role informally for more than a decade. Back in 1953, when AFSC leaders Josephine and Frank Duveneck embarked on a tour of northern California Indian rancherias to ascertain termination sentiment, they met first with the Sacramento Indian Agency. There they acquired a map, a list of rancheria contact names, and directions to Potts's house. "From her we received a detailed account of the problems as experienced by Indians, and a list of key people not necessarily on Mr. Hill's list. She explained to us that the Tribal Council was the Bureau's creation . . . the real leaders were not evident to an outsider but were recognized within the group."[4] In the urban environs of Sacramento, Marie Potts was that leader.

Her influence in the Capital City was profound. It reached into the quiet recesses of Native homes, where she recognized young mothers struggling to make ends meet, and it flowed with tremendous force into the civic sphere, where California Indian people were growing in numbers but remained largely invisible on the everyday cityscape. Recognizing the inseparable relationship between cultural tradition and political activism, Potts actively carved out Native space and place in the city; fostered revivification and respect for song, dance, and other expressive arts; and taught public school children—both Native and non-Native—about California Indian people. As the decades rolled by and her national activism brought new confidence and knowledge, she began to demand respect for ancestral heritage sites in her adopted city. Her slow and steady hand laid the early foundation upon which Sacramento's Native community now firmly rests, as this place-based chapter shows.

Urban Place-Making at Mid-Century

In 1955 AFSC fieldworker Frank Quinn was hired to interview northern California Indian people about termination.[5] He knew Marie well, but it took a while to draw

Figure 22. Tule River delegation with Marie Potts
(*second from left*) in Governor Pat Brown's office, 1962.
Courtesy Marine family.

her out. "Know any stories? Indian stories? Songs?" he began. The tape rolled in awkward silence for several seconds before he joked, "Can you draw any pictures for us?" His microphone induced some uncharacteristic bashfulness, but she was already distracted. Potts was watching her grandchildren while their mother was at work. At one point, coughing and crying erupted. "Is that Joe?" Quinn asked. "Sounds like Joe and Susie." Worriedly, Potts politely offered to close the adjoining door. This vignette from Quinn's unedited tapes is a testament to the everyday activist milieu in which FIC—the only land claims groups run exclusively by Native people—was kept afloat: by women who worked around the clock juggling family, employment, and FIC responsibilities. It also sheds some light on life in and around the household that served as Sacramento's unofficial Native community center.

Potts hit her stride as conversation turned to land claims hearings, but she was careful not to misspeak. When Quinn asked about the original impetus for the "Baker roll," by which he meant the 1928 roll, she demurred, proclaiming that she was just a busy young mother in those days. Then in afterthought, she joked self-effacingly, "There's a lot of these things I've got to find out!" He inquired about

CIJA offsets, and she offered to retrieve a book enumerating them by category—so many thimbles, so many plows, so many boarding school teachers, and so on. When Quinn reminded her that the "microphone doesn't pick up a book," she continued unfazed, citing K-344's total award value and cumulative offsets, proving she possessed not only a library of relevant documents but also knowledge of their contents. Quinn and Potts ruminated on termination. Most Indians were unprepared for it, she opined. Pressing on, Quinn asked about benefits BIA provided as leasing agent for Plumas County allotments that she co-owned with other heirs. She chuckled, admitting that one heir would be stuck doing all the work if the bureau dissolved, but already it was the heirs who forwarded the lease among one another for necessary signatures. Quinn wondered if she concurred with those who claimed BIA had done nothing for them.

> Well, what they have done has all been paid back. What I mean is that when they got that partial settlement in 1944 they paid it all back by deducting the offsets and I don't know where they did anything really for them . . . where you could say that the Indian Bureau did this for the people, for the Indian people. They've always . . . the Indians have always had to pay for anything that was given to them. . . . And in the offsets, why, it's even mentioned that they had to pay for the soldiers that had to quell some of the Indians that went on the warpath. That was also deducted!

Eventually they talked about her move to Sacramento. "Have you found there are many Indians down here?" She affirmed that there were, including veterans employed or living near McClellan Air Force Base. He asked about residential enclaves. "No, they just live all over town. Some of them own their own homes. Some of them enrolled in 1928 are still at that same address." Quinn assumed that Indian people stood out in the cityscape, and Potts corrected him, saying that the broad diversity of nationalities made it difficult to peg one's neighbors. Yet stereotypes prevailed once people learned her identity: "They just think about the Indians as being reservation Indians and they just take it for granted that that's where they should be. Our next-door neighbor here, told me one day because she was a little bit sore at me, she says 'why don't you go back to the reservation?'"

These revelations, that Native people were abundant and broadly dispersed, attest to Potts's success building Native community through the decades. When the ICCA became law, Sacramento had no recognized urban Indian community, although other metropolitan centers—San Diego, Los Angeles, Oakland, and San Francisco—were home to significant intertribal Indian communities with varying degrees of social and political organization, as scholars have shown.[6] In 1928, when the Meriam Commission published its landmark report, *Problems in Indian Administration*, a lengthy chapter was dedicated to migrated Indian communities. The commission had this to say about Sacramento:

> Probably a dozen Indian families live in Sacramento, but several were absent from home, and in some cases, the addresses were so indefinite that the families could not be located.... Only one home suggested an Indian origin. This family had been in the carnival business, and its several members still made and sold beadwork, arrows, and war bonnets, and occasionally joined Indian shows and carnivals. In all cases these Sacramento families participate in the social and civic life generally available to others in their own economic group.... The few Indians visited said they knew of no Indian associations or clubs in or near Sacramento.[7]

Further, while these individuals expressed an interest in Indian rights, they were neither socially nor politically organized. By 1942, when Potts moved to Sacramento, World War II was drawing California Indian people to the city.

This sociohistorical context is important to the Sacramento chapter's emergence as FIC's formidable engine, comprising its publicity and parade corps, publishing house, and administrative hub. Kitty, Pansy, and Marie initially worked in tandem, generating communication and social interaction. Gradually, Potts was left to carry on alone. Kitty's tragic death in 1951 was followed by Pansy's in 1965, an absolutely crushing blow:

> Friends, in the last issue of *The Smoke Signal* (such a long time ago), I reported that my sidekick assistant had gone to the hospital. As my tribe of people would say she took the " no looking back" journey to the "Unknown." Without her it has been real hard to get down to brass tacks and get on the ball. We were like a pair of plow mules that had pulled the plow together for years. When one is gone it is difficult for the other to pull the plow alone. No more jawing back and forth, no criticism, no moral support. What's the use?![8]

An obituary beneath this emotional outpouring acknowledged Pansy's activist legacy—her crucial help with the *Smoke Signal,* state fair exhibits, FIC corresponding secretarial work, 1928 roll updating, and hospitality to "out-of-town Indians."[9] She left six children. The recently formed San Francisco–based American Indian Historical Society (AIHS) published a touching tribute.

DEARLY BELOVED PANSY—

daughter of MARIE POTTS,
friend and comrade to
thousands of California
Indian people,
mother, sister, daughter
a dedicated and ardent Indian
woman we all will miss.
Farewell, dear heart.[10]

News of another tragically youthful loss was carried on the same page. Cahuilla leader Harry Hopkins, whom Potts knew from AICC, had died two weeks before. Uncharacteristically, Marie gave herself time to mourn and regroup. For two weeks nearly every year, the state fair booth was a magnet for Native people across the region and state—an ephemeral California Indian urban place.[11] Potts canceled the 1965 exhibit but published dates that her dance group would perform.

On the Cusp of Revival: Traditional Dance and the All-Indian VFW Post 9054

Quinn's rapid-fire queries across Potts's kitchen table in 1955—"Know any stories? Indian stories? Songs?"—were not Boasian-inspired, as this bit of dialogue shows:

QUINN: How's the dance group? How did the group get started?
POTTS: Talked it around until we got enough people interested.
QUINN: You and Dyson at the museum?
POTTS: Yes, and the Barbers. Not the Barbers, the Strongs.
QUINN: Are the dances you do authentic?
POTTS: Yes.
QUINN: How do you know they're authentic?
POTTS: Well, we're learning them from old timers, the old Indians. And Mr. Dyson, he in turn learned it from the old timers in Arizona and New Mexico.
QUINN: I imagine Dyson takes a lot of care in something like that.
POTTS: If he's interested in it he takes a lot of time to learn everything about the dances and their meanings.
QUINN: Does he ever sing?

POTTS: Oh yes. He's been one of our main singers, unless we're doing
          the California dances; then we try to get one of the California
          Indians to do the singing.

British-born Jack Dyson had spent the better part of his youth in Oakland,
where the Boy Scouts fed his interest in Native dance. Before matriculating at the
University of New Mexico as an anthropology major, he worked as a California
State Parks ranger and earned a reputation for expertise in American Indian
song and dance. Familiar with Gallup's Intertribal Ceremonial from high school
scouting trips, he continued to study Native American dance during college,
through course work and travel.[12] Prior to becoming SIM curator in June 1951,
he worked as San Juan Bautista State Historic Park's curator. In December 1951
he presented a lecture entitled "Songs and Dances of the Southwest Indians" to
the Sacramento Anthropological Society. Soon after he was embraced by FIC's
Sacramento chapter, where he taught and learned Native dance in an unlikely
milieu.

The All-Indian VFW Post 9054 was an arm of FIC's Sacramento chapter.
Kesner Flores and Kitty spearheaded its formation, inspired by the late 1940s
parade and Flag Day invitations. In May 1950, when a benefit dance was held in
nearby Wilton to defray costs for the post's banner and colors, it was referred
to as the Arrowhead Post.[13] By its July 29 installation, the name was All-Indian
VFW Post. "War Bonnets Exchanged for Caps," announced the *Smoke Signal*.[14]
Weeks later, the post displayed its colors at the state fair. (See flag on far left in
figure 14.) A women's auxiliary formed in 1951.[15] With no lodge of their own,
they were fortunate to have Post 9498 host them at its VFW Memorial Hall in
Bryte (now West Sacramento). For nearly a decade, All-Indian VFW gatherings
rivaled "the FIC tepee at 2727 Santa Clara Way" as Sacramento's most lively California Native place.[16] Benefit dances once held at Muir Clubhouse, Dante Club,
or Red Men's Hall moved out to Bryte, where "floor shows" featuring traditional
California Indian dancing portended the rush of 1960s cultural revivification.
The "old-timers" Potts referred to in Quinn's interview came from surrounding
communities to share social and ceremonial dances that landless and youthful
FIC members had not been privileged to witness or learn. Dyson and another
scouting aficionado, Wesley Nell, joined these gatherings. Loaning SIM collections,
Dyson taught southwestern dances and researched Plains traditions. Alongside
Native California youth, he learned about regalia, song, and dance indigenous
to the Central Valley and Sierra.[17]

In 1952 the Sacramento Indian Dance Group, also called the Marie Potts Dance Group, formed. The state fair was only one of many performance venues. On March 6, 1954, the group held a benefit dance at Bryte Memorial Hall, raising funds for the FIC delegates already in Washington for the joint hearings.[18] The dancers drew large audiences in public settings, including the 1954 Orangevale Youth Center Christmas party. A publicity photo for this event featured a youthful contingent decked out in mixed regalia.[19] Over the years, variations on names and group membership emerged: Mewauk Indian Dancers, Mewuk Indian Dance Group of Sacramento, and Sacramento Indian Dancers. Two things never changed: paramount interest in learning dance traditions indigenous to the wider region and the persistence with which Bill Franklin (Nisenan/Miwok) coaxed elders from the Amador, El Dorado, and Placer County foothills to participate in their revival (figure 24).[20]

Figure 23. Sacramento Indian dance group, California State Fair, circa 1959. On stage (*left to right*): Marvin Potts, Michael Marine, and Marvin Lee Marine. Seated (*left to right*): Darlene Brown, Susie Marine, Margaret Franklin, Terisa Franklin, and Sally Franklin (Miwok).
Courtesy California State University–Sacramento, Anthropology Department.

Figure 24. Lessons in traditional Nisenan and Miwok dance, featuring
Billy Villa and Guy Wallace, Bryte VFW Hall, circa 1950.
Sacramento History Center.

Potts created the Sacramento Committee on Indian Youth to support their
work.[21] In April 1958 it funded expenses for high school students Larry Marine,
Eugene Goodwin, Marjorie Franklin, and Dan Blodgett, and Sacramento State
College student Wayne Red Horse, to attend the second Regional Indian Youth
Council (RIYC) in Flagstaff, where Red Horse was elected vice president.[22] Gathering afterward at Auburn Rancheria, the students expressed their aspirations to
build a roundhouse and awaken the ceremonial and big time traditions that had
slumbered in the foothills for a quarter century. Stories of these days loomed
large in youthful imaginations, but RIYC endowed them with political import. A
deep longing to be anchored to the ancestral world and embraced by the powerful
Indigenous landscape surfaced with new urgency in these city-dwelling youths.
Already committed to the third RIYC in Brigham, Utah, two weeks later the
Mewauk Indian Dance Group of Sacramento announced a Fourth of July fund-
raiser. A morning and afternoon set of "old style Indian dances" would be followed
by noon and 6:00 P.M. spaghetti feeds. Location? Bryte Memorial VFW Hall.[23]
Shortly before the third RIYC, they held another fund-raiser at McClatchy High
School. Potts distributed a press release and publicity photographs. The *Sacramento*

Union ran a photograph of Potts with grandchildren Marvin, Michael, and Susie Marine, and Dorene Goodwin; the *Bee* carried an image of Darlene Brown and five Franklin daughters—Sally, Clarice, Susie, Terisa, and Maggie—engaged in the "flower dance."[24]

Post 9054's founding was a unique expression of the profound patriotism World War II fostered among Sacramento-area California Indian veterans, but it nurtured something more.[25] Bryte Memorial Hall cradled the California Indian diaspora. Migrated California Indians from across the state joined rancheria residents from Wilton, east to Jackson, and north to Auburn, Clipper Gap, and Forest Hill to host contemporary social dances, participate as teachers or learners in traditional song and ceremony, and celebrate the shared culinary traditions, values, and historical experiences—including boarding school mischief and military service—that united them.[26]

Dyson's loaned museum regalia was important. Dancers donned it not only to perform the Plains or southwestern dances he was instructing but also to limn their cultural distinction from non-Native audiences and more fully inhabit a Native dancer's sensibility. This moment and practice must be understood as a "frontier" of mid-twentieth-century Indigenous resistance to settler colonialism. As Potts complained in her 1950 state fair letters, California regalia was scant. Few Native people had time or opportunity to fashion contemporary versions, although this was about to change, as the eagerness of young Sacramento FIC members was nurtured by solidarity rooted in the physical space and wide regional community that gathered at Bryte. Franklin, who occupied a crucial middle-generation position, was a relentless fanner of the ceremonial embers he had witnessed and lived in his youth, finally convincing "old-timers" that a VFW hall was a fitting place for California Indian dance and ceremonial instruction. In 1957 Post 9054 disbanded, but FIC did not abandon Bryte.[27] In 1961 Potts reported, "The Sacramento Indian Dancers participated with the Placer County Indians in giving a benefit performance in the Veterans of Foreign Wars' Hall . . . to raise funds for the expansion of the Indian cemetery in Colfax, Placer County. Between 30–40 dancers in full regalia took part in the dancing. Mr. Coyote did his share in stirring up memories of olden days. Acorn soup was on the menu."[28]

The next year, 1962, eight youths formed United Indian Youth of California, a new iteration of the earlier group. Their goal was to develop a fund for higher education. Minimal dues and fund-raising supported their efforts. "Mr. William Franklin had consented to act as Senior Advisor and taught some Indian dancing. Mrs. Marie Potts has taught some beadwork. The members are anxious to learn basket weaving, tanning of hides, to make costumes and other crafts so they can teach the younger generation."[29] She was proud to see youths carrying forward California Indian ceremony and regalia making. Theirs was a generation actively recovering traditions that had lapsed under economic stress or been forced underground in modified form. Some elders may not have participated in ceremony as adults, but they had witnessed it as children or were told its history and meanings by their own elders. Anthropologist James Clifford suggests that this recovery work is not so much transmission as translation, one that "brings out the bumps, losses and makeshift solutions of social life."[30]

Frank LaPena (Nomtipom Wintu), the late dance captain, singer, poet, contemporary artist, and professor emeritus of art and ethnic studies, wrote of and enacted such translation from a sacred and embodied perspective, one that tapped into a wider reservoir of texts and culture bearers during the late 1960s and early 1970s, when California Indigenous ceremony was championed not only for its inherent value but also as an overt act of anticolonial activism.[31] In the 1950s and early 1960s, a highly playful, tentative, and experimental quality still animated this recovery work, as Potts described in a 1963 *Smoke Signal* article:

> The Mewok Indian Dancers entertained at the Folsom Celebration July 4–7. The dancers were dressed in authentic California Indian costumes, which is a far cry from the Hollywood version. The dances performed were the "Tuda dance," a pleasure dance of some California tribes, "Buffalo Dance," of the Plains Indians, a solo "Bird dance" and a "Flower Dance," performed by a group of young girls. The finale was the Indians "scalping" of the Clown (Hollywood version) and the Folsom Rescue Squad hauling the body out of the arena. The Mewok Dancers are a group of Indians living around Sacramento and the surrounding area. William (Bill) Franklin is the leader of the group. Eighty-one-year-old (young) Lizzie Enos was the "Belle" of the show.[32]

Though Post 9054 was long gone, Post 9498 supported the Native community throughout the mid-1960s, raising twenty-five dollars in 1966 to support Tuolumne's Acorn Festival. The post commander was photographed handing a check to Franklin, "leader of the Miwuk Indian Dance Group," as Dyson—who played the Indian to the end—looked on in his feathered headdress, with George Wessel and Alvin Daniels.[33]

In 1968, after its land claims battle was over, FIC reorganized as a cultural preservation group. Soon it announced formation of the "California Indian

Dance and Cultural Group, (formerly the Mewuk Dancers)." A July 27 gathering at Franklin's Pony Brown Road home promised instruction in "singing, traditional dances, beadwork, wood carving, etc." Dyson demonstrated mask carving, Potts instructed beadwork, and Franklin taught yellowhammer headband making.[34]

A new era of activism dawned alongside this cultural recovery process. In 1969 Potts's grandson Marvin Lee Marine joined the occupation of Alcatraz. A *Bee* story about Alcatraz featured a photograph of him in "a strategy meeting" with Sonny Larvie, a Ponca from Oklahoma, and Walter Hatch, a Miwok from Sacramento.[35] Two days later, the California Indian Cultural Group of Sacramento met at Bill Franklin's, where they played bingo to raise proceeds for Alcatraz.[36] Potts kept readers in the loop, driving a Sacramento-based FIC contingent to San Francisco. Printing the "Proclamation to the Great White Father and All His People" on *Smoke Signal*'s front page, she included an account of their ferry ride to the Rock, detailing supplies needed to keep kitchen and school operations going. Recording her observations in a small spiral notepad, she knew history was being made.[37] Potts rode this new wave of activism with gusto, organizing donation drops and keeping supply lists updated: "Kindergarten would like Indian coloring books, balloons and goldfish."[38] "Stop by the FIC office," she wrote, urging readers to sign a petition asking for the government to give American Indian people title to the island. "Your signature may be the miracle."[39]

The dance and cultural group's growing popularity led Potts to author a booklet on California Indians. In May 1970, the group accepted an invitation from the Paradise Garden Club and Butte County Honey Run Covered Bridge Association to dance at the historic structure. The occasion was a fund-raiser to restore and preserve the bridge. Since it was close to her own homelands and built just a decade before her birth, she was inspired to provide some cultural and historical context. California State Parks lent assistance. Writing under the pen name Inyahnom Kulam (Indian Woman), she dedicated *A Brief History of Indians of California* "to my three daughters, Josephine, Kitty Marie and Pansy, who have taken the 'Never to look back' journey." The book is illustrated with photographs of Pansy's children—Susie, Joe, and Judy Marine—at the covered bridge in advance of the event, images from Marie's earlier SIM work with Riddell, and line drawings by granddaughter Peggy, Jeanne's daughter.[40] The book, with headings such as "Homes," "Foods," "Clothing," "Baby Baskets," "Spring Ceremony," and "Indians Today," aimed to correct the deficit in children's literature about California Native history and culture. This was a problem she knew firsthand.

Elementary School Lecturer

Potts was a popular guest speaker and cultural demonstrator in public schools all over the greater Sacramento region. She had been engaged in this work for almost a decade when, in 1965, California state school superintendent Max Rafferty asked her to serve on a committee reviewing historical and cultural representations of California Indians in school textbooks. This project was not Rafferty's idea but rather that of committee chair Rupert Costo of AIHS.[41] Potts had plenty of experience talking to historical societies and other adult organizations, but she recognized that children were the best hope for social change, and she deemed this important work.[42] Her interests in educating children about California Indian people can be traced to April 1956, when fifth-grader Katie Leon wrote the FIC, "c/o Mrs. Marie Potts," on behalf of her peers at Mark Twain Elementary School in Corcoran, California. They were "studying about Indians" and wanted "some information about Indian customs, how and where they live, and any other information you might have." Potts wrote a long response, including the following:

> Because of the very small areas for reservations for Indians, they have become integrated with other people and a good many of them have even lost their language. Very few make baskets any more. Quite a few of the younger generation still use the baby basket as they find them more satisfactory. Most of them go to established churches although a few still cling to the old way of religion. They are very religious people although they do not attend churches. Their prayers are with the Supreme Being. In my tribe, the Maidu, we call him World Maker or Creator. Every tribe has their particular name for the Supreme Being. Except for those who live on reservations, the Indians live as other people, their neighbors. You may be rubbing elbows with an Indian and not know it.[43]

Especially notable are her allusions to language loss, the decline in basket weaving, greater numbers of urban-dwelling Natives, and the younger generation's recognition that baby baskets were superior to modern contraptions. She took care to explain that traditionalists were "very religious" despite not going to church and introduced her correspondent to the Maidu World Maker. Katie requested "booklets," and Potts duly provided her with literature, including a booklet that, she explained, was probably too advanced for children: AFSC's *Indians of California Past and Present*. She also sent four SIM pamphlets and the Senate Interim Committee on California Indian Affairs report, which contained a map of California Indian reservations. Finally, Potts enclosed a *Smoke Signal*, noting that "all the work on this publication is done by Indians." Underscoring FIC's statewide, six-thousand-member base, she wrote, "Their purpose in organizing was to promote good legislation in the Congress of the United States and our State legislation, for the welfare of our Indian people not only in California but the whole United States." The closing line of her letter typifies the warmth with which Potts approached children: "If I am ever in your area, I will come to see your school."[44] Several months later, Potts accepted an invitation to speak to one hundred schoolchildren, ages six through twelve, at San Francisco's Good Samaritan Center.[45] Potts did not yet drive. Clothed in her buckskin dress and armed with teaching props, she rode the Greyhound into San Francisco. She was a hit.

By 1958 Potts was trekking with her baby baskets, clapper sticks, and samples of acorn soup to public elementary schools all over Sacramento County, teaching children that California Indians had a long history and rich culture and were still around to live it. She grasped the importance of this work—of the wide-eyed enthusiasm and curious questions that greeted her. Dozens of thank-you letters were read and carefully filed away—treasured reminders of the influence her songs, stories, and mere presence had on impressionable minds. She had once been a tiny schoolgirl, filled with curiosity and fear. Being carted off to Greenville at four years old, speaking a different language, worrying that she was about to be cooked alive, running into the forest to escape the matron's clutches—these stories were part of her opening repertoire. She quelled the children's eagerness to handle the objects arrayed before them by telling them about the most terrifying experience of her life: her first day at school. After startling them with this tale that so thoroughly defined their different status positions in settler society, she bridged the divide by chuckling with feigned embarrassment at the image she must have presented as she tore lickety-split out the school door entirely naked. In other words, she used her childhood trauma to introduce the concept of colonization to fourth- and fifth-graders. This speaks volumes about her intelligence and profound pragmatism. She was increasingly associated with Sacramento's cityscape, but the bath story embedded her birth and belonging in an ancestral place and Indigenous milieu, leading right into her discussions of traditional sweat baths and other Maidu customs.

Her narrative repertoire was object-based. She once cataloged a "List of Articles Used in Lectures" for a correspondent:

3 baskets used in processing acorns—cleaning, sifting, and cooking
1 stirring stick

1 winnowing basket
1 burden basket, small cone shaped
Several small baskets about 10 inches in diameter for various uses,
each with a story.
Deer-hoof rattle, rawhide (deer skin) rattle
2 water jugs, 1 woven over bottle
Arrowheads and obsidian rocks
Indian rouge
Authentic Maidu costume, basket cap
Moccasins, medicine bag, Sioux tobacco pouch
Bead and yarn belts, beadwork, necklaces, belts, etc.
Necklaces of deerhorn, diggerpine nuts, shells (various kinds)
3 tribal baby baskets
Miniature fish trap
Maidu ceremonial flag
A small variety of food, acorn, seeds, salt dried berries, etc.[46]

Note that each of her "several small baskets" has a story. Her own literacy does not diminish or occlude the materiality of the Mountain Maidu archive. Her Indigenous pedagogy is grounded in orality and the material force of things cobbled together, despite overwhelming loss of traditional objects, in her own, subaltern traveling museum. These things tell stories of women working: gathering, winnowing, cooking, weaving, carrying—and caring for—infants. They speak of and to seasonal and women's life cycles, from Potts's very first basket to the altered texture and pattern of a basket completed by an elderly, blind Maidu weaver. "It's an old Indian custom to never leave a basket unfinished." Potts's own first basket encompassed stories of customary practices and cultural persistence. She had gifted it to a "girl [she] admired," but it came back to her. "Not to me," she corrected herself, but to her daughters.[47] Her friend decided that baskets should be passed on, to one another, instead of being burned or buried upon death. Weaving was hard work and less common now, she explained. It relied upon places to gather, time to prepare materials and to weave.[48]

The Sioux tobacco pouch, made by Florence Harrie (Karuk) for the Heard Museum, stands out oddly in this list. Potts found it so beautiful that she talked Harrie into letting her buy it. Its porcupine quillwork elicited classroom discussion of lively trade between coastal, valley, and mountain groups for materials not locally available. It told a story, too, of female companionship. These two spent long hours together for two weeks each summer at the fair, keeping women's traditional arts alive and appreciated—Harrie twining, Potts coiling. She was not a woman of means, but here was a piece of incredible artistry she could not resist.

Potts's school lectures between 1958 and 1963 were funded by local philanthropist and ardent eugenicist Charles C. Goethe, a classic example of how colonial ambivalence plays itself out in settler society. In March 1958, J. Martin (Mike) Weber, Sacramento County school superintendent and educational consultant, wrote him at his Crocker-Anglo Bank Building office, after hearing of Goethe's generosity from SSC professor emeritus Hubert Jenkins. Weber wanted to pay Potts a five-dollar honorarium for her Sacramento County classroom talks: "Mrs. Potts is not able financially to offer these services free to the school and the schools cannot legally pay her through public funds for this kind of service because she is not a certified teacher." Goethe, who had spent decades funding research designed to build a "master race," waxed nostalgic in third person: "As to Sacramento Valley Indianology, writer recalls that in 1881, he commenced collecting Amerinds artifacts. At that time there were two exceptionally rich localities. One was south of his uncle's ranch. It included the 2 Dry Creeks now known as Rio Linda. The weeping oak forest at that time was undisturbed and offered an abundant supply of acorn bread. The other was between his uncle's ranch and the trading post at Gougeye." They eventually reached an arrangement whereby Potts could be paid from SSC's Mary Glide Goethe Memorial Fund. Goethe dispatched a check for twenty-five dollars to cover the first five talks, and Weber wrote regularly for replenishment. Correspondence between Goethe and Weber details the former's "delight at having a share in Mrs. Potts's work," which included TV and radio talks. Goethe sent regrets to every single invitation offered to see her lecture, and in November 1960 he suddenly decided he could not spare a single dime. "Tragically," he moaned, the year's tomato crop had to be plowed under due to "labor trouble." In 1962 these activist stirrings coalesced into the National Farm Workers Association, precursor to United Farm Workers, calling attention to the fortunes harvested from stolen Native land by workers laboring under inhumane conditions.

A week later, Goethe had a change of heart. Joyous over the founding of the Idaho Academy of Sciences, new fruit of earlier philanthropic efforts, he told Weber, "Upon reflection, it seems the dramatic value of one of Redskin descent and the impact that she makes on the receptive minds of school children is something so very important that I am warranted in almost 'pawning my watch.'" Another "widow's mite," as he called his contributions, put food on Potts's table for a while longer.[49] He funded a daylong, Sacramento County teachers' workshop she gave at SIM and, as her reputation grew, multiple lectures per day at the same school. Teachers booked Potts by phoning her directly. At Weber's suggestion, she shared thank-you letters with Goethe, feeding his sense of benevolence and importance. Unaware of his eugenicist commitments, she would have taken his money regardless. She was doing important grassroots education and activism; she deserved and needed to be paid for her work. The latter point occasionally had to be driven home. Too often, non-Natives saw Indian people as novelties in the city, forgetting they had to earn a living.

In 1967 Potts wrote *Pacific Historian* editor Leland Case at University of the Pacific (UOP). He was organizing the twentieth annual California History Institute, themed "Ethnic Contributions to California History and Culture." Potts received a preliminary program and was taken aback to see that a casual conversation with a third party about her possible participation had been formalized without further discussion. She politely ticked off errors and "misinformation": she was not (yet) an instructor in basketry at SSC, though she occasionally guest-lectured in anthropology; the California Indian dancers were not sitting around waiting to dance for free at the drop of a hat: "the adults work and the children attend school. It would be very difficult for them to leave their jobs to take part in the program, unless they were compensated equal to their day's wages and cost of travel. The dance team is about twenty in numbers, adults and children. Transportation is generally made in four or five cars. It takes the entire group to put on a good program." Moreover, she was not the contact person. "Bill Franklin is our dance leader," she wrote, providing his address. As to her own time, "I give talks on Indian culture and other subjects. . . . I have my artifacts that I talk about and show. I could make myself available for March 17, for the nominal sum of $25 and mileage."[50] She could excoriate with devastating charm.

After Pansy's death in 1965, Potts struggled to support herself and her grand-children.[51] School lectures and public appearances helped pay the bills and occasionally drew her farther afield. In October 1971, great-granddaughter Kitty DuFresne showed Potts off to her Nevada Girl Scout troop. Potts took her objects up to Carson City, taught the girls about traditional ways, and confessed that she missed having Mountain Maidu speakers to talk with, as this was essential to keeping language alive.[52] The annual Bear Dance, or Wédam, at the Mankins ranch in Janesville, grounded her spiritually but also reminded her that fellow speakers of Mountain Maidu grew fewer in number every year.[53] One of them, Herb Young, passed away in an Oroville hospital during the 1970 event, which saddened all at what was otherwise deemed to be the best Bear Dance to date: "Herby had been working with anthropologists to record songs and cultures of the Indian people. He was a strong worker among Indian people helping them to understand the many problems prevalent among the Indians."[54] A generation was passing on, and it was hers. For some time, she had been writing ethnographic and historical vignettes placed "above the fold" on the paper's front page. This is where she shared Tom Epperson's sunrise service prayer. "The sun rises so that birds may sing, flowers may grow," he began, poetically working his way through an abundant and interdependent universe of forest life and beings, before asking "that the Bear do no harm to our people . . . we ask that the rattlesnake do no harm to our people . . . watch over our people as they go their separate ways to their homes . . . we are thankful for all things . . . *Heoh wah nye!*"[55]

Figure 25. Marie Potts and Frank Joseph with bearskin and maple bark flag at the 1967 Bear Dance, Janesville, California.
Dorothy M. Hill Collection, Meriam Library Special Collections, California State University–Chico.

"World Premier Features Chen-Kut-Pam"

In 1969 work began on a 16-mm film called *Chen-Kut-Pam*, documenting Potts's classroom visits.[56] Weber funded this with a $5,000 Title IIB grant from the National Education Defense Act. Conceived and produced by Arcohe Elementary School teacher Robin Swift and SSC graduate student photographer-filmmaker Gerald Heine, *Chen-Kut-Pam* opens with a clip from a classroom Q&A session: "Mrs. Potts, do you have an Indian name?" Affirming that she did "as a child," Potts tells them about it while the film title, her Maidu name, scrolls by. The setting is a classroom at Arcohe Elementary in nearby Galt, California. Children heard about her first day at Greenville Indian School, baby and winnowing baskets, and a twined collection plate with a cross marking a break in its border. Reminding students that Christianization brought money, "the root of all evil," she revealed that this gap permitted evil to escape. She talked about gathering pine nuts, acorns, and juniper for smoking—smoke that carried their prayers "up to the Creator in the unknown valley above." Noting that religion and environmental stewardship permeated daily life, she explained that Hukespem never killed ducks if he could tell they were about to lay eggs. Fishing was for subsistence, not sport. People gave thanks after catching fish. Deer were important; all parts were used. Acorn was on the classroom menu. "Your people usually offered visitors coffee," she remarked, while hers offered acorn soup. The camera zoomed in on the children's expressive faces as they sampled the soup, before heading up to her table and artifacts, which she encouraged them to handle. Some children tried on basket caps. A boy modeled a cone-shaped burden basket, feeling right at home with this original backpack.

Heine and Potts headed up to Plumas and Lassen Counties in June 1970 to film scenes to be spliced into this classroom footage: the maple bark flag and bearskin from the Spring Ceremony, Tom Epperson emerging from a dance house, Lake Almanor's shoreline near Hukespem's allotment, ducks paddling in marshy sloughs, Potts harvesting manzanita berries. Near Sutter Buttes, she shelled and pounded acorn in bedrock mortars. Footage from Alcatraz was already in the can. Indians of All Tribes, Inc. allowed Heine to film Potts exiting a cell block into the glaring sunlight. She waved shyly at the camera while crossing the barren cement court. Prefacing the voice-over for this segment with the statement that children would not find her next story in their textbooks, Potts then recounted how California Indian people were herded onto barges, like so many cattle, and shipped up the coast to a Mendocino County reservation.[57]

The film debuted in March 1971. CLAI, whose board of directors now included Potts, proclaimed, "World Premier Features Chen-Kut-Pam" in its newsletter

Indian Affairs in California. This screening at the Sacramento County Office of Education was followed by many more, including one at a local church hosting a six-week study series titled "American Indians in California."[58] Invitations to appear in person at these screenings kept seventy-six-year-old Potts busy.

Three Places in Time: Speaking Up for Sacramento's Ancestral People and Places

In 2006, when California's Native American Heritage Commission (NAHC) was celebrating its thirtieth anniversary, UC Davis Native American studies professor Jack Forbes lamented that much of the footwork leading to the commission's creation was forgotten. In 1975, he, Potts, David Risling Sr., and Dave Risling Jr. had partnered with the California Indian Education Association (CIEA) and United Native Americans to write the enabling legislation: AB 4239. An original provision giving the commission jurisdiction over SIM was vigorously opposed by California State Parks and eventually sacrificed to gain the bill's passage. Forbes said, "I think that it is important that we as Indian people, do not constantly forget our history and the key people who made things we take for granted possible. Dave Risling Sr. and Jr. and Marie Potts have passed on, as has Vivien Hailstone, whom we persuaded Governor Brown to appoint as the first Indian to the California Parks Commission. Many other key leaders are gone, but we should still honor their memory accurately."[59] Potts pushed—and published in the *Smoke Signal*—the leading edge of California Indian activism, but like her own sensibilities and expectations, that edge transformed radically over the course of her eight-decade life. Three places in time attest to this.

On March 29, 1956, hundreds of Native people from six western states and forty nations gathered at Bethel Temple in downtown Sacramento for the second annual American Indian Fellowship of the Assemblies of God Convention. Not five minutes away, an archaeological excavation was taking place along the Sacramento River's eastern bank, at the edge of the South Land Park neighborhood. The public had learned of the site's existence several days earlier, through a front-page story, "Ancient Indian Village Crops Up South of City."[60] The headline was somewhat disingenuous. It was indeed an ancient village, complete with a dance house, but SSC professors Brigham Arnold and Richard Reeve, and their students, had been excavating it for more than a year, with others from UC Berkeley. Perched precariously atop a ladder, a photographer documented the scene: Heizer stood chest-deep in a long trench while Reeve, on the ground above, peered into the deep cut where a student worked. They were racing against time. A suburban home developer was pouring foundations nearby. Asked how much time they needed to complete excavations, Arnold sighed, "about 10 years."[61] Press coverage continued throughout the week. As convention delegates began arriving, one newspaper declared, "Redmen Not Excited about Finding Old Graves."[62] The story was illustrated with individual portraits of George McPherson (Cherokee), Manuel Cordova (Pomo), George Effman (Klamath), and his father, John (Karuk), each adorned in a feathered headdress, seemingly passed between them at the photographer's request. Potts is quoted liberally throughout. The Reverend George Effman and his father were longtime Sacramento residents and FIC members, who probably directed press queries to her as the organization's publicity chair. Despite her own friendship with Reeve, who regularly asked her to speak in his anthropology classes, the limits of her concordance with his work rang clear: "We are curious but we will not go there. Indians believe the dead should be left in peace, though we do not object to digging up old camps to learn more about Indian culture." Reeve earlier speculated on the site's antiquity, and Potts wondered aloud if the remains might be Maidu before asserting, "If they are not that old, then they are probably from the Miwok (or Mewok) tribe, which inhabited the area at a later date. Maidu Indians are now considered to be from an area farther north." She would respect Reeve's interpretation but was "not going there to inspect the site herself."[63]

That summer, field classes in archaeology worked briskly, one step ahead of cement mixers.[64] Fritz Riddell was now SIM curator. Sacramento highway and housing development, as elsewhere across the nation, was obliterating Native heritage: sacred sites, villages, and cemeteries. In 1959 the Central California Archaeological Foundation (CCAF) had formed to further what was then called salvage archaeology—trying to recover whatever information could be gained before bulldozing. In 1960 Riddell became California's first state archaeologist. The next snapshot is prologue to this.

In late 1959, the historic Nisenan village of Kadema was disturbed by housing development along the American River at Watt Avenue. Archaeologist John Clemmer, CCAF treasurer, used this opportunity to educate state senator Albert Rodda and state assemblyman Edwin Z'berg about the need for regulations to prevent site destruction.[65] The remains of six individuals were identified. A *Bee* article identified their closest descendants as Lillie Williams and her brother, James Adams, of Healdsburg. [66] Williams, born at the village of Pusuni near downtown Sacramento, pinpointed the gravesite of her uncle Mike Cleanso and several others after excavations began. She had long before moved to Broderick but returned many times to visit the cemetery, fording the river on foot since no bridge existed in those days.[67] Newspapers and archaeologists failed to connect contemporary descendants with the 1956 excavations, but Kadema coverage established that descendants existed and wished to preserve the sanctity of ancestral remains. Williams chose to have her relatives reinterred at East Lawn Cemetery, where Kitty and Hensley Potts were buried and Pansy would soon be laid to rest. Developer Jones, Brand, and Hullen, Inc. purchased plots and FIC took a lead role in reburial services, scheduling them for June 11, the Saturday preceding FIC's monthly meeting. Effman would officiate. Potts announced that Native traditions would be incorporated.[68] A June 4, 1960, *Smoke Signal* flyer informed members that graveside services were set for 11:00 A.M., followed by a potluck picnic at McClatchy Park. The developers, who halted construction until excavation was complete, supplied drinks and dessert.

The flyer told Kadema's story. The village was occupied until 1930 by "the once numerous Valley Nisenan," a branch of her own Maidu people, "it was at this village that some of Captain Sutter's faithful Hawaiian companions found their Indian wives. And it is here that they established a cemetery for their departed loved ones. The bodies being reinterred are: Captain Mike Cleanso, wife Dolores Cleanso, daughter Ida Cleanso, John L. Cook, daughter Lillie Cook, Ellen Adams, daughter of Fred Adams, deceased."[69] Ten years later, the California Environmental Quality Act (CEQA), modeled on the 1969 federal law, was passed. CEQA recognized cultural and historical resources as part of the environment writ large but rarely extended those protections to Native American cultural resources. NAHC was legislated to remedy this. As the final snapshot reveals, it was slow to gain traction.

In April 1973, a reporter sat down with Potts: "You were born on Indian land?" Seventy-seven years old and full of fight, she replied sweepingly, "This was all Indian land."[70] Her retort reflected more than her maternal lineage and a quarter century of land claims reporting. She was in the eye of another Native land maelstrom and righteously protesting plans to desecrate an ancient cemetery. As the interview progressed she remarked, "We were subjugated, beaten down, then our people began to study law . . . we work now through Congress and the courts whenever we can—but, of course, we have to have militants to bring about these things . . . to get the attention of Congress and the courts." Her court reference foreshadowed things to come. A coalition of Ronald Reagan supporters, Citizens for Construction of a Governor's Mansion, had recently purchased eleven acres of Carmichael land along the American Rivers bluffs. When preliminary archaeological investigation established it was a Nisenan Maidu village and burial site, protests erupted immediately. Democratic opposition to a governor's mansion situated twenty-one miles from the capital was already afoot. Two pieces of pending legislation, one requiring the mansion to be sited downtown and another appropriating $110,000 to fund archaeological mitigation, reflected polar ends of the controversy. Meanwhile Native people, dumbfounded by this brazen demonstration of California's enduring colonial power, opposed both mansion construction and archaeological excavation. On April 22, six armed American Indian Movement (AIM) protesters were jailed for entering and attempting to occupy the fenced and gated site. They carried a three-page flyer railing against Reagan, who aimed "to bring bulldozers to vandalize and destroy that which is ours . . . in order to construct another hideous European structure alien to our land."[71] Riddell and Potts, along with many Native people, attended multiple hearings and legislative committee meetings hoping to force Reagan's hand, but to no avail.[72]

Potts's relationship with Riddell was soon tested. In early July, an employee tracking mansion development for Secretary of State Edmund G. (Jerry) Brown Jr. discovered that Riddell's office planned to commence excavation on July 16, 1973, believing that no environmental impact statement (EIS) was necessary. Brown, Potts, and Red Horse responded by filing for a preliminary injunction.[73] In her declaration, Potts explicated, "I believe in the Indian religion." She continued,

> According to our religion the land is our mother, because it is where we get our food and everything else that we have. The land where they want to build a governor's mansion is especially holy, because it is where Indians lived, worshiped and are buried. We think of all our cemeteries with reverence. It breaks our heart to have this land disturbed. . . . Even though the archaeologists say the village is 3,000 years old, the Indians say it was being used up until the gold rush. At that time the white settlers drove the Indians away. The Carmichael cemetery is sacred to me. I have gone there to pray. I have even thought of being buried there, but I told my family to have my remains cremated so I will not be dug up in a thousand years. We Indians have been neglected for a long time. It has been hard for us to defend ourselves, but I hope now the courts will respect our religion and our feelings. . . . This ground is sacred to me and as an Indian is particularly important to me because of my Maidu upbringing and because I live so close.

Riddell awaited the court's decision. On July 31, it ruled that no EIS was necessary and work could proceed. Naming her granddaughter Judy and the FIC as codefendants, Potts sued in the Eastern District Court for a permanent injunction under the First and Fourth Amendments. Jettisoning all solicitude, she asserted, "The burial grounds are wanted by the defendants for the sole purpose of the construction of a 'MANSION' type dwelling for a 'PALEFACE,' namely a Governor of the State of California. . . . We, the MAIDU NATION, simply ask, let our dead rest in the peace they are entitled to."[74] With construction set to commence on October 1, Reagan offered to reinter and memorialize human remains in a protected spot on-site. Then, demonstrating that he was utterly incapable of apprehending the emotional or sociopolitical stakes for Native people, he cavalierly stated that assertions by protestors that their relatives were being disrespected seemed "far-fetched. If there is such a village there, archaeologists seem to agree that it is 3,000 years old and I doubt there is anyone alive today who can trace back ancestors of his particular family or even ethnic group back 3,000 years."[75] With legal and legislative options soon extinguished by the superior court, Potts wrote Reagan a letter, asking to hold a prayer ceremony on-site. He forwarded her letter to the police. Offended and disgusted, Potts mocked, "I don't think I'll fool with him anymore. Reagan's not for us. He's scared. He's afraid of too many Indians coming together at once. After all, how many did he kill in the movies?"[76]

Elected governor in November 1974, Jerry Brown refused to inhabit the mansion. Never furnished, it was sold by the state in 1983 for $1.53 million.[77] The site was listed on the National Register of Historic Places in 1978. In 1990 the Point Vicente chapter of DAR purchased a brass plaque reading, in part, "Site of Nisenan Indian Village and Burial Ground, Middle Horizon Period (1000 B.C.–A.D. 500), Registered Archaeological Site CA-Sac-99L." Affixed to a boulder at the site's entrance, the plaque is now partially obscured by a manicured boxwood hedge that serves as an intentional blind, relieving passersby and residents entering this now gated community from having to grapple daily with this Indigenous place in time.

More Than a Matriarch

The term "urban clan mother" was coined by anthropologist Susan Lobo to describe women whose households provided an anchor and source of sustenance for Native people in Bay Area cities. It offers a good point of departure for analyzing Potts's work cultivating Native presence and community in Sacramento. Lobo writes, "The women who head these key households and extend many services to urban community members are strong but low-profile activists."[78] For a certainty, 2727 Santa Clara Way was Grand Central Station for Native people, the city's unrivaled California Indian urban place, for the better part of three decades. Yet Lobo's concept, valuable in the historical Bay Area context, cannot do full justice to Potts's work in Sacramento. Oakland and San Francisco were BIA relocation centers, serving tribal people from across the country. And while many California Indian people migrated to Sacramento to be with family, for military service, or for other work, they did not coalesce into community until Potts came on the scene. She fed and hosted them and played the "oral newspaper" role that one Native scholar ascribes to first wave relocated Bay Area Indians.[79] Yet she also maintained a high profile in the city due to her print journalism, state fair exhibit, national activism, and pithy commentary on the never-ending disappointments Native Californians suffered at the hands of state and federal government. Although widely sought out for her dance group, school lectures, and capacity to represent the Native community before state and nongovernmental agencies, she was equally and always engaged in the low-profile activism Lobo identifies as foundational to urban community building, an activity she maintained well into her late seventies:

> A sewing class meets once a week at the home of Marie Potts, who is teaching them. First the group are taught to use the electric and treadle machines and to sew a straight seam. So far, they have completed two quilt tops and each girl is making a quilt—for herself. The next step is to put the quilt together. Our motto is "As you sew, so shall you rip." We have done a lot of that—rip. The girls are very enthused about their sewing and attended classes pretty regularly. Later we will go into making garments.[80]

Her home was an ad hoc cultural center, where she instructed young women in life skills. Two generations removed from Greenville, where five-year-old Marie demanded that Emma Trubody give her a needle so she could stitch a doll, Potts was still sewing, but she was doing something more as well. She was sowing and seeding urban community among a new generation of Native girls while teaching them how to stitch clothing and quilts. Some of those young girls are still living in Sacramento today. In their own high- and low-profile activism, they carry her legacy forward. So do the many Native California people who gather at the capitol each September on Native American Day to dance and pay tribute to a living monument she helped establish there. The dancing, no less than the monument, forms an unbroken link to her work building Native presence and place in Sacramento.

Conclusion

It knows. Oak trees know what we are trying to do in California for all Indian people and they also know it is not at all certain we will live long enough to do it.

—*Marie Potts, 1974*

The sentiments above, expressed in reference to a small oak tree, a living monument planted in September 1968 on Capitol State Park grounds, evince Potts's grounding in an Indigenous epistemology. Pratt was wrong. One could not kill the Indian in her and leave the woman. Potts remained Native. She could draw inspiration from Disraeli's notion of constancy to purpose yet still be Mountain Maidu. English-language literacy was a Native resource, not simply a settler colonial form. Like the generations of Native women from whom she was descended, whose lives were not defined by patriarchal training in the domestic arts that aimed to circumscribe family forms and women's socioeconomic contributions, Potts continued to labor, to mother, and to keep kin and community together.[1]

A bedrock mortar and plaque beneath the small oak celebrate the mighty acorn. The little sapling always struggled to reach the sun under the expansive canopy of mature trees. Its planting predated her quarrels with Reagan, who in 1968 signed a proclamation designating the fourth Friday in September as California Indian Day. Potts was inspired to action after years of trekking to the capitol across park grounds where Junipero Serra, father of the brutal Spanish mission system, was memorialized with a monument, while none acknowledged Native people whose stolen lands financed California's colonial power and wealth. Announcing the tree-planting in June, community members came from across the state to take part.[2] Reagan declined to attend, but two government representatives were there. They turned the soil with silver ceremonial shovels, while California Native leaders used abalone shells.[3] Cognizant that archiving was a form of activism, Potts preserved a list of FIC participants.

Two months later she was sitting in the Kroeber family home on Arch Street in Berkeley, leafing through black-and-white photographs of the old ones who had come before. It was November 22, 1968, the publication party for *Almost Ancestors: The First Californians*, by Theodora Kroeber and Robert Heizer.[4] According to David Brower's dust cover introduction, the title was an allusion to extinction, as if the portraiture inside represented people who left no descendants. Potts knew this oblique and euphemistic reference to genocide was too broad a gloss. These *were* ancestors, no "almost" about it. California was carved from their labor and land, and their descendants continued to shape it. Still, she knew her own time was drawing to a close: "Oak trees know what we are trying to do in California for all Indian people and they also know it is not at all certain we will live long enough to do it."[5] Their land claims case was finally over, and her disappointment was profound.

A Predictably Bitter Pill: California's Land Claims Case Is Settled

California Indian people rode a roller coaster of optimism and despair for two decades, and Potts was there with *Smoke Signal* coverage to the very end. Following the 1954 hearings for Indians of California (Dockets 31 and 37), a second round of hearings took place in 1955 for the remaining dockets. In 1959 ICC ruled that "Indian title" was established. It was now incumbent upon the United States to take responsibility for its immoral actions a century earlier by awarding equitable compensation, but a plethora of tedious delays ensued. ICCA's life had to be extended; the plaintiffs had to mount another defense when the defendants challenged ICC's 1959 ruling in the court of claims; original petitions had to be amended because named representatives (including Calac, Miller, and Treppa) had died; attorney contracts had to be renewed. As Frederic Baker had predicted in 1946, the process was relentlessly plagued by technical problems and "splinter cases," so named because they were separate from Indians of California. These cases were tribally based, some straddling adjoining states. FIC had pushed valiantly for a unified claim in 1947; now attorneys for the groups who fought against this were desperately pursuing this strategy. The Shasta, Yana, and Yokiah Nations agreed to consolidate, but the Pit River and Mission dockets pressed forward independently. ICC then divided the state into Area A (31,000,000 acres comprising splinter group claims) and Area B (69,000,000 acres comprising Indians of California claims). Land valuation was next. Defendants argued that K-344's blanket value of $1.25 was too high given low occupancy and vast unirrigated acreage in 1853. Plaintiff attorneys countered that values were equalized by K-344's undervaluing of timber, mineral, and agricultural lands. Any land appraisal expenses would, like attorney fees and roll preparation costs, comprise offsets against the award, with appraisal potentially lasting a decade. In December 1963, attorneys for all groups whose claims were fully within California decided to press for joint settlement.

Examining recent awards, attorneys contended that $29,100,000 was the maximum recovery possible, with a smaller award and/or reversal of original finding of "Indian title" possible if the cases were fully litigated. Plaintiff attorneys proposed a compromise settlement projected at forty-seven cents per acre and won it through fear and arbitrary policing of local referenda. Attorneys began holding informational meetings and votes in early 1964. Two decisions were at stake for Area A groups: whether to consolidate with Indians of California and whether to accept the compromise settlement. Four meetings held among forty-six Mission bands yielded a positive vote on both counts, by 56 percent of eligible voters. When a negative vote was rendered in Alturas by 24.5 percent of eligible Pit River voters, their attorneys and the BIA consulted with ICC. A contentious extension via absentee balloting won the outcome now desperately sought by both the settler state and its surrogates, the plaintiff attorneys—with the exception of Baker. Meetings and absentee balloting continued until the settlement was declared accepted on July 20, 1964.

Attention then turned to imponderable distribution issues. The last roll, updated in 1950 for K-344 per capita distribution, contained descendants whose claims crossed state boundaries. Congressional legislation, informed by meetings throughout the state in 1966, tackled this problem. Introduced in 1967, H.R. 10911 called for a new roll, enumerating all descendants (born on or before the date of H.R. 10911) and ancestral affiliations for Indians residing in the state on June 1, 1852. Adult members (age twenty-one or over), except those whose ancestry derived solely from nations straddling state borders, received referendum ballots to accept or reject per capita distribution. No alternative was offered. By this means, ICC grievances came to an inglorious close in 1968, twenty-two years after Docket 12's filing. Baker shared Injun Louie's disgust.

From 1969 to 1972 the *Smoke Signal* carried reminders that February 1972 was the filing deadline for California Indian adults and their children to apply to the new roll. When $668.50 per capita checks arrived, some descendants refused to cash them. Others could ill afford to protest.[6] Many California Indian people who had dedicated their lives to fighting for land claims compensation died without a penny or even an apology from the federal government. Injun Louie had always known deep down that dreams of just compensation were nothing more than that—a fantasy that the federal government would square its debt to Native people for the land and labor on which the wealth of California had been built. Still, it is important to recognize that the labor of front-line land claims activists yielded other political and cultural rewards.

Her Final Years

In February 1974, Potts suffered a stroke while watching Frank Day and the Maidu Dancers rehearse at Pacific Western Traders, a Native art gallery that had opened its doors in nearby Folsom in 1971 and quickly became an ad hoc cultural center. This slowed her down for a few months, but she continued instruction by voice alone in the California Indian basket making courses she was teaching for CSUS's nascent Ethnic Studies Program.[7] As summer arrived, she joked self-effacingly, "Since school is not in session, Mrs. Potts would like to report that her basket class did very well. Some of the students made pine needle baskets, some made willow baskets, and all of them made very good grades, considering their helpless teacher!" The timing could have been much worse. She, Bertha Wright, Mabel McKay, and Vivian Hailstone had just completed demonstrations and appearances at a Chico State University basket weaving seminar taught by PAHMA's Larry Dawson (figure 26).[8]

She kept at the things that mattered most to her, including the *Smoke Signal*. AIPA press releases, her grandchildren's labor, and stalwart volunteers—including expert typist and consummate speller Leona Miranda Begay—kept the newspaper on track. Her gratitude overflowed with the editor's thanks to Beryl Cross, Jeanne O'Taylor, Susie Yanes, Judy and Joe Marine, Wally and Butch Gorbet, Aglaee DuFresne, CSUS students, and so many others. Every now and then, a grandchild speaks of reviving the *Smoke Signal*. That it has never been done is a testament to the incredible amount of intellectual and physical labor it took. Potts never ran short of energy for either: "I've had many inquiries about my health since my stroke last February," she wrote in December 1974. "This hasn't kept me completely tied down. . . . Every time I hear of an Indian meeting, I'm right there!!!"[9] The 1974 Bear Dance was a different kind of gathering, but she was not going to miss it: "The California Dance Group performed after lunch with Frank Day as their singer, after which Mabel McKay performed a healing ceremony on Marie Potts

Figure 26. Marie Potts peers through a mortar hopper at a
Chico State basket weaving seminar, January 1974.
Dorothy M. Hill Collection, Meriam Library Special Collections, California State University–Chico.

with the assistance of the Dance Group. During the bear dance, Marvin, Marie's
grandson, and Freda Hedricks, a friend, helped her out to the dance area where
she could get in at least a few steps in the ceremony. Freda took Marie's wormwood
down to the water because she could not go there and Freda brought back her
hands full of water so that Marie could wash her face and say a prayer."[10]

During his first gubernatorial term, Jerry Brown paid tribute to Native artists in California with an exhibit featuring examples of traditional and contemporary visual culture. *I Am These People* opened in the governor's office on April 14, 1975. Buffy Sainte-Marie sang a few verses for the featured artists and press. Potts exhibited a basket she began coiling at SIM in the late 1950s and a utilitarian sifter. During the press tour, she gifted the latter to Brown. She had begun weaving it back in the early 1920s, after Josie's house burned. "It took me 47 years to finish that basket and I'm giving it to you," seventy-nine-year-old Potts exclaimed.[11] Like all around her, she knew her days were numbered.

In May 1977, SIM named Marie its first Honored Elder and her book *The Northern Maidu* was published. The slender volume's cover image is from her 1964 fair exhibit. She poses before a cedar bark lodge, with a yellowhammer headband perched on her head and a baby basket on her arm. The photograph perfectly captures her pride and willingness to do just about anything to promote the exhibit and Native culture.[12] Her book was produced with assistance from Margery Greenleaf, a non-Native who cold-called Potts one day after reading about Pansy's death. Recently widowed and two years Potts's junior, she needed something to keep her busy. "Come on over!" Potts replied. Greenleaf accompanied her to school lectures and even tagged along on the Tulsa NCAI trip. Naturegraph Press publisher Vinson Brown's invitation to author a book came after Potts's stroke. Having lost command of her left side, she was unable to hunt and peck on her typewriter, so Potts dictated and Greenleaf transcribed. Here was an ironic state of affairs—a seeming return to the oral Native and the writerly settler.[13] Yet Potts continued to exercise her literacy and control over the manuscript, staying true to the voice she cultivated to teach—and reach—children. Reworking some materials from her 1970 booklet, she added new insights into her own childhood and culture: "The Maidu shared their land with the miners and ranchers who followed, not understanding the white man's concept of ownership, intending only to loan them the land. As more white men came, they drained the land. Ranches developed so fast that we, having had this country of mountains and meadows to ourselves, were left to become either laborers or homeless wanderers. Being peaceable and intelligent people, we adapted as best we could."[14] Three generations removed from ancestral appeals to California's Supreme Court that their oral agreement with David Blunt be honored, she was writing the story of dispossession, hoping youthful settler descendants would awaken to the injustice of their forebears' actions.

Despite her frail condition, Potts insisted on going to the 1978 Bear Dance. Ceremony always called her home. While there, she took a turn for the worse.

Hospitalized in Susanville, she died on June 24, 1978. The North American Native and mainstream press carried her obituary. Lengthier versions trace her path from a humble Big Meadow birth at Yotium to her AIPA cofounding role. All ran under the headline "Indian Publisher Dies."[15]

Carrying Tradition into Modernity

In her last years, Potts regularly conceded that hers had been a wondrous life. Counting her blessings in public venues and a variety of epistolary forms, she credited a host of benefactors, from Hukespem and Helen Peterson to her daughters and many grandchildren. She was a generous giver of thanks, always ready to acknowledge those who opened doors, loaned time and materials, typed for her, laughed with her, or carted her to the "Indian meetings" and gatherings she held so dear—the Intertribal Council of California, the Sacramento Indian Center, the California League for American Indians, California Indian Day at the state capitol, NCAI and AIPA conventions, dance practices at Pacific Western Traders, the Bear Dance in Janesville. In the 1970s, these opportunities to mingle with, work for, and celebrate Indian people multiplied at an astonishing pace, due in no small part to three decades of her own steady and selfless work.

Potts blazed trails across the city, state, and nation. She was the embodiment of a California Indian activist in the mid-twentieth century: a grandmother in homemade dresses and sturdy shoes, with cat-eye glasses framing the same mischievous twinkle that shone forth in her Greenville School days (figure 2). On May 16, 1975, Secretary of Health and Welfare Mario Obledo dedicated the second-floor lobby in State Office Building One to Potts, observing that she "has been a vital force working to overcome isolation and return needed unity to the Indian people . . . at the same time, she has helped revive in the minds and hands of young Indians the culture and skills which transmit their history."[16] A few months short of eighty years old, she was overwhelmed with pride and gratitude: "I'm glad you didn't wait until I died to do this."[17] The young men and women there to honor her had come of age in the 1960s and early 1970s. They represented fruits of her long labor to revivify and animate the cityscape with the California Indian song, dance, and ceremony—to make a place for it in contemporary lives. Here she was, three decades later, listening and watching as it filled the lobby and reverberated throughout the building's marble corridors. New activist forms and organizations were on the rise, but she had long ago made the critical link between cultural expression and political activism, and had been working to advance them both in her own way, and in her own time.

Figure 27. Portrait of Marie Potts placed in the second-floor lobby of California State Office Building One (now the Jesse M. Unruh State Office Building) following the lobby's dedication to her in March 1975.
Plumas County Museum, Quincy, California.

In Her Own Time

Potts's life embodied the full universe of possibilities and limitations facing Mountain Maidu children born in the last decades of the nineteenth century. The assault that her remote and tranquil homelands suffered after statehood is the story of her conception writ large. Her grandparents, Hukespem and Mariah, knew life in a prior time, before the ambitions of Big Meadow settlers and the wider state drew their children into a social vortex of intercultural disarray. Marie and her generational peers spanned a very different divide. They were the first generation to be formally schooled in English-language literacy, the first to face the risks and rewards of the Mission Indian School, the first to be separated from families and indoctrinated into religious beliefs and practices that challenged the traditions into which their grandparents and parents had been enculturated.[18] They were the first experts in Mountain Maidu modernity, and Potts was the most lettered one of all—Carlisle graduate, editor, publisher, author, and activist.

A Lettered Life

Marie became a boarding school pupil at four years old. This milieu soon became familiar territory, inhabited as it was by the half siblings and cousins with whom she was now reunited. We cannot know why Josie let her youngest child go off to Greenville at this age, but given the lively personality and boundless energy she exhibited well into her golden years, it is easy to imagine what a handful she must have been for her grandparents. Between the exigencies of daily life laboring for white homesteaders and hoteliers, and concern for her aging parents' ability to keep up with their ever-curious and nimble charge, Josie may have decided that having Marie join her siblings at Greenville was a sensible, if difficult, choice. Certainly, pressure to do so came from both the Aments and her Piazzoni cousins. Marie adapted. She learned her letters, she played house and games with her siblings and cousins, and she made trips home to Big Meadow. She went back and forth for brief visits and spent two years in Prattville's elementary school. Unlike many off-reservation boarding school pupils, she never suffered complete cultural rupture or isolation.

And luck was on her side. She survived. She did not come down with a deadly pathogen like her Piazzoni cousins had. By sheer accident of timing, she arrived to become acclimated while the Aments, local residents whom her cousins and other Maidu trusted, were still there. By the same token, she left not long after Greenville gained agency status, becoming perpetually understaffed and eternally overwhelmed. Her first teachers were local residents. They employed and were familiar with Maidu families. Marie was a vivacious little child. She charmed them. She was intelligent and excelled at her studies. As her siblings and cousins left for other schools, fictive kin filled the void: girlfriends like Ellen Reeves, Louise Eddelbuttel, the Peconum sisters; beaus like Hensley Potts; teachers, superintendents, and Indian Service employees like Twoguns and Curtis—all of whom influenced her future.

Marie was drawn east to Carlisle and her Piazzoni cousins like a moth to a flame, dazzled as much by their lives and letters home as she was by the school's propaganda and heady reputation. She plainly aspired to be part of that institution and its legacy. She remained fond of it and proud of her achievements there to the end. The adventurous disposition so evident in her activist years was not birthed at Carlisle, but it blossomed there. Though illuminated to heights not possible in the rural environs of Big Meadow, it was already a precious possession in September 1912 when she hopped aboard the Western Pacific, chugging its way along the Scenic Feather River Route, bound for Denver and beyond.

Once again, the odds were in her favor. Carlisle was in its waning years. It had its share of troubles during her tenure there, but authoritarian abuse of children kidnapped from reservations and leveraged away from families was not one of them. Carlisle and surrounds proved to be a stimulating environment; Marie was able to realize her full potential. Suffering a minor setback in her placement exams, she gained a new understanding of her Greenville education and place within a broader pool of academically inclined Native students. She used her outings to catch up with them and stay on track to graduate in three years. Outings endowed her with a taste of autonomy and sense of resourcefulness that she would need in middle age. They expanded the boundaries of her universe. Potts first laid eyes on an ocean in May 1913. Seventeen years old and twenty-eight hundred miles from her Mountain Maidu homelands, she was absolutely mesmerized. As she drank in the balmy air and the remarkable sight of young women in elegant bathing costumes frolicking waist-deep in the surf, the shimmering blue horizon reflected the wondrous array of possibilities she could now envision for herself. Carlisle offered her a sense of scale and perspective. It watered innate seeds of cosmopolitanism that she kept alive for six decades more, despite material and personal circumstances that would have quashed an average person's wanderlust. Most importantly, Carlisle fostered her social skills and literary talents—two passions she translated into activist forms.

From the Center to the Margins and Back Again

Despite her love of Philadelphia, the lure of a teaching career, and Eli's own example of prosperity, Marie was drawn back home. Rose returned to care for her father, but Marie came back to her mother, Hensley, and her Mountain Maidu homelands. Life was hard. Marriage and motherhood were marred by reservoir displacement, racism, and her husband's struggle with alcohol. At Carlisle, Native people were celebrated for their rich culture and intelligence. Back home, they were tolerated at best. A vital resource for the local economy, they were pushed to the literal and figurative margins of society—segregated in public schools and unwelcome in white churches. Even the federal government turned its back on them, refusing to reinvest in a site that many alumni associated with Indigenous place and belonging. Flooded out of Big Meadow, struggling to hold household and home together, striving to ensure that her girls reached their full potential, she had a lifeline in the self-sufficiency she had learned on outings.

Following her daughters to Sacramento, Marie found sanctuary from marital strife and a new purpose in life. After twenty-five years of patching together a bare living as a tenant and domestic worker on her own stolen and flooded ancestral homelands, land claims compensation could not have resonated more deeply. Like a gravitational force, FIC pulled her back into the center of a Native sphere with creative and dynamic people at its core. She expanded its influence and boundaries with the *Smoke Signal*, forging a sense of diasporic belonging and common purpose among diverse California Indian peoples. More than a vehicle for Native news reporting, it was a site of California Indian cultural production—a place to identify and celebrate shared ceremony and culinary delights, to narrate shared histories of dispossession and persistence, to turn Injun Louie loose on the settler state, and to tickle funny bones with Indian humor. The land claims factionalism that gave birth to the *Smoke Signal* paled by comparison to Potts's epic accomplishment of engaging California Indian people; she pioneered California Native journalism as a cottage industry and mode of grassroots activism well ahead of the 1960s underground and alternative press.

Coaxed onto the stage of national activism, she fought for California Indian causes and brought visibility to a Native population frequently left out of important national conversations or forgotten altogether, just as their treaties had been. And she lent her shoulder to activist projects benefiting American Indian people more broadly, through her NCAI volunteerism and AIPA work. Potts declined to pursue a college degree and teaching career after Carlisle, but she was a teacher in practice and at heart. An interpreter of California Indian and Mountain Maidu histories and cultures, she stepped eagerly into the roles of exhibit curator, museum consultant, and cultural demonstrator. Hundreds of schoolchildren in the greater Sacramento region learned from her gentle presence, repertoire of stories, collection of artifacts, and samples of acorn soup that California Indian people had histories and societies long before white people ever stepped foot in the state.[19] And she taught everyone, from apprentice anthropologists to governors, that Indian people were modern, in the countryside, on reservations, and in urban environs. She adapted to Sacramento as she had to Greenville and Carlisle. She made it her own, carving out a California Indian way of being in the city to the lasting benefit of future generations.

Leader, Activist, Wise One

Potts's life was so richly variegated and her activism so extensive that she overflows the practical confines of any book.[20] Her presence, voice, and writing spill forth in widely dispersed archival forms, from census records to missionary publications to the deep stratigraphic debris of settler colonial surveillance largely comprising the National Archive and Record Administration's Record Group 75. Read against and along the archival grain, her lettered Mountain Maidu life emerges as representative of Native women's experience at the turn of the last century yet also distinct, a portrait of Native exploration and agency exercised within and across multiple, interpenetrating domains of indigeneity and settler colonialism. Exhibiting an early desire to see and know other people, places, and things, by adolescence she was already charting—and funding—her own life course. Determined to satisfy her adventurous spirit and academic ambitions, she exploited every opportunity to advance these goals within the context available to her: off-reservation boarding school. Already accustomed to intercultural dynamics within her own extended family and Big Meadow landscape, she acquired new perspectives and tools at Carlisle that lent strength to her later years of land claims work and Native community building. Government hearings, the mainstream press, the *Smoke Signal*, Native newspapers, and reams of personal and professional correspondence document her steadfast conviction that California Indians deserved just compensation for their stolen ancestral lands, a decent standard of living, the right to practice their traditions, and a political voice in their own affairs. Traces of her extraordinary life animate the dusty recesses of humble historical societies, the voluminous Smithsonian archives, and piles of paper still languishing in garages and forgotten corners of California Native homes. Like the skills and knowledge cultivated at Carlisle, these seemingly mundane documents have too long been laid aside. In the coming decades, they and others like them will be recognized as testaments to the tidal wave of cultural and political projects—humble and grand—that land claims fostered across California during the long and tumultuous arc of the twentieth century.

Potts's life history demonstrates that settler colonialism is chaotic, unpredictable, and ongoing. In one generation, it leaped forward in leagues and bounds, claiming California Native land and lives through bloodshed and federal failure to protect even the merest rights of occupancy. Two generations later, along came Marie Mason Potts. Using the tools of detribalization in spaces of colonial ambivalence to wage a war of California Indian land claims activism and cultural revival, she pushed settler colonialism back a stride or two. A seemingly compliant boarding school pupil on first glance, in fact, she was taking control over her own destiny, exploring the wider world, and advancing a youthful agenda that never entailed transposing herself into a settler body or consciousness. Known throughout her lifetime by many names and personal attributes—Chenkutpem, "an excellent girl," Carlisle graduate, newspaper editor and publisher, "a grand, wise lady," "a happy warrior"—to the very end, she was most proud of being Hukespem's granddaughter, a Big Meadow Maidu. She succeeded in carrying his reputation and legacy forward as a strong, intelligent, and generous leader of her people. She was a modern "wise one."

Notes

Abbreviations

CCHS	Cumberland County Historical Society
CSA	California State Archives
CSH	Center for Sacramento History
CSUS	California State University–Sacramento
DMP	D'Arcy McNickle Papers, Ayer Modern Manuscripts, Newberry Library
EWG	Edward W. Gifford Papers, Bancroft Library, University of California–Berkeley
FARP	Francis A. Riddell Papers, California State Archives
HLPP	Helen L. Peterson Papers, National Museum of the American Indian
MP	Marie Potts
MPP	Marie Potts Papers, Donald and Beverly Gerth Special Collections and University Archives, California State University–Sacramento
NAA	National Anthropological Archives
NARA-DC	National Archives and Records Administration
NARA-PR	National Archives and Records Administration, Pacific Region
NMAI	National Museum of the American Indian
PAHMA	Phoebe A. Hearst Museum of Anthropology
SCRC	Special Collections Research Center, University of Chicago
SC-UNR	Special Collections, University of Nevada–Reno
SCUA, CSUS	Donald and Beverly Gerth Special Collections and University Archives, California State University–Sacramento

SCUA, UCR   Special Collections and University Archives, University of
             California–Riverside
UCB   University of California–Berkeley
UCDSC   University of California–Davis Special Collections

Introduction

1. Delilah Friedler, "Activist LaNada War Jack of the Bannock Nation Details Her Time
   Occupying Alcatraz," *Teen Vogue*, March 21, 2019, https://www.teenvogue.com/story
   /activist-lanada-war-jack-details-occupying-alcatraz (accessed December 13, 2019).
   Blansett, *A Journey to Freedom*, and War Jack, *Native Resistance*, shine new light on
   California Indian voices and women's critical contributions.
2. Rupert Costo was among these frustrated California Native leaders. See Soza War
   Soldier, "Positive and Effective Action." Following the prison's decommissioning and
   classification as surplus federal property, a group of Lakota occupied and filed claim
   to it. Smith and Warrior, *Like a Hurricane*, 10–11.
3. Vine Deloria Jr. skewered and feasted upon anthropologists for their fetishizations of
   Native American people and culture at more than one event Potts attended.
4. Self-archiving her land claims and newspaper work stands out among the many other
   settler practices she adopted to Native advantage.
5. Terri Castaneda, "American Indian Lives and Voices: The Promise and Problematics
   of Life Narratives," *Reviews in Anthropology* 39 (2009): 132–65; Alisse Waterston,
   "Intimate Ethnography and the Anthropological Imagination," *American Ethnologist*
   46 (2019): 7–19; Zeitlyn, "Life-History Writing."
6. Walter L. Hixson, *American Settler-Colonialism: A History* (New York: Palgrave
   MacMillan 2013); Stoler, *Along the Archival Grain*; Veracini, *Settler Colonialism*; Wolfe,
   "Settler Colonialism."
7. Per Hixson, *American Settler-Colonialism*, 4. He also defines Argentina, Australia,
   Brazil, Canada, Israel, New Zealand, and South Africa as settler states.
8. Veracini, *Settler Colonialism*, offers an A–Z guide to population transfer strategies.
9. Further, settler colonialism keeps settlers, capitalism, and colonial power squarely in
   the equation, front and center. I write as a descendant of dispossessors—as a settler. This
   term defines my positionality. As the acknowledgments note, my ancestors settled in
   present-day Mississippi and Louisiana, and I write from Nisenan territory, in Carmichael,
   California. My university sits on a Nisenan village site called Yalěs, near Plains Miwok
   and Patwin territory. These are ancestral territories to which enslaved peoples were
   taken and to which refugees from still other Indigenous communities escaped.
10. Settler colonialism is a highly productive analytic concept. Witness the growth of
    academic programs and departments of Indigenous and/or Native American studies.
    Sites of prolific scholarly production, they are equally laboratories of refusal, resistance,
    and decolonial praxis.

11. Mountain Maidu people are defining, mapping, and reclaiming homelands under the aegis of the Maidu Summit Consortium: https://www.maidusummit.org (accessed March 25, 2019); Middleton, "Seeking Spatial Representation."
12. This phrasing is borrowed from Zeitlyn, "Life-History Writing."
13. Stoler, *Along the Archival Grain.*

Prologue

Epigraph: Marie Potts, "A Lesson from the Indians," *Oakland Tribune-Parade*, January 8, 1961. This feature story and quotation are from Potts's fall 1960 appearance at the Lowie Museum at University of California–Berkeley.

1. *Thompson v. Doaksum et al.*, California Supreme Court, Case No. 9546, April 23, 1884, 10–12 (CSA). Seagraves misread VanNorman's first initials as D. W. An overland emigrant from New York, he was named Nathaniel Daniel, though he went by the initials D. N.
2. Blunt (b. 1816, Norridgewock, Maine) ran a stage line connecting Augusta and Skowhegan, Maine, with Boston from 1845 to 1865. With his wife, Lucinda, and four children, he came west in 1869. By fall 1876, his eldest daughter, Mary, was a Big Meadow schoolmistress. Lucinda died in Big Meadows in 1877; Blunt died in Quincy on May 29, 1885.
3. Scottish-born (b. 1833) Thompson (also spelled Thomson) immigrated to New York in his youth, apprenticing in cabinet making. Arriving in California in 1852, he then moved to Wisconsin in 1862, married, and began a family. In 1869 they moved to Plumas County—first Quincy, then Big Meadow, and then, by 1888, Greenville, where Thompson died in 1913. Census records for 1880 show that Kloppenberg (Thompson's future son-in-law) was a servant and miner residing in the household of Thompson (mine owner).
4. Kelsey complained that "frontiersmen" intentionally filed on homesteads wherever Indians had successful gardens. C. E. Kelsey, *Report on the Condition of California Indians, March 21, 1906* (Carlisle, Pa.: Indian School Print, 1906), 9.
5. Per their client's assertion, attorneys for the Nahkomahs, or Big Meadow Maidu, contended that they were not represented at treaty negotiations at Bidwell's ranch on August 1, 1851. For signatories, see Charles C. Royce, *Indian Land Cessions in the United States, 18th Annual Report of the Bureau of American Ethnology* (Washington, D.C.: Printing Office, 1900), 784. For now, rumors of possible Big Meadow Maidu participation in the Reading (or Redding) treaty remain just that.
6. *Plumas National*, February 27, 1886.
7. "Justice as She Is Delivered," *WASP*, March 1886, 3.
8. Francis A. Riddell, "Maidu and Konkow," in *Handbook of North American Indians*, Vol. 8, *California*, ed. Robert F. Heizer (Washington, D.C.: Smithsonian Institution, 1978), 387–97.
9. Nevins, *World-Making Stories.*

10. Regarding Big Meadow Maidu intermarriage, see R. B. Dixon, "Notes on Achomawi and Atsugewi Indians of Northern California," *American Anthropologist* 10, no. 2 (1908): 208–20.

11. It was reported that Big Meadow Maidu killed two brothers of Pit River chief Shave Head during a June big time attended by some four hundred Indians. *Daily Alta California*, July 8, 1860.

12. Potts reported that Hukespem established summer camp in nearby Mountain Meadow, or Saipku. William S. Evans Jr., "Ethnographic Notes on the Honey Lake Maidu," *Nevada State Museum Occasional Papers* 3 (1978): 6; James H. McMillin, "Aboriginal Human Ecology of the Mountain Maidu Area in Southwestern Lassen County" (master's thesis, California State University–Sacramento, 1963), 64. An 1870 visitor marveled at robust stands of sugar pine, pitch pine, cedar, and tamarack. *Feather River Bulletin*, July 4, 1874.

13. Marie Potts, "A Friend to All," unpublished manuscript, n.d., MPP, Box C, SCUA, CSUS.

14. According to Potts, Hukespem's twin was known by a Maidu term (possibly a nickname), roughly translated as "going fast in a canoe." MPP, Box A, SCUA, CSUS.

15. The settler also commented on how pleased he was to see men (perhaps some Native) grading a new road along this route under the direction of Gen. Allen Wood. *Plumas National*, August 18, 1866. The *Daily Alta California*, April 3, 1866, reports a mid-March battle in Tehama County. Big Meadow Maidu killed five Mill Creek women and three men and took one woman prisoner. Reprisals continued. *Plumas National*, November 10, 1866.

16. *Plumas National*, October 29, 1866. Dixon documents this pattern of blood revenge and fasting (no meat or acorn). Hukespem was still alive during his fieldwork, and battles with the Mill Creeks were only a generation removed. Dixon, "Huntington California Expedition," 227. The twigs were wormwood, a powerful medicine for warding off malevolent forces and beings.

17. Potts, *Northern Maidu*, 39–41. Other accounts include Richard Burrill, *Stolen by the Mill Creek Indians* (Chester, Calif.: Anthro Company, 2003); Coyote Man, *The Destruction of the People* (Berkeley: Brother William Press, 1973), 68–70; Ogle, *Whisper of the Maidu*, 16–17.

18. Dixon, "Huntington California Expedition," 227. It is entirely possible that Dixon was told the story of Phoebe's death and Hukespem's retaliation.

19. Maidu observed both the sororate (taking a deceased wife's sister in marriage) and the levirate (marrying a deceased brother's widow). Presumably Phoebe was Mariah's older sister.

20. Early census data trends toward exaggerating Indian people's ages. Mariah's census data shows her at age forty-five in 1880, age seventy-eight in 1900, and age seventy-five in 1910. A conservative birth estimate is 1855, based on loose historical coordinates tied to capture and children's (estimated) ages at enumeration. Bill is enumerated in 1880 with an 1835 birth year but in 1900 is assigned an 1809 birth date, suggesting he was a centenarian at death in 1909, as some suggest, though a descendant-informed

genealogy suggests an 1845 birth. Phoebe is not enumerated in known records. On occasion, Bill family enumerations record incorrect generational relations for children and grandchildren. Neither Mariah nor Hukespem was enumerated in 1860 or 1870 federal censuses. Some Plumas townships enumerated Native people; Seneca did not.

21. Big Meadow homesteaders developed an astonishingly productive dairy ranching economy. By 1882 it churned out seven hundred pounds of butter daily. *Record-Union*, September 5, 1882, 4.

22. Seneca Township boundaries were modified twice to minor effect. Fariss and Smith, *Illustrated History of Plumas, Lassen and Sierra Counties* (San Francisco: Howell-North, 1882).

23. See *Plumas National*, July 4, 1874, for commentary originally penned for the *San Francisco Post* on the dubious legality of this rampant practice.

24. Jaime Moore, in "Mountain Maidu Acculturation" (master's thesis, California State University–Sacramento, 2002), proposes a two-stage model.

25. Joel R. Hyer, *We Are Not Savages: Native Americans in Southern California and the Pala Reservation, 1840–1920* (East Lansing: Michigan State University Press, 2001).

26. Public Domain Acts of March 3, 1851, and March 3, 1853, opened Mountain Maidu and other Indigenous territory in the new state of California to settler preemption by homesteaders like Blunt. The Public Lands Commission, established pursuant to the 1851 act, provided a two-year period for holders of private titles granted under Spanish or Mexican sovereignty to submit them for evaluation. New states were often rewarded a percentage of federal surplus land sales, further discouraging state protection of Native occupancy rights. The 1862 Homestead Act changed the instrument of dispossession but not the effect. The 1891 Land Revision Act (or General Revision Act) brought an end to the 1841 Preemption Act. But this wreaked additional havoc on Mountain Maidu, as it called for cancelation of allotments situated on forested, ancestral land.

27. Lindsay, *Murder State*; Madley, *American Genocide*.

28. See Hixson, *American Settler-Colonialism*, 125.

29. Robert F. Heizer, *"They Were Only Diggers": A Collection of Articles from California Newspapers, 1851–1866, on Indian and White Relations* (Socorro, N. Mex.: Ballena Press, 1971); Linsday, *Murder State*; Madley, *American Genocide*.

30. Heizer speculates that "hundreds" were left out. See Robert F. Heizer, "Treaties," in *Handbook of California Indians*, Vol. 8, *California*, ed. R. F. Heizer (Washington, D.C.: Smithsonian Institution, 1978), 701–4.

31. George H. Phillips, *"Bringing Them under Subjection": California's Tejon Indian Reservation and Beyond, 1852–1864* (Norman: University of Oklahoma Press, 2004).

32. Bauer, *California through Native Eyes*.

33. Kimberly Johnston-Dodds and Chris Kuzak, "The History of the Northern California Indian Association, the 'Lost' California Indian Treaties, and Federal Indian Policy, 1891–1906," paper presented at the California Indian Conference, Davis, October 26–27, 2007. The OIA soon discovered they possessed copies all along.

34. Khal Schneider, "Making Indian Land in the Allotment Era: Northern California's Indian Rancherias," *Western Historical Quarterly* 41, no. 4 (2010): 429–50.

35. Material acquisitions, such as "silver watches," supposedly made them "high livers." *Greenville Bulletin*, November 18, 1885.

36. "Amelia's Body," a historical analysis set in Shasta County, reminds us that Native women were not alone in suffering gold rush–era violence. Hurtado, *Intimate Frontiers*, 115–28.

37. Adams and DeLuzio, *On the Borders of Love and Power*; Hurtado, *Intimate Frontiers*; Theda Perdue, *"Mixed Blood" Indians* (Athens: University of Georgia Press, 2003); Sousa, "An Influential Squaw."

38. Katherine Ellinghaus, *Blood Will Tell: Native Americans and Assimilation Policy* (Lincoln: University of Nebraska Press, 2017); Garroutte, *Real Indians*; Stoler, *Along the Archival Grain*; Veracini, *Settler Colonialism*.

39. *Plumas National*, December 22, 1877. It is telling that Chinese–Mountain Maidu intermarriage did not register in the "half breed" discourse of late-nineteenth-century Plumas County; it was intermarriage with whites that constituted a scandalous breach of racial divides. Formal documentation of Mountain Maidu–Chinese unions among a first generation remains elusive, but later examples include Gee Que and Big Meadow Maidu Celia Jenkins, whose son Aike was born at Nevis in 1911 (*Feather River Bulletin*, February 1, 1940), and Gee Ben and Edith Goon. (See the 1900 census for Seneca Township residents Gee B. and "Ada" [b. 1877] Goon.) I want to thank William Bauer for encouraging me to search these out.

40. Surnames were sometimes based on current or former employers. Albert H. Kneale, *Indian Agent* (Caldwell, Idaho: Caxton Printers, 1950), 41. Josie did not work for a Mason family; John and Lizzette were given this name at school (and there was no biological connection to the older "Indian John Hamilton").

41. Josie was born around 1873. The 1900 census estimates the year as 1870. She is listed as age forty on the 1916 U.S. Indian census. Her 1926 death certificate states that she was sixty.

42. Becraft began managing the ranch in May 1894, moving his family there in 1895. *Plumas National*, May 23, 1895. Hamilton remarried in 1898 and returned to Plumas County.

43. *Sacramento Bee*, April 22, 1973.

44. Guy S. Métraux, "Social and Cultural Aspects of Swiss Immigration into the United States in the Nineteenth Century" (PhD diss., Yale University, New Haven, Conn., 1949); Maurice E. Perret, *Les Colonies Tessinoises en Californie* (Lausanne, Switzerland: F. Rouge, 1950); H. F. Raup, "The Italian-Swiss Dairymen of San Luis Obispo County, Calif.," *Yearbook of the Association of the Pacific Coast Geographers* 1 (1935): 3–8; Jacqueline Hall and JoEllen Hall, *The Italian-Swiss Settlement in Plumas County, 1860–1920* (Chico: Association for Northern California Records and Research, 1973).

45. Caribou was a mining camp just downriver from Seneca. "Raging Waters," *Greenville Bulletin*, May 14, 1890.

46. Seneca was so named because it "was the Indian name for beautiful scenery." *Plumas Memories*, June 1967, 27.

47. Perini's status probably reflected indenture for immigration.

48. Veracini, *Settler Colonialism*, 26–27.

Chapter 1

Epigraph: Marie Mason, *Indian's Friend*, February 1901, 12.

1. Big Meadow boasted five hundred apple trees by 1892. Like her maiden surname, her birth date was arbitrarily selected: "I was born in apple-picking time, later a Bureau of Indian Affairs fellow came around and asked me to pick a date, I chose September 30, as it was close to apple-picking time." *Intertribal Council of California, Inc.* 1, no. 1 (November 1969). On assigning English names, see Kneale, *Indian Agent*.

2. Between 1883 and 1916, Quaker A. K. Smiley's upstate New York resort annually drew the commissioner of Indian affairs, legislators, social reformers, and Christian missionaries together for the Lake Mohonk Conference of Friends of the Indian. Paul Prucha, *The Churches and the Indian Schools, 1888–1912* (Lincoln: University of Nebraska Press, 1979).

3. Wolfe argues that settler colonialism is inherently incomplete. Defined as a structure versus an event, the process of replacing the Indigenous population with one of settlers is dialectical and adaptive, constantly recalibrating in relation to Indigenous resistance, shifting sociopolitical and economic ideologies, and new material circumstances. Like settler colonialism, the concepts of ethnocide and forced assimilation are after-the-fact labels and heuristic devices. In his A–Z explication of settler colonial transfer strategies, Veracini lists assimilation under the letter *F* (*Settler Colonialism*, 37–39).

4. Lindsay, *Murder State*; Madley, *American Genocide*.

5. The hypocrisy of this movement is at the core of Jacob's comparative analysis of American and Australian settler colonialism. Jacobs, *White Mother to a Dark Race*.

6. Middleton Manning, *Upstream*.

7. *Smoke Signal* 29, no. 6 (December 1970). Many Bill children and grandchildren were allotted. Some, such as Charley Gould, sought land in proximity to homes and work. Two Bill daughters chose land near their marital residences, but Hukespem, Mariah, two daughters, and each of their children were allotted on Big Meadow's east side.

8. Government records show Mariah's name as Maria, Mary, Marie, and so on. I follow the spelling in Potts's book, which helps differentiate Marie from her grandmother, as spelling varied for both women's names. The name Mariah likely reflects a distinct pronunciation.

9. The chapel remained WNIA property until 1907.

10. Earlier efforts and motivations to extend schooling to Indian people are eclipsed by Martin and Hall narratives. Maidu were quick to acculturate in areas of their own choosing. This inspired donations of two hundred dollars in 1873 for a Greenville-area Indian school and three hundred dollars in a separate effort on the "north side of

Indian Valley." *Plumas National,* June 7, 1873, 2. Again in 1879, the need for "an Indian School" is raised. *Plumas National,* June 21, 1879, 3. Only three Indians compared to 831 whites attended the county public schools in 1884. *Plumas National,* December 13, 1884.

11. *Indian's Friend,* February, March, and May 1891.

12. Cahill, *Federal Fathers and Mothers*; Mathes, *Divinely* Guided; Helen M. Wanken, "'Woman's Sphere' and Indian Reform: The Women's National Indian Association, 1879–1901" (PhD diss., Marquette University, Milwaukee, 1981).

13. *Indian's Friend,* January 1898, 10. Clouded title plagued the transfer for months as several individuals donated portions of their homesteads to WNIA and quitclaims were required of patent heirs. See Mathes, *Divinely Guided,* and Juliann Elizabeth Giles-Rankin, "An Ethnohistorical Reconstruction of the Greenville Indian Industrial School" (master's thesis, California State University, Chico, 1983).

14. Hall's departure and Ament's hiring were announced in the *Indian's Friend* in December 1891. Ament's father, Hiram, emigrated from Kentucky during the gold rush and settled on the Mad River in Humboldt County, where Edward was born in 1859. After "Indian troubles" drove him out, the family moved to Chico and then San Jose, where they maintained a homestead even after Hiram bought Hall Ranch, where the twenty-by-forty-foot schoolhouse stood.

15. *Plumas National,* August 9, 1894.

16. *Plumas National,* November 2, 1893.

17. A mere three decades later, as World War I raged and food shortages arose, physician and naturalist C. Hart Merriam touted two California acorn species for "their high fuel value." C. Hart Merriam, "The Acorn, a Possibly Neglected Source of Food," *National Geographic* 34, no. 2 (1918): 129–37.

18. *Plumas National,* November 2, 1893. A letter from Floy reveals that Lights Canyon families were earlier hostile to MIS, "told we are unfriendly," though a father came that month to ask for his three children to be enrolled. *Indian's Friend,* December 1897, 8.

19. *Indian's Friend,* May 1892. During this time, British-born S. W. (Samuel William) Albone was a circuit preacher assigned to Indian Valley by the Methodist Episcopal Church (*Plumas County Bulletin,* September 10, 1891). By 1899 he was living in Bodie, California (*Feather River Bulletin,* August 31, 1899).

20. Missionaries knew that literacy was vital to their subjects' conversion and scriptural study, leading the charge to translate oral tongues into written forms the colonial world over. Jacobs suggests that nearby Mechoopda Indians continued ceremony out of missionary sight. Margaret D. Jacobs, "Resistance to Rescue: The Indians of Bahapki and Mrs. Annie E. K. Bidwell," in *Writing the Range: Race, Class and Culture in the Women's West,"* ed. E. Jamison and S. Armitage (Norman: University of Oklahoma Press, 1997), 230–51.

21. Boarding potential was based on Ament's survey of nearby valleys. Big Meadow had seventeen families and sixty children. *Indian's Friend,* February 1892.

22. *Indian's Friend,* July 1892, 1.

23. *Plumas National*, June 2, 1892. Bidwell suggested a boarding school at either Big Meadow or Indian Valley not long after construction of a federal school in Perris Valley (Sherman's forerunner) was announced. *Plumas National*, September 10, 1891. The April 7, 1892, *Plumas National* reported that some Big Meadow parents moved down in early spring 1892 to take advantage of the school. It is unclear which set of parents this article references: the parents mentioned in the July 1892 *Indian's Friend* who did find work or those returning home without success.

24. *Plumas National*, July 14, 1892.

25. Regarding Quinton's "cold potato" reference, see *Indian's Friend*, May 1892, 36; September 1894, 9.

26. Assistant commissioner of Indian affairs to Edward Ament, February 12, 1900, NARA-PR, RG 75, Box 67. Six years earlier, Ament had confessed, "It was only by a continual round, from camp to camp, that I managed to keep a good average." U.S. Office of Indian Affairs, *Annual Report of the Commissioner of Indian Affairs for the Year 1984* (Washington, D.C.: Government Printing Office, 1894), 371. Greenville superintendents were constantly pressured to increase enrollment until around 1911, when they were expected to force Native students into public schools, where white society was unaccepting of them. Many Native parents therefore declined to send them.

27. Greenville Quarterly Attendance Records, March 1896–1898, NARA-PR, RG 75, GIS. *Plumas National*, February 11, 1897. In adulthood, John spelled his last name "Peazzoni."

28. Edward Ament, "Teaching California Indians," *Pacific Educational Journal* 11, no. 2 (1895): 59–61.

29. He previously stated, "I sometimes fear that this work will turn me yet into a professional beggar. *Indian's Friend*, February 1894, 6.

30. Ament, "Teaching California Indians," 1895.

31. Ament, "Teaching California Indians," 1895.

32. Alice Piazzoni is visible in the center of the same row. Marie's friend Ellen Reeves is several rows back.

33. Laura Graham, "How Should an Indian Speak? Amazonian Indians and the Symbolic Politics of Language in the Global Public Sphere," in *Indigenous Movements, Self-Representation, and the State in Latin America*, ed. K. Warren and J. Jackson (Austin: University of Texas Press, 2002), 181–228.

34. Mathes, *Divinely Guided*, 109. Students assumed a measure of agency in the process of English immersion, both encouraging one another to speak English and defending those who did not. When Ament reminded Johnnie Jim not to "talk Indian," another pupil remarked, "Maybe he's learning." *Indian's Friend*, December 1894, 9.

35. Until 1910, Greenville was lighted by dangerous coal oil.

36. Ament had earlier given this surname to Marie's half siblings. The Big Meadow community knew that Hamilton had fathered John and Lizzette, but Ament preserved Hamilton's "good name."

37. On pride in kindergarten, see *Feather River Bulletin*, May 17, 1900.

38. A string of replacements came between November 1900 and Marie's September 1912 departure. Classified personnel in the federal boarding school system were regularly shifted between schools, carrying with them academe's latest racial theories and taxonomies, and mandates to enact federal assimilation policy, such as cutting long hair, weeding the school of "decidedly white" Indians, and forbidding tribal dancing and languages. Acting commissioner of Indian affairs to Greenville superintendent, March 11, 1902, NARA-PR, RG 75, Box 68. Millard Holland was interim superintendent until Charles Shell arrived (from November 14, 1900, to January 2, 1901).

39. *Indian's Friend*, February 1901, 12. Even after Greenville's transition to a government school, WNIA affiliates funded Christmas treats for pupils. Employees made up gaps in funding.

40. *Indian's Friend*, July 1900, 5.

41. Bidwell moved to Chico when he became Great Western Power Company supervisor in the mid-1910s.

42. *San Francisco Chronicle*, February 23, 1902.

43. "We Remember," *Indian Valley Record*, November 4, 1937. Jamaica Plain sent magazines in donation barrels, a likely source for the clipped images Bidwell observed in their miniature camps.

44. *Smoke Signal* 29, no. 6 (December 1970).

45. *Indian's Friend*, November 1895, 6. Other ceremony was also retained right under the Aments' noses. They believed these were "games."

46. "We Remember," *Indian Valley Record*.

47. "We Remember," *Indian Valley Record*. Bumgarner's remembrance of Marie as a Piazzoni testifies to these cousins' nearness.

48. *Indian's Friend*, October 1901, 4.

49. Estelle Reel, *Course of Study for Indian Schools* (Washington, D.C.: Government Printing Office, 1901), 54.

50. *Indian's Friend*, June 1895, 1.

51. *Indian's Friend*, June 1895, 6–7. This was Roxy Jakes's mother.

52. L. G. Moses, *Wild West Shows and the Images of American Indians, 1883–1933* (Albuquerque: University of New Mexico Press, 1999), 65.

53. Reel regularly solicited domestic arts products—sewing, embroidery, and fancywork—to bolster public perception of federal boarding schools. In 1901 she asked Superintendent Shell to send Greenville fancywork for a Department of Indian Education exhibit. He mailed doilies, a dresser scarf, and mended hose as examples of girls' work. Estelle Reel to Charles Shell, December 7, 1901, NARA-PR, RG 75, Box 68.

54. Frank Mann to CIA, typescript annual report, 1911, Section IV–Industries, NARA-PR, RG 75, Box 70; quarterly attendance report, December 31, 1911, NARA-PR, RG 75, Box 119. See also Superintendent McChesney to CIA, "Re: Promotion of Native Industries," August 4, 1914, NARA-PR, RG 75, Box 71.

55. Cahill, *Federal Fathers and Mothers*, 82–103.

56. *Indian's Friend*, December 1896.

57. This work had commodity value for older girls; one sold lace to fund a San Jose vacation. *Indian's Friend*, July 1896, 3.

58. *Indian's Friend*, December 1895, 3.

59. The Bert Trubody Collection, Plumas County Museum and Historical Society, includes an image (circa 1905) of girls with hoops. The masculine counterpart was a marching band organized in 1905 by Frances Mansfield, a cornet player and assistant industrial teacher. The band ended in 1907 with his transfer. A White River Indian from Fort Apache, Mansfield attended Chilocco and later Haskell, where he completed a course in shoe and harness making in 1901. He died of typhoid fever in 1917 while employed at Sherman. *Indian Leader* 21, no. 6.

60. Katrina A. Paxton, "Learning Gender: Female Students at the Sherman Institute, 1907–1925," in Trafzer, Keller, and Sisquoc, *Boarding School Blues*; Robert A. Trennert, "From Carlisle to Phoenix: The Rise and Fall of the Indian Outing System, 1878–1930," *Pacific Historical Review* 52, no. 3 (August 1983).

61. Cahill leads this call, but see also Bauer, "Family Matters"; Gram, *Education at the Edge of Empire*; and Trafzer, Keller, and Sisquoc, *Boarding School Blues*.

62. In 1911 Greenville gained agency status and began drawing students from farther afield.

63. *Indian's Friend*, May 1895, 9. The Rogers sisters were the only set of three Big Meadow siblings enrolled.

64. *Indian's Friend*, May 1899, 10.

65. Potts reported this while working on her book *The Northern Maidu*.

66. *Plumas National*, September 22, 1898. Floy suffered a stillbirth two years prior, and Ament's health was poor. They retreated to San Jose and Berkeley but returned to their Greenville ranch in June 1903, building a new house. Many residents, including MIS alumni, welcomed them back. *Plumas National*, June 15, 1903.

67. Students whose transportation was government-funded were returned home in two to three years at school expense. The Aments typically vacationed in San Jose in July and August. Orphaned pupils posed potential problems for staff leaves. News stories reveal that superintendents and their wives sometimes took such "scholars" with them (separately, by gender) if no one could supervise them on-site. See, for example, "On a Vacation," *Plumas National*, June 30, 1904, 8.

68. Pupils distinguished "Indian" from "white talk." *Indian's Friend*, May 1899, 10.

69. Janet Carsten, "'Knowing Where You've Come From': Ruptures and Continuities of Time and Kinship in Narratives of Adoption Reunion," *Journal of the Royal Anthropological Institute* 6 (2000): 687–703.

70. *Indian's Friend*, January 1907. Clara Bidwell conveyed this news to Quinton.

71. In Greenville's twilight years, mothers were often propelled to exert their authority over school administrators. Dobkins, "Strong Language, Strong Actions."

72. *Plumas National*, June 14, 1906. Greenville records indicate that Josie was sick, but Marie later suggested that her stepfather was dying. MP, oral interview by Francis Riddell and James Bennyhoff, state archaeologists, May 17, 1972, Francis A. Riddell Papers, CSA. This is corroborated by a letter published in the *Indian's Friend* in March

1907. Genealogical notes made by Potts indicate that Josie was married to Abe Lowry (also spelled Lowery) and was stepmother to Mollie and Freda. Abe Lowry (older brother to Bob Schaeffer) was a baby when his Mountain Maidu mother died. He was raised by Jack Lowry and his wife, Julia. MPP, Box C, SCUA, CSUS.

73. William "Billy" Lowry and Mason were kin via Josie's marriage to Abe. My thanks to Lorena Gorbet for helping me verify this connection.

74. "Bad marksmanship is responsible for the fact that the notorious Billy Lowery did not go to the happy hunting grounds last Saturday. He was shot and wounded by another bad Indian." *Plumas National*, August 19, 1907, 1.

75. On alcohol and land dispossession, see "Give Preacher Sound Trouncing," *Plumas Independent*, November 3, 1909.

76. *Plumas National*, August 29, 1907; September 5, 1907; and September 16, 1907. The earlier altercation involved Lowry and George Peconum. *Plumas National*, March 26, 1903. More gun violence befell the family in 1908. A young Greenville pupil playing with a gun in the boys' dormitory shot Billy and Lena Peconum Lowry's five-year-old son. He died days later. *Plumas National*, March 9, 1908.

77. This appellation had yet to be turned on its head as a poetic badge of Indigenous honor. Miranda, *Bad Indians*.

78. In 1903 the commissioner said that two eighteen-year-old seventh-graders were too old for Greenville, instructing Superintendent Shell to either transfer them to another non-reservation school or to "relieve" the school of their presence. In this same letter, Shell was soundly reprimanded for taking several older boys (John Peazzoni, among them) to Chemawa instead of Stewart in Carson City, Nevada. Acting commissioner of Indian affairs to superintendent, March 24, 1903, NARA-PR, RG 75, Box 68.

79. Two years later, during a transition in superintendents, the acting commissioner of Indian affairs urged Greenville to establish a "grade and promotion" system similar to that used in public schools. Acting commissioner of Indian affairs to Harwood Hall, Supervisor-in-Charge, Greenville Indian School, November 2, 1909, NARA-PR, RG 75, Box. 69.

80. See Adams, *Education for Extinction*; Coleman, *American Indian Children at School*; Pearl Lee Walker-McNeil "The Carlisle Indian School: A Study of Acculturation" (PhD diss., American University, Washington, D.C., 1979).

81. After Chemawa, he worked as a lumberman in Washington State, married, and raised a family. He enlisted in the air force in September 1917, serving sixteen months. Chemawa supplied many lumber industry laborers. Kate McKinney's son Joaquin (Joseph) also moved from Chemawa to Spokane, not returning to Plumas County for forty years. *Smoke Signal* 9, no. 6 (June 1950).

82. Quarterly reports record consecutive days in attendance, including summer boarding.

83. *Plumas Independent*, November 25, 1908. Editorials urging pity for older Indians inevitably entreated readers to remember their peaceable nature during early statehood days (e.g., "Aid Needed," *Plumas Independent*, December 3, 1896; "Our Senators and Representatives," *Plumas National*, March 6, 1902). A "Plumas Yesterdays" column

enumerated the individuals to whom the county gave aid beginning in November 1908: "Wilson's wife, Old Williams and two sisters, Old Lady Alick, Big Meadows Bill and wife, Coyote Jim and Wife, Sadie Blueskin." *Feather River Bulletin*, November 16, 1933.

84. Mariah was enumerated on May 10, 1910, and estimated to be seventy-five, several years younger than her 1900 census–reported age.

85. Enumerated as "Tillie," this is Alta Roy Thomas. A half brother, Charles, was born in 1914.

86. The two were first cousins once removed. Rob Roy, Johnny Robert Roy's father, was Hukespem's older sister's son.

87. In his annual report to the commissioner of Indian affairs, Superintendent Campbell reported very limited success in extinguishing prejudice among white parents. NARA-PR, RG 75, Greenville Agency Annual Report, 1912, Box 70.

88. Superintendent Mann to commissioner of Indian affairs, NARA-PR, RG 75, Greenville Agency Annual Report, 1911, Box 70.

89. Lomawaima, *They Called It Prairie Light*.

90. Louise (Eddlebuttel) Maurizzio to MP, September 1950, MPP, Box A, SCUA, CSUS.

91. Marie and Ada must have been especially drawn to the massive dam project at Big Meadow. *Plumas Star*, July 1, 1912.

92. One of the 512 "living graduates" Carlisle boasted of in its 1912 catalog, she was among 85 who had secured employment in the U.S. Indian School Service and one of 20 classified as "disciplinarians" or "matrons," gendered nomenclature reflecting the role that these nonteaching personnel fulfilled as parental surrogates or guardians for boarding school pupils. Cahill, *Federal Fathers and Mothers*.

93. Twoguns student file, NARA-DC, RG 75, Series 1329, Box 2.

94. Twoguns student file. On loyalty, affect, and nostalgia in boarding school contexts, see Child, *Boarding School Seasons*; Harkin, "Emotional Archive"; Ronald Niezen, *Truth and Indignation: Canada's Truth and Reconciliation Commission on Indian Residential Schools* (Toronto: University of Toronto Press, 2015).

95. Twoguns's education began at Thomas Boarding School on the Cattaraugus Reservation, near her Gowanda, New York, home. She entered Carlisle in October 1902, just shy of her fourteenth birthday. Carlisle student contracts timed out after five years. Discharged on June 3, 1907, she was readmitted in September and then discharged again in April 1911 to take up her Greenville duties. Twoguns student file, NARA-DC, RG 75, Series 1329, Box 2. On Thomas Indian School, see Keith R. Burich, "'No Place to Go': The Thomas Indian School and the 'Forgotten' Indian Children of New York," *Wicazo Ša Review* 22, no. 2 (2007): 93–110. Settler colonial practices alienated children from families in myriad ways. See Jacobs, *White Mother to a Dark Race*; Lewandowski, *Red Bird, Red Power*; Parker, *Singing an Indian Song*; Willard, "A Study of Colonial Surrogates."

96. Adams, *Education for Extinction*; Bahr, *Viola Martinez, California Paiute*; Coleman, *American Indian Children at School*; Jacobs, *White Mother to a Dark Race*.

97. "Beaten by the Indians," *Feather River Bulletin,* November 19, 1903, credits the former Carlisle players on a local (Loyalton, California) Native team with their win: "Wilson says the white boys were no match for the Indians, the latter beating them badly."

98. Hoxie corresponded with Twoguns at Greenville. After graduating, Hoxie worked as Round Valley Indian School cook. In 1911 she married a Round Valley farmer and Sherman alumnus. In March 1913 she expressed fondness for "dear Carlisle" while sending regrets to Friedman regarding Carlisle's upcoming reunion. She had resigned her position and was "home attending to general house work. I have a comfortable home. It is not of a modern model but it is neat and nice." Hoxie student file, NARA-DC, RG 75, Series 1329, Box 1. Hoxie later helped fund one of Marie's state fair exhibits. In the 1960s her stepson wrote Marie about Hoxie's failing health.

99. Selina Twoguns to Moses Friedman, July 1, 1912, NARA-DC, RG 75, Series 1329, Box 2; Curtis student file, NARA-DC, RG 75, Series 1327, Box 93, Folder 4154.

100. Emma DeHaven was a Big Meadow Maidu fathered by a Kentucky soldier and was the first cousin of Tucker's mother, Flora (and Josie, Susie, and Jennie Bill). Emma and Cap DeHaven also served as guardians for Flora and William "Billy" Dick's daughters, Grace and Catherine.

101. Moses Friedman to Selina Twoguns, August 9, 1912, NARA-DC, RG 75, Series 1329, Box 2.

102. Willard Campbell to Moses Friedman, August 14, 1912, NARA-PR, RG 75, GIS. A postscript mentions that the two women would be traveling with Twoguns, "a graduate of Carlisle," headed east the following month. Campbell was apparently oblivious to correspondence between Twoguns and Friedman. His predecessor, Frank Mann, hired Selina and received Friedman's April 1911 package of Carlisle applications. Moses Friedman to Frank Mann, April 17, 1911, NARA-PR, RG 75, GIS.

103. Campbell to Friedman, August 22, 1912, NARA-PR, RG 75, GIS. On parental signatures, see United States Indian School, *Carlisle Indian School Catalogue* (Carlisle, Pa.: Carlisle Indian Press, 1912), 12. The catalog states that non-reservation students would be provided transportation; reservation agents were expected to fund transportation for their students.

104. Campbell to Friedman, August 29, 1912, NARA-PR, RG 75, GIS.

105. Friedman to Campbell, August 22, 1912, NARA-PR, RG 75, GIS. The cost was approximately sixty to sixty-five dollars (per 1915 statistics for students returning to California homes).

Chapter 2

1. Field notes (interview with Joe Marine and Marvin Lee Marine), March 2009.

2. After delivering Marie to campus, Twoguns continued on to New York. *Arrow* 9, no. 3 (September 20, 1912): 3.

3. This ledger includes 1,204 girls who entered between 1905 and 1918. This consecutive series begins with the number 2,057 and runs to 3,262. It continues a list of female

students begun elsewhere. "Consecutive Record of Enrolled Students," NARA-DC, RG 75, Series 1325. Although the bulk of my Carlisle-related research predates it, the Carlisle Indian School Digital Resource Center (http://carlisleindian.dickinson.edu), developed by Dickinson College in Carlisle, Pennsylvania, has been an invaluable resource for fact-checking and accessing new materials, including this ledger.

4. This was atypical of boarding school students, who often had white living fathers and deceased Native mothers.

5. These statistics were invasive, but off-reservation boarding schools were under intense scrutiny, having shown themselves to be sites of malnutrition, starvation, and epidemics of smallpox, TB, and countless other pathogens—not to mention physical, emotional, and sexual abuse.

6. Commissioner of Indian Affairs Robert Valentine was to blame for this squabbling, having forwarded Lipps's *Southern Workman* article on this topic to Friedman and more or less demanding he publish it. He did so in *Red Man* 4, no. 1 (1911): 21–40, sandwiching it between his own lengthy editorializations so as to not undermine public support of Carlisle. Robert G. Valentine to Moses Friedman, NARA-DC, RG 75, Carlisle. Carlisle was not a high school equivalent; college-bound students had to complete high school elsewhere. This is noteworthy because the public generally perceived it to be a collegiate institution, perhaps because its football team competed (and won) against college teams. Carlisle athletes captured limelight wherever they went. The school's football team and famous Olympians personified Carlisle for mainstream society. Years later, the *Smoke Signal* occasionally carried Marie's memories of being at Carlisle with Jim Thorpe and Lewis Tewanima.

7. The freshman course included "Literature and History: (a) Reading of Subjects for Composition (b) Character Study of Famous Indian Leaders; Language: Penmanship, Orthography, Business Forms; Elementary Science: General Lessons." United States Indian School, *Carlisle Indian School Catalogue*, 40.

8. *Arrow* 9, no. 20 (January 17, 1913): 4; *Arrow* 9, no. 23 (February 7, 1913): 2. Curtis, who arrived on December 28, 1912, enrolled at Carlisle specifically for this training. By mid-March she was promoted to the Domestic Arts Department. *Arrow* 9, no. 29 (March 21, 1913): 3.

9. MP, oral interview by Francis Riddell and James Bennyhoff, state archaeologists, May 17, 1972, Francis A. Riddell Papers, CSA.

10. Dunbar-Ortiz, *An Indigenous Peoples' History of the United States*; Lindsay, *Murder State*; Madley, *American Genocide*; Wolfe, "Settler Colonialism."

11. R. H. Pratt, "The Advantages of Mingling Indians with Whites," *Americanizing the American Indians: Writings by the "Friends of the Indian" 1880–1900* (Cambridge, Mass.: Harvard University Press, 1973), 260–71.

12. Lomawaima and Ostler, "Reconsidering Richard Henry Pratt."

13. *Twenty-Second Annual Report of the Board of Indian Commissioners, 1890* (Washington, D.C.: Government Printing Office, 1891), 170–71.

14. Veracini (*Settler Colonialism*, 37–39) assigns assimilation the letter *F* in his A–Z explication of settler colonial population transfer strategies.

15. United States Indian School, *Carlisle Indian School Cutulogue*, 12–13. On rare occasion, students beyond this age were admitted to pursue a well-defined course of training. The catalog also notes that students were provided with clothing and board. Enrollment approximated one thousand students during the years Marie attended.

16. Lomawaima, "Domesticity in the Federal Indian Schools"; Stoler, *Carnal* Knowledge; Stoler, *Haunted by Empire*; Robert A. Trennert Jr., "Educating Indian Girls at Non-reservation Boarding Schools, 1878–1920," *Western Historical Quarterly* 13, no. 3 (1982): 271–90.

17. Christian, monogamous marriage was central to this. See Fear-Segal, *White Man's Club*.

18. Other schools copied Carlisle's outing program to less effect. They were not in robust urban settings and lacked the sophisticated patronage Pratt cultivated. See Lomawaima, *They Called It Prairie Light*; R. A. Trennert, "From Carlisle to Phoenix: The Rise and Fall of the Indian Outing System, 1878–1930," *Pacific Historical Review* 52, no. 3 (August 1983): 267–91; Whalen, *Native Students at Work*.

19. Pratt, *Battlefield and Classroom*.

20. Richard Henry Pratt, "American Indians: Chained and Unchained: Being an Account of How the Carlisle Indian School Was Born and Grew in Its First 25 Years," *Red Man* 6, no. 10 (June 1914): 404–5.

21. Bell, "Telling Stories Out of School."

22. Correspondence between Friedman and Commissioner Sells confirms that Carlisle's outing agents showed regard for the wishes and well-being of girls and sometimes had to defend themselves to the OIA in relation to would-be patrons who were unsuccessful in acquiring household help, as when a Mrs. Ziegler complained on July 23, 1913, to U.S. representative Thomas Scully of New Jersey that she had been unable to obtain the "services" of a Carlisle schoolgirl. He passed this on to the commissioner of Indian affairs, who wrote to Friedman, who in turn checked with outing agent Lida Johnson. She explained that she had conducted a site visit upon receipt of Ziegler's application and found nothing wanting in the house except that it was way out in the country, far from any other patrons, and she feared students would be lonely. Indeed, she later "called in several girls who it was thought would answer the requirements . . . each girl objected to going. They either wanted to live in a home *with* some girl friend or in the same town or with a certain family." Moses Friedman to commissioner of Indian affairs, July 24, 1913, NARA-DC, RG 75, Carlisle.

23. The economics of outing are relevant here as well. See Carmelita Ryan, "The Carlisle Indian Industrial School" (PhD diss., Georgetown University, Washington, D.C., 1962); Walker-McNeil, "Carlisle Indian School."

24. United States Indian School, *Carlisle Indian School Catalogue*, 28–29.

25. United States Indian School, *Carlisle Indian School Catalogue*, 28–29.

26. Rapp was a pharmacist.

27. MP, oral interview by Francis Riddell and James Bennyhoff, state archaeologists, May 17, 1972, Francis A. Riddell Papers, CSA.

28. Another student, Nan Saunooke, from Cherokee, North Carolina, assured Gaither that Mrs. Rapp was very protective of the girls. NARA-DC, RG 75, Series 1327, Box 140, Folder 5519.

29. *Arrow*, in order of discussion: 10, no. 5 (October 3, 1913): 2; 10, no. 8 (October 21, 1913): 4; 10, no. 13 (November 28, 1913): 2; 10, no. 19 (January 9, 1914): 2; 10, no. 27 (March 6, 1914): 2.

30. Oral interview, Clifford Curtice, October 27, 1971, Francis A. Riddell Papers, CSA.

31. *Arrow* 10, no. 31 (April 10, 1914): 2.

32. Pauline was always a guest on outing, with no work obligations.

33. Student file, NARA-DC, RG 75, Series 1327, Box 147, Folder 5697.

34. *Arrow* 9, no. 3 (September 20, 1912): 4.

35. Bauer, "Family Matters"; Gram, *Education at the Edge of Empire*; Matthew Gilbert Sakiestewa, *Education Beyond the Mesa: Hopi Students at Sherman Institute* (Lincoln: University of Nebraska Press, 2010); Trafzer, Keller, and Sisquoc, *Boarding School Blues*.

36. *Carlisle Daily Herald*, April 5, 1907, 1

37. *Indian Craftsman* 2, no. 2 (October 1909): 35.

38. *Arrow* 7, no. 1 (September 9, 1910): 1, reports her new assignment and salary of $660 per annum. The next month an announcement amended the earlier notice, reporting that she was now principal of nearby Bristol High School. *Arrow* 7, no. 2 (November 18, 1910). Beatrice married Henry Harding Ridge in 1913.

39. "Expressions from Graduates and Ex-Students Who Had Outing Privileges," *Arrow and Red Man*, June 7, 1918, 17. Fear-Segal and Rose's *Carlisle Indian Industrial School* is a recent addition to a large literature on Carlisle and its alumni.

40. "Expressions from Graduates and Ex-Students Who Had Outing Privileges," *Carlisle Arrow and Red Man*, June 7, 1918, 17. These two publications merged in Carlisle's final year.

41. *Arrow* 11, no. 4 (September 25, 1914).

42. *Arrow* 11, no. 5 (October 2, 1914).

43. *Arrow* 11, no. 6 (October 9, 1914).

44. *Arrow* 11, no. 8 (October 23, 1914); *Arrow* 11, no. 18 (January 8, 1914).

45. *Arrow* 11, no. 32 (April 16, 1915): 4.

46. *Arrow* 11, no. 5 (October 2, 1914); *Arrow* 11, no. 6 (October 9, 1914); *Arrow* 11, no. 10 (November 6, 1914).

47. *Arrow* 11, no. 19 (January 15, 1915).

48. *Arrow* 11, no. 13 (December 4, 1914).

49. Marie's graduating class read a variety of works, including *Pushing to the Front* by O. S. Marden (1894) and Shakespeare's *Julius Caesar*.

50. Roll call as verse recitation also showed up elsewhere: "The [YWCA] meeting last Saturday afternoon was conducted by Marie Mason. After the opening hymn, roll was called and each member responded with a verse from the Bible." *Arrow* 11, no. 26 (March 5, 1915): 2.

51. *Arrow* 11, no. 22 (February 5, 1914) *Arrow* 9, no. 9 (November 8, 1912) reported a like-minded Susan's debate: "*Resolved:* That a Carlisle student derives more benefit from the Outing System than from his regular school work."

52. *Arrow* 11, multiple issues. Henry left Carlisle on June 1, 1915, when her second contract was up. Watson went to work in June for a family in Massillon, Ohio, where she married, had children, and hosted Marie in 1953.

53. *Arrow* 11, no. 11 (November 13, 1914).

54. United States Indian School, *Carlisle Indian School Catalogue*, 81. "Instruction in laundering is carried on in a separate building which is equipped for work in steam laundering and for hand work. The building is large and well lighted and well ventilated, both by natural and by artificial means. The girls not only receive instruction in machine work, but a large amount of diversified training in washing, ironing, and dyeing by hand. They are carefully taught all the details of laundry work, including rinsing, bluing, starching, and the preparation of clothes for ironing. Fine ironing is also taught them."

55. *Arrow* 11, no. 30 (March 12, 1915).

56. *Arrow* 11, no. 33 (April 23, 1915).

57. Seniors anticipating graduation were announced in March. This list comprised Charles Apekaum, Kiowa; Ovilla Azure, Chippewa; Hiram Chase, Omaha; James Garvie, Sioux; Henry Hayes, Creek; Kenneth King, Sioux; Alanson Lay, Cuyuga; Edward Morrin, Chippewa; Fred Morrisette, Chippewa; Frank Paul, Sioux; Thomas Terrence, Mohawk; William Thayer, Chippewa; Michael Wilkie, Chippewa; Wilson Wyley, Cherokee; Cora Battice, Sac and Fox; Margaret Brown, Alaskan; Minnie Charles, Cayuga; Julia Frechette, Chippewa; Bessie Gilland, Sioux; Naomi Greensky, Chippewa; Josie Holmes, Chippewa; Ella Israel, Cherokee; Della John, Seneca; Mary Kewaygeshik, Ottawa; Nettie Kingsley, Winnebago; Theresa Lay, Seneca; Minnie O'Neal, Shoshone; Mary Raiche, Chippewa; Rose Snow, Seneca; and Lillian Walker, Ottawa. *Arrow* 11, no. 26 (March 5, 1915). Not listed but graduating with his class was Paul Baldeagle, Sioux, who had left campus a year earlier to complete the full curriculum at Quarryville High School (graduating in 1915) before matriculating at Yale.

58. *Arrow* 11, no. 37 (May 28, 1915). The Friday following commencement featured competitive drills, a parade, and an alumni banquet.

59. *Arrow* 11, no. 38 (June 4, 1915): 17.

60. *Arrow* 11, no. 38 (June 4, 1915): 34.

61. This trip is first mentioned in March. *Arrow* 11, no. 26 (March 5, 1915): 2.

62. *Arrow* 11, no. 38 (June 4, 1915): 23–24.

63. The month after Marie first arrived at Carlisle, the weekly covered a similar trip: "Oh, the University Museum! Everything you ever dreamed of and more there. Some of our ancestors, well arranged as to surrounding, make a very good showing. So do their weapons, used in early warfare, tell their own story very plainly." *Arrow* 9, no. 8 (October 25, 1912).

Chapter 3

Epigraph: Marie Potts, oral interview with Frank Quinn, 1955, UCDSC.

1. MP, oral interview by Francis Riddell and James Bennyhoff, state archaeologists, May 17, 1972, Francis A. Riddell Papers, CSA.
2. Marie left for Greenville on September 4, 1915. *Arrow* 12 (September 10, 1915): 2.
3. "Lassen Again in Eruption," *Harrisburg Telegraph*, May 24, 1915.
4. Jessica Teisch, "The Drowning of Big Meadows: Nature's Managers in Progressive-Era California," *Environmental History* 4, no. 1 (January 1999): 32–35.
5. *Smoke Signal* 24, no. 6 (December 1970).
6. Teisch, "Drowning of Big Meadows."
7. These were Maidu allotments and portions of the R. L. Barnes ranch. "Condemnation Suits," *Plumas National*, May 15, 1902.
8. Tim L. Purdy, *The Lake Almanor Story* (Susanville, Calif.: Lahonton Images, 2007); Marilyn Morris Quadrio, *Big Meadows and Lake Almanor* (Charleston, S.C.: Arcadia Publishing, 2014); Jim Young, *Plumas County: History of the Feather River Region* (Charleston, S.C.: Arcadia Publishing, 2003).
9. *Plumas National*, July 8, 1909. Great Western Power acquired and closed Bunnell's Resort and Prattville Hotel. Purdy, *Lake Almanor Story*.
10. Now called Canyon Dam.
11. Great Western Power, stymied by development restrictions on national forestland until 1911, when it obtained a temporary congressional permit, hoped that all local, state, and federal stakeholders would simply fall into step. *Feather River Bulletin*, October 7, 1976.
12. Prattville's cemetery fell outside the lake's original contours and was not moved until 1926. Purdy, *Lake Almanor Story*, 32.
13. Robert M. Hanft, *Red River: Paul Bunyan's Own Lumber Company and Its Railroads* (Chico, Calif.: Center for Business and Economic Research, Chico State University, 1980).
14. Charley Gould had since moved to Westwood.
15. Lillian Porterfield attended Stewart Indian School from 1899 to November 1908, before heading to Carlisle. In April 1913 she took the civil service exam. Leaving Carlisle at the term's end, she visited her father in Reno, toured her old school in Carson City, and headed over to Greenville. In mid-September, she reported her new status and change of address using the "returned students" postcard that Carlisle mailed each fall. Under "Present Occupation," twenty-three-year-old Lillian gushed, "Employed in the Service as seamstress and am getting along splendidly so far." The *Arrow* reported, "Lillian Porterfield writes from Greenville, Cal., that she is employed as seamstress in the Indian School and getting along splendidly so far." *Arrow* 9, no. 36, May 1914: 4. Another update followed in fall 1914, when she married Edgar Parrett, Greenville's farm instructor.
16. *Plumas Independent*, March 22, 1911.

17. Levi Newton Potts was enumerated here in the 1860 census.

18. Census records of 1870 enumerate her as "Ellen" and her daughter as "Mary Ellen." Hensley provided this data on his 1930 application (no. 4863) for California Indian enrollment.

19. Alice died around 1900. Henry later married Hattie Smith, who divorced him in 1920. Hensley's death certificate records his mother's maiden name as Taylor. His daughters may (or may not) have confused his mother's maiden name with that of his grandmother. In other words, *Taylor* may be a corruption of *Toley*, his paternal great-grandparents' surname.

20. MP, oral interview by Francis Riddell and James Bennyhoff, state archaeologists, May 17, 1972, Francis A. Riddell Papers, CSA.

21. MP, oral interview by Francis Riddell and James Bennyhoff, state archaeologists, May 17, 1972, Francis A. Riddell Papers, CSA.

22. *Plumas National*, January 6, 1916.

23. *Arrow*, January 21, 1916, 5.

24. Jacqueline Emory, *Recovering Native American Writings in the Boarding School Press* (Lincoln: University of Nebraska Press, 2017), 273.

25. E. K. Miller, "Making Printers of Young Indians," *American Printer* 56, no. 4 (June 1913): 471.

26. "Wedding at the Mission," *Plumas Star*, June 23, 1911.

27. *Plumas National*, December 14, 1916.

28. *Honolulu Star Bulletin*, February 2, 1916.

29. Named for Marie's mother and friend Nellie Marie Berg, one of Marie's Big Meadow schoolteachers, with whom she remained friends after Berg's divorce from Charles Stover and after Potts moved to Sacramento.

30. *Plumas National*, November 7, 1918.

31. *Sacramento Bee*, December 24, 1917. Divorce was still rare in these days, but Ellen's gumption set a precedent that his second wife followed in 1920.

32. *Plumas National*, July 26, 1909.

33. *Sacramento Bee*, January 9, 1918.

34. Oral interview, Frank Quinn, 1955, UCDSC.

35. *Feather River Bulletin*, September 8, 1921.

36. In old age, Potts seemingly misremembered this as her aunt Susie Buckley (also known as Barclay), but it must have been Flora, as Susie was enumerated in 1910. This aunt died and was buried at "the old Indian cemetery a few miles north of Nevis . . . now under water." *Smoke Signal* 24, no. 6 (December 1970).

37. Tucker (363rd Infantry) registered with Selective Service in Riverside on May 25, 1917, while attending Sherman. He was Lassen County's first World War I casualty; Susanville's American Legion post bears his name.

38. Holmes died in Shasta County. *Plumas National*, May 12, 1898.

39. Emma was a Big Meadow Maidu fathered by a rapist who lived in local infamy as "Kentucky Ellis." He had assaulted Emma's mother, Hukespem's younger sister, in

the 1850s or 1860s. He is associated with legends of soldiers singing "My Lizard Girl," apparently to lure women out of trees where they tried to hide.

40. Paul C. Rosier, *Serving Their Country: American Indian Politics and Patriotism in the Twentieth Century* (Cambridge, Mass.: Harvard, 2009).

41. This spelling of the family's last name is distinctive to John and the branch that remained in Pennsylvania.

42. An Eldorado judge committed Baptiste to the Stockton Mental Hospital in June 1870. Observed for one month, he was released on July 22, 1870. He was naturalized on August 27, 1877.

43. No relation to Levi Potts's family.

44. In 1970 Potts remembered that an aunt was being treated by John Jenkins, a Native doctor, which is why the family lived on his property in those days. Josie was caring for her sister, who likely had TB. *Smoke Signal* 24, no. 6 (December 1970).

45. Alta died on December 19, 1942, one month into a hospital stay for strep throat. *Feather River Bulletin*, December 24, 1924, 3.

46. Miller's predecessors knew that most allotted lands were unsuitable for subsistence and aimed to protect allottees from nefarious entities. Miller saw economic development as the sole index of progress and modernity. He facilitated the fee-simple patenting of scores of allotments for sale to Great Western Power and the Red River Lumber Company.

47. Title to Mariah's allotment cleared in January 1921.

48. *Plumas National*, December 2, 1920.

49. E. K. Miller to L. Dorrington, November 12, 1918, NARA-PR, RG 75, GIS, Box 62.

50. E. K. Miller to O. H. Lipps, January 10, 1922. O. H. Lipps, General Correspondence, NARA-DC, RG 75, Box 157. Pupils were polled about transfer school preference. Most were sent to their parents' choice of Indian school, but forty-nine went home: "That means about two-thirds of those are without school advantages now."

51. E. K. Miller to H. B. Peairs, January 11, 1922, NARA-PR, RG 75, Box 77.

52. Confiding to Lipps that he did not share this vision, Miller revealed that they were "getting busy with petitions to Johnson, Shortridge, Curry and Raker and the thing may be put up to the Congress independently of the Office." E. K. Miller to O. H. Lipps, January 10, 1922, NARA-PR, RG 75, Box 68.

53. *Plumas National*, April 30, 1925.

54. *Plumas National*, June 11, 1925.

55. *Plumas National*, June 11, 1925.

56. The *Plumas National* of June 28, 1923, reported graduations and promotions. Alta and Charley advanced to fourth and third, respectively; Josephine to second.

57. *Plumas Independent*, June 12, 1941.

58. *Plumas National*, July 14, 1892.

59. *Plumas Independent*, February 19, 1920.

60. Oral interview, Frank Quinn, 1955, UCDSC.

61. *Plumas National*, January 18, 1879.

62. For instance, in 1933 total enrollment was fifteen (*Indian Valley Record*, August 31, 1933). During the 1930s, longtime teacher Mary Schiese proudly continued to submit her Native students' work to the local paper for publication.

63. *Plumas Independent*, July 22, 1926; *Feather River Bulletin*, April 21, 1927.

64. *Plumas National*, March 14, 1918.

65. *Plumas Independent*, September 8, 1919. Hensley's father was also making news during these years. Henry Potts was jailed in Susanville for alimony nonpayment in December 1920. Shortly after, Hensley sold Henry's Lights Creek property, containing two quartz mine claims, for the exorbitant sum of $33,000. Engels Copper Mining Company planned a two-mile tunnel across the property. Hensley aided the company's engineer in surveying it—his last job for Engels. Sale of "Gold Wedge No. 1 and No. 2" did nothing to enhance the couple's material lives. Perhaps Hensley was merely a conduit for liquidation of his father's assets.

66. Merriam was chairman of the U.S. Board on Geographic Names during this period. His field notes and journals are now archived at the Bancroft Library at UC Berkeley.

67. *San Francisco Chronicle*, October 23, 1927. An adjacent photograph shows these San Francisco "nimrods" with their bounty: two massive mule deer perched atop the car hood, facing the camera. Sprawling antler racks dominate the frame. Juxtaposition of the sleek automobile with rugged wildlife was clearly crafted to entice buyers.

68. Although Native fishing talents were celebrated as natural inheritances, the business was also regulated and subject to the law, as when Hensley and Walter, "Indian Guides at Big Springs Camp," were arrested for "selling game fish." Each was fined fifty dollars for peddling trout (*Plumas National*, August 12, 1926). State and federal regulation of forests, lakes, and game resources trampled right over traditional ecological practices and claims of the Mountain Maidu to materials they had exploited and astutely conserved for generations.

69. *San Francisco Chronicle*, October 10, 1928.

70. *San Francisco Chronicle*, June 24, 1930. Interestingly, a Chester "correspondent" wrote this story.

71. Marie must have worried that this would happen. In 1924 Hensley's brother Levi and another man were arrested for running an Engelmine still.

72. Gay also enumerated Hensley, who identified himself as married. Few Indian people lived right in town, although Ellen Reeves Laurence, Hensley's former sister-in-law, did. Many others (including the Henry, Foreman, Jackson, and Salem families) were within the Seneca Township boundary, which incorporated the east shore of Lake Almanor. Hensley died in Sacramento in January 1952. Pansy and Marie cared for him at their home during his final days. He was buried at East Lawn Cemetery next to Kitty and Josephine. (Pansy was later laid to rest alongside them.) Marie and Hensley never divorced.

73. These shallow lake waters were put to good use during the frigid winter months. In March 1930, Rube and Hensley announced that they had stored away "50 tons of ice to keep Chester cold in the summer months" (*Plumas National*, March 6, 1930).

74. MP, oral interview by Francis Riddell and James Bennyhoff, state archaeologists, May 17, 1972, Francis A. Riddell Papers, CSA.

75. C. Bates, personal communication. On Thieler's divorce, see *Oakland Tribune*, February 3, 1928.

76. Josephine graduated from Stewart in 1933, and Jeanne was there through 1934. The two then moved briefly to Los Angeles; Beryl stayed at Sherman through 1935. Rhoda Silverthorne graduated from Westwood High School in 1940. She was boarding in a private home and working as a domestic.

77. Several of Pansy's children told me that their grandfather was well-known for his musicianship. In addition to playing drums in the Mechoopda Indian Band when he was a young man, he was considered the "best fiddler around" (field notes). Also see *Indian Valley Record*, December 8, 1932.

78. MP, oral interview by Francis Riddell and James Bennyhoff, state archaeologists, May 17, 1972, Francis A. Riddell Papers, CSA.

79. *Indian Valley Record*, February 6, 1936.

80. *Indian Valley Record*, December 7, 1937; October 28, 1938.

81. MP to Sacramento Indian Agency, December 9, 1938, Fort Bidwell, Box 45B, RG 75, NARA-PR.

82. *Feather River Bulletin*, June 6, 1940. Marie tried to reproduce her own experience of having family at boarding school and counted on her daughters to look after one another (field notes).

83. Born in Cincinnati, DuFresne was adopted by a French Canadian woman. He worked in Sacramento as a shoemaker, salesman, gas station attendant, and deliveryman, and later as a ship fitter in Vallejo. The couple married in Reno. *Nevada State Journal*, June 14, 1938.

84. Years later, Marie revealed that the ceremony was performed by Judge Joseph Shell, son of former Greenville superintendent Charles Shell. *Smoke Signal* 24, no. 2 (May–August 1965).

85. For example, "Mrs. Marie Potts, a former resident of Chester, now of Sacramento, is visiting friends and incidentally brought her rifle; of course, none of the hunting enthusiasts can understand why." *Indian Valley Record*, October 12, 1944. Marie also used her gun for protection, once shooting Hensley in the leg according to Don Thieler (field notes 2001).

86. Only twenty-seven years old, she was laid to rest on July 5 in Sacramento's East Lawn Memorial Park. *Plumas Independent*, July 6, 1944. A niece believes that TB was the cause.

87. *Sacramento Bee*, August 31, 1944.

88. In 1945 the household comprised Pansy and her children, Kitty, Marie, Jeanne, and her son.

89. Around 1897 Wilgus (1842–1934) came to Sacramento, where he met and married Mary VanNorman, who had several grown children from two earlier marriages. Around 1919 they adopted a three-year-old boy, Charles Irvin Wilgus, inspiring the Santa

Clara Way purchase. Adding a kitchen, an enclosed porch, and a detached garage, he expanded the one-story home to 1,280 square feet. Mary died in 1941 and Charles, then serving in the navy, sold the property.

90. Also see Dwight Dutschke, "American Indians in California," in *Five Views: An Ethnic Historic Site Survey for California* (Sacramento, Calif: Office of Historic Preservation, 1988).

91. Expressions of frustration and resistance grew stronger as Greenville drew students from farther afield (Dobkins, "Strong Language, Strong Actions").

92. In January 1902, eighteen months after Marie's arrival, a little girl, Lola Allen, died there, perhaps from TB. She was not the first. Runaways were reported almost every year, starting in Ament's day. An inquiry into Allen's death was inconclusive. Commissioner Jones to Greenville superintendent, January 28, 1902, NARA-PR, RG 75, Box 68. Wanken argues that Quinton falsely accused Shell's wife of abuse and neglect because the couple was more permissive than the Aments (Wanken, "Woman's Sphere and Indian Reform").

93. For example, *Plumas National*, May 8, 1902, 3.

94. Utter tragedy befell five girls who fled on December 1, 1916. Miller sent out eight different search parties. The Westwood postmaster and WNIA missionary R. C. Green found the three older girls around ten the next night, in Coppervale, forty miles distant by road; they had trekked the shorter route over the mountains and suffered severe frostbite. These three reported that the two younger girls had changed their minds and turned back somewhere along the way. Three days later, eight-year-old Margaret (Mollie) Lowery was discovered by a stage driver near Westwood, at the summit of Clear Creek Hill, frozen to death. Eloisa Stonecoal, found alive nearby, lost both feet. An older pupil, Edith Buckskin, suffered partial leg amputations, dying several weeks later of toxemia at the school hospital. Catherine Dick, Flora (Bill) Dick's youngest, was also among the runaways. *Plumas National*, December 16, 1916; *Portola Sentinel*, December 16, 1916; Giles-Rankin, "An Ethnohistorical Reconstruction." Descendants of boarding school alumni often report that their parents could not, or would not, pass down Native tongues. Today these serve as vehicles for cultural sovereignty and regeneration, but they were cause for punishment, ranging from shame to beatings, in earlier times. Some alumni who retained their fluency reluctantly concluded that speaking "Indian" was anachronistic and that their children were better off without it (e.g., Leonard Lowry, 1993 oral interview, University of Nevada Oral History Program, no. 179, Reno, 1999).

95. Lizzette discovered this when she was hired as Greenville's temporary laundress in August 1915. (In 1914 she also served as the temporary cook.) Miller summarily fired her seventeen days later, ostensibly for refusing to complete her full scope of duties, but her separation documents reveal something more: "She interfered with discipline and encouraged the girl students to rebel at regular intervals." She was written up for being "dictatorial," refusing to launder clothing soiled by young children, and causing problems among employees. Report of Separation of Temporary Employees, August 20, 1915, NARA-PR, RG 75, Box 69.

96. Harkin "Emotional Archive."

97. Marie was in her seventies before she could articulate the emotional cost of her Greenville education, suggesting that she had been "a real brat" to her mother because she suffered from not having her love on a daily basis, something school matrons could not replace (oral interview, Clifford Curtice, 1971, Francis A. Riddell Papers, CSA). See also her article that begins, "Remember when the Department of the Interior wanted all the American Indian students to forget their native languages, their songs, their religion and heritage? Well! It has come about. The Indians are so educated in the white man's ways that they speak well with forked tongues now." *Smoke Signal* 27, no. 3 (April 1969): 8.

Chapter 4

Epigraph: "Brief Summary of the Collett Convention (Indians of California, Inc.) Held at the Friends Church, Berkeley California, September 25 and 26, 1945," Indians of California, Rupert and Jeannette Costo Papers, MS 170, Box 92, Folder 092.005.001, SCUA, UCR. Stewart chose the title "A California Indian" to demonstrate her distinction from non-Native land claims leaders.

1. C. S. Goodrich, "Legal Status of the California Indian," *California Law Review* 14, no. 2 (January 1926): 95.
2. The United States did not recognize Indigenous title to land as defined by English common law. Thus, aside from "rancheros," "pueblos," and other habitations of "civilized Indians"—language connoting sedentary agricultural life—Native land rights were not recognized by the Public Lands Commission. In *We Are Not Savages* (Michigan State University Press, 2001), Joel Hyer argues that because the 1824 Mexican constitution extended citizenship to Native people, they should have become American citizens within a year (a Treaty of Guadalupe Hidalgo proviso), thereby subverting wholesale American appropriation of Native lands. This interpretation draws on distinctions between Ibero-American versus Anglo-Saxon colonial practice (Sherburne F. Cook, *The Conflict between the California Indian and White Civilization* [Berkeley: University of California Press, 1976], 258), but regardless of how Native citizenship was interpreted under Mexican rule, the long-standing tradition of allowing Indigenous people to reside upon their lands ended with American conquest.
3. California's 1850 Act for the Government and Protection of Indians, Statute 133, must be recognized as a tool of genocide. It stripped Native people of rights to their land, their labor, their power to testify against settlers in court, and their very lives—rendered all the more vulnerable by a handy provision allowing orphaned children to be pressed into settler servitude.
4. By the time of the 1944 judgment, most Sherman Institute pupils were not California Indians, demonstrating another CIJA inequity.
5. Thomas Le Duc, "The Work of the Indian Claims Commission under the Act of 1946," *Pacific Historical Review* 26, no. 1 (1957): 1–16.
6. See Nancy O. Lurie, "The Indian Claims Commission Act," *Annals of the American Academy of Political and Social Science* 311 (May 1957): 56–70.

7. Ulrich, *American Indian Nations*.

8. Kenneth M. Johnson, *K-344 or the Indians of California vs. The United States* (Los Angeles: Dawson's Book Shop, 1966).

9. Bills aiming to improve prospects for equitable recovery were also introduced. Webb watched them progress through committee only to be rejected on the floor (Johnson, *K-344*, 67).

10. Tim Wright, "We Cast Our Lot with the Indians from That Day Forward: The Indian Welfare Work of the Reverends Frederick G. Collett and Beryl Bishop-Collett, 1910–1914" (master's thesis, California State University–Sacramento, 2004).

11. Wright, "We Cast Our Lot with the Indians." IBC incorporated in 1914; Beryl Bishop divorced Collett in the 1920s.

12. Throughout the 1930s, Frederic A. Baker (who headed CIJA's enrolling commission) and Winnifred R. Codman (social worker and BIA fieldworker) documented countless stories of confused Indians, some elderly and impoverished, who had paid Collett to be on "the State roll," or so they thought; there was no fee associated with the roll. Whether Indian people should pay Collett to lobby Washington for their right to have private attorneys represent them in the U.S. Court of Claims was a very different issue than Collett's verbal and print assertions that Indians had to belong to one of his auxiliaries to partake in any award. After all, there was no stipulation for per capita payment.

13. "The Ghost," April 1932. NARA-PR, RG 75, Central Classified Files, Collett.

14. Letters complaining about Collett had been pouring into the Indian Defense Association for years. Collett later sued for defamation and lost. NARA-PR, RG 75, Central Classified Files, Collett.

15. See article by CIRA delegate and California Indian Brotherhood spokesperson Stella Von Bulow, written in Washington: "Appeal to Indians to Avoid the Racketeer in Bill Before Congress," *Ukiah Redwood Journal*, March 31, 1938.

16. Von Bulow (CIRA) and attorney Charles Johnson recounted a story told by Purl Willis (Mission Indian Federation) about efforts to bribe him into supporting such bills in exchange for a house and cash payments. Baker to Von Bulow, May 14, 1947, Indians of California, Rupert and Jeaneatte Costo Papers, MS 170, Box 92, Folder 092.005.001, SCUA, UCR.

17. On the Mission Indian Federation, see Damon Akins, "Line on the Land: The San Luis Rey River Reservations and the Origins of the Mission Indian Federation, 1850–1934" (PhD diss., University of Oklahoma, 2009); Thorne, *El Capitan*.

18. *Sacramento Bee*, March 25, 1946.

19. Following ICCA passage, FIC scrapped its bill, which did not conform to claim procedures.

20. ICCA established a five-year filing deadline. Originally given a ten-year life, the commission was extended many times. Lurie, "The Indian Claims Commission Act."

21. "Report of Subcommittee of Committee on Governmental Efficiency and Economy of Investigating Conditions of Indian Affairs in the State of California," California Legislature, 57th Session, *Assembly Daily Journal* (January 15, 1947): 82–94.

22. *Sacramento Bee*, August 19, 1946.

23. *Sacramento Bee*, August 30, 1946.

24. Allen initiated an investigation, but the attorney general's office soon closed it due to budget issues.

25. Knight testified about Collett before the 1928 Meriam Commission and by 1930 had written the Sacramento Indian Agency for action, exclaiming, "When Collett goes on government land for the purpose of fleecing the poor Indians of their small earnings, I think it is time for the Federal Indian agents to get into action and order him off. S. Knight to Indian agent, Sacramento, California, November 12, 1930, NARA-PR, RG 75, Sacramento Indian Agency, Collett File, Box 090.

26. "Report of Subcommittee," *Assembly Daily Journal*, January 15, 1947.

27. *Sacramento Bee*, August 30, 1946.

28. Elkus, Codman, and Lipps also testified (Subcommittee of the Senate Committee on Indian Affairs, 73rd Congress, San Francisco, July 2, 1934).

29. George LaMotte to Bertha Stewart, July 1, 1946, Rupert and Jeannette Costo Papers, Del Norte Indian Welfare Association Correspondence, 1940–1950, Box 006.022-031, Folder 006.031, SCUA, UCR.

30. When FIC convened its December 7, 1946, meeting, Fuller, Stewart, and Baker stayed with Codman at her substantial country estate in Fair Oaks, northeast of Sacramento, where they burned the midnight oil planning this convention.

31. Committee members were Ethan T. Anderson, William Fuller, Frank Gorbet, Sam Lopez, Thomas Pete, Joseph Red-Horse, Cleve Ray, Grover Sanderson, Bertha Stewart, Ernest U. Scott, Arthur Treppa, Albert Wilder, and Victor Williams." Several left FIC in 1947.

32. Indians of California, Rupert and Jeannette Costo Papers, MS 170, Box 92, Folder 092.005.001, SCUA, UCR.

33. Indians of California, Rupert and Jeannette Costo Papers, MS 170, Box 92, Folder 092.005.001, SCUA, UCR.

34. Quoted in Stewart's meeting summary, January 1947, MPP.

35. Quoted in Stewart's meeting summary, January 1947, MPP.

36. Agenda, Indians of California, Rupert and Jeannette Costo Papers, MS 170, Box 92, Folder 092.005.001, SCUA, UCR.

37. Agenda, Indians of California, Rupert and Jeannette Costo Papers, MS 170, Box 92, Folder 092.005.001, SCUA, UCR.

38. House Resolution No. 36, California Legislature, 57th Session, *Assembly Daily Journal* (January 14, 1947): 53–54.

39. "To Committee Members," Indians of California, Rupert and Jeannette Costo Papers, MS 170, Box 92, Folder 092.005.001, SCUA, UCR.

40. *Sacramento Bee*, March 31, 1947. Kitty left Moesch in February 1947; they divorced in May.

41. *Sacramento Bee*, April 10, 1947. The group met in Judge Percy West's courtroom.

42. Frederic A. Baker memo, May 14, 1947, Indians of California, Rupert and Jeannette Costo Papers, MS 170, Box 92, Folder 092.005.001, SCUA, UCR. Ernest Risling later

forced Red-Horse out of the Council of California Indians. Baker's experience producing the 1928 roll (and others, such as that of the Eastern Band of Cherokee) schooled him to watch for reciprocal acknowledgment of claims to Native identity. Though a popular "Indian" figure in Napa and Sonoma Counties, Pomo Stephen Knight was adamant that Red-Horse was not a California Indian. Baker queried BIA contacts and ex-wives (one of Mission descent and another from Covelo), who confirmed Knight's contention. Red-Horse asserted that he was acting on his children's behalf.

43. Stella Von Bulow to Fredric A. Baker, August 31, 1947, Indians of California, Rupert and Jeannette Costo Papers, MS 170, Box 92, Folder 092.005.001, SCUA, UCR.

44. This could have been from Morro, but other indicators point to Frank Gorbet, ad hoc Sacramento FIC representative, writing to Stewart. "Just a little note . . . ," Indians of California, Rupert and Jeannette Costo Papers, MS 170, Box 92, Folder 092.005.001, SCUA, UCR.

45. CCI incorporated on March 19, 1948. Ellen Ramsaur, "An Historical Narrative of the Land Claims of the Federated Indians of California" (master's thesis, California State University–Sacramento, 1975).

46. Indians of California, Rupert and Jeannette Costo Papers, MS 170, Box 92, Folder 092.005.001, SCUA, UCR.

47. FIC rolls 1–28, MPP, Box J, SCUA, CSUS.

48. Baker used this technique to vet 1928 CIJA roll applicants.

49. *Sacramento Bee*, September 19, 1947.

50. These were canceled. FIC *News Letter*, November 19, 1947.

51. Minutes, July 17, 1947, MPP, Box J, SCUA, CSUS.

52. Stewart worked in San Francisco but used Smith River Rancheria as her mailing address, delaying her ability to respond to developments in Sacramento and Washington. Furthermore, the Sacramento chapter had been discussing the need for a post office box to handle dance ticket sales and other business. The office solved both needs.

53. *News Letter*, November 19, 1947, MPP, Box O, SCUA, CSUS.

54. *News Letter*, November 19, 1947, MPP, Box O, SCUA, CSUS.

55. Minutes, December 19, 1948. MPP, Box J, SCUA, CSUS.

56. Victor Williams later reported that Auburn was "through with Collett." Minutes, November 1948, MPP, Box J, SCUA, CSUS.

57. Gorbet may not have been up to running the chapter, but he was working the cause. The evening before being asked to resign, he sent Baker news that his Susanville contact was collecting Collett circulars. Sacramento chapter minutes, April 14, 1947, MPP, Box J, SCUA, CSUS.

58. Space was freed up in June 1948 when Kitty remarried and moved out, but FIC work expanded to fill the void.

59. *Smoke Signal* 1 (January 1948).

60. The paper's smoke-signaling figure was clearly adapted from an early logo (changed by September 1941 to a Native man at the printing press) of the print shop at the Sherman Institute, which Beryl, Pansy, and Kitty had attended. This was just one way FIC sought to distinguish the *Smoke Signal* from materials targeting but not

published or authored by California Natives. For example, George Wharton James edited the first issue of Collett's *California Indian Herald* in January 1923. This publication was eventually abandoned, and Collet introduced the *Indian Arrow*, at fifteen cents per issue, in September 1929. It was not owned and published by Indians either.

61. *Smoke Signal* 1 (January 1948).
62. *Smoke Signal* 3 (March 28, 1948).
63. FIC *News Letter*, November 19, 1947, MPP, Box O, SCUA, CSUS.
64. The Collett petition, "Selection, Authorization, Confirmation of Representatives of the Indians of California," inclusive of a certification essentially assigning power of attorney to ICI delegates, to be signed and witnessed by a notary public, was reproduced in a single-spaced copy and then explicated and critiqued, paragraph by paragraph. *Smoke Signal* 8, no. 2 (September 21, 1948): 3, 4–6.
65. Kitty Potts Flores to BIA, April 1948, MPP, Box L, SCUA, CSUS.
66. FIC *News Letter*, November 19, 1947, MPP, Box O, SCUA, CSUS.
67. Building inspector's report, May 25, 1948, 2727 Santa Clara Way, Center for Sacramento History.
68. Minutes, November 1948, MPP, Box J, SCUA, CSUS.
69. Raised to $1.50 (1954), $2.50 (1961), and $3.50 (1976).
70. By April 1, there were ninety-seven subscribers; Kitty reported that they continued to pour in daily. *Smoke Signal* 5 (April 11, 1948).
71. *Smoke Signal* 8, no. 6 (February 26, 1949).
72. *Indian Valley Record*, April 1, 1948.
73. *Smoke Signal* 8, no. 1 (August 27, 1948).
74. *Smoke Signal* 8, no. 1 (August 27, 1948).

Chapter 5

1. Not an *Arrow* reporter; the byline "One of the Guests" appears to be hers.
2. Robert Warrior, *The People and the Word* (Minneapolis: University of Minnesota Press, 2005), 104.
3. Bernadette A. Lear, "Libraries and Reading Culture at the Carlisle Indian Industrial School, 1879–1918," *Book History* 18 (2015): 166–96.
4. For example, James Danky and Wayne Weigand, eds., *Women in Print: Essays on the Print Culture of American Women from the Nineteenth and Twentieth Centuries* (Madison: University of Wisconsin Press, 2006). Given Quaker influence at Carlisle and within the Indian Service, some historical instruction might have provided exposure to the abolitionist press. Burgess, an unmarried Quaker, was surely inspired by the suffragist press, where women made significant print culture strides.
5. Some were also essayists. See Daniel F. Littlefield Jr. and James W. Parins, *A Bibliography of Native American Writers, 1772–1924* (Metuchen, N.J.: Scarecrow Press, 1984).
6. Patricia Okker, *Our Sister Editors: Sarah J. Hale and the Tradition of Nineteenth-Century American Women Editors* (Athens: University of Georgia Press, 1995). See also Jillmarie

Murphy, "The Humming Bird; or Herald of Taste (1798). Periodical Culture and Female Editorship," *American Periodicals* 26, no. 1 (2016): 44–69.

7. Genevieve Bell, "Telling Stories Out of School: Remembering the Carlisle Indian Industrial School, 1879–1918" (PhD diss., Stanford University, Stanford, Calif., 1998); Jacqueline Fear-Segal, "The Man on the Bandstand at Carlisle Indian Industrial School," in Trafzer, Keller, and Sisquoc, *Boarding School Blues*, 99–122.

8. Warrior, *People*, 104.

9. Joseph McMillan, *Smoking Typewriters: The Sixties Underground Press and the Rise of Alternative Media in America* (New York: Oxford University Press, 2011), 13.

10. *Smoke Signal* 8, no. 4 (December 1, 1948).

11. *Carlisle Arrow* 11, no. 14 (December 4, 1914): 3. The winner was Otie Henry (Davis), Potts's Greenville schoolmate.

12. Meadows: *Smoke Signal* 9, no. 6 (June 1950); Anderson: *Smoke Signal* 8, no. 7 (March 26, 1949); Flores: *Smoke Signal* 10, no. 6 (August 1951); William: *Smoke Signal* 14, no. 2 (February/March 1955).

13. *Smoke Signal* 8, no. 13 (November 1949).

14. *Smoke Signal* 8, no. 13 (November 1949).

15. *Smoke Signal* 10, no. 1 (December 1950/January 1951).

16. *Smoke Signal* 8, no. 11 (August/September 1949); *Smoke Signal* 9, no. 2 (February 1950); *Smoke Signal* 9, no. 4 (April 1950), respectively.

17. *Smoke Signal* 7 (June 13, 1948).

18. *Smoke Signal* 9, no. 6 (June 1950).

19. MP to Genevieve Golsh, October 13, 1942, MPP, Box M, SCUA, CSUS.

20. Florence McClintock to MP, November 1, 1950, MPP, Box N, SCUA, CSUS. For more on McClintock, see Trafzer, *Fighting Invisible Enemies*.

21. MP to Frederic A. Baker, July 13, 1960, MPP, Box A, SCUA, CSUS; for membership numbers, see *Sacramento Union*, June 12, 1960.

22. Injun Louie's inspiration remains a mystery, despite efforts to discover the real-life Louie or Louis (for example, Louie Oliver or Mountain Maidu Dr. Louie). Louis (Louie) Sitting Crow, who figures into Vine Deloria Jr.'s work, hailed from South Dakota and postdates Injun Louie (Deloria, *Custer Died for Your Sins*).

23. Deborah A. Poole, *Vision, Race and Modernity: A Visual Economy of the Andean Image World* (Princeton, N.J.: Princeton University Press, 1997).

24. Barbara Meek, "Indian English in White Public Space," *Language in Society* 35, no. 1 (2006): 93–128.

25. For instance, see *Smoke Signal* 14, no. 2 (February/March 1955): "Injun Louie No Unnerstand."

26. *Plumas Independent*, June 5, 1930.

27. Arndt, "Making and Muting."

28. *Smoke Signal* 9, no. 6 (June 1950). This brings to mind an interview in which 2016 Pulitzer Prize winner Jack Ohman, *Sacramento Bee* editorial cartoonist, remarked that "political cartooning isn't a drawing job, it's a writing job." Capital Public Radio,

"Insight with Beth Ruyak," April 21, 2016, Capradio, http://www.capradio.org/70569 (accessed March 25, 2019).

29. *Smoke Signal* 9, no. 1 (December 1950/January 1951).

30. *Smoke Signal* 7, no. 7 (March 26, 1949); *Smoke Signal* 22, no. 3 (June/July 1963).

31. Ricardo Caté, *Without Reservations* (Layton, Utah: Gibbs Smith, 2012). Other Native comedy genres and forms were making their mark in FIC's founding years. At Bronson and LaMotte's behest, FIC endorsed NCAI's campaign to have humorist Will Rogers appointed BIA commissioner. The late Oneida comedian Charlie Hill proved that Native humor, though barbed with anticolonial critiques, was prime-time material. Similarly, the late performance artist James Luna (Luiseño) used humor to highlight the colonial violence Natives continue to suffer.

32. Richard B. Lee, "Twenty-first Century Indigenism," *Anthropological Theory* 6, no. 4 (2006): 470–71.

33. Deloria, *Custer Died for Your Sins.*

34. *Smoke Signal* 9, no. 4 (April 1950). The paper was still full of wit in its final decade: "PS: I do enjoy the *Smoke Signal* and especially the bits of humor you throw in sometimes." Mary Thornton to MP, January 6, 1971, MPP, Box N, SCUA, CSUS.

35. It appears that Kitty and Kesner Flores were first to sketch Injun Louie, but others did so as well.

36. In 1975 Potts heard from an old friend named Velma, who wrote for a photograph and asked if she ever visited Chester. Potts explained her recent stroke and fall, enclosing a photograph (circa 1967) and a *Smoke Signal.* Humble as ever, she added, "I edit this paper, so I keep busy even for my hardship." Archives, Chester Library and Museum, Plumas County.

37. MP to Frederic A. Baker, November 2, 1953, MPP, Box A, SCUA, CSUS.

38. Benedict Anderson, *Imagined Communities: Reflections on the Origin and Spread of Nationalism* (New York: Verso, 1983).

39. By now, land claims were over, FIC had evolved into a cultural organization, and Potts was dedicating three weeks a month to publishing the *Smoke Signal. Spokesman-Review* (Spokane), July 24, 1970.

Chapter 6

Epigraph 1: California Centennial Commission, *California Centennials 1948, 1949, 1950* (Sacramento: State Printing Office, 1948).

1. Bertha Stewart to Hap and Sadie Gorbet, February 9, 1948, Del Norte Indian Welfare Association Correspondence, 1940–1950, Rupert and Jeannette Costo Papers, Box 006.022-031, Folder 006.031, SCUA, UCR.

2. *Sacramento Union*, February 7, 1948.

3. *Oakland Tribune*, June 1, 1947.

4. *Petaluma Argus-Courier*, January 23, 1948.

5. Jack Norton, *Genocide in Northwestern California: When Our Worlds Cried* (San Francisco: Indian Historian Press, 1979).

6. James Scott theorizes that subordinate groups respond to oppression on two planes. One he identifies as the "infrapolitics" of everyday resistance, entailing actions that operate below the radar of state power (for example, reducing the pace of labor/production or feigning inability to comprehend the oppressor's language). Veiled as otherwise compliant behaviors and performances, they conceal a more subversive "hidden transcript" that plays out and gains momentum in private before erupting into the public sphere. James Scott, *Domination and the Arts of Resistance* (New Haven, Conn.: Yale University Press, 1992), 188. Injun Louie, who groused, joked, and skewered his way through the *Smoke Signal*'s pages, bitterly critiquing Uncle Sam, gives robust expression to that hidden transcript, but a cleverer discourse and demeanor were necessary in face-to-face interactions with power—whether embodied in the ICC, the Indian Office, the state of California, or the federal government.

7. Warren was also appropriating them. See *Modesto Bee*, February 7, 1948.

8. *Sacramento Bee*, February 9, 1948.

9. Kitty Potts Flores to FIC membership, January 29, 1948, MPP, Box M, SCUA, CSUS.

10. *Sacramento Bee*, February 9, 1948.

11. Bertha Stewart, February 9, 1948. Del Norte Indian Welfare Association Correspondence, 1940–1950, Rupert and Jeannette Costo Papers, Box 006.022-031, Folder 006.031, SCUA, UCR.

12. Goddard's photographs are in the Phoebe A. Hearst Museum of Anthropology at UC Berkeley.

13. Bertha Stewart, February 9, 1948, Del Norte Indian Welfare Association Correspondence, 1940–1950, Rupert and Jeannette Costo Papers, Box 006.022-031, Folder 006.031, SCUA, UCR.

14. Chapter minutes, March 1948, MPP, Box J, SCUA, CSUS.

15. *Smoke Signal* 3, March 7, 1948.

16. Stuart J. Little, "The Freedom Train: Citizenship and Postwar Political Culture 1946–1949," *American Studies* 34, no. 1 (Spring 1993): 35–67.

17. The newest document was the United Nations Charter. *Sacramento Bee*, March 19, 1948.

18. James Gregory Brashear, "The Freedom Train Story," *Prologue* 17 (Winter 1985): 229–45.

19. Little, "Freedom Train," 56.

20. *Sacramento Bee*, March 20, 1948, 1.

21. The five were named in the March 7, 1948, *Smoke Signal* and the March 12, 1948, *Sacramento Bee*. Stewart expressed excitement in a letter to Sylvia Forrest on March 11, 1948. Del Norte Indian Welfare Association Correspondence, 1940–1950, Rupert and Jeannette Costo Papers, Box 006.022-031, Folder 006.031, SCUA, UCR.

22. Hathaway was not alone in lending museum objects. The Oakland Museum did this for the Federation of Women's Clubs (e.g., *Oakland Tribune*, January 20, 1927).

23. Bates, "Dressing the Part," 55–66.

24. For McKay, see *Sacramento Union*, January 23, 1934; for *Tabuce*, see Craig D. Bates and Martha J. Lee, *Tradition and Innovation*.

25. After Collett's Indian Board of Co-operation formed, the June 16, 1914, *Oakland Tribune* announced, "Indians in Costume Will Attend Church."

26. Observed when FIC photographs were featured in the West Sacramento Historical Society's *First Families* exhibit (2012–14).

27. Further, anthropologists have been known to "correct" Native people who borrow from other traditions, even those who are intermarried, as if they are gatekeepers of culture and tradition.

28. Carolyn Butler Palmer, "Renegotiating Identity: 'Primitivism' in 20th Century Art as Family Narrative," *Frontiers* 29, no. 2/3 (2008): 186–223.

29. *Oakland Tribune*, January 8, 1952.

30. Michel-Rolph Trouillot, *Global Transformations* (New York: Palgrave MacMillan, 2003).

31. *Chester Progressive*, April 1, 1948; *Lassen Advocate*, March 26, 1948. The press release also carried word of FIC's position relative to per capita payments of $250 and their appearance at a Senate subcommittee meeting held at the Capitol. Discussion of payment was invariably tied to early discussions of termination, which Kitty also covered in her story, stating that the FIC delegates had voted in favor of a resolution to abolish the BIA. The *Chester Progressive* quoted former Susanville resident Kesner Flores, who invoked the discourse of citizenship and "freedom" from BIA wardship so common during this period.

32. *Smoke Signal* 5 (April 11, 1948).

33. April 12, 1948, NARA-PR, RG 75, Central Classified Files. Ironically, this is evidenced by his own advance apology and qualification of their "important role" as "very passive."

34. No record of dancers has been found. *Smoke Signal* 6 (May 9, 1948).

35. *Sacramento Bee*, May 10, 1948. Growing celebrity status was not the *Sacramento Bee*'s sole reason for covering FIC's meeting; the organization also passed a resolution endorsing a bill calling for $250 per capita payments from K-344 funds, versus the $150 amount preferred by the federal government.

36. *Smoke Signal* 7 (June 13, 1948). FIC's float was staged right behind the NAACP's. *Sacramento Bee*, March 26, 1938.

37. *Smoke Signal* 3 (March 7, 1948).

38. Minutes, March 7, 1948, MPP, Box J, SCUA, CSUS.

39. *Smoke Signal* 7 (June 13, 1948); crowd estimate from *Folsom Telegraph*, June 18, 1948.

40. *Smoke Signal* 8 (July 25, 1948).

41. *Smoke Signal* 6 (May 9, 1948).

42. *Smoke Signal* 6 (May 9, 1948).

43. Parading was not Stewart's cup of tea. She told Hostler that she feared she "would have to march in the [Flag Day] parade," affirming to Happy Gorbet two days later that "even I marched in the parade in Indian costumes. We got Harrison in it also, in a big trailing head-dress." Bertha Stewart to Joseph Hostler, June 14, 1948; Bertha Stewart to Happy Gorbet, June 16, 1948; Del Norte Indian Welfare Association Correspondence, 1940–1950, Rupert and Jeannette Costo Papers, Box 006.022-031, Folder 006.031, SCUA, UCR.

44. *Smoke Signal* 7 (June 13, 1948). Outside greater Sacramento, Fuller was taking a lead role in the Tuolumne Jubilee and Centennial, where the FIC voted to have a concession. This three-day centennial extravaganza featured a July 3 dance, a July 4 barbeque, and Indian dances on July 5. FIC's float won an award in the "family" category. Ione's Mother Lode chapter hosted dances and fund-raisers, as did the Del Norte Indian Welfare Association chapter and the Mission chapter of NCAI.

45. Berkhofer, *The White Man's Indian*; Philip J. Deloria, *Playing Indian* (New Haven, Conn.: Yale University Press, 1998); Huhndorf, *Going Native*.

46. The Sacramento chapter rented the Red Men's Hall at 1127 Twenty-First Street. MPP, Box K, SCUA, CSUS.

47. Scott, *Domination*, 198.

48. *Smoke Signal* 8, no. 2 (September 21, 1948).

49. *Smoke Signal* 8, no. 2 (September 21, 1948).

50. For a discussion of ceremonial recuperation and hybridity across northern California during the late twentieth century, see LaPena, *Dream Songs and Ceremony*.

51. Bertha Stewart to Joseph Hostler, August 30, 1948, Del Norte Indian Welfare Association Correspondence, 1940–1950, Rupert and Jeannette Costo Papers, Box 006.022-031, Folder 006.031, SCUA, UCR.

52. Bertha Stewart to Sadie Gorbet, September 17, 1948, Del Norte Indian Welfare Association Correspondence, 1940–1950, Rupert and Jeannette Costo Papers, Box 006.022-031, Folder 006.03, SCUA, UCR.

53. Bertha Stewart to Sadie Gorbet, September 19, 1948. Del Norte Indian Welfare Association Correspondence, 1940–1950, Rupert and Jeannette Costo Papers, Box 006.022-031, Folder 006.031, SCUA, UCR.

54. *Sacramento Bee*, September 10; *Sacremento Bee*, September 27, 1948, 5.

55. *Smoke Signal* 8, no. 3 (October 25, 1948). Marie bought the baby basket from Hazel Sanchez, a Flores relative in Susanville.

56. Minutes, January 23, February 13, 1949, MPP, Box J, SCUA, CSUS.

57. Minutes, May 1948, MPP, Box J, SCUA, CSUS.

58. Winnifred R. Codman to Kodak, April, 30, 1949; Codman to Pyramid Lake Women's Club April 27, 1949; Codman to Carson Trading Post, March 23, 1949, MPP, Box A, SCUA, CSUS.

59. Codman to Ernest Hodge, May 1, 1949, MPP, Box A, SCUA, CSUS.

60. Codman to William Fuller and MP, May 1, 1949, MPP, Box A, SCUA, CSUS.

61. Codman, pamphlet, MPP, Box A, SCUA, CSUS.

62. Codman to MP, May 10, 1949, MPP, Box A, SCUA, CSUS.

63. Press release, Fair Oaks Centennial Committee, MPP, Box A, SCUA CSUS. Codman also invited Edward Gifford, UC Berkeley Anthropology Museum curator, explaining that William Graves and Fuller would be singing in the concession. Friends for nearly a decade, Graves and Harry Holmes, two noted medicine men, had been inviting Codman to Lake County events since the late 1930s. Winnifred R. Codman to Edward Gifford, May 18, 1949, Edward W. Gifford Papers, Bancroft Library, UCB.

64. *San Juan Record*, May 19, 1949.

65. *San Juan Record*, May 26, 1949.

66. *Smoke Signal* 8, no. 8 (May 26, 1949).

67. MP to Robert Massey and George Frazier, May 25, 1949, MPM, Box M, SCUA, CSUS.

68. *Smoke Signal* 8, no. 8 (May 26, 1949).

69. *Sacramento Bee*, June 6, 1949, 8.

70. MP to *Auburn Journal*, June 17, 1949.

71. *Smoke Signal* 8, no. 10 (July 26, 1949).

72. *Smoke Signal* 8, no. 11 (August/September 1949).

73. Minutes, August 14, 1949, MPP, Box J, SCUA, CSUS.

74. Minutes, August 14, 1949, MPP, Box J, SCUA, CSUS.

75. *Ione Progress*, September 8, 1949; *Smoke Signal* 8, no. 12 (October 1949).

76. FIC's mid-century publicity appearances foreshadow contemporary strategic essentialism in bids for tribal acknowledgment. This entails performing behaviors, sensibilities, and discursive forms imagined by dominant society, in a racialist fashion, to be innate traits or "essences" subject to neither the vicissitudes of time nor the ravages of imperial rule. In their appearances as "real Indians," FIC members inhabited identities that squared with settler conceptions but denied them coevality and distinct tribal origins. Contemporary multicultural statecraft makes similar demands. As a legal status conferred by the state, recognition acknowledges distinct nationhood with circumscribed sovereignty and limited rights inherently conjoined to peoplehood. To qualify for such status, groups must meet thresholds of sociopolitical and cultural continuity that often deny the conditions of survival exacted by colonialism. For example, see Les W. Field, "Unacknowledged Tribes, Dangerous Knowledge: The Muwekma Ohlone and How Indian Identities Are 'Known,'" *Wicazo Ša* 19, no. 2 (Fall 2003): 79–94; Townsend Middleton, *The Demands of Recognition: State Anthropology and Ethnopolitics in Darjeeling* (Stanford, Calif.: Stanford University Press, 2015); Elizabeth Povinelli, *The Cunning of Recognition: Indigenous Alterities and the Making of Australian Multiculturalism* (Durham, N.C.: Duke University Press, 2002); Tolley, *Quest for Tribal Acknowledgment*.

Chapter 7

Epigraph: MP to Genevieve Golsh, October 13, 1952, MPP, Box M, SCUA, CSUS.

1. George Jones to MP, March 6, 1950, MPP, Box M, SCUA, CSUS.

2. *Daily Independent Journal*, March 7, 1950, 9.

3. For more on Rancho Nicasio, see Goerke, *Chief Marin*. See also Tsim D. Schneider and Lee M. Panich, "Landscapes of Refuge and Resiliency, Native Californian Persistence at Tomales Bay, California: 1770s–1870s," *Ethnohistory* 66, no. 1 (2019): 21–47.

4. Lucas Valley Road predates and is unrelated to Lucas.

5. Codman to Helen McGregor, June 18, 1949, Earl Warren Papers, Administrative Files, 1949–50, CSA.

6. Codman's Lake Tahoe place was in South Lake's Al Tahoe subdivision. Her Michigan Bluff residence near Forest Hill was reputed to have been owned by Stanford.

7. Codman to governor's office, July 3, 1949, Earl Warren Papers, Administrative Files, 1949–50, CSA.

8. *Smoke Signal* 8, no. 14 (December 1949); *Smoke Signal* 9, no. 1 (January 1950).

9. James Stewart to Myrthus Evans, January 1, 1950; Evans to Stewart, January 25, 1950, MPP, Box M, SCUA, CSUS.

10. Lewis Morrill to MP, March 7, 1950, MPP, Box M, SCUA, CSUS.

11. James W. Pool to MP, March 10, 1950, MPP, Box M, SCUA, CSUS.

12. N. W. Armstrong to MP, May 27, 1950, MPP, Box M, SCUA, CSUS.

13. Edith Beck to MP, March 16, 1950, MPP, Box M, SCUA, CSUS.

14. Alton Wilder to MP, March 25, 1950, MPP, Box M, SCUA, CSUS.

15. Wilder designed and printed FIC's letterhead for free. MPP, Box K, SCUA, CSUS.

16. Alton Wilder to MP, March 21, 1950, MPP, Box M, SCUA, CSUS. Wilder recommended contacting Spade Cooley and Will Rogers. Wilder's parents, from Orleans, were Klamath. Albert Wilder and Fuller were contemporaries and former IBC members. Boarding school connections were also involved. They shared a Carlisle connection; Alton's mother, Lillian, attended Carlisle from 1897 to 1901. Wilder and Clyde "Spade" Cooley were Chemawa alums.

17. Codman to Charles Deterding, March 29, 1950, MPP, Box A, SCUA, CSUS.

18. Codman to Charles Deterding, March 29, 1950, MPP, Box A, SCUA, CSUS.

19. Codman to Charles Deterding, March 29, 1950, MPP, Box A, SCUA, CSUS.

20. *Sacramento Bee*, May 18, 1950, 1.

21. One grandson related how fed up Potts was that FIC was always placed immediately behind horses in parade formations, forcing them to dodge manure. She was savvy; nuance did not escape her.

22. In 1917 Miller took Greenville students to the state fair, where they were invited by the Native Sons to participate in Admission Day celebrations. The paper reported, "[Fair] Secretary Paine will try to . . . have the Indians don war paint and feathers during the celebration." *Plumas Independent*, March 28, 1917.

23. BIA employed Kitty, and later Pansy, as part-time assistants on roll updating, a process that continued through 1955.

24. *Smoke Signal* 9, no. 2 (February 1950): 7.

25. *Ukiah Daily Journal*, March 13, 1958, 5. Murphey misremembered the year; Major traveled to Sacramento in 1934. *Ukiah Republican Press*, November 28, 1934.

26. MP to Josie Atwell, July 6, 1950, MPP, Box M, SCUA, CSUS.

27. MP to Roland Vasquez, July 6, 1950, MPP, Box M, SCUA, CSUS.

28. MP to Peter Rojas, July 7, 1950, MPP, Box M, SCUA, CSUS.

29. MP to Harrison Williams, July 7, 1950, MPP, Box M, SCUA, CSUS.

30. *San Bernardino County Sun*, July 13, 1950.

31. Winnifred R. Codman to MP, July 13, 1950, MPP, Box A, SCUA, CSUS.

32. MP to Valeria Navarro, July 17, 1950, MPP, Box M, SCUA, CSUS.

33. Awards were based on a point system: 40 for education ("that is the effectiveness of the exhibit in educating the public to the organization's function"), 30 for originality, and 30 for attractiveness "as a whole." MPP, Box M, SCUA, CSUS.

34. MP to Richard E. Barrington, July 17, 1950, MPP, Box M, SCUA, CSUS. Abe Benner (also known as Abel Alvin or A. A.) was Potts's age and was briefly enrolled at Greenville.

35. MP to Carl and Rose Salem, July 17, 1950, MPP, Box M, SCUA, CSUS.

36. Jennie Meadows, born around 1835, died in 1930. Pat Lindgren-Kurtz, interpreting Daisy Baker's comment that she was born in Big Meadow, has suggested that Jennie Meadows was Bill's second wife (see Lindgren-Kurtz, *Picking Willows with Daisy and Lilly Baker*). This seems highly unlikely. Hukespem had two daughters named Jennie, one each by Phoebe and Mariah.

37. Marie and Otie were Greenville schoolmates before Otie's transfer to Phoenix Indian School. They grew close at Carlisle.

38. Frank Joseph was the son of Freda Davis Joseph, one of Johnny Davis's sisters.

39. Henry was married to Selena Davis, sibling to Johnny and Freda.

40. Edna (Johnson) Calac (daughter of Eliza Wicket) was an Achumawi from Modoc County and was married to Saturino Calac (Luiseño), enrolled at Rincon Reservation. The Calacs lived in Escondido. Edna attended Stewart.

41. MP to Johnny Davis, July 7, 1950, MPP, Box M, SCUA, CSUS. Davis's mother, Mary (Mottie) Yatkin, married a Welsh immigrant.

42. MP to Abe Benner, July 7, 1950, MPP, Box M, SCUA, CSUS. Benner was among those reported as an FIC office visitor in the May 1950 *Smoke Signal*, as were Herb Young, John Davis, E. E. Mankins, and Rose (Piazzoni) Walker.

43. MP to Gladys Mankins, July 1, 1950, MPP, Box M, SCUA, CSUS.

44. George helped build and rode on FIC's float for Placer County's August 1949 Gold Rush Revival. *Smoke Signal* 8, no. 11 (August/September 1949): 2. Potts and George's aunt met as Fort Bidwell Hospital patients in 1939.

45. Codman spearheaded development of the Weimar Joint Sanatorium in the early 1930s while state and national chair of the DAR Indian Committee. John Collier awarded WPA funds to this project and a partner site, Wish-i-ah.

46. *Lassen Advocate*, July 25, 1950.

47. For example, she asked the Reverend Ernest DeFord of Covelo about quilts and other handiwork but now earnestly sought traditional material: "Do they have relics that they would put on exhibit? I found some real old things in Lassen Co." MP to Ernest DeFord, July 26, 1950, MPP, Box M, SCUA, CSUS.

48. MP to Thelma McVay, July 26, 1950, MPP, Box M, SCUA, CSUS.

49. MP to Thelma McVay, July 26, 1950, MPP, Box M, SCUA, CSUS. McVay's group was Del Norte Indian Welfare Association.

50. MP to Elsie Allen, August 6, 1950, MPP, Box M, SCUA, CSUS.

51. Club women, field agents, and reformers were critical conduits for Native women participants in the market economy (e.g., Bates and Lee, *Tradition and Innovation*; Mathes, *Divinely Guided*; Jacobs, *White Mother to a Dark Race*; Usner, "An Ethnohistory of Things"). It was not unusual for adventurous women who stepped outside the gendered expectations of early twentieth-century society to know one another. Murphey visited Codman at her Lake Tahoe home in the 1940s.

52. Elsie Allen to MP, August 9, 1950, MPP, SCUA, CSUS. Allen and Burke came for Admission Day.

53. MP to Lilly Baker, August 22, 1950, MPP, Box M, SCUA, CSUS. Kate Meadows McKinney, Lilly's maternal grandmother, was too elderly to make the trip down, but at least one of her baskets did. She passed away four years later, at ninety-four.

54. Stewart apparently reported this likelihood to Potts in late July. See Sylvia Hostler to MP, August 24, 1950, MPP, Box M, SCUA, CSUS.

55. Sylvia Hostler to MP, August 24, 1950, MPP, Box M, SCUA, CSUS. Hostler, president of Del Norte Indian Welfare Association, was Stewart's daughter and shared her take-charge spirit. Pansy and Kitty knew Hostler and Bowen (and Florence Harrie's son) from Sherman.

56. A letter to the Sacramento mayor and city council cited food and housing costs, hoping they would support the cultural demonstrators. MPP, Box M, SCUA, CSUS.

57. The County, State and National Affairs Committee of San Francisco provided her with a list of potential donors. She sent letters to four automobile dealerships on Van Ness Avenue: George Daniels (Pontiac), James McAlister (Plymouth-Chrysler), James F. Waters (De Soto), and a used car broker, Horsetrader Ed. Potts opened her letter to the latter dealer with a play on his advertising tagline, writing, "This is meant for you because you never turn your back 'on a deal' so we hope you will give this particular 'deal' your special attention." In addition to service organizations, Potts wrote the women's professional and business clubs. See MPP, Box M, SCUA, CSUS.

58. MP to Native Daughters of the Golden West, August 18, 1950, MPP, Box M, SCUA, CSUS.

59. In late August, Potts and Stewart logged smaller contributions from friends and associates. Stewart gained permission from San Francisco's chief of police to solicit donations in the city. A letter to Carl's Barber Shop (owned by the husband of Lela Dunlap, who loaned a Pomo basket) yielded an offer to collect donations (listing patron names and addresses). These totaled $20.50. Additional donations (five and ten dollars each) came from Dunlap and others. MPP, Box K, SCUA, CSUS.

60. *Smoke Signal* 9, no. 8 (September/October1950). The fairground's proximity to Santa Clara Way meant that Potts and volunteers she housed could walk to the fair. In 1951 Sacramento artist Gregory Kondos assisted exhibitors with booth design. Grant Duggins to MP, Summer 1951, MPP, Box M, SCUA, CSUS.

61. Potts penciled exhibitor names on her schematic: PTA, Girl Scouts, U.S. Navy, Amateur Radio Club, USGS Mental Health Association, Mosquito Abatement, Capital City Coin Club, Red Cross, U.S. Treasury, Model Airplane, Infant Paralysis, Sierra Club, and others. MPP, Box M, SCUA, CSUS.

62. MP to Rose Montague Johnson, Yuma, Arizona, August 20, 1950; *Del Norte Triplicate*, September 22, 1950. Conceiving of each lender's contributions as its own exhibit, she had commitments for six by August 20 and eleven upon opening. MPP, Box M, SCUA, CSUS.

63. "Federated Indians Will Offer Exhibit," *Sacramento Bee*, August 30, 1950. Drawn verbatim from press release.

64. "Federated Indians Will Offer Exhibit," *Sacramento Bee*, August 30, 1950. Drawn verbatim from press release.

65. Craig Bates (personal communication, July 2001) notes that George and Brown were friends and performed together occasionally.

66. County guest registers were labeled Almeda–Imperial, Inyo–Merced, San Bernardino–Sonoma, and Siskiyou–Yuba. An out-of-state register featured the outline of the state of California on its cover. MPP, Box M, SCUA, CSUS.

67. Sherman's was originally prepared for the 1949 Indian Day and includes a list (filed in back) of about fifty non–boarding school Native attendees. MPP, Box M, SCUA, CSUS.

68. Potts and Harry Bonser overlapped at Carlisle. Student file, NARA-DC, RG 75, Series 1327, Box 142, Folder 5569.

69. Davis loaned objects, including, "1 water jug, 1 Hat Creek basket, 2 Indian hats, 1 porcupine quill basket, 1 winnow basket, 1 Cedarville basket, 1 beaded buckskin bag, 1 beaded purse, 1 Pit River basket with cover, 1 panel of arrowheads, 1 papoose basket, 2 beaded baskets, 1 plaque matching basket by Salina Jackson, 1 bow and arrow and 1 quiver." MPP, Box M, SCUA, CSUS.

70. *Smoke Signal* 9, no. 8 (September/October 1950). Potts apologized in this issue for being unable to produce a September edition, citing her state fair work. Records show that she was still shipping objects back to owners and following up with the state fair, which was anxious for them to come back in 1951. MPP, Box M, SCUA, CSUS.

71. Florence Harrie (Karuk) first joined Potts in 1961. She lodged with Potts for two weeks each year while demonstrating twined basket weaving to all comers, near and far. Potts is often pictured at her side, working on a large coiled basket that made yearly appearances over the course of a decade.

72. MP to Grant Duggins, October 28, 1951, MPP, Box M, SCUA, CSUS. In 1955 the exhibit moved to the natural resources area and displayed plants and minerals used in daily life. The fair quoted Potts: "Through the annual exhibits at the State Fair, revived interest has been stimulated in Indian arts and crafts." The new location was near the Outdoor Theatre, where "each evening during the 11-day run of the fair the organization will present authentic Indian dances and will use native costumes and use the surrounding wooded area to advantage." "Special Evening Feature Has Been Arranged by Indians," *Sacramento Bee*, August 31, 1955. Small snapshots from the 1950s show visitors in street clothes joining Native people dancing in buckskin and feathers under the moonlight. In time, Native California dance and regalia were common.

73. MP to Genevieve Golsh, October 13, 1952, MPP, Box M, SCUA, CSUS. The young woman to whom she refers is Rosalie Nichols, whose mother, Katie, exhibited paintings in the booth. Golsh was a ceramicist married to a Luiseño FIC member and contributed pottery to the exhibit.

74. *Smoke Signal* 32, no. 4 (July/August 1974). Potts's memory was fading. In *Smoke Signal* 22, no. 3 (June/July 1963) she reported a three-year hiatus (1958–60).

75. Valuable introductions to this topic can found in Lonetree, *Decolonizing Museums*, and Sleeper-Smith, *Contesting Knowledge*.

76. Visibility as modern people was hard-won. In 1964, reminding *Smoke Signal* readers why the exhibit had educational value, she reported, "The booth was manned at all times by Indians, but one invariably heard children say, 'Where are the Indians?' TV has educated our younger generation that Indians all wear feathers. One four-year-old almost cried his heart out because his sister wanted to show him the Indians. He was afraid he was going to be killed. It took a lot of persuasion by his sister and the Indians to convince him that he was not going to be hurt and that these were the real Indians." *Smoke Signal* 23, no. 3 (July–October 1964).

Chapter 8

Epigraph: Robert A. Littlewood, "A Pomo Dance Ceremony and Northeastern Maidu Acorn Technology," term paper, University of California–Los Angeles, May 20, 1957. Copy obtained through personal communication, March 2003.

1. Oral interview, Clifford Curtice, October 27, 1971, Francis A. Riddell Papers, CSA. Curtice met Potts at the 1950 fair. His 1961 CSUS master's thesis is dedicated to her. She also spoke at Sacramento Junior College on May 20, 1971.

2. Bonnin lectured in tribal regalia in the mid-1920s. This drew large audiences, but her celebrity and billing as an Indian princess distracted from her cause. Lewandowski, *Red Bird, Red Power.*

3. Indian Agency director Walter Woehlke was the headliner. *Sacramento Bee*, March 30, 1949.

4. *Sacramento Bee*, April 5, 1949.

5. Mary Hubbard to MP, August 23, 1950, MPP, Box A, SCUA, CSUS.

6. *Sacramento Bee*, April 5, 1954. Following her travel to Washington as an FIC delegate, she was increasingly sought out for speaking engagements.

7. *Sacramento Bee*, May 28, 1954; October 1, 1954. This was not Codman's DAR group.

8. *Sonoma West Times and News*, October 27, 1955, *Madera Tribune*, March 29, 1956.

9. *Petaluma Argus-Courier*, October 26, 1955, 2.

10. "Custer Died for Your Sins" bumper stickers were "a dig at the National Council of Churches." Deloria, *Custer Died for Your Sins*, 148.

11. *Smoke Signal* 9, no. 5 (May 1950). She signed this and other prayers "M. P."

12. She later asserted that the Bahai faith was closest to that of Native people. MP, oral interview by Francis Riddell and James Bennyhoff, state archaeologists, May 17, 1972, Francis A. Riddell Papers, CSA.

13. Boas's first professorial appointment was at Clark University (1889–1982). Curtis M. Hinsley Jr. and Bill Holm, "A Cannibal in the National Museum: The Early Career of Boas in America," *American Anthropologist* 78 (1976): 306–16.

14. See Donald Collier and Harry Tschopik Jr., "The Role of Museums in American Anthropology," *American Anthropologist* 56 (1955): 768–79. Boas was repelled by earlier generations' theoretical commitments to unilinear evolution, which judged societies to be "primitive" or "savage" if they were oral rather than literate, hunters

and gatherers rather than food producers, stone rather than iron tool users, and so forth. Evolutionism lingered overlong in museums, where typological displays of material culture were inexpensive and readily lent themselves to this paradigm. Further, trustees and expedition funders could more easily measure productivity in object (versus song, story, or language) acquisition. Boas's theoretical commitment was to inductive, fine-grained historical analysis in service to the concept of cultural relativism.

15. Among the many self-taught or self-styled anthropologists working in northern California Indian Country were Clinton Hart Merriam, J. P. Harrington, John Hudson, and Jaime de Angulo.

16. On California collectors and museum founders, see S. K. Krech and Barbara A. Hail, eds., *Collecting Native America, 1870–1960* (Washington, D.C.: Smithsonian Institution, 1999).

17. Cora Du Bois, "Studies in an Indian Town," in *Women in the Field*, ed. Peggy Golde (Berkeley: University of California Press, 1970), 21.

18. This was a very different project than decolonization.

19. MP, oral interview by Francis Riddell and James Bennyhoff, state archaeologists, May 17, 1972, Francis A. Riddell Papers, CSA.

20. S. A. Barrett Papers, Bancroft Library, UCB.

21. *Sacramento Bee*, October 14, 1950.

22. Lillard Museum (founded 1936), not Lillard Hall (built in 1963), comprised four purpose-built rooms in the library. Lillard's 1939 retirement and 1941 death ended the museum and archaeological program. In 1942 Sacramento Junior College alumnus and Berkeley graduate student Franklin Fenenga packed and transported the central California materials to UC Berkelely. In 1959 the State Indian Museum was given the rest of Lillard's collection. Zallio withdrew his collection upon retirement, hoping to sell it. After his 1951 death, his daughter donated it to Sacramento State College. Reeve announced that it would form the basis for a teaching and exhibit collection on the new campus. *Pony Express*, May 15, 1942; December 16, 1949; May 19, 1959.

23. Anthony Zallio to Alfred L. Kroeber, April 11, 1929, Box 184, Bancroft Library, UCB.

24. Holly Lamb, "Collecting at the Margins of Professional Anthropology: The Native American Basket Collection of Anthony G. Zallio" (master's thesis, California State University–Sacramento, 2012).

25. Lillard earned his bachelor's degree in physiology and histology from Stanford (1899) and his master's from University of Southern California (1911). He was state supervisor of agricultural education when he accepted the Sacramento Junior College presidency in 1923. *San Francisco Call Bulletin*, May 23, 1899; *Sacramento Bee*, June 29, 1923. USC later awarded him an honorary doctorate of pedagogy. *Sacramento Bee*, May 30, 1940. Encountering the detritus of earlier habitations while rambling across rangelands and plow furrows on his family's Santa Barbara ranch unquestionably fostered Lillard's archaeological curiosity.

26. Benjamin W. Hathaway, State Capitol Indian Museum, "To Whom It May Concern," April 24, 1931 (in author's possession).

27. For a contemporaneous review of Sacramento Junior College excavations and reports, see *American Antiquity* 6, no. 4 (April 1941): 360–63.

28. Thomas Hester, "Robert Fleming Heizer," *American Antiquity* 47, no. 1 (1982): 100. Lillard courted Heizer on Sacramento Junior College's behalf after seeing newspaper coverage of his excavations as a Nevada high schooler. Heizer donated skulls and burial objects to SJC's museum upon matriculation ("College Given Indian Relics from Nevada," *Sacramento Bee*, October 15, 1932). Some claim that Lillard had abandoned pot hunting by Heizer's time. See "Roundtable Discussion: Some Thoughts on California Archaeology: An Historical Perspective," *Society for California Archaeology Occasional Papers 4* (March 1984).

29. *Sacramento Union*, September 26, 1949. Geography later replaced speech.

30. *Express* (Sacramento Junior College's newspaper), October 17, 1952.

31. Packard left the State Indian Museum in 1951 to become curator at Will Rogers State Park. An accomplished artist, he illustrated several State Indian Museum pamphlets, stayed in touch with Potts, and was a *Smoke Signal* subscriber. *Sacramento Bee*, March 20, 1951; *Los Angeles Times*, October 24, 1951.

32. *Express* (Sacramento Junior College's newspaper), November 30, 1951. The 1940 census lists Dyson as an Oakland resident, "relic collector," and museum worker. See chapter 10 for his FIC involvement.

33. *Smoke Signal* 10, no. 1 (December 1950/January 1951).

34. Francis A. Riddell, "Climate and the Aboriginal Occupation of the Pacific Coast of Alaska," *Kroeber Anthropological Society Papers* 11 (1954): 60–123.

35. Oral interview by the author, July 28, 2000.

36. Franklin Fenenga and Francis A. Riddell, "Excavation of Tommy Tucker Cave, Lassen County," *American Antiquity* 14, no. 3 (January 1949): 203–14.

37. This course was Anthropology 250 A-B.

38. Meighan and Seibert married three years later.

39. Several of Pansy's children told me that Potts spent many years collecting clothing and food to help homeless Native people who frequented this area before its redevelopment.

40. A dancer collapsed and was attended by "Mrs. Burris." This was undoubtedly Edith Burrows, identified verbally by Barrett. Littlewood misheard the name.

41. This may be the source of the photo of Herb Young with Selena's baskets published by Patricia Lindgren-Kurtz in *Picking Willows*.

42. Littlewood, "Pomo Dance Ceremony."

43. *Kroeber Anthropological Society Papers* 19 (1958): 67–84. The presentation was at the Southwestern Anthropological Association Conference in Long Beach, December 7, 1957.

44. Riddell to Robert Euler, January 28, 1957, Francis A. Riddell Papers, CSA. Riddell shot this footage in 1949. Riddell continued to employ Marie as a cultural consultant. His field notes informed his own and others' research. For example, her memory of summering in Mountain Meadow, and specific fishing and cooking practices prior to Big Meadow's inundation, appears in William S. Evans Jr., "Ethnographic Notes on the Honey Lake Maidu," *Nevada State Museum Occasional Papers* 3, no. 2 (1978).

45. Littlewood, "Pomo Dance Ceremony."

46. *Plumas National*, August 24, 1899.

47. Bernstein, "Roland Dixon and the Maidu."

48. Bernstein, "Roland Dixon and the Maidu."

49. Ramsaur, "Historical Narrative."

50. Heizer and Kroeber, "For Sale"; Omer C. Stewart, "Litigation and Its Effects," in *Handbook of California Indians*, Vol. 8, *California*, ed. R. F. Heizer (Washington, D.C.: Smithsonian, 1978), 705–12. Swartz cited Beal's DOJ report, which suggested that northern Maidu exploited only 2 percent of their High Sierra territory.

51. "Indian Folklore Cited at Inquiry on Indian Land Claims," *Oakland Tribune*, June 24, 1954. Use of the word *folklore* speaks to Potts's mid-1960s critique of the hearings and the anthropological discipline: "I asked an attorney in SF why the Indians weren't allowed to testify as witnesses. I don't remember his exact words, but he insinuated that they were not truthful. He might as well have called them liars. He could be right to a certain extent. I'll tell you why. When the anthropologists bounced into an Indian home asking questions, the Indians thought he was ridiculous and gave them ridiculous answers. The anthropologists have printed the ridiculous answers as fact so the anthro students are using these ridiculous statements to earn their college degrees on. Now the Indians and non-Indians are coming up with facts that contradict some of the books now in use in colleges and universities." Untitled and undated statement on California Indian land claims case, MPP, Box C, SCUA, CSUS.

52. Stephen Powers, *Tribes of California*, Vol. 3, *Contributions to American Ethnology* (Washington, D.C.: U.S. Government Printing Office, 1877), 586. This was Powers's second Maidu country foray; the name Ná-kum was elicited from a Big Meadow Maidu.

53. See Bernstein, "Roland Dixon and the Maidu," 21.

54. Mary Gist Dornback to California Council of Indians membership, "Re: California Claims Case," March 12, 1956, NCAI Tribal Files, Box 96, NMAI.

55. Potts continued her association with Reeve, appearing with her grandson in 1957 at his Sacramento State College–Lake Tahoe class on North American Indians, with Jack Dyson in Plains headdress.

56. Oral interview, Clifford Curtice, October 27, 1971, Francis A. Riddell Papers, CSA.

57. Miranda, *Bad Indians*, 28.

58. Oral interview, Frank Quinn, 1955, UCDSC.

59. Oral interview, Frank Quinn, 1955, UCDSC.

60. Exhibit register, September 6, 1952, MPP, Box M, SCUA, CSUS.

61. Dobkins articulates this representational project as one of autoethnography (Dobkins et al., *Memory and Imagination*), while Mark Minch recognizes Day's body of work as a distinctly Indigenous and postapocalyptic self-archiving project. Mark Minch, "The Undone Petroglyph: Frank Day's Work of Nonvitalist Revitalization," paper presented at the Spirit of Pacific Western Traders Native Art Symposium, Folsom Lake College, Folsom, Calif., January 12, 2020.

62. Riddell to Frank Day, April 11, 1961, Francis A. Riddell Papers, CSA.

63. *Sacramento Bee*, May 17, 1963; *Smoke Signal* 23, no. 3 (July–October 1964); *Sacramento Bee*, September 9, 1966. Potts used the 1966 *Bee* interview to hammer home the devastation to basketry and arts that resulted from land theft: "Our arts and crafts are gradually dying out, because, for one thing, of the lack of material. Years ago, the Indians burned the brushes and when new shoots came out, they used them in basket weaving. But we can't do that anymore. Everything is private property, or state or federal parks. I went out this spring and looked for willows. I found them. But they were full of bugs. In the old days our controlled burns would have gotten rid of the bugs."

64. State Indian Museum gift/accession nos. 170–1 to 170–4. The clapper sticks were repatriated in the early 2000s. The cedar bark house was demolished in 1961, and vandals incinerated the tule house not long after.

65. S. A. Barrett, "American Indian Films," Samuel A. Barrett Papers, Bancroft Library, UCB. Following her UCLA graduation and marriage to Meighan, Seibert worked for the American Indian Films Project.

66. Samuel A. Barrett to Riddell, June 17, 1957, Francis A. Riddell Papers, CSA.

67. Riddell exhibited this at the State Indian Museum. See "Rare Tule Canoe Is Shown at State Museum," *Sacramento Bee*, November 10, 1948.

68. Norm Wilson, Riddell's colleague, shot stills while Barrett worked. Images from these sessions illustrate multiple publications, including Janet Goodrich, "Acorns and Baskets," *Pacific Historian* 16, no. 3 (Fall 1972): 18–34. Enos is pictured in Norman L. Wilson and Arleane H. Town, "Nisenan," in *Handbook of North American Indians*, Vol. 8, *California*, ed. Robert F. Heizer (Washington, D.C.: Smithsonian, 1978), 387–97. Also note the image of Barrett filming Enos (figure 6) in the same volume.

69. PAHMA catalog nos. 1–68989, 1–68990 (weaving material), 1–144994, and 1–144995 (dolls).

70. PAHMA nos. 1–211618 through 1–211621; Elsasser to Potts, November 11, 1962, PAHMA. My thanks to Ira Jacknis, Joan Knudson, and Leslie Freund for assistance in accessing these museum objects, registration records, and images.

71. "Indian Woman to Show How to Live on Acorns," September 12, 1960, and "Lost in the Wilds? Try a Delicious Acorn Dish," September 16, 1960, *Oakland Tribune*; also see "A Lesson from the Indians," *Oakland Tribune-Parade*, January 8, 1961.

72. *Smoke Signal* 24, no. 1 (January–April 1965).

73. Riddell later told Barrett that his bow tie was found in Ole's car when they were back in Sacramento. Francis A. Riddell to Samuel A. Barrett, April 10, 1960, Francis A. Riddell Papers, CSA. Bear Dance preparation and filming correspondence can be found in the Francis A. Riddell Papers (CSA) and Samuel A. Barrett Papers (Bancroft Library, UCB).

74. For example, Stephen Warren and Ben Barnes highlight methodologies for a community-engaged scholarship enabling Native communities and scholars—not mutually exclusive parties by any means—to use such material productively. "Salvaging the Salvage Anthropologists," *Ethnohistory* 65, no. 2 (2018): 189–214. Cutcha Risling Baldy (*We Are Dancing for You*) explains how women in her northern California tribe critically deciphered heteropatriarchal field notes and literature when reintroducing their Flower Dance and related ceremonies. Kenneth Holbrook grapples with the

troubling circumstances by which contemporary Mountain Maidu come by the gift of hearing Maidu stories told in their ancestral tongue while pondering the twenty-first-century possibilities that these recordings embody ("*Wéjenem Bíspadà*: A Brief History of Maidu Language Keepers and Other Thoughts on Language Revitalization," in Nevins, *World-Making Stories*, 61–74).

75. Audra Simpson, *Mohawk Interruptus: Political Life across the Borders of Settler States* (Durham, N.C.: Duke University Press, 2014).

76. Bruchac, *Savage Kin*.

77. Potts continued to collaborate and keep company with anthropologists, especially CSUS anthropologist Dotty Theodoratus. Their collaboration included activist causes, such as lobbying on and off campus in 1970 for creation of the Sacramento Indian Center, of which Potts was a founding board member.

Chapter 9

Epigraph: letter to *Smoke Signal* readers and subscribers, July 1961.

1. *Smoke Signal* 12, no. 7 (September/October 1953).

2. Helen L. Peterson, "NCAI Nostalgia: The Worst of Times, the Best of Times," *Sentinel* (Winter 1971): 36–38, 40; Chuck Trimble (personal communication, August 23, 2000).

3. *Smoke Signal* 12, no. 6 (August 1953): 1, 6; *Smoke Signal* 13, no. 1 (January/February 1954).

4. Carefully preserved maps and mementos documenting their visits to the House and Senate chambers, and tickets to television studios and the Empire State Building, give material expression to her love of travel and cosmopolitan adventure. MPP, Box C, SCUA, CSUS.

5. Gretchen Harvey, "Cherokee and American: Ruth Muskrat Bronson, 1897–1982" (PhD diss., Arizona State University, Tempe, 1996).

6. John Ranier (Taos) resigned in 1951 to attend graduate school, and Frank George (Nez Perce) resigned in 1953 under executive council pressure.

7. "Caution on Indians Asked," *New York Times*, August 15, 1953.

8. MP, oral interview by Francis Riddell and James Bennyhoff, state archaeologists, May 17, 1972, Francis A. Riddell Papers, CSA.

9. *Sentinel*, August 18, 1953.

10. Bertha Stewart to MP, December 21, 1963, MPP, Box A, SCUA, CSUS.

11. *Smoke Signal* 12, no. 7 (September/October 1953).

12. *Smoke Signal* 11, no. 5 (May 1952): 2.

13. *Smoke Signal* 12, no. 1 (December/January 1953).

14. Peterson was born in 1915 on Pine Ridge Reservation.

15. "Report of Public Relations Committee, NCAI Convention, September 1949"; enclosure, Ataloa Stone McClendon to Ruth Bronson, October 20, 1949, HLPP, Series 1, NCAI Conventions/Correspondence, NMAI. The committee included Louis Bruce (Dakota/Mohawk), Alvin Warren (Chippewa), Alcesta Murphy (Dakota), and Ataloa Stone McClendon (Chickasaw).

16. In October, Bronson penned a thank-you note but swiftly pivoted to a more pressing concern: a plea that Peterson, not McNickle, represent NCAI at a meeting in Chicago that Peterson would be attending for the Denver Mayor's Commission on Human Relations. McNickle would be there for American Indian Development, but his longtime BIA affiliation continued to cloud NCAI's reputation as an independent organization. Peterson understood and obliged. Such was the lockstep nature of their collaboration throughout the late 1940s and early 1950s as they built NCAI's fiscal resources and influence. Ruth Muskrat Bronson to Helen Peterson, October 25, 1949, HLPP, Series 1, NCAI Conventions/Correspondence, NMAI.

17. Helen Peterson to W. W. Short, August 17, 1953, HLPP, Series 1, NMAI.

18. "California Civic Unity Council Plans Education for Indians," *Oakland Tribune*, November 9, 1953, 14. Potts ran this announcement adjacent to her delegate's report about the Denver visit with McNickle. *Smoke Signal* 12, no. 7 (September/October 1953).

19. *Smoke Signal* 12, no. 8 (November/December 1953); Josephine Duveneck, *Life on Two Levels: An Autobiography* (Los Altos, Calif.: Trust for Hidden Villa, 1978). Potts and Duveneck served together on the board of the California League for American Indians.

20. *Smoke Signal* 12, no. 8 (November/December 1953).

21. Termination was legislated through the California Rancheria Acts.

22. Arthur V. Watkins, "Termination of Federal Supervision: The Removal of Restrictions over Indian Property and Person," *Annals of the American Academy of Political and Social Science* 311 (May 1957): 47–55.

23. *Termination of Federal Supervision Over Certain Tribes of Indians, Joint Hearings before Subcommittees of the Committees on Interior and Insular Affairs*, 83rd. Congress (March 4–5, 1954).

24. FIC delegates were elected on February 28. *Sacramento Bee*, March 2, 1954. XL-Ranch sent Forrest.

25. *Daily Independent Journal* (San Rafael), March 18, 1954, 7.

26. Delegates reported on hearings in the Sacramento County Courthouse on March 28. *Sacramento Bee*, March 23, 1954.

27. Harvey, "Cherokee and American."

28. This group's relationship with FIC appears to have developed as a result of Sherman and Carlisle alumni connections.

29. Ruth Muskrat Bronson to Saturino Calac, January 26, 1948, HLPP, Series 1, Conventions/Correspondence, NMAI. Bronson notes his letter of January 7. This group appears to have morphed by the mid-1950s into the Rincon Reservation/FIC–affiliated Mission Indian chapter of NCAI.

30. Ramsaur, "Historical Narrative."

31. Helen Peterson to California Indian groups, May 19, 1954, NCAI, Tribal Files, Box 96, NMAI.

32. Formally the Pitt River Home and Agricultural Cooperative Association, this band organized under IRA in 1934, a process to which McNickle was party. Janice Mecham,

"XL Reservation: A Study in New Deal Indian Politics, 1934–1946" (master's thesis, California State University–Sacramento, 1980).

33. *Smoke Signal* 13, no. 4 (May/June 1954).

34. Originally named Indian Congress of California, it had been renamed California Indians' Congress by December 1954, when Forrest testified as president before the Senate Interim Committee on California Indian Affairs. Officers included Vyola Olinger (Long Beach), Glen Moore (Hoopa), Eileen Miguel (Palm Springs), Max Mazetti (Valley Center), Frank Treppa (Upper Lake), and Cruz Siva (Palm Springs). NCAI, Tribal Files, Box 96, NMAI.

35. Their statement read, "We have probed and discussed pro and con in an effort to comprehend the meaning of those bills and their effect on our future welfare and destiny. It is our firm belief that the aims and intent of the well-meaning but misinformed Congress is, instead of restoring and emancipating the California Indians and according them the same privileges and right as accorded other citizens, but euphemism to abrogate our treaty rights, agreement, statutes, custom and precedents created for us by our ancestors by prior use thereof." Erin Forrest to William Knowland, June 20, 1954, NCAI, Tribal Files, Box 96, NMAI.

36. Helen Peterson to Ruth Muskrat Bronson, September 5, 1954, HLPP, Box 1, Subject Files, NMAI. Winnie Howell and Stewart registered at the fair on September 4, 1954.

37. Peterson to Bronson, September 5, 1954, HLPP, Box 1, Subject Files, NMAI.

38. Peterson to Bronson, September 5, 1954, HLPP, Box 1, Subject Files, NMAI. Peterson had choice words for American Friends Service Committee's Quinn, who was "real mixed up," using concepts such as "integration" to talk about termination's nefarious goals.

39. *Smoke Signal* 13, no. 6 (September/October 1954): 3.

40. Citing round-trip bus fare of $57.15, Stewart added, "No doubt those of us who go will travel by bus." Bertha Stewart to Helen L. Peterson, October 19, 1954, NCAI, Box 96, NMAI. Forrest and McNickle served on Spokane's 1955 Resolutions Committee; other FIC and/or CIC members on NCAI committees were Max Mazzetti and Vyola Olinger.

41. "Pictorial Highlights," *Bulletin*, November 1957.

42. Helen L. Peterson to Charles Elkus, February 13, 1958, NCAI, Series 16, Box 567, NMAI. Ataloa was copied on the letter.

43. Charles Elkus to Helen Peterson, February 18, 1958, NCAI, Series 16, Box 567, NMAI. An eight-page summary of the study trip is archived. See HLPP, Series 1, NMAI.

44. Sol Tax to MP, Manuscript 4806, Box 8, Chicago Indian Advisors, NAA.

45. On "action anthropology," see Joan Ablon, "The American Indian Chicago Conference," *Journal of American Indian Education* 1, no. 2 (1962): 17–23; Daniel Cobb, "The Personal Politics of Action and Applied Anthropology," *Ethnohistory* 66, no. 3 (2019): 537–63.

46. NCAI, conference proceedings, 1960, NMAI.

47. *Smoke Signal* 20, no. 2 (February/March 1961): 3.

48. Benjamin Bearskin of the Chicago Indian Center spoke about "urban Indians as recent groups having special problems of establishing residence to be eligible for public welfare, of finding desirable social and recreational facilities as Indians, and of establishing their continuing rights in their home communities." Typescript minutes, "Fifth Session, 2/21/61," 4–6; "AICC—Meeting of Indian Advisory Committee, Feb. 10–14, 1961, Chicago, Ill," Manuscript 4806, Box 8, Chicago Indian Advisors, NAA.

49. Nancy O. Lurie to Sol Tax, February 16, 1961, Manuscript 4806, Box 8, NOL, NAA.

50. Samuel A. Barret to Nancy O. Lurie, February 3, 1961, Manuscript 4806, Box 5, B-Boc, NAA.

51. Thomas Clarkin, *Federal Indian Policy in the Kennedy and Johnson Administrations, 1961–1969* (Albuquerque: University of New Mexico Press, 2001).

52. Tax, Lurie, and Robert Reitz (Chicago Indian Center director) met in Chicago on March 8–9, 1961, to schedule the nine regional meetings. AICC, task force, and NCAI communication led to Clarence Wesley's meeting with the task force at NCAI headquarters on March 13.

53. Daniel M. Cobb, *Native Activism in Cold War America* (Lawrence: University of Kansas Press, 2011), 38.

54. D'Arcy McNickle to Sol Tax, March 25, 1961, Manuscript 4806, Box 8, NOL, NAA.

55. Sol Tax to MP, March 19, 1961, Manuscript 4806, Box 1, AICC, NAA.

56. Samuel Barrett to Nancy O. Lurie, April 4, 1961, Manuscript 4806, Box 5, NAA.

57. Clarkin, *Federal Indian Policy*; BIA press release, February 10, 1961, Robert Leland Papers, SC-UNR.

58. *Santa Rosa Press Democrat*, April 13, 1961, 4.

59. Organizing committee commentary was tape-recorded. Sol Tax Papers, University of Chicago Special Collections Research Center.

60. Including Dr. and Mrs. Richard Shutler (Nevada Museum). Barrett observed task force and regional meetings and was filming nearby.

61. *Reno Gazette Journal*, April 14, 1961.

62. *Reno Gazette Journal*, April 14, 1961.

63. Sellers and American Friends Service Committee representatives (Wesley Huss, the Duvenecks, and Virginia Perry) observed.

64. Robert Leland to Mary Sellers, April 11, 1961, Robert Leland Papers, SC-UNR.

65. "California-Nevada Regional Meetings," Manuscript 4806, Box 2, NAA.

66. April–May 1961, Manuscript 4806, Box 8, NOL, NAA.

67. Nancy O. Lurie to Samuel A. Barrett, May 18, 1961, Manuscript 4806, Box 5, NAA.

68. Her readers were never out of mind. Potts sent Tax a postcard from Washington, D.C., asking him to send Pansy the latest draft declaration for *Smoke Signal* publication. MP to Sol Tax, May 6, 1961, Manuscript 4806, Box 1, AICC, NAA. No paper was published in her absence.

69. Four purposes, including adult and youth education, were detailed in the declaration of trust adopted by the executive council at the 1957 convention. The fund's trustees were the NCAI's elected officers, so fiduciary and managerial distinctions were symbolic at best. *NCAI Fund Report* 1, no. 1 (1961).

70. Helen Peterson to Emily F. Morrison, August 26, 1960, NCAI, Correspondence, Box 71, NMAI.

71. Helen Peterson to Rose Mandan, February 26, 1960, NCAI, Correspondence, Box 71, NMAI.

72. Helen Peterson to Earl Boyd Pierce, October 27, 1960, NCAI Correspondence, Box 71, NMAI.

73. Helen L. Peterson to John Ranier, April 18, 1960, NCAI, Executive Council, Correspondence, Box 71, NMAI.

74. Dorothy Davids (Stockbridge-Munsee Band of Delaware Indians), a schoolteacher, was the second "Indian leader observer-trainee," working July 1 to August 15. *NCAI Fund Report* 1, no. 1 (1961). Interns typically earned a modest salary and stipend for travel, room, and board.

75. Helen Peterson to Betty Jane Powell (Chippewa), Lowell, Michigan, May 18, 1961; MP to Betty Jane Powell, May 18, 1961, NCAI Correspondence, 1960–61, Box 71, NMAI.

76. The May 7 *Oakland Tribune* headlined its coverage "Tribal Committee to Propose Abolition of Indian Commission at Parley." This interpretation was way off the mark.

77. Privately, Peterson expressed exasperation over the time this took from pressing business, especially given the blizzard-reduced parade attendance. She was not convinced that the five tribally sponsored floats garnered Indian Country goodwill in proportion to NCAI staff time expended to gain them entry. The story aimed to extend publicity given NCAI's investment.

78. Potts began working on June's issue, but it was November before those stories saw the light of day. By then, the publication was a post-convention/resignation *Bulletin* 6, no. 2 (1961). The proposed 1957–58 budget shows publication costs for ten to twelve *Bulletins* per year projected at $3,600. See HLPP, Series 1, Box 2, NMAI.

79. Helen Peterson, "Dear Friends," June 7, 1961, NCAI, Chronological Files, Box 71, NMAI.

80. Potts sold twenty-four copies, mailing six dollars to Peterson. MP to Helen L. Peterson, August 10, 1961, HLPP, NCAI Correspondence, NMAI.

81. "Freberg Hones His Needles," *Minneapolis Star Tribune*, May 5, 1961; "The Unplayed Record," *Pittsburgh Press*, May 14, 1961; "Inhospitality to Funnyman," *Marion Star* (Ohio), May 22, 1961.

82. Potts and Peterson knew one of them, Russell "Big Chief" Moore, Sherman alumnus and jazz trombonist, whose fall 1958 tour of South Dakota secondary schools the NCAI Fund sponsored.

83. MP, oral interview by Francis Riddell and James Bennyhoff, state archaeologists, May 17, 1972, Francis A. Riddell Papers, CSA.

84. Stan Freberg, *It Only Hurts When I Laugh* (New York: Random House, 1988), 208–11.

85. Stachowiack anticipated an annual seminar on Indian affairs. Dr. George Blue Spruce (Pueblo), Forrest Gerard (Blackfeet) Dr. Angie Debo, and Dr. Mari Sandoz were among the speakers. *Daily Courier*, May 18, 1961.

86. *Smoke Signal* 22, no. 3 (June/July 1963): 5.

87. *Smoke Signal* 29, no. 1 (January/February 1970): 1.

88. "Report of the Steering Committee," HLPP, NCAI Subject Files, NMAI.

89. "Committee Meetings: Drafting, Steering, Regional Organizers," Manuscript 4806, Box 1, AICC, April 1961, NAA.

90. Besides Potts and Forrest, several delegates, including Cahuilla workshop student Harry Hopkins and Katherine Saubel, represented California. Stewart wanted to attend but did not. Manuscript 4806, Box 2, Yellow Suggestion Sheets, NAA. Hopkins returned home after AICC and did not attend the Boulder portion of the workshop. Viola Pfrommer to D'Arcy McNickle, June 30, 1961, D'Arcy McNickle Papers, Box 19, Folder 162, Ayer Modern Manuscripts, Newberry Library, Chicago.

91. Cowger, *National Congress of American Indians*.

92. Burnette replaced Peterson, quickly learning that there were many ropes to fund and climb. Explaining that the *Bulletin* had been last printed in November 1961, that Peterson had left the treasury "badly broke," and that he'd resorted to a newsletter to disseminate legislative news, he exclaimed "Now we are printing the first issue of the new *NCAI Sentinel Bulletin* that you will have next week. . . . It will be printed every month hereafter, in fact we will be printing 15,000 copies so we can build up the NCAI membership. . . . THE FIRST ISSUE WILL SHOCK A FEW PEOPLE." Robert Burnette to Ruby F. Nahlstadt, June 19, 1962, NCAI, Box 71, NMAI.

93. Vine J. Deloria Jr. and Clifford M. Lytle, *The Nations Within* (Austin: University of Texas Press, 1984).

94. McNickle agreed to send the students to AICC on the conditions that Chicago room and board would be billed at twenty-five dollars per week (the same rate American Indian Development was paying for the remainder of its stay at the Boulder workshop) and that no other costs (registration, transportation, and so on) could be incurred by AID. AID board minutes of November 30, 1961, clarify that Tax was anxious for the students to attend. Box 21, Folder 181, D'Arcy McNickle Papers, Ayer Modern Manuscripts, Newberry Library.

95. McKenzie-Jones, *Clyde Warrior*. Deloria and Lytle cite NIYC as an AICC by-product.

96. Shreve, *Red Power Rising*.

97. MP to Helen L. Peterson, August 10, 1961, HLPP, NCAI Correspondence, NMAI; *Smoke Signal* 21, no. 3 (October 1962): 2–3; Viola Pfrommer to D'Arcy McNickle, November 11, 1962, Box 19, Folder 162, McNickle Papers, Ayer Modern Manuscripts, Newberry Library.

98. *Smoke Signal* 24, no. 1 (January–April 1965).

99. *Smoke Signal* 24, no. 3 (September/October 1965).

100. *Chicago Sun Times*, June 14, 1961; *Saint Louis Post Dispatch*, June 25, 1961.

101. "The American Indian Chicago Conference," *American Behavioral Scientist* 5, no. 2 (October 1961): 36.

102. Parker, *Singing an Indian Song*, 190.

103. *Klamath Falls Herald and News*, June 14, 1961, 8.

104. William Rickard, "Report on AICC," Robert Leland Papers, SC-UNR; see also Laurence Hauptman and Jack Campisi, "The Voice of Eastern Indians," *Proceedings of the American Philosophical Society* 132, no. 4 (1988): 316–29.

105. MP to Helen L. Peterson, August 10, 1961, HLPP, NCAI Correspondence, Box 4, NMAI.
106. A candid shot showed Potts and Irma Bahnsen inspecting an antique Nez Perce teepee pitched at Hotel Lewis-Clark.
107. Charles Trimble, *Iyeska* (Indianapolis: Dog Ear Publishing, 2012).
108. *Smoke Signal* 30, no. 1 (January/February 1971).
109. *Smoke Signal* 30, no. 1 (January/February 1971).
110. MP, oral interview by Francis Riddell and James Bennyhoff, state archaeologists, May 17, 1972, Francis A. Riddell Papers, CSA.
111. *Smoke Signal* 30, no. 1 (January/February 1971).
112. *Riverside Daily Enterprise*, January 5, 1971.
113. In 1972 Ada Deer was NCAI's keynote speaker at the Tulsa convention, where she gifted Potts a beaded necklace. This gesture made a lasting impression on Potts. Asked to give the prayer and award diplomas to D-Q University's first graduating class on June 26, 1976, Potts went prepared with beaded necklaces. It was a good thing, since diplomas were not ready on time (*Smoke Signal* July/August 1976). Potts, David Risling Sr., Ben Black Elk, Katie Nichols, and Elsie Allen were named to D-Q's Hehaka Sapa College Council of Honored Elders in 1972. *Smoke Signal* 31, no. 2 (March/April 1972).
114. *Smoke Signal* 31, no. 5 (September/October 1972).
115. *Rocky Mountain News*, November 17, 1972. The next year it went to Alaska's *Tundra Times*, and in 1974 to AIHS's *Wassaja*. AIPA operated from 1970 to 1976. It was unable to attract sufficient revenue from the fledgling Native press to sustain itself.
116. Some Mountain Maidu people are today affiliated with Susanville Indian Rancheria or Greenville Rancheria. Many more continue to struggle for federal recognition. For more on Olinger, see Ortner, *You Can't Eat Dirt*.

Chapter 10

Epigraph: *Sacramento Bee*, August 5, 1974.
1. *Smoke Signal* 20, no. 2 (February/March 1961).
2. *Smoke Signal* 21, no. 1 (January/February 1962) and *Smoke Signal* 21, no. 3 (October 1962). This camp was at the Duveneck estate. *Los Altos Town Crier*, August 4, 1971.
3. Mildred Van Every replaced Quinn (now California Federation for Civic Unity executive director) and hired Potts. These two, working with the California League for American Indians, fostered legislation to establish the State Advisory Commission on Indian Affairs, created in July 1961 and renamed the California Indian Affairs Commission in 1968. It dragged its feet and never seated any Native people due to internal squabbles. For this reason (and despite the fact that some Native people, including Potts, advocated for prioritizing Native representation) some Native people successfully called for its abolishment in late 1968. This greatly angered Potts, who had worked long and hard to get a foot in the door for rural and non-reservation Indians. She noted that it was the large, federally acknowledged tribes that pushed for abolishment, leaving smaller groups and federally unrecognized Native people with

no point of contact for their needs and voices to be heard by the legislature. *Smoke Signal* 26, no. 1 (November 1966–January 1967); *Smoke Signal* 27, no. 3 (April 1969); *Smoke Signal* 27, no. 4 (June/July 1969).

4. Duveneck, *Life on Two Levels*, 271.

5. *Indians of California: Past and Present* (San Francisco: American Friends Service Committee, 1955).

6. Lobo, *Urban Voices*; Nagel, *American Indian Ethnic Renewal*; Ramirez, *Native Hubs*; Rosenthal, *Reimagining Indian Country*.

7. Brookings Institution, *The Problem of Indian Administration* (Baltimore: Johns Hopkins Press, 1928), 725.

8. *Smoke Signal* 24, no. 2 (Summer 1965); *Sacramento Bee*, May 17, 1965. Pansy died on May 14 from cirrhosis of the liver (Susie Bear Yanes, personal communication, August 24, 2009). This revises another descendant's remembrance of death from TB.

9. *Smoke Signal* 24, no. 2 (Summer 1965).

10. *Indian Historian* 2, no. 5 (May/June 1965).

11. Sometimes dances were scheduled to coincide with the fair. See, e.g., *Smoke Signal* 9, no. 6 (June 1950).

12. "Visiting Scouts," *Gallup Independent*, August 26, 1932; "Pageant Given with Skill," *Oakland Tribune*, October 29, 1934; "High School Pageant," October 2, 1941; "Indian Museum Curator," *Sacramento Bee*, December 3, 1951.

13. *Smoke Signal* 9, no. 5 (May 1950).

14. *Smoke Signal* 9, no. 7 (July/August 1950).

15. It was installed on June 16, 1951, six weeks after Kitty's death; Kesner was guest speaker. Beryl and Pansy were charter members.

16. Potts and Pansy used this to describe the venue for the sixteenth anniversary party. *Smoke Signal* 12, no. 1 (January/February 1963).

17. Guy Wallace, Billy Villa, Ida Starkey, Ramona Burris, Henry Miller, John Porter, Albert Clifford, and Louie Oliver, among others.

18. *Sacramento Bee*, March 2, 1954. This article suggests that Fuller traveled to Washington; he did not.

19. Pictured were Ernest and Cecil Cheeka; Larry, Michael, and Marvin Lee Marine; Dorene and Eugene Goodwin; and Danny, Clarice, and Susie Franklin. Potts, Julie James, Harriett Kelly, Joyce Cheeka, Bill Franklin, Eugene and Genevieve Paddy, Marvin Potts, and non-Natives Dyson and Nell were listed as additional participants. *Roseville Press-Tribune*, December 10, 1954. The *San Juan Record* caption for story of this same performance read, "West Coast and Plains Tribes." Photographs featuring float banners reading "Mewauk Dancers" are from the Folsom Pioneer Festival. *Folsom Telegraph*, June 21, 1956. A *Sacramento Union* photograph (September 5, 1954) identifies two Miwok dancers as Juliet Jones and Lucetta Cheeka.

20. Minor chronological revisions aside, this account draws upon two decades of *Smoke Signal* articles; William Franklin, oral interview, 1983, Sacramento Ethnic Sites Survey, SHC; Brian Bibby, "Still Going: Bill Franklin and the Revival of Miwuk Traditions," *News from Native California* (Summer 1993): 21–36.

21. *Sacramento Bee*, March 27, 1958.

22. *Santa Fe New Mexican*, April 23, 1958.

23. *Auburn Journal*, May 15, 1958; *Auburn Journal* May 29, 1958.

24. *Sacramento Union*, April 13, 1959; *Sacramento Bee*, April 15, 1959.

25. Northern California veteran experiences are richly documented in Chag Lowry, *The Original Patriots* (Eureka, Calif.: Chag Lowry, 2007).

26. Following Lorraine Roberts, this can also be likened to "hub-making." Ramirez, *Native Hubs*.

27. My thanks to Thom Lewis (West Sacramento Historical Society), who tracked down official documentation of its disbandment as part of the society's recent campaign to preserve Bryte Memorial Hall.

28. *Smoke Signal* 20, no. 2 (February/March 1961). Fred Baker passed away in November 1968. Bryte Memorial Hall was the site of FIC's memorial service, led by Effman. *Smoke Signal* 28, no. 1 (January 1969).

29. *Smoke Signal* 21, no. 3 (October 1962).

30. Clifford, *Returns*, 48.

31. LaPena, *Dream Songs*.

32. *Smoke Signal* 22, no. 3 (June/July 1963).

33. *East Yolo Record*, March 30, 1966.

34. "Action . . . Fun . . . Heritage," Dance Files, MPP, Box M, SCUA, CSUS. Lorraine Dyson was the cultural group's secretary. This meeting offered yellowhammer headband instruction and discussed needing more regalia and male dancers at the state fair. *Smoke Signal* 27, no. 4 (July 1968). Gerald Paiute Davis, FIC president, headed the group; Franklin was culture and dance captain; Pat Celli was legislative captain; and Jack Dyson was treasurer. *Sacramento Bee*, May 23, 1968.

35. *Sacramento Bee*, December 4, 1969.

36. *Smoke Signal* 27, no. 7 (December 1969).

37. On June 1, 1970, an AP story announced the federal government's plan to force evacuation by cutting water and electricity. Quoting David Risling Jr., who said that this continued a long pattern of genocide, the article was illustrated with photographs of headdress-wearing men and "Sioux peace pipes." Because Risling's status as California Indian Education Association president was cited, readers from Albuquerque to Oshkosh learned that California Indian people existed and were engaged in educational self-determination. Hundreds of national papers (including the *Albuquerque Journal* and the *Oshkosh Northwestern*) ran this story.

38. *Smoke Signal* 29, no. 3 (May–July 1970).

39. *Smoke Signal* 29, no. 3 (May–July 1970).

40. She also incorporated Dyson's essay "Why Indians Dance," edited to include California dance traditions.

41. *San Francisco Chronicle*, July 14, 1965. Original committee membership included two Native teachers and seven California Indian people, though some change later occurred. (See Soza War Soldier, "Positive and Effective Action.") AIHS's governance model was inflexible on some points. Several Tuolumne board members were booted

in 1965 for not paying dues and for maintaining what Costo saw as competing board commitments (such as holding FIC office). Like Potts and FIC, the Costos shouldered most of the organization's labor and costs. George Wessel and John Porter both sat on AIHS's board, though Wessell lost his position and Porter almost left with him. Costo Papers, 012.017, AIHS Correspondence, SCUA, UCR. Costo founded AIHS in October 1964 with his wife, Jeanette Henry, and thirteen charter members, including Stewart, a board member from 1964 to 1969. Stewart's imprimatur is evident in *Indian Historian*'s 1965 FIC coverage.

42. For example, the World Affairs Council, American Association of University Women, DAR, and church groups.
43. MP to Katie Leon, April 24, 1956, MPP, Box A, SCUA, CSUS.
44. MP to Katie Leon, April 24, 1956, MPP, Box A, SCUA, CSUS.
45. Beatrice Corash to MP, July 6, 1956, MPP, Box A, SCUA, CSUS. This was a Quinn referral.
46. MP to Lloyd P. Hiatt, William S. Hart Park, December 15, 1978, MPP, Box A, SCUA, CSUS.
47. MP, oral interview by Francis Riddell and James Bennyhoff, state archaeologists, May 17, 1972, Francis A. Riddell Papers, CSA.
48. *Smoke Signal* 31, no. 4 (July/August 1972); Anderson, *Tending the Wild*.
49. Correspondence cited in reference to Goethe and Potts includes J. Martin Weber to C. M. Goethe, March 4, 1958; "Statement of C. M. Goethe" to J. Martin Weber, n.d.; C. M. Goethe to J. Martin Weber, November 16, 1960; C. M. Goethe to J. Martin Weber, November 22, 1960; and J. Martin Weber to C. M. Goethe, November 19, 1958. Public School Records, Box 1, California State Archives. On October 26, 1959, Potts received a thank-you letter from Mary Parker, chair of the Committee on Indian Affairs, regarding her talk at the "recent Indian Conference held in Oakland. One hundred sixteen people were in attendance with a fine percentage of Indian leadership and participation." MPP, Box A, SCUA, CSUS. The letter was written on Northern California–Nevada Council of Churches letterhead, which boasted twenty-six denominations united in serving one-half million church members. Dr. and Mrs. C. M. Goethe are listed as "Founders of the Church Council Movement in California."
50. MP to Leland Case, February 17, 1967, MPP, Box M, SCUA, CSUS. Potts did teach Sacramento State College basket weaving classes in the 1970s.
51. In April 1966 she penned a letter to the editor of the *Bee*, after taking her grandchildren to see *Hansel and Gretel* at a local theater: "A pink wallet was lost. The money in the wallet belonged to four orphaned children and their grandmother. The wallet was turned in . . . emptied of all the money. The orphans were denied their Easter holiday and groceries for the next two weeks. They join their grandmother in prayer that whoever took the money will enjoy it to the fullest—MARIE POTTS." *Sacramento Bee*, April 15, 1966.
52. *Carson Review*, April 14, 1971.
53. See "Welcome to our Bear Dance," *Smoke Signal* 22, no. 3 (May/June 1974); Marvin Benner, "Jamáni Maidu Wédam: Mountain Maidu Spring Rite," *News from Native*

California, May–June 1989; Leigh Ann Hunt, "Rite of Spring: A History of the Mountain Maidu Bear Dance" (master's thesis, California State University–Sacramento, 1992).

54. *Smoke Signal* 29, no. 3 (May–July 1970).

55. *Smoke Signal* 29, no. 3 (May–July 1970).

56. A variant spelling of her Maidu name.

57. See Bauer, *California through Native Eyes*.

58. *Sacramento Bee*, September 9, 1973.

59. Email to author and others, August 30, 2006.

60. *Sacramento Bee*, March 24, 1956. Nearby, discovery of another possible site occurred when a house foundation excavation revealed a skull (*Sacramento Bee*, March 20).

61. *Sacramento Bee*, March 24, 1956, 4.

62. *Sacramento Union*, March 29, 1956.

63. *Sacramento Union*, March 29, 1956.

64. *Sacramento Bee*, June 25, 1956.

65. *Sacramento Bee*, February 10, 1960. Reeve and Dyson had conducted many excavations between 1952 and 1956, introducing Sacramento State College students Richard Simpson, Clifford Curtice, and Sam Payen to archaeology.

66. *Sacramento Bee*, June 5, 1960.

67. *Sacramento Bee*, February 5, 1960, 14.

68. *Sacramento Bee*, June 10, 1960.

69. *Smoke Signal*, June 4, 1960.

70. *Sacramento Bee*, April 22, 1973.

71. *Bakersfield Californian*, April 23, 1973.

72. *Sacramento Bee*, May 12, May 30, June 5, 1973. Potts and Riddell had been working together for nearly a decade to promote cultural preservation and archaeological awareness through the California League for American Indians.

73. *Santa Cruz Sentinel*, July 17, 1973.

74. *Potts et al. vs. State of California*, MPP, Box B, SCUA, CSUS.

75. *Sacramento Bee*, August 3, 1973.

76. *Sacramento Union*, August 5, 1974.

77. *Los Angeles Times*, October 18, 1983.

78. Susan Lobo, "Urban Clan Mothers," in *Keeping the Campfires Going*, ed. Susan A. Krouse and Heather A. Howard (Lincoln: University of Nebraska Press, 2009), 1–21.

79. William Willard, "Indian Newspapers, or 'Say, Ain't You Some Kind of Indians?'" *Wicazo Ša Review* 10, no. 2 (Autumn 1994): 91–97.

80. *Smoke Signal* 31, no. 2 (March/April 1972).

Conclusion

Epigraph: *Pony Express*, September 26, 1974, 3.

1. For example, see Carol Williams, ed., *Indigenous Women and Work: From Labor to Activism* (Urbana: University of Illinois Press, 2012).

2. *Smoke Signal* 27, no. 6 (October 1968).

3. *Smoke Signal* 27, no. 4 (July/August 1974).

4. *Smoke Signal* 27, no. 7 (November/December 1968).

5. *Pony Express*, September 26, 1974, 3.

6. Rupert Costo published a photograph of his check (for $668.50; forty-nine cents per acre) marked, "Void—Rejected, R.C." in *Wassaja* 1, no. 1 (January 1973): 9. An individual who read an early version of this book saved hers for college (personal communication, 2019).

7. Morgan Otis, Native American studies director, reported that she had a waiting list of more than one hundred the first semester. She taught one class the first semester and two classes each semester thereafter for "3–4 years" (field notes, June 29, 2000).

8. *Smoke Signal* 27, no. 1 (January/February 1974); *Chico Enterprise Record*, January 29, 1974.

9. *Smoke Signal* 50, no. 6 (December 1974).

10. *Smoke Signal* 32, no. 3 (May/June 1974): 3.

11. *Redlands Daily Facts*, April 10, 1975. An exhibit catalog, *I Am These People: Native American Art Exhibit*, was published in 1975. Frank LaPena spearheaded this publication project after the exhibit closed. His correspondence with the exhibiting artists and other interested parties is a testament to his desire to bring contemporary Native American art to a wider audience. Frank R. LaPena Papers, Governor's Indian Art Show, Box 28, Folder 32, SCUA, CSUS. See also Rosenthal, "Rewriting the Narrative."

12. The yellowhammer headband may have been borrowed from Roxie Peconum, who often wore one at the Lassen County Fair. Cropped from the image is Florence Harrie, seated at Potts's lower right, and infant Joanna Ahern in the baby basket. *Sacramento Bee*, September 13, 1964.

13. Lest literary critics pounce on this as an "as told to" biography or proof that the subaltern cannot speak, this serves as a reminder that she did so regularly in the *Smoke Signal*. Writing as Injun Louie, she deployed settler "injun speak" as a sophisticated form of postcolonial mimicry and critique, but she also wrote in her own Native woman's voice.

14. Marie Potts, *Northern Maidu*.

15. Papers included the *Brunswick News* (Georgia), *Kansas City Star* (Missouri), *Omaha World-Herald*, *News Palladium* (Benton Harbor, Michigan), *San Francisco Chronicle*, and *Ottawa Journal*.

16. *Tribal Spokesman* (Inter-tribal Council of California, Inc.), June 1975.

17. *Alabama Journal*, July 3, 1975. In 2001 Larry Myers (then executive secretary of the California Native American Heritage Commission) contacted me to learn more about Potts's portrait, hanging in the lobby just outside their offices. In short order, he organized and installed an exhibit honoring Native California women. In 2019 renovations to the building required Potts's portrait to be moved to another site. Office Building One (also known as OB-1) is now called the Jesse Unruh Building.

18. English and English-speaking settlers now thoroughly dominated the socioeconomic landscape. It was one thing to speak English, as did John Peconum when he translated for *Doaksum et al.* a decade prior, and quite another to ensure that future generations

were safeguarded against dishonesty and trickery based on English language illiteracy. As recently documented, many Mountain Maidu people were disenfranchised from their allotments by such means (Manning, *Upstream*).

19. Still teaching young people through the *Northern Maidu*, Potts continues to be a role model to current generations of Maidu and California Indian people engaged in new forms of activism in the academy: developing decolonizing methodologies; earning doctorates in Indigenous and Native American studies; advocating for repatriation; and training to promote and lead tribal museums, cultural centers, and cultural resource management firms. These are twenty-first-century destinations she could hardly imagine when she began paving pathways into museums and universities nearly a century ago.

20. Zeitlyn, "Anthropology in and of the Archives."

Selected Bibliography

Archives and Manuscript Collections

California State Railroad Museum Library and Archives, Sacramento
Center for Sacramento History
Chester Library and Museum, Plumas County, Calif.
Cumberland County Historical Society, Carlisle, Pa.
D'Arcy McNickle Papers, Ayer Modern Manuscripts, Newberry Library, Chicago
Edward W. Gifford Papers, Bancroft Library, University of California–Berkeley
Francis A. Riddell Papers, California State Archives, Sacramento
Frank R. LaPena Papers, Donald and Beverly Gerth Special Collections and University Archives, California State University–Sacramento
Helen L. Peterson Papers, National Museum of the American Indian, Washington, D.C.
Marie Potts Papers, Donald and Beverly Gerth Special Collections and University Archives, California State University–Sacramento
Meriam Library Special Collections and University Archives, California State University–Chico
National Anthropological Archives, Smithsonian Institution, Suitland, Md.
National Archives and Records Administration, Washington, D.C.
National Archives and Records Administration, Pacific Region, San Francisco
National Congress of American Indians, National Museum of the American Indian, Washington, D.C.
Phoebe Apperson Hearst Museum of Anthropology, University of California–Berkeley
Plumas County Museum and Historical Society, Quincy, Calif.
Robert Leland Papers, Special Collections, University of Nevada–Reno
Rupert and Jeanette Costo Papers, Special Collections and University Archives, University of California–Riverside
Samuel A. Barrett Papers, Bancroft Library, University of California–Berkeley
Sol Tax Papers, University of Chicago Special Collections Research Center, Chicago

Special Collections, University of California–Davis
State Indian Museum, California State Parks, Sacramento

Books and Articles

Adams, David Wallace. *Education for Extinction: American Indians and the Boarding School Experience, 1875–1928*. Lawrence: University Press of Kansas, 1995.

Adams, David Wallace, and Crista DeLuzio, eds. *On the Borders of Love and Power: Families and Kinship in the Intercultural American Southwest*. Berkeley: University of California Press, 2012.

Anderson, M. Kat. *Tending the Wild: Native American Knowledge and the Management of California's Natural Resources*. Berkeley: University of California Press, 2005.

Arndt, Grant. "The Making and Muting of an Indigenous Media Activist." *American Ethnologist* 37, no. 3 (2010): 499–510.

Bahr, Diana Meyers. *The Students of Sherman Indian School: Education and Native Identity since 1892*. Norman: University of Oklahoma Press, 2014.

———. *Viola Martinez, California Paiute: Living in Two Worlds*. Norman: University of Oklahoma Press, 2003.

Bates, Craig. "Dressing the Part: A Brief Look at the Development of Stereotypical Indian Clothing among Native Peoples in the Far West." *Journal of California and Great Basin Anthropology* 4, no. 1 (1982): 55–66.

Bates, Craig, and Martha J. Lee. *Tradition and Innovation: A Basket History of the Indians of the Yosemite-Mono Lake Area*. Yosemite National Park, Calif.: Yosemite Association, 1990.

Bataille, Gretchen M., and Laurie Lisa. *Native American Women: A Biographical Dictionary*. New York: Routledge, 2003.

Battaille, Gretchen M., and Kathleen Mullen Sands, eds. *American Indian Women: Telling Their Lives*. Lincoln: University of Nebraska Press, 1984.

Bauer, William, Jr. *California through Native Eyes: Reclaiming History*. Seattle: University of Washington Press, 2016.

———. "Family Matters: Round Valley Indian Families at the Sherman Indian Institute." *Southern California Quarterly* 92, no. 4 (2010–11): 393–423.

———. *We Were All Like Migrant Workers Here: Work, Community and Memory on California's Round Valley Reservation, 1850–1941*. Chapel Hill: University of North Carolina Press, 2009.

Bell, Genevieve. "Telling Stories Out of School: Remembering the Carlisle Indian Industrial School, 1879–1918." PhD dissertation, Department of Anthropology, Stanford University, Stanford, Calif., 1998.

Berkhofer, Robert, Jr. *The White Man's Indian*. New York: Knopf, 1978.

Bernstein, Bruce. "Roland Dixon and the Maidu." *Museum Anthropology* 17, no. 2 (1993): 20–26.

Bibby, Brian. *Essential Art: Native Basketry from the California Indian Heritage Center*. Berkeley: Heyday Books, 2012.

Blansett, Kent. *A Journey to Freedom: Richard Oakes, Alcatraz, and the Red Power Movement.* New Haven, Conn.: Yale University Press, 2018.

Brayboy, Bryan McKinley Jones, K. Tsianina Lomawaima, and Malia Villegas. "The Lives and Work of Beatrice Medicine and Vine Deloria Jr." *Anthropology and Education Quarterly* 38, no. 3 (2007): 231–38.

Bruchac, Margaret M. *Savage Kin: Indigenous Informants and American Anthropologists.* Tucson: University of Arizona Press, 2018.

Brumble, David H. *American Indian Autobiography.* 2nd ed. Lincoln: University of Nebraska Press, 2008.

Burrows, Jack. *Black Sun of the Miwok.* Albuquerque: University of New Mexico Press, 2000.

Buss, Joseph James. "Imagined Worlds and Archival Realities." In *Beyond Two Worlds: Critical Conversations on Language and Power in Native North America,* ed. James Joseph Buss and C. Joseph Genetin-Pilawa, 97–115. Albany: SUNY Press, 2014.

Cahill, Cathleen. *Federal Fathers and Mothers: A Social History of the United States Indian Service.* Chapel Hill: University of North Carolina Press, 2011.

Castaneda, Terri. "Making News: Marie Potts and *The Smoke Signal of the Federated Indians of California.*" In *Women in Print: Essays on the Print Culture of American Women from the Nineteenth and Twentieth Centuries,* ed. James P. Danky and Wayne Wiegand, 77–125. Madison: University of Wisconsin Press, 2006.

Cattelino, Jessica. "Thoughts on the U.S. as a Settler Society." *North American Dialogue* 14, no. 1 (April 2011): 1–6.

Child, Brenda J. *Boarding School Seasons.* Lincoln: University of Nebraska Press, 1995.

Clifford, James. *The Predicament of Culture: Twentieth-Century Ethnography, Literature, and Art.* Cambridge, Mass.: Harvard University Press, 1988.

———. *Returns: Becoming Indigenous in the Twenty-First Century.* Cambridge, Mass.: Harvard University Press, 2013.

———. *Routes: Travel and Translation in the Late Twentieth Century.* Cambridge, Mass.: Harvard University Press, 1997.

Cobb, Daniel M., and Loretta Fowler, eds. *Beyond Red Power: American Indian Activism since 1900.* Santa Fe, N. Mex.: School for Advanced Research, 2007.

Coleman, Michael C. *American Indian Children at School, 1850–1930.* Jackson: University Press of Mississippi, 2009.

Cowger, Thomas W. *The National Congress of American Indians: The Founding Years.* Lincoln: University of Nebraska Press, 1999.

Crum, Steven J. "Almost Invisible: The Brotherhood of North American Indians (1911) and the League of North American Indians (1935)." *Wicazo Ša Review* 21 no. 1 (2006): 43–59.

Curtis, Molly, ed. *Lela Rhoades: Pit River Woman.* Berkeley: Heyday Books, 2013.

Danky, James P., and Maureen E. Hady. *Native American Periodicals and Newspapers 1828–1982: Bibliography, Publishing Record, and Holdings.* Westport, Conn.: Greenwood Press, 1984.

Danky, James P., and Wayne Wiegand, eds. *Print Culture in a Diverse America.* Chicago: University of Illinois Press, 1998.

De la Cadena, Marisol, and Orin Starn, eds. *Indigenous Experience Today*. New York: Berg, 2007.

Deloria, Philip J. *Indians in Unexpected Places*. Topeka: University Press of Kansas, 2004.

Deloria, Vine L., Jr. *Custer Died for Your Sins: An Indian Manifesto*. New York: McMillan Company, 1969.

DeMaille, Raymond J. "'These Have No Ears': Narrative and the Ethnohistoric Method." *Ethnohistory* 40, no. 4 (1993): 515–38.

Dixon, Roland B. "The Huntington California Expedition: The Northern Maidu." *Bulletin of the American Museum of Natural History* 17, no. 3 (1905): 119–346.

———. "Maidu Texts." *American Ethnological Society* 4 (1912).

Dobkins, Rebecca J. "From Vanishing to Visible: Maidu Indian Arts and the Uses of Tradition." PhD dissertation, University of California–Berkeley, 1995.

———. "Strong Language, Strong Actions: Native American Women Writing against Federal Authority." In *Reinventing Identities: The Gendered Self in Discourse*, ed. Mary Bucholtz, A. C. Liang, and Laurel Ann Sutton, 181–99. New York: Oxford University Press, 1999.

———. "Art and Autoethnography: Frank Day and the Uses of Anthropology." *Museum Anthropology* 24, no. 2–3 (2000): 22–29.

Dobkins, Rebecca J., Carey T. Caldwell, and Frank R. LaPena. *Memory and Imagination: The Legacy of Maidu Indian Artist Frank Day*. Oakland: Oakland Museum of California, 1997.

Dunbar-Ortiz, Roxanne. *An Indigenous Peoples' History of the United States*. Boston: Beacon Press, 2014.

Eastman, Charles. *From the Deep Woods to Civilization*. New York: Little Brown, 1916.

Eastman, Elaine Goodale. *Pratt: The Redman's Moses*. Norman: University of Oklahoma Press, 1935.

Edmunds, R. David. *American Indian Leaders: Studies in Diversity*. Lincoln: University of Nebraska Press, 1980.

Ellis, Clyde. *To Change Them Forever: Indian Education at the Rainy Mountain Boarding School 1893–1920*. Norman: University of Oklahoma Press, 1996.

Fear-Segal, Jacqueline. *White Man's Club: Schools, Race, and the Struggle of Indian Acculturation*. Lincoln: University of Nebraska Press, 2007.

Fear-Segal, Jacqueline, and Susan D. Rose, eds. *Carlisle Indian Industrial School: Indigenous Histories, Memories and Reclamations*. Lincoln: University of Nebraska Press, 2016.

Field, Les W. "Complicities and Collaborations." *Current Anthropology* 40 (1999): 193–209.

———. *Abalone Tales: Collaborative Explorations of Sovereignty and Identity in Native California*. Durham, N.C.: Duke University Press, 2008.

Finn, Janet L. "Ella Cara Deloria and Mourning Dove: Writing for Cultures, Writing against the Grain." *Critique of Anthropology* 13, no. 4 (2009): 335–49.

Fixico, Donald L. *The Urban Indian Experience in America*. Albuquerque: University of New Mexico Press, 2000.

Frank, L., and Kim Hogeland. *First Families: A Photographic History of California Indians*. Berkeley: Heyday Books, 2007.

Garroutte, Eva Marie. *Real Indians: Identity and the Survival of Native America*. Berkeley: University of California Press, 2003.

Goerke, Betty. *Chief Marin: Leader, Rebel, and Legend*. Berkeley: Heyday Books, 2007.

Gram, John R. *Education at the Edge of Empire: Negotiating Pueblo Identity in New Mexico's Indian Boarding Schools*. Seattle: University of Washington Press, 2015.

Harkin, Michael E. "The Emotional Archive: The Formation of Social Memory of the Residential School Experience in British Columbia." *Ethnohistory* 63, no. 3 (2016): 459–68.

Harmon, Alexandra. "Wanted: More Histories of Indian Identity." In *A Companion to American Indian History*, ed. Vine Deloria Jr. and Neal Salisbury, 248–65. New York: Blackwell, 2004.

Harwood, George. *Indians and Indian Agents: The Origins of the Reservation System in California, 1849–1952*. Norman: University of Oklahoma Press, 1997.

Heizer, Robert F., and Alfred L. Kroeber. "For Sale: California at 47 Cents per Acre." *Journal of California Anthropology* 3, no. 2 (1976): 38–65.

Hertzberg, Hazel. *The Search for an American Indian Identity*. Syracuse: Syracuse University Press, 1971.

Hopkins, Sarah Winnemucca. *Life among the Piutes: Their Wrongs and Claims*. 1883. Reprint, Reno: University of Nevada Press, 1994.

Horne, Esther Burnett, and Sally McBeth. *Essie's Story: The Life and Legacy of a Shoshone Teacher*. Lincoln: University of Nebraska Press, 1998.

Hoxie, Frederick E. *This Indian Country: American Indian Activists and the Place They Made*. New York: Penguin Press, 2012.

Huhndorf, Shari M. *Going Native: Indians in the American Cultural Imagination*. Ithaca: Cornell University Press, 2001.

Hurtado, Albert L. *Indian Survival on the California Frontier*. New Haven, Conn.: Yale University Press, 1988.

———. *Intimate Frontiers: Sex, Gender, and Culture in Old California*. Albuquerque: University of New Mexico Press, 1999.

Jacobs, Margaret D. *White Mother to a Dark Race: Settler Colonialism, Maternalism, and the Removal of Indigenous Children in the American West and Australia, 1880–1940*. Lincoln: University of Nebraska Press, 2009.

Jewell, Donald P. *Indians of the Feather River: Tales and Legends of Concow Maidu of California*. Menlo Park: Ballena Press, 1987.

Johnson, Susan Lee. "'My Own Private Life': Toward a History of Desire in Gold Rush California." *California History* 79, no. 2 (2000): 316–46.

Kroeber, Karl, and Clifton Kroeber, eds. *Ishi in Three Centuries*. Lincoln: University of Nebraska Press, 2003.

Kroeber, Theodora. *Ishi in Two Worlds*. Berkeley: University of California Press, 1961.

Krupat, Arnold. *For Those Who Come After: A Study of Native American Autobiography*. Berkeley: University of California Press, 1985.

LaGrand, James B. *Indian Metropolis: Native Americans in Chicago, 1945–75*. Urbana: University of Illinois Press, 2002.

LaPena, Frank R. *Dream Songs and Ceremony: Reflections on Traditional California Indian Dance*. Berkeley: Heyday Books, 2004.

Laverty, Philip. "The Ohlone/Costanoan-Esselen Nation of Monterey, California: Dispossession, Federal Neglect and the Bitter Irony of the Federal Acknowledgment Process." *Wicazo Ša Review* 18 no. 2 (2003): 41–77.

Lee, Gaylen D. *Walking Where We Lived: Memoirs of a Mono Indian Family*. Norman: University of Oklahoma Press, 1998.

Lewandowski, Tadeusz. *Red Bird, Red Power: The Life and Legacy of Zitkala-Ša*. Norman: University of Oklahoma Press, 2016.

Liberty, Margot. *American Indian Intellectuals of the Nineteenth and Early Twentieth Centuries*. Norman: University of Oklahoma Press, 2002.

Lightfoot, Kent. *Indians, Missionaries, and Merchants: The Legacy of Colonial Encounters on the California Frontiers*. Berkeley: University of California Press, 2005.

Lindgren-Kurtz, Pat. *Picking Willows with Daisy and Lilly Baker: Maidu Basket Makers of Lake Almanor*. Bloomington, Ind.: iUniverse, 2011.

Lindsay, Brendan. *Murder State: California's Native American Genocide, 1846–1873*. Lincoln: University of Nebraska Press.

Littlefield, Daniel F., Jr., and James W. Parins, eds., *American Indian and Alaska Native Newspapers and Periodicals, 1826–1924*. Westport, Conn.: Greenwood Press, 1984.

Lobo, Susan. "Urban Clan Mothers: Key Households in Cities." *American Indian Quarterly* 27 no. 3/4 (2003): 505–22.

———, ed. *Urban Voices: The Bay Area Indian Community*. Tucson: University of Arizona Press, 2002.

Lomawaima, K. Tsianina. "Domesticity in the Federal Indian Schools: The Power of Authority over Mind and Body." *American Ethnologist* 20, no. 2 (1993): 227–40.

———. *They Called It Prairie Light: The Story of Chilocco Indian School*. Lincoln: University of Nebraska Press, 1995.

Lomawaima, K. Tsianina, Brenda Child, and Margaret Archuleta, eds. *Away from Home: American Indian Boarding School Experiences, 1879–2000*. Phoenix: Heard Museum, 2000.

Lomawaima, K. Tsianina, and Jeffrey Ostler. "Reconsidering Richard Henry Pratt: Cultural Genocide and Native Liberation in an Era of Racial Oppression." *Journal of American Indian Education* 57, no. 1 (2018): 79–100.

Lonetree, Amy. *Decolonizing Museums: Representing Native America in National and Tribal Museums*. Chapel Hill: University of North Carolina Press, 2012.

Lurie, Nancy Oestreich. "The Voice of the American Indian: Report on the American Indian Chicago Conference." *Current Anthropology* 2, no. 5 (1961): 478–500.

Madley, Benjamin. *An American Genocide: The United States and the California Indian Catastrophe*. New Haven, Conn.: Yale University Press, 2016.

Mathes, Valerie Sherer. *Divinely Guided: The California Work of the Women's National Indian Association*. Lubbock: Texas Tech University Press, 2010.

McKenzie-Jones, Paul R. *Clyde Warrior: Tradition, Community, and Red Power*. Norman: University of Oklahoma Press, 2015.

McNenly, Linda S. *Native Performers in Wild West Shows: From Buffalo Bill to Euro Disney.* Norman: University of Oklahoma Press, 2012.

Medicine, Bea, and Sue Ellen Jacobs, eds. *Learning to be an Anthropologist and Remaining Native.* Urbana: University of Illinois Press, 2001.

Middleton Manning, Beth Rose. *Upstream: Trust Lands and Power on the Feather River.* Tucson: University of Arizona Press, 2018.

Middleton, Elisabeth Rose. "Seeking Spatial Representation: Reflections on Participatory Ethnohistorical GIS Mapping of Maidu Allotment Lands." *Ethnohistory* 57, no. 3 (2010): 363–87.

Mihesuah, Devon A., ed. *Natives and Academics: Researching and Writing about American Indians.* Lincoln: University of Nebraska Press, 1998.

Miller, Larisa K. "The Secret Treaties with California's Indians." *Prologue* (Fall/Winter 2013): 39–45.

Miranda, Deborah. *Bad Indians: A Tribal Memoir.* Berkeley: Heyday Books, 2013.

Moses, L. G., and Raymond Wilson, eds. *Indian Lives: Essays on Nineteenth and Twentieth-Century Native American Leaders.* Albuquerque: University of New Mexico Press, 1993.

Nagel, Joane. *American Indian Ethnic Renewal.* New York: Oxford University Press, 1996.

Nevins, M. Eleanor. *World-Making Stories: Maidu Language and Community Renewal on a Shared California Landscape.* Lincoln: University of Nebraska Press, 2017.

Ochs, Eleanor, and L. Capps. "Narrating the Self." *Annual Review of Anthropology* 25 (1996): 19–43.

Ogle, Beverly Benner. *Whisper of the Maidu: My Indian Ancestors of Hum Bug Valley.* Self-published, 1998.

Ortiz, Bev. *It Will Live Forever: Traditional Yosemite Indian Acorn Preparation.* Berkeley: Heyday Books, 1991.

Ortner, Sherry B. *Anthropology and Social Theory: Culture, Power and the Acting Subject.* Durham, N.C.: Duke University Press, 2006

Ortner, Vyola J. *You Can't Eat Dirt: Leading America's First All-Women Tribal Council and How We Changed Palm Springs.* Palm Springs: Fan Palm Research Project, 2011.

Parker, Dorothy. *Singing an Indian Song: A Biography of D'Arcy McNickle.* Lincoln: University of Nebraska Press, 1992.

Pels, Peter, and Oscar Salemink, eds. *Colonial Subjects: Essays on the Practical History of Anthropology.* Ann Arbor: University of Michigan Press, 2000.

Perdue, Theda, ed. *Sifters: Native American Women's Lives, Viewpoints on American Culture.* New York: Oxford University Press, 2001.

Potts, Marie. *The Northern Maidu.* Happy Camp, Calif.: Naturegraph Press, 1977.

Pratt, Mary Louise Pratt. *Imperial Eyes: Travel Writing and Transculturation.* New York: Routledge, 1992.

Pratt, Richard Henry. *Battlefield and Classroom: Four Decades with the American Indian, 1867–1904,* ed. Robert Marshall Utley. New Haven, Conn.: Yale University Press, 1964.

Prucha, Francis P. *American Indian Policy in Crisis: Christian Reformers and the Indian, 1865–1900.* Norman: University of Oklahoma Press, 1976.

Purdy, John Lloyd, ed. *The Legacy of D'Arcy McNickle.* Norman: University of Oklahoma Press, 1996.

Ramirez, Renya K. *Native Hubs: Culture, Community, and Belonging in Silicon Valley and Beyond.* Durham, N.C.: Duke University Press, 2007.

Risling Baldy, Cutcha. *We Are Dancing for You: Native Feminisms and the Revitalization of Women's Coming-of-Age Ceremonies.* Seattle: University of Washington Press, 2018.

Roberts, Charles. "A Choctaw Odyssey: The Life of Lesa Phillip Roberts." *American Indian Quarterly* 14, no. 3 (1990): 259–76.

Rosenthal, Nicolas G. *Reimagining Indian Country: Native American Migration and Identity in Twentieth-Century Los Angeles.* Chapel Hill: University of North Carolina Press, 2012.

———. "Rewriting the Narrative: American Indian Artists in California, 1960s–1980s." *Western Historical Quarterly* 49 (Winter 2018): 409–36.

Sanchez, Susan Lynn. "The Selling of California: The Indians Claims Commission and the Case of the *Indians of California v. the United States.*" PhD dissertation, University of California, Riverside, 2003.

Sarris, Greg. *Mabel McKay: Weaving the Dream.* Berkeley: University of California Press, 1997.

Schnieder, Khal. "Making Indian Land in the Allotment Era: Northern California's Indian Rancherias." *Western Historical Quarterly* 41, no. 4 (December 2010): 429–45.

Shipek, Florence, ed. *Delfina Cuero: Her Autobiography—An Account of Her Last Years and Her Ethnobotanic Contributions.* Menlo Park, Calif.: Ballena Press, 1991.

Shipley, William. *The Maidu Indian Myths and Stories of Hánc'ibyjim.* Berkeley: Heyday Books, 1991.

Shoemaker, Nancy, ed. *Negotiators of Change: Historical Perspectives on Native American Women.* New York: Routledge, 1995.

Shoup, Laurence, and Randall Millken. *Inigo of Rancho Posolmi: The Life and Times of a Mission Indian.* Menlo Park: Ballena Press, 1999.

Shreve, Bradley B. *Red Power Rising: The National Indian Youth Council and the Origins of Native Activism.* Norman: University of Oklahoma Press, 2011.

Simpson, Richard. *Ooti: A Maidu Legacy.* Millbrae, Calif.: Celestial Arts, 1977.

Sleeper-Smith, Susan, ed. *Contesting Knowledge, Museum and Indigenous Perspectives.* Lincoln: University of Nebraska Press, 2009.

Smith, Linda Tuhiwai. *Decolonizing Methodologies: Research and Indigenous Methodologies.* Auckland, New Zealand: Zed Books, 1999.

Smith, Paul Chaat, and Robert Allen Warrior. *Like a Hurricane: The Indian Movement from Alcatraz to Wounded Knee.* New York: New Press, 1996.

Smith, Sherry L. "Francis Laflesche and the World of Letters." *American Indian Quarterly* 25, no. 4 (2001): 579–603.

Smith-Trafzer, LeeAnn, and Clifford E. Trafzer. *Creation of a California Tribe: Grandfather's Maidu Tales.* Newcastle, Calif.: Sierra Oaks Publishing, 1988.

Sousa, Ashley Riley. "An Influential Squaw": Intermarriage and Community in Central California, 1839–1851." *Ethnohistory* 62, no. 4 (2015): 707–27.

Soza War Soldier, Rose D. "'To take positive and effective action': Rupert Costo and the California-Based American Indian Historical Society." PhD dissertation, Arizona State University, Tempe, 2013.

Spivak, Gayatri. "Can the Subaltern Speak?" In *Marxism and the Interpretation of Culture*, ed. Cary Nelson and Lawrence Grossberg, 271–313. London: Macmillan, 1988.

Standing Bear, Luther. *My People: The Sioux*. 1928. Reprint, Lincoln: Bison Books, 2006.

Starn, Orin. *Ishi's Brain: In Search of America's Last "Wild" Indian*. New York: W. W. Norton, 2004.

Stoler, Ann Laura. *Along the Archival Grain: Epistemic Anxieties and Colonial Common Sense*. Princeton, N.J.: Princeton University Press, 2009.

———. *Carnal Knowledge and Imperial Power: Race and the Intimate in Colonial Rule*. Berkeley: University of California Press, 2002.

———, ed. *Haunted by Empire: Geographies of Intimacy in North American History*. Durham, N.C.: Duke University Press, 2006.

Swann, Brian, and Arnold Krupat. *I Tell You Now: Autobiographical Essays by Native American Writers*. Lincoln: University of Nebraska Press, 2005.

Szasz, Margaret Connell. *Education and the American Indian: The Road to Self-Determination since 1928*. Albuquerque: University of New Mexico Press, 1991.

Thompson, Lucy. *To the American Indian*. Eureka, Calif.: Cummins Print Shop, 1911.

Thorne, Tanis C. *El Capitan*. Banning, Calif.: Malki-Ballena Press, 2012.

Tolley, Sara-Larus. *Quest for Tribal Acknowledgment: California's Honey Lake Maidus*. Norman: University of Oklahoma Press, 2006.

Trafzer, Clifford E. *Fighting Invisible Enemies: Health and Medical Transitions among Southern California Indians*. Norman: University of Oklahoma Press, 2019.

Trafzer, Clifford E., Jean A. Keller, and Lorene Sisquoc, eds. *Boarding School Blues: Revisiting American Indian Educational Experiences*. Lincoln: University of Nebraska Press, 2006.

Trahant, Mark. "American Indians at Press: The Native American Journalists Association." In *American Indians and the Mass Media*, ed. Meta G. Carstarphen and John P. Sanchez, 212–21. Norman: University of Oklahoma Press, 2012.

Trennert, Robert A., Jr. *The Phoenix Indian School: Forced Assimilation in Arizona, 1891–1935*. Norman: University of Oklahoma Press, 1988.

Ulrich, Roberta. *American Indian Nations: Termination to Restoration, 1953–2006*. Lincoln: University of Nebraska Press, 2010.

Usner, Daniel, Jr. "ASE Address 2011: An Ethnohistory of Things: Or, How to Treat California's Canastromania." *Ethnohistory* 59, no. 3 (Summer): 441–63.

Valandra, Edward. "The As-Told-To Native [Auto]biography: Whose Voice Is Speaking?" *Wicazo Ša Review* 20, no. 2 (2005): 103–19.

Veracini, Lorenzo. *Settler Colonialism: A Theoretical Overview*. New York: Palgrave MacMillan, 2010.

War Jack, LaNada. *Native Resistance: An Intergenerational Fight for Survival and Life*. Brookfield, Mo.: Donning Publishers, 2019.

Whalen, Kevin. *Native Students at Work: American Indian Labor and Sherman Institute's Outing Program, 1900–1945.* Seattle: University of Washington Press, 2016.

Willard, William. "A Study of Colonial Surrogates and Indigenous Others." *Wicazo Ša Review* 9, no. 2 (1993): 70–78.

Wilson, Darryl Babe. *The Morning the Sun Went Down.* Berkeley: Heyday Books, 1998.

Wolfe, Patrick. "Settler Colonialism and the Elimination of the Native." *Journal of Genocide Research* 8, no. 4 (2006): 387–409.

Zeitlyn, David. "Anthropology in and of the Archives: Possible Futures and Contingent Pasts. Archives as Anthropological Surrogates." *Annual Review of Anthropology* 41, no. 1 (2012): 461–80.

———. "Life-History Writing and the Anthropological Silhouette." *Social Anthropology* 16, no. 2 (2008): 154–71.

Index

Page references in *italics* refer to illustrative matter.

9 780806 167190